THE TRIALS
CHARLES I

THE TRIALS OF CHARLES I

Ian Ward

BLOOMSBURY ACADEMIC
LONDON • NEW YORK • OXFORD • NEW DELHI • SYDNEY

BLOOMSBURY ACADEMIC
Bloomsbury Publishing Plc
50 Bedford Square, London, WC1B 3DP, UK
1385 Broadway, New York, NY 10018, USA
29 Earlsfort Terrace, Dublin 2, Ireland

BLOOMSBURY, BLOOMSBURY ACADEMIC and the Diana logo are trademarks of
Bloomsbury Publishing Plc

First published in Great Britain 2023

Cover image: Portrait of King Charles I of England, Scotland and Ireland (1600–1649),
end 1630s. Found in the collection of Statens Museum for Kunst,
Copenhagen © Getty Images
Cover design: Graham Robert Ward

A catalogue record for this book is available from the British Library.

A catalog record for this book is available from the Library of Congress.

ISBN: HB: 978-1-3500-2497-7
PB: 978-1-3500-2514-1
ePDF: 978-1-3500-2498-4
eBook: 978-1-3500-2499-1

Typeset by Newgen KnowledgeWorks Pvt. Ltd., Chennai, India
Printed and bound in Great Britain

To find out more about our authors and books visit www.bloomsbury.com
and sign up for our newsletters.

For Ross, fellow historian, with whom I enjoyed so many great conversations about the trials of Charles Stuart

CONTENTS

List of Illustrations ix

Introduction: An evening in Hampstead 1

1 The casebook of Sir Edward Coke 5

2 The triumphs of King Charles I 37

3 The trial of Charles Stuart 77

4 Milton's war 119

5 The histories of Edward Hyde 159

Notes 199
Select Bibliography 233
Index 243

ILLUSTRATIONS

1   Sir Edward Coke 5

2   Battle of Naseby 37

3   Eikon Basilike 77

4   Milton at his desk 119

5   Sir Edward Hyde 159

INTRODUCTION

An evening in Hampstead

We will start in the tranquil surroundings of north Hampstead. On the evening of 18 October 2012. The opening night for a new play by the celebrated British dramatist Howard Brenton. In his youth, Brenton had earned a reputation as a fiery, left-leaning, writer. Determined, in his words, to 'toss a petrol-bomb through the proscenium arch'.[1] A theatre-loving Leveller, we might say. In more recent years, Brenton has written a number of plays revisiting significant historical moments, and personalities. The play which was about to be premiered that evening was one of these. *55 Days* was about the final eight weeks, minus a day, in the life of King Charles I. The events leading up to his trial, which commenced on 20 January 1649, and culminated in his execution ten days later.

The time frame is more closely set by the purge of Parliament, named after Colonel Thomas Pride, on 6 December 1648. On that day, Pride excluded around a 140 MPs, chiefly Presbyterian, with a scattering of Levellers, who were likely to oppose the intended trial of the king. The idea of putting the king on trial had bounced around for a while. Certainly months, in some quarters years. But Pride's 'purge' represented the first concerted move to make a reality of the idea. It also represented something else, as apparent as it was prosaic. In the end, the fate of the king, and the nation, would be decided by the sword. By the army, more closely a small group of senior officers, headed by Oliver Cromwell and his son-in-law Henry Ireton. This is not to say that they somehow 'caused' the king's trial and execution. Questions of causation are rarely so easily resolved. But they made it happen.

Brenton's play invites us to consider a series of questions regarding both the writing of history and the writing of the trial of King Charles I. The first is that history in dramatic form seems a little different. We expect to find history written in textbooks and monographs, critical essays perhaps. We also expect it to make certain claims to veracity, to how things really happened and why. We are less comfortable with the idea that the historian is free to imagine things, in order to create dramatic coherence. Which is what Brenton does. Whilst much of *55 Days* is drawn from original sources, much is not. At this point we find ourselves approaching a defining distinction in historical writing. Between those who are more easily reconciled to the idea that history is an art-form, and those who prefer to think that it might be reduced to scientific principles.

This distinction finds familiar shape in the alternative arguments of 'Whig' and 'revisionist' historians. Put very simply the Whig historian tends to write larger histories which assume a narrative form. A species of story-telling, or so their revisionist critics suppose, which tends to rub away the contingencies. In his seminal critique, *The Whig Interpretation of History*, Herbert Butterfield likened it to history written by 'strolling minstrels', and urged historians to write the 'vicissitudes' back in.[2] The underlying concern with veracity is understandable. But also potentially delusional. All history takes narrative form, and all history is written around contingencies. Something which is perhaps better appreciated by historians who assume a more ironic approach to their art. Realizing that what they do is not, in the end, that different from what any other story-teller does. Neither are they so concerned that the story they tell must be coherent. On the contrary, the ironic historian embraces all the contingencies that make the story interesting, and human. History with some 'colour in its cheeks', as Thomas Carlyle put it, in his excoriating critique of seventeenth-century historical writing.[3] Whether Carlyle can be properly termed an ironist is debatable. But Brenton is, writing a particular story of the trial and execution of Charles I, which is, on its terms, perfectly credible, and indeed coherent. Whilst not supposing that it is the only credible account, or indeed the most credible.

The next insight is the matter of choice. Any historian is faced with choices, most commonly of place and moment. The same choices which face the dramatist. Brenton chooses just the fifty-five days, and centres his story around the character of Charles Stuart. It is, in a sense, the obvious choice. The events of January 1649 lend themselves to dramatic presentation. We might reasonably assume that Shakespeare, had he been alive, would have written his 'Tragedy of King Charles' around the same. There again, if discretion militated towards a 'history' instead, he might have chosen a different moment.[4] Or at least included a few more moments. The murder of the Duke of Buckingham perhaps in 1628. The execution of Strafford, the battle of Naseby, the Putney debates, the siege of Colchester. Various possibilities which might attract a different historian in a different moment. Various contingencies which would write a different history. We will revisit all of these, and plenty more, in our history.

Of course, the original choice was to decide to write a play about Charles Stuart at all. It might seem obvious. Few events in English history seemed more remarkable, to contemporaries at least, than the trial and execution of their king. A world 'turned upside down', heralding, some supposed, the Second Coming. Time contextualizes. But even so. Three and a half centuries on, it still seems a remarkable occurrence. Well worthy of a play, and some history. Of course, the broader moment has always fascinated. The 'great seventeenth-century time', as

Carlyle and Dickens variously called it. The England of cavaliers and roundheads, roaming the country disembowelling one another. Oddly relatable. There is, as Sellars and Yeatman intimated in their wonderful pastiche, *1066 and All That*, something of the 'wrong but wromantic', and the 'right but repulsive', in all of us. And within this 'great' time, the events of January 1649 assume a pivotal place. And not just for reason of chronology. The place of the Crown in the English Constitution was never the same again.

The 'most extraordinary judicial body' in English history, it has been suggested, of the court assembled at Westminster Hall.[5] Quite a claim. A salutary, and spectacular, lesson in 'how lawlessness seeks to impersonate the rule of law'.[6] Another claim which should give us pause for thought: true or not. The event which persuaded the Framers, Benjamin Franklin and James Madison in particular, that the nascent American Constitution must have provision for holding supreme magistrates to account, for their sakes and that of everyone else.[7] And the 'framers' of the English Bill of Rights too, and the 'great' reform acts to follow. We will revisit the 'glorious' revolution of 1688 in due course. A history that can only be imagined, and written, in the shadow of January 1649.

And yet, despite this, the nagging sense remains that the trial of Charles I has been, ever so slightly, 'neglected'.[8] Like indeed Charles himself. A famously diffident king, struggling to impose himself amidst a starry cast. Up against the 'greatest, because the most typical Englishman of all time', as Samuel Rawson Gardiner described Oliver Cromwell. Victorian England, as we shall see, was far more intrigued by the king-killer, than the king killed. The 'heroic' Oliver, pitched by Carlyle, against the 'baffled' Charles.[9] The first modern biography of Cromwell was written by Gardiner's pupil, Charles Harding Firth. And whilst interest in Charles has recovered, that in Cromwell has not lessened. Christopher Hill's *God's Englishman*, Antonia Fraser's *Our Chief of Men* – the Devil has the best lines. In retrospect a critical moment arrived in the 1960s with C. V. Wedgwood's magisterial three-volume history of Charles during the 1640s. Starting, in fact in 1637, and running through to that moment in January 1649. Not necessarily Whig in its politics but irreducibly Whig in its writing. The final volume was originally entitled *The Trial of Charles I*. Published in 1964, and still in many ways the definitive account.

The argument should not be pressed too fervently. There have been other biographies of Charles, some of the 'personal' variety, others more critical. And plenty of scholarly articles on different aspects of Charles and his kingship. And there have been other accounts of the trial too. Some close, such as Geoffrey Robertson's *Tyrannicide Brief*; in effect, redrafting the case for the prosecution. Others more glancing, enveloping the trial into various political and cultural histories of the larger moment; David Underdown's *Pride's Purge*, Sean Kelsey's *Inventing a Republic*, Clive Holmes's *Why Was Charles I Executed?* The trial of Charles Stuart is present in any history of the 'great seventeenth-century time'. It could hardly be other. But only occasionally is it centre stage. Which bring us to this book; and an essential irony.

Which is captured in the title. *The Trials of Charles I* flirts with the same temptation; to envelop the trial itself within a larger history. What is different, however, is that this larger history is still a history of the trial. It is simply the fact that, for us, fifty-five days is not enough. That the 'trials' of Charles I started well before November 1648, and finished long after; if indeed they have finished at all. We can adopt a juridical conceit, distinguishing the five chapters to come in terms of preliminary hearings, the trial itself and subsequent appeals. In doing so, of course, we are being immediately ironic. First, because we are inventing a coherence. And second, because our history of the trials of Charles Stuart will be written, not just in prose but in poetry and performance. A cultural event as much as a jurisprudential. And a spiritual, a king not just judged but also crucified. All of which will make for a particular and prejudiced set of histories: like any other.

Chapter 1 focuses on the 'casebook' of Sir Edward Coke, Jacobean Lord Chief Justice and author of a celebrated set of *Reports*. A first preliminary hearing, for the constitutional arguments which would be heard again in Westminster Hall in January 1649. The trial of Charles Stuart was, after all, a legal event. But it was also something more, as we will see in Chapter 2, which turns its attention to the person and kingship of Charles Stuart. The various 'triumphs' of the 1630s, leading to the catastrophic defeats of the 1640s. Plenty more trials, in court, on the battlefield, in Parliament. Before we move on, in Chapter 3, to the trial itself, in January 1649. We will, in fact, start a few months earlier, with some preliminaries. A slightly longer history than just fifty-five days. But not that much longer. The two remaining chapters will revisit a couple of the appeals. Both of which, on closer inspection, will be more about their authors than the events they purport to describe. The focus of Chapter 4 is John Milton. The man to whom the authorities turned in early 1649 to draft a first brief in the anticipated appeal of Charles Stuart. Drafting and then redrafting this brief would occupy Milton for the rest of his life. Our second testament, and the focus of Chapter 5, is Sir Edward Hyde. Restoration Lord Chancellor and then, following his enforced retirement in 1667, author of a celebrated *History of the Rebellion*. Credibility, more than anything, animated Hyde: the need to believe that he would be believed. Of course, the same can be said of Coke and Milton, and all the rest who played a role, leading and supporting, in the various trials of King Charles I.

1 THE CASEBOOK OF SIR EDWARD COKE

Engraved by J. Posselwhite from a Picture in the Hall of Sergeants Inn Chancery Lane.

FIGURE 1 Sir Edward Coke.

We will start 3662 miles away, the distance from the Palace of Westminster to the Supreme Court in Washington DC. Where we will find some very impressive doors.[1] If we look closely we will see a series of eight bronze reliefs, one of which depicts the Lord Chief Justice of England, Sir Edward Coke, barring King James I from entering the 'King's Court'. Of course, Coke never physically barred his king from anywhere. But it is the impression that counts, literally and figuratively. The 'founding fathers' were enchanted by Coke. A 'sounder Whig never wrote', according to Thomas Jefferson. When John Adams stood up in Congress to argue the 'natural rights' of the colonialists, he brandished a copy of Coke's *Institutes*. The 'oracle of the law', he proclaimed.[2] The metaphor preferred, closer to our particular moment, by the notorious Leveller radical, John Lilburne, when he was prosecuted for sedition in early 1649. The 'great Oracle of the Laws of England'.[3] More of Lilburne and his brandishing in a later chapter. It brought the house down, literally.

Our present concern is, though, with Coke. And what we might term his 'casebook'. It is here that his brilliance lies, or so we are told. In thirteen volumes of *Reports*, written 'for the common good', for the 'quieting' of confusion, the blurb confirmed.[4] To which might be added four volumes of *Institutes*, written a little later during his retirement. We will come to the matter of Coke's retirement in due course. It is these collected writings that 'established the common law on its firm foundations'.[5] It is why Coke is the 'greatest lawyer in English history'.[6] The champion of the 'ancient' constitution, and chronicler of its 'mind'.[7] And it is not just later jurists who have been inclined to fawn. His near contemporary William Prynne thought much the same. The 'patron and pillar of the common law', the man whose 'quotations' are 'received, and relied on by a mere implicit faith, as infallible oracles'.[8] Prynne is another we will revisit, railing against French 'whores' and getting his ears cut off as a consequence. As for his teeth, they were cut in writing an extended essay on Coke's brilliance. But the brilliant jurist is only one Edward Coke. There are others.

There is Coke the self-promoting fantasist, busy rewriting history to make himself look good. Caricatured, it has been surmised, in the shape of Shakespeare's pompous buffoon, Sir Andrew Aguecheek, in *Twelfth Night*.[9] Something of a gamble it might have been thought, especially given the repeat performances of the play at Court in 1601 and 1602. But Shakespeare was probably assured by thought that there were plenty in the audience who did not much like Edward Coke. Such as Francis Bacon. In a facetious *Letter of Advice*, Bacon would accuse Coke of fabricating many of his famed *Reports*. 'You make the law to lean a little too much to your opinion', the *Letter* 'advised', such that 'you show yourself a legal tyrant'.[10] Something we might bear in mind as we proceed. Bacon was not alone in his suspicions. And then there is Coke the courtroom boor, who thought nothing of screaming abuse and barristers, and jurymen, who had the temerity to argue against him. Such, indeed, as Bacon. 'The less you speak of your greatness', an exasperated Bacon was driven to exclaim, in one of their many courtroom jousts, 'the more I will think of it'. Coke's reply, according to Bacon at least, was 'a number of disgraceful words'.[11] The enmity was long-standing, nurtured by years of professional jealousy.

And thwarted romance. Back in 1597, Bacon and Coke had been rivals for the hand of Lady Elizabeth Hatton. A serious catch; recently widowed, still young and beautiful, and now fabulously wealthy. In the end she married Coke. A bit of a 'mystery', as one contemporary noted.[12] Scurrilous rumour had it that she was already pregnant. Which brings us to Coke the family man. Who bore an unfortunate similarity to Coke the courtroom bully. A predictably tempestuous marriage collapsed predictably. By 1606 Lord and Lady Coke were living apart. A bit of a rubbish dad too. Who would beat his distraught teenage daughter into marrying an insane nobleman, in the hope that it might help his flagging career? More of that later. 'We shall never see his like again', Lady Elizabeth remarked, on hearing of her husband's death in 1634, 'praises be to God'.[13] It had been a fair old wait. Coke was eighty-two when he passed on. It was, perhaps, the bitterness that kept him going. Blaming Bacon for his downfall in 1616, he would take pleasure in drafting the impeachment charges which would be laid against his old enemy in 1621.

Not an easy man then. And not every Whig historian was a fan. A 'pedant, bigot and brute', Macaulay concluded.[14] But most were. Enchanted by all the glitter. Solicitor General in 1592, promoted to Attorney General two years later, in which capacity he represented the Crown in a series of high-profile treason cases, including those of the Earl of Essex, Sir Walter Raleigh, and the surviving Powder Plotters. Rewarded for the latter service, he was appointed Chief Justice of Common Pleas in 1606, and then Lord Chief Justice of the Kings Bench in 1613. Rising and rising. Until summer 1616, when it all came to a dramatic end. A decade of semi-retirement would follow, during which he would compose his *Institutes* and plot. And then a second career, drafting an English constitution. Quite a career.

Before we take a closer look, we should address an obvious question: why does Coke matter to us? The conjecture is this. We will better understand what happened to Charles Stuart if we can better understand what Edward Coke thought. It is for this reason that we are going to take an extended dip into his 'casebook'. To include not just cases which he wrote up, but those other in which he played a part, drawn from both his first and his second career. First, though, we might pause to take a glance across the broader constitutional landscape. The civil war might have been a generation away, but the battle lines were already being drawn up.

Metaphors of kingship

King James I came to the throne in 1603. He called his first Parliament the following year. It became known as the 'Blessed' Parliament, chiefly because it avoided being blown up by Guy Fawkes in November 1605. It sat intermittently through to 1611, spending much of the time frustrating James's desire for a 'union of crowns'. There would be three more Jacobean Parliaments, all short, in 1614, 1621 and 1624. Put simply, when James could do without Parliament, he did.[15] A place of 'private devices', as his Lord Chancellor put it, of 'privy conventicles and conferences'.[16] Which is where proclamations, executed under the prerogative authority of the Crown, came in so useful. No need for all the bother of Westminster. We will take a closer look at a couple of proclamations shortly. First, though, we should acquaint ourselves with a rather concerning essay.

The Trew Law

Published in 1598, it was entitled *The Trew Law of Free Monarchies*. What made it concerning was the prospect that its author, King James VI of Scotland, was soon to become King James I of England. James was a man of many opinions, with a propensity to write about them. A first essay on the *Divine Art of Poesie* before he had even turned twenty. Another, a few years later, on the same subject. After which he moved on to write a handbook on witch-hunting entitled *Daemonology*. Written from experience, its author having played a part in the 'discovery' of a coven based in North Berwick. In this instance, welcome; for England, as Lord Chief Justice Anderson had recently confirmed, was a 'land full of witches'.[17] Less welcome were disapproving essays on duelling and tobacco. 'The wisest fool in Christendom', it was famously said of England's new king. In modern vernacular, James Stuart was a bit of a 'know-all'.

He certainly seemed to know a lot about kingship. Wisdom which he was keen to spread. Which brings us to the *Trew Law*. An essay on the 'divine right' of kings; purposed, more especially, to rebut incipient theories of civil 'resistance'. Of which there were a troubling number circulating in late-sixteenth-century Scotland. Including George Buchanan's *De Jure Regni apud Scotus*, published in 1579. Written as a piece of 'mirror' literature, to better inform other princes, and necessarily ironic, given Buchanan's position as tutor to the young Prince James. Buchanan apparently instilled a love of learning in his charge. His view of kingship was though challenging. According to Buchanan 'whatever rights the populace may have granted' their sovereign, 'they can with equal justice rescind'.[18] An incipient idea of contractual kingship. Proscribed by successive Stuart monarchs, *De Jure* would be burned by the public hangman in 1683. Just five years before the 'glorious' revolution which would, finally, prove Buchanan right.

James thought very differently, about kingship and accountability. A 'divine right' indeed, beyond human question.[19] Later, in 1610, he would famously remind Parliament that 'Kings are not only God's lieutenants upon earth, and sit upon God's throne, but even by God are themselves called God'. And as a consequence are 'accomptable to none but God alone'.[20] Becoming by then contentious, but not intended to be in 1598. Scriptural authorities aplenty sprinkled liberally around the *Trew Law*. James particularly liked *Psalms* 82. 'Kings are called Gods' because 'they sit upon God his throne in the earth'. The purpose of the coronation, and the ceremony of anointment, was to bear witness, so that God might then hold His sovereign accountable. Kings are 'countable' to God alone, each to reign 'upon the peril of his soul'.[21] This did not, of necessity, mean that James had a catholic view of kingship, at least not a Catholic one. But there was, in the eyes of some, an insinuation. It certainly felt somehow un-English, and a bit popish.

The extent to which the coming revolution, which would destroy his son, might be termed a 'war of religion' remains contestable.[22] But there can be little doubt that, in espousing a 'divine right' theory of kingship, James twisted the Reformation tail. Reinvesting himself with 'priestly' authority, to go along with the secular reinforced in Reformation statute law. Not, again, explicitly Roman. But assuming a semblance. And completely out of step with the idea of 'elective' kingship recommended, not just by Buchanan but by an increasing number of protestant writers. There could, James assured his readers, be no sensible idea of a 'mutuall paction' between king and the 'headlesse multitude'.[23] Which, to extend the jurisprudential metaphor, might be dissolved by either party. A Christian king should certainly respect the law, and indeed has a duty to protect it. But he is never subject to it.

In a companion text, the *Basilicon Doron*, James confirmed that a 'good king will frame his actions to be according to the law, but he is not bound thereto but of his good will'.[24] More of the *Basilicon* in due course. A manual of fatherly advice mainly about dressing up and looking good. And indeed being a 'loving father' to his realm. As James affirmed in the *Trew Law*. The patriarchal metaphor was a favourite amongst political theorists of an absolutist persuasion: English or Roman. In his *Patriarcha*, composed during the 1630s, Sir Robert Filmer traced the Stuart dynasty right back to the patriarchs of the Old Testament. The 'first kings were fathers of families'.[25] Lots of helpful scripture again, unsurprisingly. All leading to the same conclusion, shared by later royalist apologists such as Claudius Salmasius, that the king 'takes the place of a parent among his subjects'.[26] We will encounter Salmasius again in a later chapter, annoying Milton.

Needless to say James liked all this. He particularly liked the renowned injunction from 1 *Peter* 2:17: 'Fear God, Honour the King.' And the bit that came before, 2:14–15, an especial favourite of Filmer too: 'Submit yourself to every ordinance of man for the Lord's sake: whether it be to the king as supreme; Or unto governors as unto them are sent by him … For so is the will of God.' And another bit *Psalms* 82, especially usefully in explaining the 'duties' of kingship. Amongst which is 'maintaining and putting to execution the old lowable laws of the countrey'. James never disputed the authority of the common law. He did though dispute the idea that it might define his prerogative. 'You should not go to the root and dispute my prerogative', he would warn Parliament in his 1610 address, not for the first time, or the last. Do not 'meddle with such ancient rights of mine', privileges 'derived' from 'grace'. As 'God standeth in the congregation of the mighty' his anointed sovereign 'judgeth among the gods'.[27] Echoes of the Byzantine *dominus mundi*. And 1 *Samuel* 8:5: 'And Samuel judged Israel all the days of his life.' James rather liked the idea of being the new Samuel, almost as much as he liked the idea of being the new Justinian.[28]

In time, as we will see, the contestability of James's view of kingship would be resolved in successive revolutions. For now, we should note a couple more points, necessarily related. First, different absolutists believed differently. The *Trew Law* matters most because of its author. Second, it was not aberrant, regardless of what later Whig historians might have intimated. There were plenty of clerics and jurists who thought much as their new king thought. The future Archbishop of Canterbury, William Laud, put it plainly: 'God's power is in the King.'[29] A 'Prince of this Realme is the immediate minister of Justice under God', the antiquarian William Lambarde agreed.[30] Seriate Lord Chancellors too. The 'king's majesty', Lord Ellesmere sought to assure his newly arrived sovereign, 'as it were inheritable and descended from God, hath absolute monarchical power annexed inseparably to his crown and diadem, not by common law nor statute, but more anciently than either of them'.[31] A view shared by his successor. The 'king holdeth not his prerogatives mediate from the law, but immediately from God', the coming Lord Chancellor Bacon confirmed.[32]

The extent to which Bacon was intellectually tuned to an evidently more naturalistic, even Roman, idea of kingship remains a matter of conjecture.[33] But he certainly appreciated its prescience, and how much it appealed to his master. Moreover, there was precedent in the common law, some distant, some less so. Back in 1514, the court in *Hunne's Case* had obligingly confirmed that 'Kings of England in time past have never had any superior but God alone'.[34] A perception again reinforced by the logic of Reformation: the king of England as governor of its Church. More recently, in 1591, *Caudry's Case* had confirmed that 'by the ancient laws of this realm, this kingdom of England is an absolute empire and monarchy'. Chief Baron Fleming gestured similarly in *Bates's Case* in 1606. The king's 'power to govern', coming directly from God, is 'ordinary and absolute'.[35]

This need not, though, mean that an English king ruled by 'licence'. As Sir John Eliot confirmed in his *Monarchie of Man*. It simply meant that there was 'not superiority above' the crown.[36] It was sort of what James said; and sort of not. So much, as ever, depended on metaphorical feint. Here, two in particular. First, the exercise of royal prerogative to correct perceived injustices of the common law. Most apparent in the jurisdiction of prerogative courts, such as Star Chamber and the High Commission. Lord Keeper Williams supplied the poetry. The 'sweet temper of equity' had saved the English from the 'oppressions' of the 'customs of Normandy, which we call our Common Law', for six hundred years.[37] A contestable history, as we will see. And second, rule without the bother of Parliament. More contentious still, as we shall also see. Though Bacon did his best, all part of the same 'garland of prerogative'.[38]

Hooker's law

Plenty of counter-metaphors of course. A number refined in the rectory at Bishopsbourne on the Kentish Weald. Home, by the later 1590s, of a semi-retired cleric named Richard Hooker. At that moment writing up a vast commentary on the governance of Church and Crown, entitled *Of the Laws of Ecclesiastical Polity*. The final volume appearing just a few months before the *Trew Law*. The younger Hooker had led a more exciting life. Rector of the Temple Church in the Inns of Court during the latter part of the 1580s. Amongst his regular congregation was a young Edward Coke.[39] A prestigious appointment, if wearying. The Temple had become a hot seat of theological contention during the closing decades of the sixteenth century, as the late Elizabethan Church struggled to accommodate competing conformist and Presbyterian factions.

Which meant that it was also a hot seat of constitutional contention. The entire purpose of the Reformation, aside from saving a 'chosen' people, was to bring Church and commonwealth into alignment. So that one could 'never subsist but in the other', as Laud would later confirm.[40] All of which meant a lot of work for a generation of bright young lawyers. Looking back on the Reformation 'settlement', all Lambarde could see was 'stacks of statutes'. Beginning with an *Act in Restraint of Appeals* in March 1533, to be followed by acts *Concerning Ecclesiastical Appointments*, in *Restraint of Annates*, *of Supremacy*, *of Succession* and so on. A couple of *Dissolution Acts*. And a new *Treason Act* too, just to keep everyone honest. And a recurring business, for each successive sovereign seemed to want to fiddle with it. Which meant more statutes; and more contention. Hooker's *Laws* were designed to put an end to all that.[41]

Not that there was anything radical in the *Laws*, still less unfamiliar. Quite the opposite. Any young gentleman pitching up at the Inns of Court in late Elizabethan England would have found, on his reading list, Aristotle's *Ethics*. A few might even have read it. Hooker founded his 'polity' here, on the Aristotelian 'common good'.[42] Which he then reshaped to fit Reformation England and its 'chosen' people. The 'common good' of a commonwealth, secured by a common law. Here again, the invocation was hardly original. Legions of scholastic and antiquarian jurists had laid the ground; all situating the common law in the founding mythologies of the 'ancient' constitution. A famous statement could be found in Sir John Davies's *Irish Reports*. The 'common law of England is nothing, but the common custome of the realme'. Which was 'the most perfect and most excellent, and without comparison the best, to make and preserve a Commonwealth'. A conclusion proved 'time out of mind'.[43]

Commonalty was defining.[44] Time out of mind, perhaps, but also chiming nicely with the closer sentiment of Reformation. A 'chosen people' with common purpose, out and about doing His work. A defining assurance. Cherished half a century on by a very different cleric, in a very different moment. 'God seemes to call for somethinge att our hands about Religion, and that only because wee are Englishmen'. So the incendiary army chaplain Hugh Peter advised the Council of Officers on 15 December 1648, as it wrestled with the possibility that what He wanted now was for them to kill their king.[45] A little less heated on the Kentish Weald in the mid-1590s, and accordingly a little more measured in Hooker's Aristotelian idyll. Part of a greater harmony. Hooker sought recourse to a musical metaphor:

> Happier the people, whose law is their king in the greatest things than that whose King is himself their law. Where the King doth guide the state and the law the King, that commonwealth is like an harp or melodious instrument, the strings whereof are tuned and handled all by one hand, following as laws the rules and canons of Musical science.[46]

The harp was said to be Queen Elizabeth's favourite instrument.

As to the vexed matter of prerogative, Hooker adopted a sensibly light touch. In the eighth book of the *Laws* he discussed the prerogative to call church 'assemblies'. Easier in regard to the Church, absent any competing claims on 'supremacy'. Otherwise, it was simply a matter of deploying more diversionary metaphors. Such as the king's 'two bodies', made familiar to English audiences in Plowden's *Commentaries*.[47] It supposed that a king had two 'bodies', a public and a private; that he was, in effect, 'twice-born'.[48] Thus certain prerogatives might be personal, vested by God, whilst others might be bound by rules of public law; such, critically, as tax-raising. Coke, as Attorney General, had accepted the principled distinction, that there were 'two manners of prerogatives', one 'absolute' and the other 'ordinary'; the latter only being 'determined by the law'. A fiction approved by Chief Baron Fleming in *Bates's Case*.[49] And implicit, again, in Coke's account of *Calvin's Case*; the 'natural body, being descended of the blood royal', and the body politic, which 'framed the policy of man'.[50] Peter Heylyn would twist the distinction slightly; so that a king possessed powers *in abstracto*, which were 'above the lawes', and powers *in concreto* which were not. Sir John Dodderidge would do similarly, and, a little later, Samuel Rutherford in his 1644 tract *Lex Rex*.[51]

Tricky though. The margins were never really clear, and whilst Coke would praise Queen Elizabeth for her dexterity, ensuring that any 'commandement' should 'agreeth with the ancient Law of England', there was no guarantee that any successor would be so sensitive to metaphorical nuance.[52] Interestingly, as the case against Charles was taking shape, during the later 1640s, both sides would continue to work with the corporeal metaphor. Thus a royalist pamphlet, published in 1647, would reframe the thesis as a 'Gemini, Inseperable, and individuall', whilst the radical parliamentarian Henry Marten would sharply distinguish the office of king from the 'will of Charles Steuart'. John Lilburne was plainer still. 'Charles Stewart as Charles Stewart' was 'different from the King as King'. The latter was an office of state, the former a 'meer man'. A sentiment revisited in Henry Robinson's later defence of the regicide. The public body of 'Kings are but meer chargeable Ceremonies'.[53] Levelling kings, and levelling metaphors.

The aligned idea that the monarch was the 'fountain of justice' was beyond argument. Though Archbishop Bancroft's metaphorical extension, that the king might, from time to time, 'draw' on the fountain to give the courts a good 'clean', would not have washed with Coke.[54] Likewise the 'measuring' of the prerogative. Another ubiquitous metaphor, around which, as we will shortly see, Shakespeare would write an entire play. Selden famously jibed the 'measure' of the Chancellor's 'foot'.[55] Coke would deploy a 'metewand'.[56] At a slight variant, Sir Roger Twysden wrote of a 'tempered' constitution.[57] The measuring of the past too, endless tracts surmising the meaning of 'ancient'. Taking his lead from Geoffrey of Monmouth, Coke plumped for Brutus, who had written a first book of laws, amended by Dunwallo of Molmutius. Fun to surmise, of course. But not really the point. Time out of mind was not supposed to have a start.

As to the mind of James Stuart. Not always that much easier to read, despite everything that he had written on the subject; or perhaps because. In his 1610 speech, James confirmed that would indeed rule 'according to my Lawes'. A perception which, at first glance, seems to chime. 'It is neither permitted unto Prelates nor Prince to judge or determine at their own discretion', Hooker's *Laws* confirmed, 'but law hath prescribed what both shall do'. For 'what power the King hath he hath it by law, the bounds and limits of it are known'. It is for this reason that any royal 'grant' made 'contrary to law is void'.[58] So far so good. It is the second glance which imports doubt, and made for some awkward moments. The proprietary sentiment; 'my' laws. Thirty years later, Charles would berate those who 'have gone about subtilly to distinguish betwixt our person and our authority'. The consequence, most likely, of an awkward few days at Hull, and a parliamentary declaration urging the king to 'remember that his resolutions do concern kingdoms, and therefore ought not to be moulded by his own'.[59] We will return to Hull in due course.

By which time the metaphors, at least those of 'divine' kingship, had begun to lose their charm. Selden coined a rather earthier alternative. A 'king is a thing men have made for their own sakes, for quietness sake. Just as in a family, one man is appointed to buy the meat'.[60] A loaded insinuation. A makeable king could be unmade. We might skip briefly forward to January 1649, by which time the acuity of Selden's prophesy had become brutally apparent. The night before his execution, Charles was visited by his youngest children. Some fatherly advice and a reading list. For spiritual sustenance, the sermons of William Laud and Lancelot

Andrewes. For some tips on governance, the *Laws* of Richard Hooker. A daunting list, for children of any age; or their parents. Time now for another daunting read; the 'casebook' of Sir Edward Coke.

The casebook of Edward Coke

There are thirteen volumes of Coke's *Reports*. A first appeared in 1600. The last was published in 1613. Selective, of course, for reason of authorial discretion. But still, plenty from which to choose. Not all touched on matters of kingship and governance. But many did, not least because Coke twisted them into that shape. We only have time to revisit a few. Starting with the case which, it has been suggested, signalled the opening of Coke's 'offensive' against the jurisprudence of 'divine right'.[61]

The case of the fractious barrister

Many things annoyed Nicholas Fuller, Member of Parliament for the City of London and barrister of Gray's Inn. Not a man of easy temper, nor one inclined to keep his opinions to himself. The idea of 'union' with Scotland, for example. A nation of 'pedlars', Fuller advised his fellow parliamentarians, 'infidels and pagans'. Hardly an observation calculated to win much favour at the Court of James Stuart. A 'rash and headlong' man, according to Gardiner.[62] A vehement critic of monopolies, Fuller had built a lucrative practice disputing patents and impositions.[63] Hostile to anything which smacked of prerogative abuse, zealous in his faith. The common law 'mind' and the puritan 'conscience' in testy alignment.[64]

A shaded conscience, in truth. Puritanism, as we will discover, came in various forms. In 1641, Henry Burton would coin the term 'independency' in a tract entitled *England's Bondage and Hope of Deliverance*. Not that he was an admirer. We will next encounter Burton propped up in a pillory next to a similarly doubtful William Prynne. The 'spirit of independency', in the opinion of both, being no less troubling than the damnable heresies of Rome. Prophetic, given what would occur in January 1649. That, though, is another story. For now, we can identify Fuller as an advocate of Presbyterianism; literally. Someone who thought in similar terms as the later regicide, Thomas Scot, in whose opinion it was 'against conscience' for all 'judicious puritans' to 'yield obedience to tyrannical and lawless commands'.[65] And lawless courts.

We will, in a later chapter, take a closer look at the writings of John Milton. A champion of 'independency', of course, as well as regicide. But sharing the same belief, that the Reformation had been corrupted by the creation of 'grinding courts', purposed to reinvest 'priestly machinations'. The most grinding of all being the court of High Commission, established in 1559 to enforce the 'Uniformity of Common Prayer'. And do some tidying-up. The preamble to the Act which established the Commission aspired to root out 'all and singular heretical opinions, seditious books, contempts, conspiracies, false rumours, tales, seditions, misbehaviours, invented or set forth by any person or persons against us, contrary or against the laws or statutes of this our realm, against the quiet governance and rule of our people'. Catholics were an obvious concern. But so too, increasingly, were puritans of the more zealous variety; which, by definition, was most of them.

The Commission operated in a quasi-judicial capacity, presided over by a mixture of bishops, lay commissioners and canon lawyers. The 1593 *Seditious Sectaries Act*, which treated it as a 'court', vested closer authority to discipline persistent non-attenders at church, as well as 'seditious sectaries and disloyal persons'. Reason enough for resentment. Exacerbated by three further features. First, the lack of jurisdictional determination. Second, the fact that proceedings could be held *in camera*. And third, the imposition of an ex officio oath which required accused parties to provide incriminatory evidence. The oath caused especial resentment, touching so directly on the matter of conscience. A popish affectation, resonant of the Inquisition. A 'bloody and broyling law', in the words of the puritan barrister Roger Morice.[66] In simple terms, the Commission was a policing institution, intended to enforce the Reformation 'settlement'. Which is what made it 'grinding'.

Not the only 'grinding' court, of course. Of older vintage were the prerogative courts of Chancery and Star Chamber. Both of which had developed during the later middle ages, with the intention of relieving the administrative burden on the *curia regis*. An entire body of equity law had grown up in Chancery; the preferred court of any litigant who did not fancy their chances in the common law courts of Common Pleas or King's Bench. The 'court' of Star Chamber, meanwhile, had become synonymous with protecting Crown interests.[67] It was where those who fell foul of monopoly and patent licences might expect to be brought. Doubtful doctors too, as we will shortly see, and those accused of sedition, who wrote horrid things about the king and his wife, and his archbishop.[68] Lightening rods for the collected resentment of puritans and common lawyers. In 1641, the Long Parliament would abolish both Star Chamber and the Commission, for having 'undertaken to punish where no law doth warrant'. Now though, back to the case of Nicholas Fuller.

A man with something of a reputation. Not just for baiting his king in Parliament but for representing puritan ministers brought before the Commission. Fuller had been annoying for a while. In 1589, he represented the notorious Presbyterian preacher John Udall, accused of sedition, having written a tract entitled *A Discovery of the Discipline*.[69] A couple of years later, he represented Thomas Cartwright and other ministers before the Star Chamber, ending up in the Fleet prison for his efforts.[70] By 1603, Fuller was very much the barrister of choice for harassed preachers accused of heresy or sedition. And things were about to get busy, with the appointment, in December 1604, of a new Archbishop of Canterbury. Richard Bancroft had made his name hunting down pesky puritans during the 1590s. And the purge of the Church, which followed the discovery of the Powder Plot a year later, gave him just the excuse he needed, to flush out a few more.

Such as Richard Mansell and Thomas Ladd, two recently deprived ministers who Fuller agreed to represent in early 1607. Mansell had presented a rather pointed petition to the House, which argued that 'all the late proceedings against the ministers, in repressing of their ministry, and in depriving them of their free holds, is contrary to the laws of this kingdom, both the Charta Magna and to many statutes'. As a consequence of which he was arrested and placed in the Clink. Where he remained for nine months. At which point Fuller went to the Court of King's Bench and obtained a writ of habeas corpus. As he did for Ladd. Who had been arrested for refusing to take the oath ex officio, as part of a Commission investigation into a 'conventicle' in Norfolk. The Commission did have arrest powers, under the provisions of the governing Elizabethan statute. But the general consensus, amongst common lawyers at least, was that these were reinvested powers.[71]

Which, importantly, did not extend to imprisonment. As Fuller argued, a little too hotly, advising the court that history revealed only one comparable instance, of an ecclesiastical body seeking to over-reach the common law in order to detain subjects of the Crown. Back in the reign of Henry IV, 'procured by popish prelates in the time of darkness'. The desire to imprison men 'without showing any cause or matter' was ultra vires, 'popish and antichristian'. 'Granted an ynch', diocesan officers will 'take an ell'. Fuller was committed for his 'offensive words' and 'schismatical and factious humour', and despatched to the Fleet.[72] A blatant breach of the 'precious liberty' enshrined in Chapter 29 of *Magna Carta*, according to his counsel. Meanwhile Fuller urged his parliamentary colleagues to investigate the apparent breach of privilege. 'At every renewing', the Commission 'increaseth and encroacheth more power and more', something which 'by the Law is not warrantable nor can be granted'.[73] The following summer, having been released and then rearrested, Fuller entered a writ of prohibition at King's Bench. Such writs were issued to stay proceedings, in this case, Fuller's arrest.

The stakes were high. A moment of 'great peril to the state', the newly appointed Master of Requests soberly advised the Commons.[74] A perception shared, albeit differently, by his king. Fuller was a 'villain' threatening the very 'dignity' of the Crown. An 'evil' personified, his Lord Chancellor agreed.[75] Fuller was going nowhere, and was ordered to be kept in chains. Meanwhile there would be a 'consultation' between the king and his judges. Who, sitting as a full bench, replete with barons of Exchequer, sought to cut some kind of compromise. The jurisdiction of the Commission in matters of heresy was unarguable. But matters of 'scandal' and contempt against the 'King or his Government, Temporal or Ecclesiastical' fell to the common law courts. A resolution easily enough predicted by anyone who had read Coke's recent judgement in *Sir Anthony Roper's Case*:

> The ecclesiastical court is like a fountain of sweet water to refresh all the earth, but if the fountain does not contain itself within its banks it will flood the lower lands. The policy of this state has always been that the common law should be the bounder, to reduce it within its channel when it runs over.[76]

A familiar metaphor. And a hint taken. The Commission proceeded to prosecute Fuller for heresy, fining him £200.

The position, to Coke at least, was clear. The Commission was established by statute, the 'construction' of which 'belongs to the judges of the common law'. And if the Commission over-reached its 'cognizance', then a writ of prohibition could be granted.[77] But if Coke thought the matter was settled, he was wrong. Another invitation, to Privy Council on 10 November. Accounts vary as to the temper of this 'consultation', and precisely what was said.[78] Coke, as Chief Justice of Common Pleas, was certainly in no mood to be malleable, at least not according to his own report of the proceedings.[79] Rather than seeking his king's forgiveness, he launched into a diatribe against Bancroft, and the supposition that judges were simply the 'delegates' of the king. The matter, the archbishop had suggested, was 'clear in Divinity'. Not so, Coke replied; apparently on behalf of 'all' the assembled judges. Their authority lay in the common law, and it 'protecteth the king'. To which James had apparently replied, in heated tones, that 'he was not defended by his laws but by God'.[80] Which gave him the authority to 'maketh the Judges', and unmake them.

Rarely averse to a bit of intellectual fencing, James had then engaged Coke directly. Given that 'the law was founded on reason, and that he had reason as well as judges', he wondered why he should be precluded from assuming a judicial authority clearly invested in him by God. The answer was simple, but hardly tactful. Coke agreed entirely that reason was the 'life of the law'. But it was a particular kind of reason, an 'artificial perfection' that was only 'gotten by long study'. Which James had not done, and so did not possess:

> True it was that God had endowed his Majesty with excellent science and great endowments of nature; but His Majesty was not learned in the laws of the realm of England; and causes which concern the life, or inheritance, or goods, or fortunes, of his subjects are not to be decided by natural reason, but by artificial reason and judgement of law, which requires long study and experience before that a man can attain to the cognizance of it; and that the law was the golden mete-wand and means to try the causes of his subjects; and which protected His Majesty in safety and peace.

A famous bit of Bracton to close: 'The king ought not to be under any man, but under God and the law.' Coke liked to cite Bracton at such moments; when elevating opinion into something apparently beyond argument. Such a principle, he continued, 'delights the honour of the king, whose person they represent as they sit in justice'.[81]

James did not seem very delighted. On the contrary, reported to be 'greatly offended'. Hardly surprising; the inference being that he was probably bright enough, but not sufficiently learned in the common law. James wondered loudly if his Chief Justice was too 'full of craturity', his body of judges too ready to embellish the 'obscuritie' of their jurisprudence. Like the 'papistes' indeed, who 'alleadge scriptures and will interpret the same'. A dark insinuation. It was, James concluded, a 'traiterous speech'. According to one report, 'his Majestie fell into that high indignation as the like was never knowne in him, looking and speaking fiercely with bended fist, offering to strike' his Chief Justice. And was only pacified when Coke 'fell flatt on all fower; humbly beseeching his Majestie to take compassion on him and pardon him'. Along with the Lord Treasurer, Sir Robert Cecil, who likewise 'kneeled down' and 'prayed' the king forgive his wayward nephew.[82]

If Coke was cowed, it was not for long. The following year he would repeat the aspersion in *Calvin's Case*. Only 'reverend judges' could be properly trusted to interpret the scriptures of the law, for only they had undertaken the necessary 'diligent study'.[83] And he would do so again, more famously still, in the final book of *Institutes*: 'For reason is the life of the law, nay the Common Law it selfe is nothing else but reason, which is to be understood as an artificiall perfection of reason.'[84] Meantime, writs of prohibition continued to issue out of Common Pleas. An alleged adulterer released in 1611, a tardy alimony-payer in 1614, assorted tithe-disputants. Not though a couple of Brownists. There were limits, and the nature of their heresy was just too damnable.[85]

James bided his time, whilst Bancroft continued to whisper in his ear. Of the common lawyers who 'come with such an absolute and ravenous cause of power like a keyte and take and teare all Ecclesiastical Courts', and the judges, who behave like the 'Ephori'.[86] As for Nicholas Fuller, a cursory apology and a release from the Fleet, in January 1608; 'very frolic' it was reported. By the end of the month he was back inside. More 'offensive words', found in a printed account of his defence, entitled *The Argument of Nicholas Fuller*. The 'laws of England are the high inheritance of the realm, by which both King and subjects are directed'. And 'kings are made for commonwealths, not commonwealths for kings'. And so on, replete with various invocations of *Magna Carta* and 'divers other statutes after'.[87] Out again in April, under 'restraint'. Though not so restrained that he was prevented from attending Parliament. Where, amidst the heated debates of late 1610, he could be heard quoting choice bits of his *Argument*. We will leave Nicholas Fuller, by now an elder statesman at sixty-seven years of age. Energies undimmed he would remain in Parliament until his death in 1620. And turn our attention to a couple of cases which revisited the same essential contention, but from a rather different perspective.

The case of the floppy ruff and the overrunning stew

We noted before James's liking for ruling by prerogative decree. A hundred or more proclamations in the first half dozen years of his reign. Many uncontroversial. Various proclamations for chasing down those implicated in the notorious Powder Plot, for example, or for apprehending enclosure rioters. Proclamations forbidding 'infected persons' from attending Court made sense too, as did those intended to remove 'hangers-on in Court'. And there was not much controversy in the 1609 proclamation 'forbidding any person to carry letters' except 'such as are allowed by Authority'. At least not at first glance. James had no principled objection to entrepreneurial postmen; but he did want a cut.

Which brings us to a real reason why James issued so many proclamations. Money, the blight of English kings. Or the saving, according to Sir John Fortescue. In his fifteenth-century treatise, *In Praise of the Laws of England*, Fortescue had identified two particular characteristics of a country governed *dominium politicum et regale*. We have just come across a first; that the king ruled in accordance with the law. The second was that the king could only levy taxes with the approval of Parliament. There could be no 'strange impositions', on domestic business at least. The upside for the king was that his people would 'rejoice'.[88] The downside was that he was constantly in need of submitting an account to Parliament, and asking for a favour. Or indulging in some very creative accountancy. There were alternative means of raising finance. Various customary or 'incident' fines, such as distraint of knighthood. Hardly popular, as we will discover. And not especially lucrative either. King and Parliament would spend much of 1609–10 negotiating the possibility of the Crown relinquishing its customary incomes in return for a more regular parliamentary grant. The 'Great Contract', it would have been called, if they had managed to agree terms. Which they did not.

Other possibilities included 'forcing' loans, even less popular, or raising money through 'impositions' on imported goods. A broad authority could be granted, again by Parliament, under provisions of 'tonnage and poundage'. Queen Elizabeth had laid a precedent, with an imposition on tobacco and currants in 1601. Not, she hastened to add, in any way purposed to 'the hurt of my people'. Exchequer Court would later approve the legality of the imposition in *Bates's Case*. But whilst it demurred in the moment, Parliament remained vigilant, especially where it suspected that proclamations purporting to correct 'disorderly' trading practices were really vehicles for creating domestic monopolies.[89]

Accordingly, when King James proposed a couple more proclamations in 1607, one intended to 'prohibit' new buildings in London, and another the making of starch, there were mutterings. Both tapped into growing markets, and were intended to protect revenue streams. Which, it was reported, brought 'considerable sums' to the Exchequer.[90] But it was not just economics. Government by proclamation touched on questions of law and constitution too. In asking his judges to establish the legality of his proclamations, James was thus inviting them to muse on something rather greater; on what it meant to be a king of England. Before we find out what Coke, and his judicial brethren, concluded, we might take a closer look at the two markets in question.

First the starch. The proclamation was intended to reinforce the recent incorporation of the Company of Starchmakers, which had been granted a monopoly in the manufacture of starch, along with an authority to 'fine' imports. The Company would get half the 'fine', the Exchequer the rest. Private starch-making monopolies had been a matter of contention since the granting of a first patent in 1588. There was money in starch, alongside all the glycosidic bonds which made it so usefully sticky. Commonly used in baking, as well as fermenting and malting. And in the making of a paper, an increasingly lucrative market. And in fashion. No self-respecting Jacobean gentleman could be seen wandering the streets of London with a floppy ruff. Originally designed to counter the hazards of the unbecoming dribble, the ruff had become quite the fashion item by the mid-sixteenth century. James, himself a notoriously messy eater, and very much a follower of fashion, took great pride in the size of his ruff. When he really wanted to impress, he wore one that was nearly a foot in radius. Useful too in helping to protect his neck from any knife-wielding assassin. James Stuart was as paranoid as he was dribbly and vain. Eventually the wing-collar would replace the fancy ruff. But not yet. And in the meantime there were lots of 'fines' to be levied.

The second proclamation addressed building regulation. There was a lot about his new realm that James rather liked. But London disappointed. A city of 'sticks'. Which he intended to replace with 'bricke, being a material farre more durable, safe from fire and beautiful and magnificent'.[91] Less likely to fall down, or promote the spread of disease. And there was something else, something even more dreadful than crumbling masonry. Crumbling morality. The Proclamation of 1607 aimed at a more particular kind of construction; the conversion of existing houses into what we would term multi-occupancy units. And for the housing of a particular kind of resident. Demography again, and the demand curve. More bored gentlemen resident in the City meant more prostitutes in gainful employment. And needing somewhere to reside.

Henry VIII had tried to shut down the Southwark 'bawdy houses' in 1546. A proclamation intended to suppress 'Whore-houses' with 'sound of Trumpet'. Not entirely successful. A City full of 'licenced stews', so the puritan Thomas Nashe described late Elizabethan London, a haven of 'six-penny whoredom'.

Queen Elizabeth expressed a measure of disapproval, at the proliferation of 'stews' at the margins of her capital.[92] Dreadful indeed; especially the consequence of the 'French welcome', as syphilis was more commonly known. But nothing if not a pragmatist, Elizabeth was well aware that markets are difficult to buck. Prostitution was business. The Earl of Warwick liveried his pimps; marketing for a more discerning gentleman. And there was a further connection; with another thriving business. A slap-up meal at the local tavern, followed by a half-hour fumble in the brothel next door, were two parts of a cracking night out for most Jacobean gentlemen. The third part was a couple of hours spent in the nearby theatre, hurling profanities and rotting vegetation at the stage. Unsurprising then that late Elizabethan actor-managers, such as Philip Henslowe and Edward Alleyn, should dabble in the brothel business.

Morality and money, never an easy accommodation. As anyone in attendance at Court for the Christmas festivities in 1604 would have been reminded. To watch the first production of a new play performed by the recently appointed Company of King's Men. The Company manager was William Shakespeare, and the play was entitled *Measure for Measure*. Intended for instruction as well as entertainment. In the next chapter we will take a closer look at the fashion for didactic 'mirror' literature. *Measure for Measure* was a contribution. Familiar in a sense. The struggles of an inept prince would not have been much of a surprise to Shakespearian audiences; the lighter comedies of the 1590s were full of them. But different shading. The commonwealth created in *Measure for Measure* is a dark and dangerous place. Coleridge would later call it 'horrible'.[93] No more frolicking in the forest of Arden. Joyous muddle gives way to a politics of vicious hypocrisy. The main plot turns around a duke distressed by the apparent collapse of morality in his commonwealth, the sub-plot around a magistrate driven to distraction by a brothel-owner and his clients. A familiar Shakespearean conceit, the mirroring of high and low politics.

There are three magistrates in *Measure for Measure*. The first is the duke. Baffled by jurisprudence. Possessed of 'strict statutes and most biting laws', but seemingly unable to enforce them. Now 'more mock'd than fear'd' (1.3.19, 27–9).[94] So he abdicates and goes about his commonwealth in disguise in the hope of discovering the cause. James had famously done similar the previous summer, visiting the Exchange *incognito*. Risky though, as the courtier Lucio observes. Playing the 'fantastical duke of dark corners' (4.3.156). The second magistrate is the duke's brother Angelo. A strident puritan, and prospective rapist, in whom the duke vests regency powers during his absence. Evil counsel was a constant hazard for any prince. We will encounter plenty of evil counsellors in the coming pages. The third magistrate in the play is Escalus, the local Justice who struggles to impose some kind of order on the ground. A man of measure and moderation, he just about manages.

We can assume that James caught the gist. A Court and a commonwealth drowning in a sea of sexual impropriety; threatening, as the returning duke admits, to 'oe'errun the stew' (5.1.316–17). The 'duke of dark corners', struggling to impose himself on his new realm. And not, according to some critics, setting much of an example. A 'nursery of lust and intemperance', the puritan Lucy Hutchinson would later say of the Jacobean Court. A place 'grown scandalous', Lady Anne Clifford agreed.[95] Time perhaps for a Royal Proclamation that made it look like the new king cared. Remember though, as Lucio again observes, there is measure to be had: 'Grace is grace, despite of all controversy' (1.2.24–5). For which reason, it might be best to check with the judges. A 'conference' was called in Privy Council. Coke's account of what transpired is found in the twelfth volume of *Reports*.[96]

Along with Coke, as Chief Justice of Common Pleas, James invited Lord Chief Justice Fleming, Chief Baron Tanfield and Baron Altham. A starry bench. Greeted by a similarly starry cast of royal sycophants. Headed by Coke's uncle, Sir Robert Cecil, presently Lord Treasurer and Secretary of State, and Lord Chancellor Ellesmere. Who, on behalf of the king, requested an 'opinion' on the legality of the proclamations and, by inference, the credibility of various 'grievances' which had been brought to the king's attention. His view, as 'keeper of the king's conscience', was predictable. He would enforce any 'decree accordingly'. But the king wished to know that his common law judges would do similarly. That they too would respect the 'power and prerogative of the King', recognizing that in 'cases in which there is no authority and president' they must 'leave it to the King to order in it according to his wisdome'. Otherwise the king would indeed be 'no more than the Duke of Venice'. The Lord Privy Seal chipped in with a familiar metaphor. A king, like a physician, is best placed to 'apply his Medecine according to the quality of the disease'. Allusions, and questions, of the loaded variety.

Which did not elicit an especially helpful response; as the Council, deep down, probably feared. Speaking on their behalf, Coke requested time to consult his judicial 'brethren'. The questions were of 'great importance', and touched on a matter of 'novelty'. Precedent appeared 'wanting', which necessitated 'great considerations'. He would though venture a preliminary 'opinion'. That a 'King cannot change any part of the Common Law, nor create any offence by his Proclamations, which was not an offence before, without Parliament'. Enough to raise a few alarm bells. A few weeks later Coke was back, having consulted with his 'brethren'. His preliminary opinion now confirmed. And, despite the 'novelty', now apparently unarguable. Finding authority in Fortescue and Holinshed and various statutes, including a Henrician Act of 1539 which confirmed that proclamations enjoyed the same status as Parliamentary Acts. Which also meant that they were comprehended within the jurisdiction of the common law. Coke did not challenge the existence of the prerogative. But it was 'resolved that the King hath no Prerogative, but that which the Law of the Land allows him'. To rub it in a bit, Coke cited various proclamations which he had, on closer study, discovered to be 'utterly against Law and reason'. At least he did not list any of James's.

A modern public lawyer would recognize a declaratory ruling. A statement of the law which, by custom, would be respected by the executive body in question.

King James, though, perceived something more: a threat. For now, he just fumed. And, of course, carried on with his proclamations. A further on building regulation appeared in early 1611. Followed by similar on cloth-dyeing and vegetable pricing, 'abuses' in the tin-trade, the making of 'gold and silver thread', and the 'garbling of spices, and all other things garbleable'. And dozens more over the coming decade. All seeking to regulate 'disorderly' trade, and keep the Exchequer afloat. The builders kept building, the prostitutes plying their trade. And the actors acting. A breed of men, as Coke declared at the Norwich Assize in 1606, of which the 'country' was 'much troubled'.[97] Not though the starch-making monopoly. It proved unworkable and would be revoked in 1619.

A dodgy dealer and a missing vicar

Our final two cases will take us through to the summer of 1616, a 'year to consecrate justice', as Bacon described it.[98] And the spectacular fall of the now Lord Chief Justice of England. Neither case, we might note, made it into Coke's final volumes of *Reports*; a 'greatest hits', in the main selected by the artist himself.[99] Cases which, in practical terms, were conjoined. And, again, not much about matters of kingship; at least not at first glance. But Coke made them so. Similar might be said of *Dr Bonham's Case*, decided in 1610. A squabble about the licencing of a supposed doctor, and the jurisdiction of quasi-public bodies established in Crown charters. And again in the *Earl of Oxford's Case*, decided in King's Bench in 1615. A troublesome conveyance this time. Which ended up with James instructing his Attorney General to remind his Lord Chief Justice of a few home truths. More precisely, that the office of Lord Chancellor existed precisely to 'correct Men's Consciences for Frauds, Breaches of Trusts, Wrongs and oppressions, of what nature soever they be, and to soften and nullify the Extremity of the Law'. In other words, when the common law got it wrong. Coke was reported 'vexed'.[100]

Patience wearing thin, on all sides. Which brings us to these final two cases. Starting with another dodgy deal. Early-seventeenth-century England was full of dodgy dealers, as anyone who had attended a performance of Ben Jonson's *Bartholomew Fair* would have been fully aware. As Robert Dallington, indeed, advised his young charge, the future Charles I. Beware of 'novelty', and those 'desirous' of it.[101] Deaf ears, as we will see. Charles could rarely resist a pretty novelty. The novelty in *Glanvil's Case* was 'paste' jewellery, sold to gullible gentlemen and their ladies. Most of whom, it seems, either never noticed, or just put it down to experience. Unfortunately for Glanvil one of his clients took particular exception to being conned. Mr Courtney had agreed to pay £360 for a presumably very nice diamond. Instead he received a piece of 'topaz' that was supposed to look a lot like a diamond. There were reasons to wear topaz; good for curing lunacy, it was commonly believed, and warning off the 'evil eye'.[102] But it was not what

Mr Courtney wanted, and it was not worth £360. Nearer to £20. Understandably perhaps he refused to pay up. Glanvil, hardly lacking in boldness, decided to sue for payment in King's Bench and succeeded in getting an order. Courtney retaliated by suing in Chancery for rescission of the contract of sale.

And received judgement, Chancery issuing a declaration halting the judgement of King's Bench. Which, needless to say, Glanvil ignored. All very predictable, as was the consequence. Glanvil was arrested and placed in the Fleet. But not for long, immediately entering a writ of habeas corpus in King's Bench. Another Chief Justice might have left well alone. Glanvil was hardly deserving of judicial favour. Not Coke though. The writ was granted; on the grounds that the reasons for the 'return' of Chancery were not stated. A triumphant Glanvil apparently returned to the Fleet, this time of his own free will, to encourage other incumbents to seek similar recourse. Lord Chancellor Ellesmere immediately ordered his re-arrest, whilst making 'greevous complaint' to the king. He had his suspicions. Not enough of what was going on seemed to surprise the Lord Chief Justice.

By this point Glanvil had adopted a new strategy, preferring bills of *praemunire* against Courtney and his lawyers, and a range of other legal officers, including the warden of the Fleet. The *Statute of Praemunire* had been enacted, back in the fourteenth century, to prevent the remitting of tax direct to Rome, and had proved very useful at the time of the Reformation. It was not intended to save conmen from prison. But Glanvil gave it a go. Back to King's Bench, where Coke was invited to exercise his imagination. The thought that an action in Chancery might be analogous to an appeal to Rome was something of a stretch. But Coke, it seems, was persuaded. Not though the jury, which declined to follow his direction. It was reported that a furious Coke tore into the 'varletts and knaves' assembled in his court, giving all 'faire warning' that the hand of the Chief Justice would 'fall heavy' on any who attempted to interfere with the run of a King's Bench writ.[103] 'We must looke about or the common lawe of England will be overthrown', he concluded, to his presumably startled audience of lawyers and clerks; or maybe they had heard it all before. The declamation was of course reported back to the king, who certainly had. Shortly after, Glanvil was 'clogged' in 'irons', and hauled before Star Chamber to answer some very awkward questions.[104] Chiefly about Coke. Who, it was wondered, might just have put Glanvil up to the whole charade.

At much the same time as Glanvil was pushing his luck in King's Bench, it became apparent that a parish near Lichfield was missing a vicar. Not itself unusual. There were lots of absent vicars in early modern England. In 1589 Convocation petitioned the queen, claiming that 'not more than 600' out of nearly nine thousand 'livings' were fit, held singly, to provide for 'learned men'. Which was why, the petition argued, ministers should be allowed to hold 'pluralities' of livings.[105] Not, it seems, an attractive career. There is a story of the essayist Sir John Harrington inviting the new bishop of Bath and Wells for a stroll in 1608. He waited for a rainy day, so that they might seek shelter in the abbey, only to discover that the roof had rotted away. The bishop was so horrified that he ordered immediate repairs, to the tune of £1000. The Reformation Church might have been spiritually uplifted, but it was physically shattered. Tithing disputes as common as leaky chancels.

So, no great surprise that a vicar was missing. And not much prospect of getting another. Not just because applicants were sparse but because there was a financial incentive in dithering. Which bring us to the famous *Case of Commendams*, which should never have been famous at all. A *commendam* was a means of transferring an ecclesiastical benefice in trust to the custody of a bishop. The grant was in the gift of the governor of the Church, in other words the king, and was supposed to facilitate the exaction of tithes in parishes temporarily divested of a vicar. Somewhat arcane, then, but also lucrative. And not especially controversial. At least not until 1616. When a Staffordshire landowner named Colt arrived at court armed with a writ challenging a *commendam* granted to the bishop of Lichfield. An obliging kind of prelate, Bishop John Overall had played a principal role in drafting the 'Authorized Version' of the Bible, and published some very helpful comments on the 'divine' nature of kingship in his *Convocation Book* in 1610. Worthy of patronage then, when the pesky Colt pitched up with his annoying writ.

The matter was remitted to the Court of Exchequer sitting as a deliberative assembly.[106] Meanwhile, the bishop of Winchester was despatched to listen in. His report was not encouraging. Serjeant Chibborne had already advised the court that a *commendam* could only be issued in cases of 'necessity' and, the implication ran, this particular absent vicar was hardly that. And the Lord Chief Justice had been seen to nod. A message was sent, asking that judgement be deferred until the king 'be first consulted with'. Which was ignored. The case, the judges returned, was of 'private interest'.[107] Time for Attorney General Bacon to draft another brief.

To be read out at another 'consultation' in Privy Council, on the morning of 6 June. The judges had of late 'entertayned' a 'greater boldness to dispute the heigh pointes of his Majesty's prerogative'. A 'reverend' body, James admitted of his judiciary, but also 'corrigible', as 'all subjects are'. And now over-reaching themselves, misusing a common law that had 'growne so vast and transcendent'. More particularly, 'ever since comeinge to this Crowne the popular sorte of lawyers have ben men that most affrontedly in all Parliament have trodden upon his prerogative'. The 'supreme and imperial power' was not something to be disputed in 'vulgar argument', in court or out.[108] The judges had probably sensed what was coming. It was reported that they 'fell downe upon their knees' and 'asked pardon for their error' and each in turn confirmed the king's authority to grant the *commendam*.

Except, it seems for one. Coke explained that the king's request to defer judgement had threatened a 'delay of justice' and was itself 'contrary to law'. As to the particular question, the legality of the transfer, there were a 'multitude of particulars' which could not be easily answered. All Coke could promise was that he 'would doe that should be fit for a judge to do'.[109] The king was reported furious, again. The judges were recalled a week later, for further admonishment. Beginning in plain and uncompromising terms: 'As Kings borrow their power from God, so judges from Kings: And as Kings are to accompt to God, so Judges unto God and Kings.' Continuing,

> And as no King can discharge his accompt to God, unlesse he make conscience not to alter, but to declare and establish the will of God: So Judges cannot discharge their accompts to Kings, unlesse they take the like care, not to take upon them to make the Law, but joyned together after a deliberate consultation, to declare what the Law is. For as Kings are subject unto God's Law, so they to mans Law. It is the Kings Office to protect and settle the trew interpretation of the Law of God within his Dominions: And it is the Judges Office to interpret the Law of the King, whereto themselves are also subject.[110]

The king then moved on to the familiar complaint. Too many judges were inclined to 'meddle with the King's Prerogative', as a consequence of which prerogative courts, most especially those of Chancery and High Commission, had been much 'shaken of late'. Too much 'Incertaintie and Noveltie'. Henceforth respective courts must 'keepe' within their 'owne bounds, and nourish not the people in the contempt of other Courts'. If they did there would be 'sweete harmony' once more. He then departed.

Six days later, Coke was charged with corruption relating to *Glanvil's Case*. The Lord Chief Justice had, for a number of months, displayed a 'perpetual, turbulent carriage' to the prejudice of 'crown, parliament and subjects'. Coke was duly suspended from Privy Council, and withdrawn from the summer Assize circuit. Sent on his way with the suggestion that he spend his enforced leave correcting the 'manie exorbitaunt and extravagant opinions sett downe' in his published *Reports*; necessary so that 'our crown and people be not secretly snared by conceit of laws'. Bacon, it transpired, had already found seventeen. A truculent Coke would later admit to just five, all 'minor'.[111] No-one seemed inclined to compromise. In November, the Lord Chief Justice was fired, receiving his writ of dismissal 'with dejection and tears'.[112] An extraordinary consequence of a case which might otherwise have been so trivial. But it had been a long time coming. The consequence, John Chamberlain surmised, of 'Pride, Prohibitions, Praemunire and Prerogative'.[113]

The retirement of Edward Coke

Timothy Tourneur contemplated darkly. The 'liberty of the subjects of England' hung in the balance and, unless the 'breeding mischiefs' were 'redressed', there would be 'no law practised upon them but prerogative'. Only Parliament could now save the kingdom. With the benefit of some useful hindsight, Tourneur would later suppose that 'the alterations that followed upon King Charles' started here, in summer 1616.[114] As for Coke, now in his sixty-fifth year, time for more reflective pleasures perhaps. Potter about his new knot-garden at Stoke Poges, play with the grandchildren. Except that Sir Edward was more the grudge-bearing than the hedge-trimming type. And not much of a family man. Which brings us to what should have been a lovely day.

Steenie's case

Frances Coke was aged just fourteen when her father was removed from office. Young, pretty and more or less available; give or take a year or two. Prospective matches were already under consideration. Her mother, Lady Hatton, had in mind the young Henry de Vere, 18th Earl of Oxford.[115] Sir Edward, however, had other ideas. Better still might be a match with Sir John Villiers. The fact that Sir John was more or less broke, and more or less mad, was outweighed by the simple fact that he was the brother of George, 1st Duke of Buckingham. Coke made his offer: Frances, plus £10,000 in dowry. Lady Elizabeth tried to intervene, sheltering her daughter at Hatton House, and affirming that she was already pre-contracted to Henry. She knew what it was like, being married to an ill-tempered boor.

But Coke was having none of it. Ignoring an order brought in Council instructing all parties to 'forbear all occasion of violence or disturbance', Frances was dragged out of the house and taken to her father.[116] Who, it was put about, had her 'tyed to the bed-poste and severely whipped into consent'. The big day followed in September 1617, at Hampton Court. Given away by an evidently affectionate king. A little too affectionate some thought. Unlike her husband, who was too drunk to evince any kind of emotion. It was reported that Frances spent the entire day in tears. Unsurprising. Hardly the kind of wedding day of which many teenage girls dream.

In due course she responded in the only sensible manner, by hiring a sorcerer to cast a spell on her new husband. Who retaliated in kind. Frances's sorcerer was, it seems, the more adept. The intermittently demented Purbeck finally went completely mad in 1620. Possibly syphilis, possibly schizophrenia, possibly manic depression; probably a bit of each. At which point Frances ran off and set up home with Sir Robert Howard, son of the Earl of Suffolk. And, importantly, Member of Parliament for Bishop's Castle, in Shropshire. They had a child in 1624. As a consequence of which, the duke had them both hauled before Star Chamber to answer charges of adultery. And then again before High Commission, at which point additional charges of witchcraft were added to the indictment against Frances. The trial began in 1625, and reached an eventual conclusion two years later. Amongst the trial commissioners was the Dean of St Paul's, the poet John Donne.

In due course, the lovers were both convicted and excommunicated, Frances further sentenced to do penance in a white shirt. A verdict she predictably ignored. In the meantime, Parliament took the opportunity to vent its spleen against the apparent infringement of its privileges. Not only had one of their Members been excommunicated, but so too had he been committed to the Fleet for refusing to take the ex officio oath before the Commission.[117] A bill was introduced to abolish the oath, and the House treated to a long discourse on the subject of privilege by a young lawyer named John Selden. If they did not annul the verdict, Selden advised, anyone of them might find themselves hauled before the Commission on trumped-up charges. So they did. A period of sensible discretion awaited the lovers, before Frances eventually made her way over to a Parisian convent.[118]

It comes as no surprise to learn that Coke's relations with his daughter were strained. As, we might reasonably assume, they were with his son-in-law. And the duke, fast becoming the favourite amongst the various handsome young men upon whose arms the king liked to lean as he wandered the corridors of Whitehall playing with himself. 'Christ had his John', James liked to say, 'I have my George.'[119] Or Steenie, after St Stephen, who was said to have had an 'angel face', just like George. A fast favourite of the young Prince Charles too. Almost brothers. 'Dear Dad', George used to address Charles's father. They went on holiday together, most famously venturing to Madrid in 1623, to woo the Spanish Infanta, Dona Maria. The 'codpiece point', as James had termed it; a man of prose.[120] Charles, more the poet, was particularly keen to see Dona Maria dance. So off they went on their little jape, 'Tom' and 'John', as they called themselves; along with a couple of retainers, and a pair of unconvincing false beards. Negotiations had progressed nicely enough for a while, Charles appearing suitably infatuated. But then run aground; tricky matters of Hapsburg foreign policy. Leaving a lovelorn prince to return to London. And plot his revenge.

King James died in March 1625, having spent much of the previous year incapacitated. A new age beckoned. The Earl of Dorset wondered if there might be a new 'covenant' between monarch and subjects.[121] The 'joy of so hopeful a successor', Edward Tilman tried to persuade himself.[122] A momentarily fawning Coke wondered if England would be blessed by another Henry V. It would not. Charles called his first Parliament in summer 1625, hoping to persuade Parliament to fund a war with Spain. He needed £700,000. It offered £140,000. The 'Useless' Parliament, as it became known, was dissolved after a couple of months. A second Parliament, no more useful, sat for a couple of months in early 1626. We will see what happened to it very shortly. As we will a third, which was called in early 1628 and dissolved a year later. Each parsimonious. And each distracted, by something which Charles found just as annoying; a determination to impeach Steenie. The reasons were various. No-one much liked Steenie, aside from Charles.

A closet papist, some suspected. And bit of a loser, widely blamed for the ill-fated Cadiz expedition in 1625, and the La Rochelle expedition, a year later. Sir Philip Warwick would later surmise 'too great an enterpriser'.[123] In sum, precisely the type of wicked counsellor for which the process of impeachment was designed.

In a sense. Except that the original purpose of impeachment was to display the authority of the Crown. A means for ceremonially destroying an over-mighty subject. In terms of process, charges alleging the commission of certain 'high crimes and misdemeanours' would be laid in the House of Commons; usually relating to some kind of corruption or abuse in public office. A vote would follow, rigged of course. After which the charges would be sent to the Lords, where a formal trial of the accused would take place, before his peers. Commonly rigged again. Leaving the finale in the hands of the monarch, who might deem fit to grant a reprieve. Though usually not. Different here though, where the proceedings were commenced by Parliament to the purpose of humiliating its king. We might note a statistic. Nearly three-quarters of all impeachments in English legal history occurred in the first half of the seventeenth century. We will encounter a fair few impeachments in the coming pages, including one, of a kind, in January 1649.

A first set of charges against Steenie were laid in March 1626. A series of 'queries', chiefly battles lost at sea, and money lost from the Exchequer. No need for hard evidence. The 'queries' were raised by 'common fame'.[124] As was the rumour that Steenie had, in the end, done 'dear dad' in; not just an evil counsellor but a homicidal maniac in the service of 'Romeish Priests and Popish Recusants'.[125] Convicted by public opinion; another portent for Charles. The travails of living in an emergent tabloid age.[126] The prosaic matter of saving Steenie could be served by the expedient of dissolving Parliament. Which Charles did. But it was not a good look. And as soon as Parliament assembled once again, in early 1628, it set about preparing the ground for a fresh impeachment. Drafting a *Remonstrance*, detailing the various 'evils and dangers' which faced the realm; the 'principal cause' of which was the duke. An indignant rebuttal was drafted, most probably by a different evil counsellor, William Laud, then bishop of Bath and Wells. It was a 'great wrong to ourself and government'.[127] But then contingency intervened.

An unfortunate incident at the Spotted Dog Tavern in Portsmouth. Where, on 28 August 1628, Steenie had just finished breakfast. His last. An army lieutenant named John Felton approached him with a grievance and a rapier, and, a couple of minutes later, Steenie was dead, stabbed in the heart. Now renamed the Greyhound, there is a commemorative plaque on the wall. A tourist spot, of a kind. Pepys visited in early May 1661, with his wife Elizabeth, his clerk Tom Hayter and John Creed, secretary to the Earl of Sandwich. Pepys was probably distracted by the barmaid. Hayter and Creed, puritans both, might have detected the Hand of Providence. Though Felton's grudge was of the more personal kind. He had recently petitioned for £80 back-pay and promotion to a captaincy. Both, apparently, promised by the duke, but neither gotten.

George left a wife, presumably distraught, though given the rumours of her husband's sexual dalliances with 'dear dad', maybe not that much. And a king bereft. On hearing news of the assassination, Charles had taken to his chamber 'and threw himself upon his bed, lamenting with much passion and with abundance of tears'. So Sir Edward Hyde would later confirm.[128] The fact that pretty much everyone else seemed elated would not have helped the grieving process. The Earl of Pembroke acclaimed a 'happy' moment. As soon as the news of the assassination had reached London, it was reported that the 'base multitude' were drinking Felton's health. Lord Dorchester sensed 'a sea moved by a tempest'.[129] There were riots at Tyburn, where Felton was executed. And when his mouldering corpse was taken back to Portsmouth, to be hanged in chains, it was seized by a cheering crowd and taken on a charivari round the town. Charles was in little doubt as to who or what was to blame. The 'much endeavours' of a hostile Parliament which had, time and again, sought to 'demolish' the duke.[130] Under interrogation, Felton admitted to having read the *Remonstrance*. Parliament had murdered Steenie. It would never be forgiven.[131]

We can reasonably assume that Coke was amongst those who did not much mourn Steenie. Initial hopes that the succession might bring renewed favour at Court had not lasted. Relations with the Villiers long soured. By the time that Steenie was enjoying his last breakfast, Coke was in cahoots with the 'stirring' men in Parliament. He probably helped with the drafting of the *Remonstrance*, and the impeachment proceedings. A renowned jurist with a sense of consuming bitterness was precisely what these 'stirring' men needed, in 1628. He would shortly be invited to draft something else. First though we need to pause and take note of another famous case in English legal history. Involving some surly tax-dodgers.

The case of the reluctant lenders

It started with something else which Charles had a tendency to do. Pick the wrong fights. The particular fight that he wanted to pick in 1626 was with the Hapsburgs, in support of his uncle, King Christian IV of Denmark. Who, having just suffered a devastating defeat at the battle of Lutter, was hardly investible. Charles approached Parliament for some subsidies, as he had the year before. And met with much the same response. An offer of £122,000; just about enough to get the fleet back to sea for a few months. The usual array of alternatives offered themselves, none especially convincing. Customs duties in the form of 'tonnage and poundage'. But that needed parliamentary approval too. Borrowing on security perhaps. Charles had approached the City for a loan of £100,000 in the summer of 1626. And been offered £20,000, which did not say much for the security. More land sales; £600,000 of Crown property was sold between 1625 and 1630. But once gone, beyond recovery. He could 'farm' some more monopolies, at the risk of annoying

Parliament further. And continue to extract 'fines', as his father had, from property developers and gentlemen who could not be bothered to attend his coronation. Distraint of knighthood, the latter was called. A feudal 'incident fine', worth £40 a time. Other 'incident fines' could be levied for the raising of enclosures or hunting in royal forests. It all stacked up, though not very high.

So Charles looked for a more 'speedie way' of raising some cash.[132] And alighted upon the possibility of using his prerogative to 'force' a loan from some of his better-off subjects. Some supposed it was all Steenie's idea. Perhaps. What mattered was that it was not a good idea. Nothing was more likely to raise tempers than using prerogative to threaten property. Thomas Crosfield, fellow Queen's College Oxford, likened it to Spanish 'servility'.[133] Feeding the 'palate of absolute power', the Earl of Clare was heard to observe. It was reported that the gentlemen of Kent had berated Lord Keeper Coventry at Maidstone Assizes, reminding him that such a tax was against the 'whole discourse of Fortescue'.[134] Archbishop Abbott expressed some doubts, but only to himself; 'suppressed within my soul'.[135] Other clerics weighed in to support the king, most notably Robert Sibthorpe and Roger Mainwaring, their sermons published by 'His Majesty's special command'. Kings, Mainwaring wrote reassuringly, were 'inferior to none, to no man, to no multitudes of men, to no angel'.[136]

A Royal Proclamation issued, writs sent out. The reason being 'necessitie to which no ordinarie course can give the lawe'.[137] A fair number paid up, to the tune of around £240,000. But plenty did not. For some, it was a matter of conscience. Brought before Privy Council, Sir William Corytone explained that he had long conversed with his God, before resolving that he could not pay. After some consultation, Council accepted his argument and gave him 'leave to depart with fair respect'. For others the doubts were more prosaic, wondering the credibility of the supposed 'necessity'.[138] And then there were jurisprudential concerns. Articulated by the Lord Keeper no less. As 'far as he understood the law, none were liable to martial law but martial men'. Go to law with even the more 'refractory' of the non-payers, and the king risked humiliation. Charles was, though, undeterred. The judges would do his bidding. If not he would 'sweep all their benches'.[139] So he blundered on. Into one of the most famous cases in English constitutional history, and a marketing disaster. The *Case of the Five Knights*.[140]

In March 1627, warrants were issued for the arrest of Sir Thomas Darnell, a Lincolnshire landowner, a couple of Norfolk Members of Parliament named Sir John Corbet and Sir John Heveningham, Sir Walter Earle and Sir Edmund Hampden. None have left any greater mark on history. Though the latter's nephew would, as we shall see, and Earle would raise a regiment for Parliament in 1643. The five were despatched to the Fleet prison by 'special command of His Majesty'. It was where most debtors ended up, along with truculent barristers. A hot and stuffy summer followed. A little more salubrious for a sixth 'refractory spirit', the puritan Earl of Lincoln. Sent, as befitted his rank, to the Tower instead. The earl had published a pamphlet which suggested that the king, and his 'loan', threatened the 'liberties' of Parliament.[141] It is, though, the 'five knights' who are remembered. Because of the legal proceedings which ensued.

None of the five were actually charged with a crime. The contention was their detention. They had petitioned 'for their relief out of prison' in July, and the king was said to be 'much moved'. Charles took a keen personal interest in the case, even taking the precaution of interviewing his judges, to be sure that he knew what was in their minds, and more importantly perhaps, that they knew what was in his. It was time, as the hawks in Council urged, to bring the 'factious men' to heel.[142] Charles agreed. He wanted his day in court. And he got it, a few months later, when the five issued writs of habeas corpus at King's Bench, and the bailiff, unsure of the legal position, failed to present. The Attorney General secured a second writ, in Darnell's name, and the matter was returned to court.[143] Another starry legal cast. Amongst those representing the knights were William Noy and John Selden. Noy would later switch allegiance, becoming Attorney General in 1631.

Selden would not.[144] A property lawyer by professional inclination, author of a renowned *History of Tithes*, which argued that all Church law was held under common rather than canon law, together with myriad articles on Islamic poetry, Syrian architecture and the law of the Old Testament.[145] And a champion of Chapter 29 of *Magna Carta*: 'No freeman shall be imprisoned without due process of law.' It was Chapter 29 which inspired the 'stirring men'. The root of habeas corpus, according to Selden's friend Sir Dudley Digges, and the reason why one true-hearted Englishman would always beat 'five Muscovites' in a fight.[146] And why, Selden counselled the court, the five knights had to be surrendered. If they were not, their 'imprisonment shall not continue on for a time, but for ever; and the subjects of this kingdom may be restrained of their liberties perpetually'. An observation which, it was reported, elicited 'wonderful applause' in the galleries, 'even of shouting and clapping of hands'. Attorney General Heath was lower-key, simply arguing that Selden had vouched no precedents. A view approved by Lord Chief Justice Hyde, a couple of days later. Selden might have managed to 'inveigle' the galleries, but he had not charmed Hyde.[147] Relief lay with the king who, being 'bound by law', would 'do what is right'.[148]

So the prisoners remained where they were; at least until 2 January, when they were quietly released. A kind of victory for the king. Narrow though, and tainted. A few months later, Selden uncovered a dreadful plot. The judges had given a 'declaration of judgement', in effect an interlocutory ruling. But the Attorney General had apparently sought to enrol it, thus creating a precedent from a particular, 'for ever and ever'.[149] Secretly. The Commons established a Committee to hear the complaint, and to consider the broader contention; whether a subject could be held without charge at the king's pleasure. To be chaired by Selden. Amongst those to give evidence was Sir Edward Coke. Brushing aside the fact that he had, in an earlier life, supposed that they might, Sir Edward now confirmed that they most certainly could not.[150] Meanwhile the Commons chattered excitably about the 'slavery' in which the new king clearly intended to hold his subjects. A tyranny compounded. If the common law was a scripture, the Attorney General's subterfuge was a sacrilege.[151]

The *Case of the Five Knights* should have been instructive. It certainly suggested to the 'stirring men' that there was something to be gained by contesting the king in court. It might have suggested the converse to the king. But no. Winning arguments in court, but losing them outside, would become a familiar and debilitating experience over the coming decade. Meantime the same residual problem. No money. At the end of 1627, Sir Robert Pye reported that Crown revenue was all but dried up, 'land much sold and credit lost'. Charles tried to pawn some of his jewellery, and that of his wife. But struggled to find purchasers. The royal plate was melted down, the queen's household thinned out. What else? The new Chancellor of the Exchequer, Sir Richard Weston, recommended a period of 'rest and vigilancy'.[152] If only.

Ghosts

The events which surround the *Case of the Five Knights* tell us something rather obvious about Charles Stuart, apart from the fact that he was usually broke, and had a tendency to keep making the same mistakes. He held Parliament in contempt. 'Remember that parliaments are altogether in my power for the calling, sitting and continuance of them', he warned his second Parliament in March 1626. 'Therefore as I find the fruits either good or evil they are to continue or not to be.'[153] The inference was plain enough. If Parliament did not behave, and give him the money he needed, he would do without it. Sir Dudley Carleton was under no illusion: 'Move not his Majesty with trenching upon his prerogatives, lest you bring him out of love with parliaments.'[154] The House was, though, undaunted. As was Charles. Not much liking the fruits on offer, he shut his second Parliament after a couple of months. The possibility of ruling in a 'personal' capacity was becoming ever more attractive. The king had reportedly discussed the idea with the bishop of Mende, over from France to give the queen spiritual sustenance. Charles wanted to know of 'the means used by the kings of France to rid themselves of parliament'.[155] More pertinently, perhaps, how they managed to fund themselves.

One last chance, for all concerned. A third Parliament opened in March 1628. The significance of the moment was not lost on contemporaries. Sir Benjamin Rudyerd left no-one in any doubt. It was the 'crisis of parliaments', and soon they would 'know by this if parliaments live or die'. Give the king the excuse, and he would be rid of them for good. It was only a few months since the resolution of the *Five Knights*. Barely enough. As soon as it assembled, the Commons immediately began another attempt to impeach Steenie. Selden at the helm, the refrain was familiar. The duke had counselled his king to 'breach of the fundamental liberties of this kingdom'.[156]

Meantime, the newly recalled Commons passed four *Resolutions*, to be conveyed to the king. A first deploring prerogative taxation, and three more relating to conditions of detention; which could only be lawful, had to be under formal charge, and were subject to the run of habeas corpus writs.[157] When Charles demurred, it was suggested that the *Resolutions* be passed into law, in the form of a petition. What it needed was a grudge-bearing jurist with time on his hands. On 8 May 1628, Coke presented a draft *Petition of Right* to the House of Lords.[158] Nothing that was really new, which was precisely the point. Written, once again, in the past tense, summoning the ghosts of the 'ancient' constitution. The hallowed 'liberties' of *Magna Carta*, the 'statute of statutes', as Francis Ashley had put it, back in the febrile summer of 1616, 'worthy to be written in letters of gold', now liberated from the 'yoke' of Norman tyranny.[159] And, by insinuation, the Stuart. A metaphor for the ages; the Norman 'yoke' proving a variant of the Egyptian 'yoke' under which the Israelites had been enslaved, until Moses led them to freedom.

As regards the 'liberties' reinvested in Coke's *Petition*, there were more particularly four, bearing close resemblance to those discovered in the *Resolutions*; habeas corpus, prohibitions against billeting on private property, and the imposition of martial law, to which was added, rather pointedly, confirmation that 'no person should be compelled to make any loans to the king against his will'. Drawn rather more obviously from English than Mosaic law, as might be expected of their author. And by now familiar. Royalists perceived a direct assault on the royal prerogative. As did 'stirring men' such as Digges. 'Prerogative only has caused it', Sir Dudley confirmed in parliamentary debate.[160] That, and the nasty incident at the Spotted Dog. Steenie might be dead, but his spirit was hardly laid to rest. Still stalking Whitehall, whispering in the ear of his distraught king.

After an agonizing dither, Charles offered instead to reaffirm *Magna Carta*. But that was precisely what Coke did not want. The *Petition* was an assertion, not a plea. And the lexicon had moved. These were 'rights', being 'liberties' now in the care of Parliament, not the gift of the Crown. Which gestures to something else, rather more familiar today. The birthing of a defining principle of English constitutional law. Parliament asserting a legislative 'sovereignty'. Or re-birthing, according to Coke, in his commentary on the 'High Court of Parliament', which appeared in the fourth volume of *Institutes*. And importing a juridical capacity too; necessary to secure its own liberties against whoever, whenever. The idea that Parliament was a 'court' would find renowned expression in Henry Parker's *Observations*, published in 1642. And would prove very useful in late 1648, as the senior officer corps of the New Model Army pondered how they might put a king on trial.

Back in 1628, Charles was faced with a dilemma. The *Petition* was hardly welcome. But the sweetener was; a conditional offer of five subsidies worth £300,000. He sought the advice of his judges. Evasive in the main, they did though confirm that the king would still retain the right to detain subjects 'in secrecie' for a 'convenient time' without cause. It seemed assurance enough. Eyeing up his subsidies, Charles gave his assent on 7 June 1628. A momentary cessation of hostilities. Until November, when the Court of Exchequer ruled in the case of five merchants who had refused to pay 'tonnage and poundage'. Their argument, that the tax was not admitted under the terms of the *Petition*, was dismissed. The Commons erupted. A fractious winter. Tax strikes in the City, the subsidies stalled. Robert Triplet, an Islington brewer, petitioned the king; held 'in my esteem like God'. A couple of pieces of advice. Convert the queen to Protestantism and take heed of Sir Edward Coke, 'as good a commonwealth man as you have in all your kingdom'.[161]

Charles, though, was distracted. He had a decision to make, driven by 'necessity'.[162] His Parliament, too 'blinded with a popular applause', would be dissolved.[163] Needless to say, it was all rather messy. Black Rod arrived at the door of the Commons early afternoon on 2 March 1629, with the king's instruction. The doors were barred, inside was chaos. The Speaker, Sir John Finch, was forcibly held in his chair whilst some of the more fractious Members, led by Sir John Eliot, chased through three further resolutions; condemning 'innovation in religion', the misuse of prerogative with an intent to 'break parliaments' and the illegal levying of 'tonnage and poundage'. Anyone who paid the latter should 'be reputed a capital enemy to the kingdom and commonwealth'.[164] We will encounter Finch again when we take a look at England in the 1630s; by then Chief Justice of Common Pleas, and scourge of tax-dodgers everywhere.

A 'tumultuary' day, Sir Simonds D'Ewes recorded, the 'most gloomy, sad and dismal day for England that happened in five hundred days'. Sir Edward Hyde would later identify himself amongst those 'scandalized at those distempers'.[165] Charles would deploy the same metaphor in his testamentary *Eikon Basilike*. By 'forbearing to convene' Parliament for 'some years', he 'hoped to have extinguished' those 'distempers'.[166] There is much about the *Eikon*, as we will see, which inclines to gloss. But D'Ewes predicted likewise, and in the moment. After the events of 2 March, he doubted that there could be another parliament for 'many years'.[167] He was right. Eleven years of prerogative, or 'personal', rule would follow. Designed to be easier on the nerves; at least the king's. But not likely to be much easier on the purse. We will take up this story in the next chapter. More doubtful taxes, more evil counsellors, lots more 'tumultuary' days.

A few pretty much straightaway. For Charles, predictably enough, could not leave well alone. On hearing of the events of the 2nd, he had nine of the more 'stirring' Members arrested and hauled before Privy Council to explain themselves, and then prosecuted in Star Chamber for their 'notable contempte'.[168] Amongst the 'vipers', as Charles called them, were Eliot, Selden and the two Members who had reputedly held Finch in his chair, Denzil Holles and Benjamin Valentine. An early airing for Coke's *Petition*. And an augury. On hearing that the judges in King's Bench were inclined to approve writs of habeas corpus, on grounds of parliamentary privilege, Charles had the prisoners removed to the Tower under royal warrant. Where they would stay, in disregard of any court order. Selden and Holles were released in 1631. A couple more had to wait until 1640. Eliot never got out, dying in the Tower in 1632. Charles especially hated Eliot who, in a characteristically splenetic speech, had compared Steenic to Sejanus.[169] Some were beyond forgiveness; and, it appeared, the law.

For now, though, we have come far enough. Time to close, with a couple more spectral conceits. Both of which require us to take a brief glimpse into the future. First to 1661. The royalist judge David Jenkins musing the extent to which Coke might have been to blame for much of what had occurred during these 'turbulent and calamitous times'.[170] Jenkins wondered if the former Chief Justice might have regretted what he had written about kingship. Many passages would have been better 'expunged', most especially those where he 'seems to bridle the Sovereign and give the reins to the people'. Were 'he to rise from the dead', Jenkins concluded, 'he would take care to expunge them'.[171] It is certainly true that Coke would have been appalled by the thought that he had given the people the reins to do anything much. It is also true that his writings would exercise a considerable influence on those who, during the 1630s and early 1640s, evinced a willingness to go to war to defend the principles of the 'ancient' constitution. But otherwise it is highly doubtful that he would have regretted much of what he had, in life, said or written. Sir Edward Coke was not the regretting type.

Our second spectre is to be found flitting about the manor house at Stoke Poges. Acquired by Coke in 1599, hastily refurbished for the pending visit of Queen Elizabeth, it was to Stoke Poges that Coke had retired in late 1616, to lick his wounds. Not, though, as we have already noted, to indulge any more reflective pleasures. He would continue to visit Stoke Poges, the residence of his second daughter, Anne, up until his death in 1634. It is surmised that he might have drafted some of his *Petition* there, edited a few more *Reports*. Determined to secure his legacy, and settle a few scores.[172] In summer 1647, King Charles would pay a visit to Stoke Poges, escorted by a troop of New Model cavalry. Recently taken into custody at Holdenby House, and now being perambulated around the 'home' counties whilst his captors tried to work out what to do with him. He would spend a night at the house. We might, as the carriage clatters its way up the drive, glimpse a ghostly face peering through a mullioned window. A grisly smile, and a slight chill in the air. Revenge, as every Jacobean theatre-goer knew, is best served cold.

2 THE TRIUMPHS OF KING CHARLES I

FIGURE 2 Battle of Naseby.

arly afternoon on 4 January 1642, King Charles I arrived at Westminster with around three hundred 'swaggerers and ruffians' recruited, John Milton would later recall, from the 'Stewes and Brothels; the spawns and shipwrack of Taverns and Dicing Houses'.[1] Hardly a partial observer, as we will see. But a common enough perception, in parliamentarian presses at least. A motley crew of 'papists … panders and rogues'.[2] A gang of 'desperadoes', according to Edmund Ludlow.[3] The previous day, an indictment had been read out charging five Members of the Commons with treason; having sought to 'deprive the King of his Royal Power'. Familiar suspects: John Pym, John Hampden, Denzil Holles, Sir Arthur

Haselrige and Sir William Strode.[4] All 'stirring' men. They had, it seems, incited war against the king, and were now actively engaged in encouraging rioting in the City. It was, Charles suggested to his Attorney General, enough to lay a charge of treason. The House of Commons refused to surrender the named Members, complaining an infringement of privilege. So Charles decided to attend the House himself. Such confrontation was hardly in his character. But the moment was exceptional, and it was reported that his wife Henrietta Maria had urged him to 'pull these rogues out by the ears or never see my face again'.[5] So he went.

'To the great amazement of all', Sir Edward Hyde would later recall.[6] Not the first poor decision reached in recent weeks and months. Later in the chapter, we will take a closer look at the case of Thomas Wentworth, Earl of Strafford. Arrested by Parliament, and executed under Bill of Attainder in spring 1641. Charles never forgave himself for failing to save Strafford. Nor did he forgive the governor of the Tower, Sir William Balfour, who had thwarted a rescue attempt. In mid-December Charles finally summoned up the courage to remove Balfour, and replace him with Thomas Lunsford. A man of undoubted loyalty but less estimable character. The Earl of Dorset described Lunsford as a 'young outlaw' and 'swaggering ruffian'.[7] Parliament put it about that he was a cannibal who feasted on children, worse still a Catholic. Predictably enough, there were riots. On 26 December the Lord Mayor visited the king, to plead for Lunsford's removal. Panicked, Charles climbed down. Needless to say, the following day Lunsford arrived at Westminster with a gang of mates, looking to start a fight. Beaten off, he escaped by wading down the Thames.

Next day, hundreds of apprentices marched on the Abbey, and laid siege. Trapping the Archbishop of York, busy inside interrogating some 'insolent' brethren. When a barge carrying more bishops approached, it was met by loud jeers and scarcely veiled threats. Sensibly, it sailed on. A rescue party managed to retrieve the Archbishop. Amongst those 'sorely wounded' in the ensuing melee in Westminster Yard was a radical young lawyer named John Lilburne. More of him later. Meanwhile, Christmas was ruined. Not least because all the shops were shut, as Captain Robert Slyngesbie confirmed, writing home. 'I cannot say we have had a merry Christmas,' the Captain observed, 'but the maddest one that ever I saw.'[8] And about to get madder.

On the 28th, Charles issued a proclamation banning assemblies, knighted Lunsford, and appointed him commander of the guard at Whitehall. On the 29th, an estimated ten thousand 'mechanic citizens and apprentices' collected outside the palace chanting 'No bishops, no papist lords'. Lunsford and his fellow 'cavaliers' pondered what to do, and then did what they were always going to do. Swords drawn, they charged out into the crowd and started hacking away at the 'roundheads', as the apprentices were now known. And then retreated back inside. Next day, twelve bishops made formal complaint to the king, claiming that it was no longer safe to attend the House of Lords. Time for a think, though not a lot. The Commons duly impeached the bishops, whilst the king had chat with the Attorney

General, and then with his wife. And somehow reached the decision that what might really help would be a personal appearance in the House.

Unsurprisingly, by the time that Charles arrived on 4 January, the accused MPs were long gone. Rumoured to be staying with Alderman Isaac Pennington, Prime Warden of the Worshipful Company of Fishmongers, and close friend of Pym. The king, evidently unaware, strode into the Commons shortly after lunch, took off his hat and asked the Speaker if he might 'borrow your chair a little'. His followers were less decorous, reportedly stood milling about in the Hall swearing 'oaths' and waving their swords around. Duly seated, Charles began: 'I must declare unto you here, that albeit no king that ever was in England shall be more careful of your privileges' they 'must know that in cases of Treason, no person hath a privilege'. He looked about. Realizing that the MPs were gone, he tried to recover the position. 'What, are all the birds flown, well, I will find them.' Adding, as he got up, 'I do expect from you that you will send them unto me as soon as they return here.' He never, he closed, 'did intend any force, but shall proceed against them in a legal and fair way'. Speaker Lenthall's reply is no less renowned: 'May it please your Majesty, I have neither eyes to see nor tongue to speak in this place but as the House is pleased to direct me, whose servant I am here.' At which point Charles left, 'in a more disconcerted and angry passion than he came in', according to Sir Simonds D'Ewes. As he departed, the benches erupted with cries of 'Privilege'.[9]

Next day, Charles went to the Common Council of the City, looking for the five. No luck again. As he retreated in his coach, a crowd gathered shouting 'Privileges of Parliament'. On the 8th, Parliament resolved to welcome back the five MPs. Three days later, they were brought up the Thames by barge, escorted by eight companies of the Trained Bands. Charles departed Whitehall for Hampton Court. And then, on the 13th, moved the Court to Windsor. Henrietta Maria was sent to the United Provinces, to explore the possibility of raising money. Many, as we will see, would protest their surprise when war finally came a few months later. Not Henrietta Maria though, and not her husband.

Meanwhile Parliament moved to restore order in the city. A new Sergeant Major of the Trained Bands was appointed. Tasked with making a credible fighting force out of all the ale-fuelled apprentices who had spent the previous few days scrapping with Lunsford's cavaliers.[10] Histories tend to neglect Phillip Skippon, paling perhaps amidst a starry cast of brilliant Parliamentary commanders. But English history would have been very different if Skippon had instead obeyed the king's call to Oxford in early 1642. Only three years earlier appointed to command the Honourable Company of Artillery. But he could not, Skippon resolved, serve Charles and 'honour God'.[11] So he fought for Parliament instead. We will encounter Skippon again, holding firm against a furious royalist assault at Naseby in June 1645. But for the present, in spring 1642, Phillip Skippon was pretty much all that stood between Parliament and the very real threat of annihilation.

Whether war was inevitable by then remains a matter of conjecture. Hindsight tempts us. It was certainly more likely. In practical terms, it was difficult to conceive how Charles might force his way back into London, unless at the head of an army which had first crushed Skippon's militia. Negotiations would continue. But positions were entrenched, and trust all but evaporated. Charles would return to London, of course, in late 1648. But as a prisoner of the New Model Army, destined for his own treason trial: a passing irony. The extent to which the events of January 1642 made those of January 1649 inevitable is subject to the same kinds of contention. But we can at least venture one conclusion with a fair degree of confidence. On the afternoon of 4 January 1642, King Charles I looked a fool; and that is the worst way for a king to look.[12]

This chapter is about looking, the consonance of the aesthetic and the constitutional. Only a few weeks earlier, Charles had pulled off a triumph, in a sense. A spectacular procession through the City on 25 November, from Moorgate to Whitehall, with a stop at the Grocer's Hall, for a lavish feast and the inevitable masque. Along with the entire royal family, 'divers Lordes and ladyes' and assorted civic dignitaries. Met, according to the *Oratio Carolina*, with 'loud and joyful acclamations'. And leaving his parliamentary opponents, Hyde supposed, 'much troubled'.[13] The performance of majesty. As promised at the start of the year; to 'reduce all things to the best and purest time, as they were in the time of Queen Elizabeth'.[14] The sentiment celebrated by Lawrence Price in his *Great Britain's Time of Triumph*. A rare event though, in the reign of Charles I. Too rare. And too late. Writing in reflective mood, during the 1650s, Peter Heylyn wondered if the civil war would ever have happened if Charles had found it possible to perform 'a little popularity', a little more often.[15] Another ponderable.

We will start this chapter by taking a look at Charles in his natural habitat, in lighter tones, with some pretty dances and brilliant portraits. After which we will contemplate the concerns of a percipient Venetian, and some anxious farmers. And the fall of a very wicked counsellor. Trials of the literal and metaphorical variety. The palate will be darkening. And it will darken further, as we take a tour of war-torn England. Very definitely not the natural habitat of Charles Stuart. A 'chosen' people on crusade, slaughtering one another. Trial by combat, we might suppose. We will close with a blood-bath in the Cotswolds.

At the court of King Charles

But first, to the northern Italy. To the city of Mantua, to be precise. Where Shakespeare sent Romeo to sort himself out. And where, in early 1628, a fabulous art collection had just come on the market. A consequence of the death of Duke Vincenzio II Gonzaga. Without a legitimate heir. Which meant a war of 'succession', and a fire-sale. Lots of Titian, including the famed *Supper at Emmaus*, Raphael and Caravaggio. Along with Andrea Mantegna's renowned set of nine canvasses, *The Triumphs of Caesar*. Most of the courts of Europe sent agents. Cardinal Richelieu was said to be keen. But not as keen as Charles, who was determined, whatever the cost. Which was, in the end, just shy of £19,000.[16] Mantegna's *Triumphs* would be installed in Hampton Court; where they would, a little later, catch the equally admiring eye of Oliver Cromwell. Lovely. But expensive, especially for a prince perennially short of cash. And a bit Roman.

Mirrors

Art was Charles's passion. Over the following decade he would collect in excess of one thousand paintings, and a further five hundred sculptures.[17] None of which he could reasonably afford. But the price of majesty was incalculable. So he kept buying. In a sense it chimed with the idea of monarchy as spectacle. Princes surrounded by lots of nice things. We will, in a later chapter, come across John Gauden, furiously spinning the myth of the martyred King Charles. If history taught Gauden anything, it was this; the plebs must be kept in a state of 'reverent awe'. Otherwise they will inevitably degenerate to 'wolves and tigers'.[18] Two centuries on, the great Victorian constitutionalist Walter Bagehot would say precisely the same. The responsibility of monarchy is to cast a little fairy-dust, to keep the 'bovine masses' enchanted.[19] In correspondence with the future Charles II, during the 1630s, the Earl of Newcastle deployed a different metaphor to the same purpose. 'What protects you kings' is the 'mist cast before us'.[20] Rather later, in 1646, the radical Henry Marten would liken 'King craft, Clergy craft, and Court craft' to witchcraft, and demand its end.[21] Again, though, easier said than done: on both counts. Making sense of the metaphors, and measuring the margins of sovereignty.

We might note the publication of a couple of texts with suggestive titles. We have already come across the first, Shakespeare's *Measure for Measure*; a play which moved precisely around the relation of public and private. The second was published in 1574, and entitled *Mirror for Magistrates*. A set of poetic histories, chiefly of assorted kings and queens, variously great and not-so-great.[22] To educate and enlighten. Very much the fashion. Similarly purposed texts included Machiavelli's *The Prince*, Erasmus's *The Education of a Christian Prince* and Thomas More's *History of King Richard III*.[23] It became known as 'mirror' literature. *Measure for Measure* was a contribution, as we noted. In fact, it might be argued that pretty much everything Shakespeare wrote was a contribution. Nothing more obviously than the 'tragedy' of *King Richard II*.[24] Queen Elizabeth certainly learned the lesson. Still recovering from the shock of the Essex rebellion in early 1600, she had visited the Tower, in the company of its antiquarian, William Lambarde.

'I am Richard, know ye not that', she had explained at one point. Eliciting, we might assume, a suitably emollient response. We can only surmise what Charles thought of Shakespeare's Richard. More particularly still the deposition scene in Act 4 Scene 1. A deluded prince wandering the chamber, 'flatt'ring glass' in hand, slowly realizing the extent of his self-delusion (4.1.279).[25] Shortly after, usurped and despatched to 'Pomfret' castle, where he will be starved to death. We will, in due course, revisit 'Pomfret'; to note a strange coincidence.

Equally, we can only conjecture what Charles thought of another renowned contribution to the genre. Which he would certainly have read, and which we have already encountered. The *Basilicon Doron*, written by his father, as a companion piece to the *Trew Law*. A commentary on the aesthetics of magistracy, to complement his treatise on the jurisprudence. The *Basilicon* was, in fact, addressed to his eldest son and likely heir, Prince Henry.[26] Charles was the second son, the spare. But the broader principles applied. Princes, the *Basilicon* confirmed, have a 'worldly glorie' which is 'given to them by God' so that they can 'glister and shine before their people'. 'Remember', above all else, a prince must present himself as a 'mirrour and law-booke' of 'earthly' magistracy to his subjects.[27] James's predecessor would have nodded. Gloriana was all about looking glorious.

James was though more temperate, at least in his advice. Dress to impress, but not over-impress; ruffs excepted. Neither like a 'Candie soldier or a vaine young Courtier', nor like a sober 'Minister'.[28] Moderation in all things. Sensible advice passed down parental generations, and usually ignored. Of course the aesthetics could never be cleanly distinguished from the politics. So, a few words on 'divine' authority and the reach of prerogative. Justice is the 'greatest vertue' that 'belongeth' to a Christian prince, and subjects will look to their kings to correct any seeming injustices. Which is why God invests His princes with prerogative powers; and allows them to levy 'fines' on property developers and unlicensed postmen. Money again. Hardly elevating, but necessary if a prince was to afford all the nice paintings.

Which brings us to a different kind of elevation that was concerning Charles. A couple of years after he acquired the Gonzaga collection, the new king decided to do something about his height. Barely more than five feet tall, even on his tippy-toes. He had previously sought the assistance of Orazio Gentileschi and Daniel Mytens. But both had struggled to make him look more Caesar-like, and taller.[29] So instead he turned his attention to Antwerp, where he had recently commissioned some spectacular ceiling paintings from the studio of Peter Paul Rubens; of which more later. And invited over his star pupil. A suitably flattered Anthony van Dyck arrived in April 1632, to see what he could do.[30] Which, in numbers, was quite a lot; roughly four hundred paintings over the next seven years. Representing a very tidy income, at around £60 for a full-length, and £30 for a half. To add to the pension of £200 pa which Charles offered, along with a rather nice Thames-side house at Blackfriars, a gold chain and, in short order, a knighthood.[31]

Sir Anthony would, in due course, paint not just a king but an entire way of courtly life. A pictorial celebration of the 'halcyon days' which the poet Thomas Carew would later recall. An aesthetics of 'personal rule'. We will encounter many of his clients in the coming pages. Some would later turn against their king, such as the Earls of Pembroke and Warwick, and Lords Russell and Wharton. Most, though, would fight for him; or at least cheer him on. Cavaliers of the more authentic variety: the Duke of Richmond, the Earls of Arundel and Newport, Viscount Falkland, Lord Goring, Sir Kenelm Digby. Falkland would die an iconic death at the first battle of Newbury, as we will shortly see. Goring would fight to the bitterest of ends, in command of the last credible royalist army destroyed at Langport in July 1645. A 'master of dissimulation', as Hyde later recorded, and usually drunk. But brave and loyal to a fault. Digby, a former pirate and passionate astrologer, was the king's master-spy; or so he liked to see himself.

Their wives and families too. A definitive portraiture in a political culture which made so much of the patriarchal unit. Amongst van Dyke's most brilliant paintings is Sir Kenelm's wife, on her deathbed.[32] Most iconic was, though, the royal family. Which van Dyck was commissioned to paint within months of arriving in London. His first portrait, entitled the *Great Peece*, was completed by the end of 1632. Followed, five years later, by the *Five Eldest Children of Charles I*. A very assertive Prince Charles, a cowed mastiff at his side, along with some similarly awed siblings. Various portraits of Henrietta Maria too. Not by repute an especial beauty; except when van Dyck painted her. Not tall either, a few inches shorter than her husband indeed. Which required some ingenuity, and some very small props. As in *Queen Henrietta Maria with Sir Jeffrey Hudson*, completed in 1633. Hudson was her dwarf. Henrietta Maria stands in front of a fluted column, whilst an adoring Hudson holds a tiny monkey. Majesty always requires a bit of imagination.

Charles had spotted Henrietta when he passed back through Paris following his disappointing trip to see the Spanish Infanta dance. He was not immediately smitten. But the match had its advantages; not least that it annoyed the Infanta's father. Charles married the fifteen-year-old Henrietta Maria, by proxy, in summer 1625. The first couple of years would not prove easy; probably because Steenie always seemed to be hanging around. The new queen refused to take part in the coronation ceremony. Instead, by an admittedly scurrilous report, spending the afternoon 'frisking and dancing' with her maids. The despatch of the said maids back to France, shortly after, did not help to ease marital tensions much. In time, though, Charles and Henrietta Maria grew genuinely fond. Perhaps too fond. Charles would become increasingly reliant on his wife's advice, especially when it was wrong. Such as in January 1642. There is no doubt that Henrietta Maria strove mightily to help her husband, not least in trying to raise funds abroad during the war. In reality, though, the 'popish brat of France', as some unkind editors took to calling the Queen of England, did far more harm to the brand than might be compensated by entreaties made and jewels pawned.

Bright majesty

It is, though, the portraits of Charles which have become definitive, of van Dyck and the age. The 'two bodies' painted in all their bright majesty: Charles Stuart and King Charles I.[33] Both taller; by the simple expedient of sitting him on a horse. In 1633, van Dyck produced his first equestrian portrait of Charles, entitled *Charles I on Horseback with M de St. Antoine*. A king possessed of strangely long legs, decked out in his finest armour, marshal's baton in hand, the sash of the Order of the Garter round his neck. Charles was obsessed with the Order; hoping that it might do for him what the Order of the Knights of the Round Table had done for the legendary Arthur. He would wear it at his trial, and on the day of his execution. Four years later, came a second equestrian portrait, on a similar theme, *Charles I on Horseback*. Same armour and legs, this time with a peculiarly long rapier. It was supposed to represent a virtuous and beneficent warrior-prince, in easy control of nature, ruling over a becalmed nation. Not for long though. The halcyon days were nearly done.

Van Dyck's Charles was not always sat on a horse. Sometimes he was just stood next to a horse. Or in front of a usefully thin column. Or beside a desk, holding his marshal's baton, or showing off his Order. But it was the equestrian Charles which looked the most majestic. Which was van Dyck's brief, in the main. Less easy was the hope that van Dyck could also make Charles seem a little less Catholic. The problem here was less tractable, a matter of taste. They both adored Titian. *Charles I on Horseback* looked a lot like Titian's *Emperor Charles V at Muelberg*; the leader of the Catholic world slaughtering all his Protestant foes.[34] In fact, pretty much every Caroline portrait that van Dyck painted was based on a Titian. And looked baroque. Charles might have taken to wearing black about Court, in order to impress his sobriety. But it was only because he had noted the fashion in Madrid; and decided to copy it. Hardly very reformed. Van Dyck's 1636 portrait of Charles dressed in black, and wearing his Garter, was inspired by Rubens's *King Phillip IV of Spain wearing the Order of the Golden Fleece*. Which was almost certainly inspired by Titian's similar of Phillip II, painted in 1553. Difficult for a painter with catholic sensibilities to do other than paint pictures which looked a bit Catholic. Difficult for his king too.

And it was not just the paintings. There was the dancing too. Most especially the Court-masque. Definitive, in many ways, of the Renaissance fashion for magisterial spectacle. A stylized form of theatre with a distinctly moralizing aspiration, intended to emphasize the kingly virtues of temperance and harmony. Though not apparently in 1606. When an appalled Sir John Harrington recorded the drunken debauchery into which both actors and audience had fallen during a performance of *Solomon and Sheba* at the Court of King James. Bit parts played by local prostitutes. Charles was determined to restore the majesty of the masque. Something which evidently required the personal touch. Not merely an appearance on stage, invariably leading the Court in a dance intended to symbolize his innate sense of justice, but also taking a hand in the production. Much as he apparently liked to trundle along to van Dyck's studio from time to time, to help out with a spot of daubing. Self-fashioning in the most 'personal' of senses.

And again, all a tad baroque. More dignified perhaps, but hardly godly. And certainly not very conciliatory. The ante-masque, originally pioneered by Ben Jonson, had become very much of the fashion by the 1630s. A pageant of the grotesque and heretical, which would precede the main event. Lots of puritans, for everyone to jeer. The 'sworn enemy of poetry', as Sir William Davenant confirmed in *The Temple of Love*, the 'great friend of murmuring, libelling and all sorts of discord'.[35] Davenant's was part of a spectacular set of masques presented in early 1634. Another was James Shirley's *The Triumph of Peace*. Famed for its production values, and expense, a vast cavalcade starting at the Inns of Court, which then proceeded along Chancery Lane and the Strand, before arriving at the palace. Where the king and queen were so impressed that they sent it off to do another circuit. And then performed again ten days later, at the Merchant Taylor's Hall, at the personal request of Henrietta Maria. Bulstrode Whitelock estimated a total cost of around £21,000, covered by the Inns. The reason why the Inns thought it a wise investment will become shortly apparent.

The ironies are only too obvious. The fashioning of an aesthetic of triumph and harmony, just as the fissures of 'personal' rule began to crack. And not a little poignant too, in van Dyck's case especially. Testament to a shattered age, so many of his dashing cavaliers shortly to be cut to pieces on the battlefields of England. Few more famously dashing than Lucius Cary, Viscount Falkland. Perhaps the greatest of the cavalier poets, who declared himself so 'weary' of his times that he rode off into a hail of musket-shot at the first battle of Newbury. A spectacular martyrdom. Another of the most iconic of van Dyck's cavalier portraits is *Lord John Stuart and His Brother Lord Bernard Stuart*, painted in 1638. Hard to imagine any cavaliers looking more dashing. Lord John would die at the battle of Cheriton in 1644. Lord Bernard, who commanded the King's Lifeguard, would die a few months later, at the battle of Rowton Heath. Another brother, Lord George, was already dead; disembowelled at Edgehill. A lost generation of extremely well-dressed young men.[36] With very curly hair. Which brings us nicely to the already familiar name of William Prynne, and the 'Case of the Notorious Whores'.

The case of the notorious whores

Of course, fashion is a variable. The Stuart brothers might have liked what they saw in themselves; or what van Dyck saw. The 'friends of murmuring' saw something different. A liking for continental affectation that was at least ridiculous, probably damnable. A Court populated by 'rattleheaded' cavaliers, as satirical news-sheets took to calling them. With their 'pretty faces' and 'ridiculous toys', their 'gingling of coach-wheel rowed spurs' and the 'French troubled straddling of the legs'.[37] At least neither Lord James nor Lord Bernard are doing any straddling. Clear evidence of gingling though, and far too much satin. And precisely the kind of hairstyle which could so easily lead to war. Lord Bernard is sporting ringlets. A style apparently admired by the king, borrowed again from France.

Which entertained the still deeper, and more dangerous, suspicion, that the King of England might be a closet Catholic. Literally indeed; given the rumours of Charles attending Catholic masses conducted in his wife's 'closet'. A bit of stretch? Not to men like John Goodwin, whose 1644 *Anti-Cavalierisme* explicitly aligned the spiritually damnable with the cultural. Do not 'exchange your quails and manna from Heaven for the garlicke and onions of Egypt'.[38] An insinuation which was, by the mid-1630s, becoming dangerously familiar; Charles Stuart as Pharaoh, his subjects held in 'cruell bondage', as Jeremiah Burroughs put it, 'as the Egyptians did the Israelites'.[39]

No surprise to William Prynne either. Whose story begins at Lincoln's Inn. Where the young William had come into contact with John Preston, a controversial 'lecturer' with a distinctly moralizing tone.[40] Preston would later become chaplain to Prince Charles; incongruous perhaps given the ferocity with which he would denounce all the things that his young charge liked. The moralizing tone evidently had little effect on Charles. But it did on Prynne. Disdaining a quiet life at the bar, William turned instead to a career in writing. Some legal tracts, such as his *Animadversions on the Fourth Part of Coke's Institutes*. But mainly writings on theology and moral dissipation. We will take a closer look at the politics, and the aesthetics, of the Caroline Church very shortly. Suffice to say that Prynne was not much impressed. All the pretty stained glass windows and brightly woven altar-cloths, and suspiciously popish prelates who packed the Caroline episcopacy. Not a man to mince his words, Prynne let it be known that the Laudian 'reformation' was something 'raised up from hell of late by some Jesuits and infernal spirits'.[41]

But what really got Prynne fired up were cavorting French maids. More specifically the maids who had accompanied Henrietta Maria over from France. A disconcerting experience for all concerned. In 1627, John Cosin, personal chaplain to the Laudian Bishop of Durham, John Neile, published a short text entitled a *Collection of Private Devotions*. Written to reassure the maids, and their queen, now marooned in a country full of men like Prynne, that there was in fact nothing really 'new' about the Reformation Church. More a tweaking. Prynne was twenty-seven, clearly still an impressionable age. He was not supposed to have gotten hold of a copy of Cosin's *Devotions*. But he did, and immediately set about writing a sharp rebuttal with a witty title: *A Brief Survey of Mr Cozen's, His Cozening Devotions*. The title of his next tract, published the following year, was nothing like so pithy.

In full: *The Unloveliness of Lovelocks; or a Summary Discourse, proving the wearing and nourishing of a lock, or love-lock, to be altogether unseemly, and unlawful unto Christians, in which there are likewise some passages collected out of Fathers, Councils and Sundry Authors, Historians, against Face-painting, the wearing of supposititious Powdered, Frizled or extraordinary long Hair; the inordinate affection of corporal Beautie; and Women's Mannish, Unnatural, Impudent and unchristian cutting of their Hair, the Epidemicall Vanities, and Vices of our Age.* It might seem a bit odd, to get quite so worked up about a hairstyle. But this was no ordinary affectation. In his satirical 1632 pamphlet *Earth's Vanity*, Samuel Rowlands had observed that 'your Gallant is no man unless his hair be of the woman's fashion, dangling and waving over his shoulders'.[42]

Some just sniggered, others took to the streets. When the London apprentices decided to take on Lunsford and his cavaliers in early 1641, they cut their hair. In part, so that they would be sure who to beat up. But also to make a point. They were 'round-headed', and serious. As was Prynne; always. There was, as readers of his tract discovered, more to the lovelock than met the eye, far more. First, because it was a gateway abomination. From such 'petty vices' flowed any number of 'heinous sins' including the 'incitation of lust' and the 'occasion of sodomy'. And second, because it was representative of a courtly culture which was brazenly licentious. Prynne did not cite Charles in person. But it was pretty clear which prospective sodomite he had in mind. Casting aspersion was Prynne's modus operandi.

Which brings us to his most famous tract, *Histriomastix*, published in 1632. An extended commentary on all the familiar 'abominations', but most especially those of the theatre, or 'devil's chapels' as Prynne preferred. The 'dancing, masks, mummeries' and 'state plays', being so obviously 'derived' from 'Roman Saturnalia and Bacchanalian festivals'. And thus so clearly deserving of the condemnation of all 'pious Christians'. Not all music was so deserving. But most was, especially the 'lascivious, amorous, effeminate, voluptuous'. The kind which Charles seemed to like. And his wife. It was the behaviour of Henrietta Maria which inspired *Histriomastix. The Player's Scourge, or Actor's Tragedy*, as the sub-title confirmed, for anyone unfamiliar with the classical Greek.[43]

Prynne was not the only Englishman concerned by female actors. Sir Benjamin Rudyerd was just as exercised, especially by those who wore false beards. The reason why Prynne decided to go into print in 1632 were reports, then circulating, that Henrietta Maria had taken part in a court-masque, entitled *The Shepherd's Paradise*.[44] Not just appearing on stage with her husband, in the customary 'dance' of harmony. But singing in French, apparently, and then dancing about with her maids dressed as the queen of the shepherdesses.[45] And so when *Histriomastix* appeared, with its pointed allusion to women actors as 'notorious whores, and the eternal shame of their sex', and the scarcely veiled insinuation that the Court of Charles Stuart bore a dreadful resemblance to the 'basely prostituted' Rome of the Emperor Nero, the authorities felt obliged to respond.[46]

It was not the first time that Prynne had come to their attention. He had been hauled before Star Chamber, charged with breaches of licensing regulations, in 1627 and 1630. This time the charges were more grievous. Accused of 'seditious, libellous railing' for the purpose of inciting 'disobedience' and 'discontent', the author had sought to 'withdraw the peoples' affections from the King and Government'. More particularly still, in directing his reader's attention to various deposed Roman tyrants, and their scandalous courtesans, he had 'imagined' the king's death. The fact that he had not actually said as much hardly mattered. Indeed, the equivocation simply affirmed his dreadful 'intention'.[47]

And, on these terms, Prynne did not have much of a defence. Contextualization hardly helped. The condemnation of female actors as 'notorious whores' alluded more generally to the incidence of French actresses recently invited to perform at Blackfriars and other London theatres. But it hardly left much to the imagination. Certainly not that of Chief Justice Heath, in whose opinion Prynne's was a 'very horrid' crime, perhaps the most horrid ever to have 'come into this court'. Various possible punishments were mooted by the arraigned judges. Heath noted that 'others have been hanged as traitors that have not gone so far'.[48] In the end Prynne was sentenced to be pilloried twice, disbarred, fined £5000 and imprisoned for life. He would also have his ears cut off. And his book would be publicly burned by the common hangman. Meantime, the Inns of Court decided that it might be appropriate to create some distance between themselves and their fractious learned friend. And decided to invest £21,000 in some more masques.

Not that the learned friend was quite so inclined to make peace. Within weeks of being returned to the Tower to serve his sentence, Prynne was composing a public letter condemning his trial as an abuse of process. Observing God's evident displeasure too. Attorney General Noy, 'intoxicated with malice', had died within weeks of the trial. Prynne then turned his attention to the recent re-issuing of the *Book of Lawful Sports*. A prerogative gesture intended to alleviate harassed hobbyists who found themselves hauled before local justices for breaking the Sabbath. Pretty much a compulsory purchase too, copies to be held in each parish church.[49] The *Book* listed various activities that the more energetic Stuart Englishman might lawfully pursue on Sunday afternoons; instead of just going to the local alehouse. Eighteen pages of possibilities, including archery, 'leaping, vaulting' and 'morris dancing'. As for women, carrying 'rushes to church for the decorating of it' was highly recommended.

But not by Prynne. Or by his fellow contrarian, Henry Burton, in whose opinions such activities were 'floodgates' to 'presumptuous sin'.[50] Or the constables of Olney in Buckinghamshire, who armed themselves with halberds before wading in to break up some offensive maypole-dancing in 1636. Another kind of civil war. Or William Whiteway, a prominent Dorchester puritan, who diligently recorded various instances of localized divine displeasure; collapsing maypoles, young lads maimed playing inter-village football matches. There was no such thing as a harmless pastime in the mind of William Whiteway. Morris dancing was still dancing, and the 'gates of heaven' would always be shut to those who skipped about waving sticks. The *Book* would be publicly burned by order of Parliament in 1643. England purged of its 'licentious' flower-arrangers, puppeteers and stick-waivers.[51]

Not, of course, that over-zealous flower-arrangers were the most pressing concern. Nor over-exuberant maypole-dancers. It was mendacious bishops. Amongst whom might be counted Matthew Wren, bishop of Norwich. Who, readers of Prynne's *News from Ipswich* were about to discover, was in league with a number of other prominent Laudians in a concerted attempt to seize control of the Church and 'usher' in popery. We will, as advertised, encounter the Laudian reformers shortly, with all their devilish attempts to smarten up local churches and make them smell a bit nicer. Interior decoration was one of the many 'intolerable usurpations' that Prynne would address in his next missive, *A Breviate of the Prelates Intolerable Usurpations*. Not that 'breviate', at three hundred plus pages, but there were so many usurpations.

Spring 1637 found Prynne back in Star Chamber. Along with Burton and another puritan contrarian, John Bastwick.[52] Familiar surroundings for each, and a familiar contempt. All three refused to plead to charges of sedition, but did take the opportunity to make a number of 'bold' and 'impudent' remarks impugning the legitimacy of the court. The verdict was not much in doubt. The pillory again. A first ear-shaving for Bastwick and Burton. For Prynne a bit more of the stump cut off. And his cheeks branded, with the letters 'SL'; to denote 'Seditious Libeller'. Prynne liked to suppose that it really meant *Stigmata Laudis*, the 'mark of Laud'. Lots of handy biblical referents too. Three pillories on a hill, Burton noted; just like the three crosses at Calvary. Bastwick compared his trial to that of St Paul before Nero, and spent his time reciting prayers. Three 'desperate mad factious fellows', John Burgh noted, all craving a 'kind of puritanical martyrdom'.[53] And getting it.

The risks were self-evident. To Sir Thomas Wentworth at least. 'A Prince that loses the force and example of his punishment, loses withal the greatest part of his dominion'.[54] Heylyn expressed similar misgivings. Few doubted Prynne's guilt. But the manner of his treatment caused 'great trouble to the spirits of many very moderate and well-meaning gentlemen'.[55] Meanwhile, a series of royal decrees were issued, vesting still tighter regulatory powers in Star Chamber; thirty-three new clauses all intended to quieten the likes of William Prynne. Who was despatched to commence his life sentence in Carnarvon castle. Along the way feasted at Barnet, St Albans and then Chester. Such was his notoriety that even Carnarvon proved too near, and Prynne was shortly moved to Mount Orgueil in Jersey. Where he would stay until his release in November 1640, by order of the newly summoned Parliament. A triumphal re-entry to London awaited, greeted by a crowd of ten thousand, streets strewn with flowers. A couple of weeks later, Parliament would commence impeachment proceedings against Archbishop Laud, at Prynne's urging. We will take up that story very shortly. Contrary as ever, we will next encounter Prynne opposing the idea of putting the king on trial, and being excluded from Parliament as a consequence. The 1650s would be spent harassing Cromwell.[56]

The rule of King Charles

Amongst the many who wondered the wisdom of chasing men like William Prynne through the courts was the Venetian envoy, Anthony Correr. Vesting a 'most exalted martyrdom', Correr observed in his end-of-year report in late 1637. A percipient man, Correr also noted that Charles was starting to look a bit weary. Still 'glorious', but a prince whose 'very face clearly betrays the passions within'. Not really the prince who could be discerned in van Dyck's *Charles I at the Hunt*, regal, assured. Nor, indeed, a prince who hunted anymore; as Correr also noted. It 'remains to be seen', the envoy surmised, 'if he will go on'. By which he meant ruling in his 'personal' capacity. It has certainly been a difficult year.[57] Made all the more 'perilous', because Charles had brought into alignment, against him, 'two great causes', those of 'religion and the diminution of the liberty of the people'. The king, Correr concluded, will 'be very fortunate if he does not fall into some great upheaval'.[58]

The case of the red-faced prelate

A simple enough concept. Government through the 'person' of the king. Where 'everyone walks within the circle of his charge and his Majesty's hand is the chief and, in effect, the sole directory'.[59] The words of Sir Dudley Carleton, Secretary of State up until 1632. The governmental complement to the 'halcyon days' promised by the poets. England was certainly in need of cheering itself up, as Laud observed in 1631. There 'is no nation under heaven so happy' he assured his king, 'if it did but know and understand its happiness'.[60] For sure, the idea of ruling without the 'hidra' of Parliament appealed to Charles. An institution which he had consistently found to be 'as well cunning, as malitious'.[61] And there was nothing essentially aberrant in ruling without it. His father had done so, as much as possible. What mattered was how Charles might deal with any crises that came his way, and more particularly how he would fund all the wars and paintings. For a while he seemed to manage, just about. Preaching at the Northampton Assizes in 1635, Edward Reynolds celebrated a 'long uninterrupted and blessed tranquillity'. Which was the 'astonishment of other nations', and probably a fair few who lived in Northamptonshire, a county which, as we will see, would assume a curiously large significance in the later history of Charles Stuart.

But then it started to go awry. In large part, a consequence of the same two 'great causes' noted by Correr. Money and faith. Faith first. A century had passed since Henry Tudor had ransacked the monasteries under the auspices of returning England to God. A generation since James had expressed his exasperation at Hampton Court; beyond giving a 'turd' for liturgical dispute. In March 1630, Charles would express a similar displeasure following a sermon given by the Calvinist Bishop Davenant. Theological niceties were 'too high for the people's understanding'. There were 'other points which concern reformation and newness of life' that 'were more needful and profitable'.[62] Politer; but point made. The greater challenge that faced Charles in 1625 was settling consciences. Partly to save souls but mainly to save the Crown. 'No bishops, no King'; the inexorable consequence of a Reformation settlement which was, as Sir Simonds D'Ewes surmised, still 'full of wrinkles'.[63] The last thing the new king needed, as Sir Philip Warwick later confirmed, was the 'chaos' of intractable religious disputation.[64]

But it was what he got. 'The Devil take him whosoever he be, that had a design to change religion', Charles was heard to mutter, on receiving Pym's *Grand Remonstrance* in 1641. He probably meant Henry Tudor. Others pointed the finger at him. A king who seemed complicit in a counter-reformation of the English Church. The king in the 'Closet', all the onions and garlic, the shepherdesses and the ringlets. Hyde would later confirm that Charles was entirely 'averse from the Romish Church'.[65] But it did not appear so. Certainly not when it came to appointing High Church ceremonialists to the Caroline episcopacy. Men like Richard Montague, John Bancroft, Thomas Morton, Richard Neile and Matthew Wren.[66] And, of course, William Laud; as Archbishop of Canterbury in 1633. Each sharing their king's perception that congregations are happier when awed. Nothing, Laud confirmed, was better designed to ensure 'quiet discipline' than lots of fancy 'ceremonies'.[67] Bowing, kneeling, candles, lots of Latin and divine service at least twice a week.

The right kit too, fancy windows and beautiful tapestry-cloths, draped over communion tables that looked like altars. And wooden-rails, to 'decently sever', as the canons of 1640 put it, the plebs from all the expensive stuff. Not that many plebs were likely to get a peek into the Royal Chapel. William Hawkins did though, attending the Palm Sunday service in 1637. He reported back to his patron, the puritan Earl of Leicester; lots of bowing and something that looked very like 'crucifix' hanging over the altar. We can assume that the earl was suitably appalled. Though whether he was much surprised is a different matter. The Queen's Chapel was already notorious. A blatant popery which now appeared to be spreading across parochial England. The 'beauty of holiness', as Richard Skinner put it, brought to the people; or near enough. The 'decency and comeliness' of the Church restored, Heylyn affirmed, by the grace of 'his sacred majesty'.[68] A matter of taste, of course.

But not only. Squabbles over interior decoration spoke to darker fears too, about the pretences of independent Church governance. In the king's opinion, 'absolutely unlawful'.[69] Catholics cleaving to Rome was a concern. More so 'independent' congregations cleaving to themselves, choosing their own decoration and their own preachers. The running riot of 'popularity', literally in some cases. The arrival of 'personal rule' was heralded by the issuance of new Royal Instructions on Church discipline. Chief amongst them being an authority to suppress puritan lecturers, 'elected' or otherwise. When Charles heard of a dispute regarding a lecturer at Great Yarmouth he intervened in person. What was at stake, he reminded the corporation, was not just 'ecclesiastical discipline' but the very basis of 'civil order and government'.[70] We might take a glance at a few more instances of parochial dispute, and vandalism. It will give us a better sense of the kinds of things which were troubling God's once-chosen people.

Such as Lady Eleanor Davies who, on discovering some 'hangings of Arras behind the altar' at Lichfield Cathedral brought a kettle of 'holy water', as she called it, composed of 'tar, pitch' and 'puddle-water'. To 'sprinkle upon the aforesaid things'. And Henry Sherfield, recorder of Salisbury, so distressed by one particular stained glass window, which purported to depict Jesus Christ as an old man dressed in a blue frock-coat, that he smashed it with a stick. And Samuel Greygoose, an Epping churchwarden, who set about breaking up the altar-rail in his local church. It was an 'idol' and in the way.[71] And dozens more, up and down the country. Later, during the Long Parliament, the vandalism would assume more organized form; with nominated commissioners touring the country tearing down all 'the relics of idolatry'. The 'work of the Spirit', as Colonel William Goffe would confirm, approvingly, which is to 'pull down all works' that are not 'of the Spirit'.[72]

Not yet though. Small wonder then that the Laudian episcopacy was keen on parochial 'visitations'. Not simply to deter amateur window-smashers and rail-strippers, but to ensure that people were chanting the right prayers, and kneeling at the right times, and standing. Thus Elizabeth Perfit of Perbeck, prosecuted by the Archdeacon of Northampton for refusing to get off her 'arse'. One of many arse-sitters. No less worrying were furtive leaners; looking like they were kneeling, but not really. And those who were unaware, or simply unwilling, to stand for the Creed. 'Can ye not stand, ye lazy sows', an exasperated John Cosin cried out on one occasion at Durham, when some of his female congregation stayed sat.[73] A less lyrical moment in the career of one of the Caroline Church's most accomplished advocates.

Ceremonialism was an acquired taste, not always acquired. And much the same was true of tighter Church 'discipline'. A bulwark against the 'many machinations of Satan', Reynolds observed in his Northampton Assizes sermon. Well maybe. Sir Francis Rous was not so sure. Laudian reform was nothing other than the 'spawn of a Papist'.[74] Sir Francis had other 'machinations' in mind. As did Prynne's chum, Henry Burton, in whose opinion the appointment of Laud had been purposed 'for the bringing in of popery'. As Cosin's not-so *Private Devotions* seemed to impute. Still the Church of our 'forefathers', Cosin assured his new Queen, and any who think differently simply 'betray their own infirmities'.[75] Cosin supposed that the Anglican Church might position itself between arrant 'popery' and the 'wild madness' of puritanism.[76] A thin margin though.

And infinitely contested. 'Innovations in religion' were a principal complaint in the dying moments of the third Caroline Parliament. And would remain so. As Correr noted in his 1637 report. Militant puritanism, the 'pest' that will likely 'disturb the repose of this Kingdom', a 'poison spreading'. The Essex minister, Samuel Hoard, deployed a variant pathological metaphor. Puritanism as 'a gangrene, if it seize and be permitted to settle but on one limb it speedily runs over and ruins all the body'. Not the first to deploy the metaphor of the diseased body politic, and certainly not the last. From a very different perspective Andrew Humfrey described Laudian decoration as a kind of 'leprosy' which had to be 'stifled'.[77] Which meant purgation; another metaphor that would become ubiquitous, and variable. It might be purging the Church of its puritans. Or it might be purging the Church of men like William Laud.

Taking the 'axe to the root' of popery, as Sir John Wray urged, in his speech to the Commons in late November 1640. Nothing mattered more. Sir Benjamin Rudyerd agreed. 'Let religion be our *Primum Quaerite*', he advised the newly assembled Members, 'for all things else are but *etcaeteras* to it'.[78] The preamble to the *Root and Branch Petition*, which arrived in Parliament a few weeks later, spoke of the 'proved prejudice' of the Laudian episcopate. The 'main cause and occasion of many foul evils, pressures and grievances'.[79] Aspersions towards Star Chamber too, a 'monster' at Laud's command, and the Commission.[80] Bills for the abolition of both would arrive in Parliament a few months later. Not everyone was persuaded, of course. Falkland turned the metaphor, advising that they 'should not root up this ancient tree as dead as it appears' until they were sure that it could not be made to 'flourish' again.[81]

But puritan blood was up. The following May, Sir Henry Vane presented a *Root and Branch Bill* to Parliament, alongside a hitherto obscure Cambridge MP named Oliver Cromwell. Formal impeachment proceedings against thirteen bishops began at the end of July. On the grounds that recent canons passed in Convocation had breached the provisions of *Praemunire* legislation. A few others too, including Cosin, then Vice Chancellor of Cambridge University. Conducting masses which made it clear that 'the pope is not far off' and having apparently confided that the king 'hath no more power over the church than the boy who rubs my horse's heels'.[82] Another of Cosin's more prosaic moments. John Hall, bishop of Exeter, had taken a rather different tack in his *Episcopacy by Divine Right Asserted*, published a year before. His king had absolute power, given by God. A familiar argument, if not well timed. Hall was another to find himself stood at the bar of the House in late 1641, defending impeachment charges.

A precipitous fall; for an entire clerisy. None steeper, of course, than that which befell William Laud. By common repute the most powerful man in England during the decade of 'personal rule'. Scurrilous comparisons with Cardinal Wolsey were irresistible. When the Marquis of Hamilton wanted a favour of the king, he checked with Laud first; no point asking otherwise. We might take a glance at van

Dyke's Laud, painted around 1638. A short man, rotund, with a slightly podgy face; apparently a good likeness. Red too, a consequence no doubt of high blood pressure. Understandable. Looking very clerical and very serious. And a lot like the Abbe Scaglia, who van Dyck had painted in 1634. Hogarth thought it was van Dyck's 'most excellent head', because he could still feel the intimidation.

Fear, and loathing. The 'sty of all pestilential filth', as Harbottle Grimstone put it, 'like a busie angry wasp, his sting is in the tayl of everything'. The 'only man' responsible for 'all our ruins, miseries and calamities' over the previous 'ten years'. Wray agreed. Laud's 'innovations' responsible for putting an entire country so 'out of joint' that only the most 'skilful chiyrurgeons' could now 'set' the fractured nation.[83] Along with some decent lawyers. Laud was arrested within days of the Long Parliament opening, and hauled off to the Tower. Pym took personal responsibility for laying impeachment charges a few weeks later. The fallen prelate had 'traiterously assumed to himself a papal and tyrannical power' and 'made the king's throne a footstool to his own … pride'.[84]

Laud waited his fate, and then waited a bit more. The impeachment strategy ran into a brick-wall in the shape of the House of Lords. Already sixty-seven, and far from well, it might be hoped that a spot of judicious neglect would anyway finish him off. But no. Instead Laud remained in the Tower, nearly forgotten, until spring 1644. When proceedings finally got underway again, with fresh impeachment charges; laid, this time, by Prynne. Seven general articles, and twenty-eight in particular, most alleging acts of treasonous 'perversion'. The second general article charging that the Archbishop had 'endeavoured to advance the Power of the Council Table, the Canons of the Church, and the King's Prerogative, above the Laws and Statutes of the Realm'. Various Council meetings recalled, in which the Archbishop had repeatedly urged the king to rule by prerogative and 'canons of the Church'. Intimations of 'popery', and an opportunity to give Fuller's *Argument* another airing. Amongst the recollections was a sermon given by the Archbishop about 'six years last past', on *Matthew* 21:44: 'That those who would not yield to the King's Power, he would crush them to Pieces.'[85]

Much made of Laud's role in the coronation too. Conducted by Archbishop Abbott, but drafted by Laud. The sentiment had not worn well; the hope that Charles would be 'endued with the mildness of Moses, armed with the fortitude of Joshua, exalted with the humility of David, beautified with the wisdom of Solomon'.[86] Not really. English kings were supposed to lead their people out of slavery, not back in. The more particular complaint moved around the coronation oath. Four rhetorical questions. A first asking the coming king to:

grant and keep, and so by your oath confirm, to the people of England, the laws and customs to them granted by the kings of England your lawful and religious predecessors; and namely the laws, customs, and franchises granted to the clergy by the glorious king St Edward your predecessor (according to the laws of God, the true profession of the Gospel established in this kingdom, and agreeable to the prerogatives of the kings thereof, and the ancient customs of this realm)?

Familiar, and not. Four words missing. Previous oaths had referred to laws granted to the 'clergy and to the people'; not just the clergy. But thirty-two added, at the end; including a conspicuous reference to prerogatives. The second oath asked Charles to preserve the peace. The third that he would secure the execution of justice. The fourth asked him to 'keep and hold the laws' of England 'to the honour of God'. Holy covenants with God. Except where they assumed exclusivity. The idea that kings were also bound, in contract, with their subjects would be worked hard in January 1649; as we will see. Laud's trial gave it an airing. Various things led Laud to the scaffold, but nothing was more damning than what he had written twenty years earlier.

No compelling evidence of treason though. Not enough to make an impeachment stick, even now, in late 1644. If anything the jurisprudence was trickier still; charges of treason against a king brought by a Parliament which was now at war with the same king. There was though an alternative, an Act of Attainder. A legislative instrument, the effect of which was to nullify the common law rights of the subject in particular instances of alleged treason or serious felony. Their greatest virtue was simplicity. Following the passage of the bill through both Houses, only royal assent would be required to secure the judicial execution of the guilty party. Henry VIII had found them handy; despatching both Thomas Cromwell and Catherine Howard by means of attainder. Expeditious then. Charles could hardly be expected to oblige. But God had. A great victory on the outskirts of York, at Marston Moor on 2 July. Providence pointed the way. Along with Prynne. The Attainder arrived in the very end of October, and was enrolled at the beginning of January. As was an Ordinance for *the Beheading of the Archbishop of Canterbury*, at the 'accustomed place', Tower Hill. To which the seventy-one-year-old prelate was conveyed on the morning of 10 January. Not the first slaughtered Archbishop in English history; Becket, Cranmer, a few medieval traitors and a very forgotten Anglo-Saxon.[87] The last though.

The case of the fainting farmers

The purpose of 'personal rule', if we recall, was to make the life of the king a bit easier. His nerves hopefully. Not, though, his purse. So many nice things to buy. Expenditure on the royal wardrobe doubled during the first decade of Charles's reign; from £13 million a year to £27 million. Neither king nor queen seemed able to stop spending, chiefly on themselves. And so many wars to fight. So many promises made. Within months of coming to the throne Charles had promised to help Uncle Christian. And then his new brother-in-law, Louis XIII of France. Both at war with the Hapsburgs. Parliament had offered barely a fifth of what he had demanded for the former endeavour, which was £700,000. His third Parliament, as we have already noted, was no more helpful. In return for assenting to the *Petition of Right* it had offered around half of what was required to refurbish the fleet for yet another attempt to relieve the Huguenots still bottled up in La Rochelle. All very irritating, and not a little embarrassing. Very 'irksome' to the 'princely honour', if the King of England was unable to get a fleet to sea.

And not likely to get much better, absent a beneficent Parliament. By 1633 the Exchequer was perilously low. The money was there, Secretary Windebank assured his king, if the 'right vein be opened'.[88] Windebank had the City in mind. But it was not feeling generous. Which left just a few familiar options, bits and pieces of customary income, mortgaging any still-uncharged Crown estate. Or recourse, once again, to prerogative taxation. The precedent was hardly encouraging, but the need was unarguable. Charles consulted his Attorney General, who suggested the idea of 'ship money', a tax to be levied on ports for the maintenance of the navy. The right to do so in times of emergency was not contested. But peace was different. The prerogative order issued in 1635 cited incidents of 'piracy'. But it was a stretch. There were always pirates around. Charles issued a declaration clarifying the need, 'for the good and safety of the Kingdom'. And emphasizing that 'in such cases' he was the 'sole judge' of the 'danger'. A variant on a familiar tension; the king's absolute authority to determine when he had absolute authority.

The 'most deadly and fatal blow' inflicted on the 'liberty of the subjects of England' in 'five hundred years last past', Sir Simonds D'Ewes observed. Before asking the same familiar question: 'What shall free men differ from ancient bondsmen and villeins', if 'their estates be subject to arbitrary taxes?' Indeed. Another given to pathological metaphors, D'Ewes closed by wondering if the 'disease' which presently afflicted the county might prove 'incurable'.[89] Sir Simonds was an inveterate worrier. But there was reason, and history. The lesson of the past was plain enough; princes short of cash tend to take chances. Better budgeting was a solution; but hardly the Stuart way. The levy was extended across the country.

And the courtrooms of England filled with fractious cattle-owners suing writs of replevin.[90] And their lawyers, looking for a fight and a decent fee. Counter-suits were pressed against constables attempting distraint. The London merchant Richard Chambers sued the Lord Mayor. When the latter checked with his lawyers, he received the disappointing advice that the levy probably was unlawful, and that settlement might be a good idea. Up in Nottinghamshire an attorney named John Coude advised the gentlemen of the county along the same lines. Any distraint should be contested. Down in Somerset, Sir William Strode received the same advice.[91] Another cow recovered, and another constable sued. Over in Lincolnshire, a couple of oxen were sequestered from the estate of Lord Saye at

Brumby. Not for long though. Saye, a prominent member of the parliamentary 'junto', was gearing up.

In the summer of 1637, the sheriff of Buckingham returned a list of non-payers. At the top of the list was the name of John Hampden. A writ of *scire facias* was issued, for failure to pay an assessment of twenty shillings. Hampden knew it was coming. The sheriff, Sir Peter Temple, was Saye's kinsman. And Saye and Hampden were mates. There is a tendency to assume the English civil war was animated by annoyance. It was also animated by amiability. Sir Edward Hyde would later write a potted biography of Hampden into his *History of the Rebellion*. A man much liked by those of 'jolly conversation' who, despite turning increasingly towards a life of 'sobriety and strictness' in later middle age, never lost his innate 'affability'.[92] Hyde rather liked John Hampden; and he knew that lots of others did. He also counselled Charles against taking Hampden and the other tax-dodgers to court. For pretty much the same reason that wiser counsel wondered the wisdom of persecuting William Prynne. Litigation is never just about winning legal cases. Charles might have recalled what had happened a decade earlier, when Hampden's uncle had been prosecuted for refusing the 'forced' loan.[93] Not a happy precedent. Undeterred though, Charles pressed on. Maybe he just felt luckier.

Hampden's Case arrived at the Court of Exchequer in early autumn.[94] Hampden's counsel, led by another close ally, Oliver St John, did not dispute prerogative power. But he did question the ability of the Crown to seize 'goods' without 'parliamentary assistance', and the presence of any 'special' case of emergency; in the absence of which 'by the fundamental laws of England, the King cannot, out of Parliament, charge the subject'. Attorney General Bankes retaliated metaphorically. The king 'is the first mover among these orbs of ours, and he is the circle of this circumference'. The power to 'defend' the realm 'absolutely inherent in the king's person'. The Solicitor General threw in some jurisprudence, of the predictable kind. The king held a 'trust', which included a duty to do 'whatever tends to the preservation' of the realm at moments of 'danger'; and if need be deal with instances of 'refractoriness'. Contemporaries sensed a close call, recognizing the skill in St John's argument, but doubting whether a full bench would go against the king. And so it proved.

The twelve justices found themselves, in fact, at considerable odds. Aside from a basic agreement that tax could only be raised through Parliament, except in moments of credible 'necessity'; something that neither side disputed. Four justices inclined towards the king on grounds of principle. Most strongly, perhaps, Sir Robert Berkeley. In whose opinion, the law was 'of itself an old and trusty servant of the King', the 'instrument of means which he useth to govern his people by'. Any attempt to challenge the prerogative would be a kind of 'king-yoking' unknown in English law. Two justices leant just as strongly the other way. According to Justice Croke 'no necessity can procure this charge without a Parliament'. Justice Hutton affirmed, simply, that the 'king had no lawful power to levy the Ship Money'. The remaining judges dodged the larger questions altogether, preferring to immerse themselves in technical arguments regarding the execution of the writ, whether it was appropriate to a tax or a 'service'. Justices Bramston and Davenport resolved that the king had the power to command the service, but not receive the money. Most thought that the judges had decided for the king by seven to five. But no-one was entirely sure. Correr thought it might be seven to four, with one abstention. Whitelock counted it ten to two.[95]

If it was difficult to be sure who had won, and by how much, it was clear who had lost. As Hyde had feared. *Hampden's Case* 'grew the argument of all tongues'. And did far more 'credit' for Hampden than it did his king. At that moment, Hampden had the 'greatest power and interest' of any man 'in the kingdom'.[96] Hampden would later die of wounds received whilst commanding a regiment of horse at Chalgrove Field in 1643. Hyde closed his potted biography by noting that Hampden had, by then, become 'much fiercer'. And by casting an intimation. If Charles had been rather more sensitive in his dealings with men such as John Hampden, he would never have gotten himself into quite such a mess. A perception shared by Sir Roger Twysden. Up until 1637, prerogative taxation was mere 'grating'. Something different now though. *Hampden's Case* had made Charles look like an 'absolute' tyrant, not dissimilar to the 'King of France or the Great Duke of Tuscany'.[97]

Fascinating though. 'All the talk in London', Anthony Mingay reported back to his friends in Norfolk. Thomas Knyvett decided to attend in person, but could not get inside the courtroom 'by two or three yards, the crowd being so great'. The future Archbishop of Canterbury, William Sancroft, managed. And was able to keep his brother in Suffolk abreast of daily events; focussing rather more on the theatre than the jurisprudence. When any justice 'gave for the country tis strange how he was hummed and applauded, and how slighted if for the King'.[98] A nation enthralled. And torn. Northamptonshire seemed confused. The chief constable of the country, William Walker, praised the 'best and most honest' of the justices for having the courage to stand up to the king. In contrast to the Reverend Thomas Harrison. A few months later hauled before King's Bench to answer charges of sedition, having accused Justice Hutton of wilfully misinterpreting the law. 'We are not to question the King's actions,' Harrison had argued, 'they are only between God and his own conscience.' When challenged by Chief Justice Finch, Harrison had admitted that kings rule not only by 'the common laws' but also by 'something else'.[99] His Reverence could be fined and imprisoned for his temerity. But the inference was clear.

The tax had re-floated the Exchequer. Raising around £750,000 in total by 1640. But at what cost. A culture of provincial recalcitrance. As Laud noted, as early as 1636, the non-payers were growing daily more 'bold'.[100] The parson of Winterbourne let it be known that 'he would lose his life rather than suffer his goods to be taken'. The Reverend Richard Northen advised his Lincolnshire parishioners that it was plain 'theft'; and found himself before the High Commission as a consequence.[101] By 1639 delinquency rates were up to 80 per cent. Lots of grumpy pastors. Along with the swathes of irritated gentlemen-farmers, now emboldened to dispute all kinds of customary, as well as 'forced', taxes. Such as Sir John Corbet, of Adderley in Shropshire. History has not made quite so much of Sir John's case. But it is no less instructive. In 1635, Sir John goaded a Grand Jury into contesting the cost, and need, of an annual militia muster. When challenged by the Earl of Bridgwater, Lord President of the Marches, Sir John had cited the *Petition of Right*. An impudence which saw him despatched to the Fleet. The Jury was meanwhile purged and payment instructed. Less easy to collect though. In 1640, Corbet could be found petitioning Parliament against payments 'unlawfully settled'.[102]

Difficult times for postmen too. Anthony Spittle, postmaster of Hampshire, was entitled to requisition horses 'upon extraordinary occasions'. But found that no-one would let him have any, in case they might be used to carry summons. And for muster-masters. The Dorset master pretty much gave up. As did his counterpart in Leicestershire, where Sir Arthur Haselrig loudly declined to muster anything. And in neighbouring Northamptonshire again, where a 'seditious refractory attorney who stands upon the letter of the law' was reported to have advised the gentlemen of the county to ignore the charge. Whether the same attorney had a word with the gentlemen-foresters of Rockingham we can only surmise. They threatened to resign en masse if they were required to pay another customary 'fine'. Isolated incidents in a sense but also suggestive of something which should have seemed more troubling. A habit of disobedience assuming a strategic potential. A decade of Personal Rule had seeded a nascent 'Country' Party. All it now needed was a Parliament to concentrate its sense of common 'grievance'.

Which is why Charles resisted calling one for so long. But here was the catch; the longer he held out, the louder the grievances became, and the emptier his coffers got. In April 1640, crippled by the terms of the Treaty of Ripon, of which more very shortly, he finally gave in. And called the famously 'Short' Parliament. Which immediately embarked on a very long discussion about the iniquities of prerogative taxation. A threat to the 'inheritance of every gentleman', Sir Nicholas Culpeper advised his fellow Members. Something which, Sir Nicholas averred, in a moment of poetic fancy, made 'the farmers faint and the plough to grow heavy'.[103] Culpeper was the most loyal of the king's supporters. But even they drew a line; around what they owned.

Black Tom's case

Back though to 1637, the morning of 23 July to be precise. Up in Edinburgh, the dean of St Giles was just getting into the swing of his sermon, reading from the newly Scottish-ized version of the Book of Common Prayer, when a 'creepie-stool' shot passed his head.[104] Thrown by a market trader named Jenny Geddes, to the accompanying comment 'Dare you say Mass in my lug?' The service ended in chaos. Shortly after, rioting broke out across the city. A few months later, the Assembly of the Kirk, gathered in Glasgow, reaffirmed its commitment to the principles of Presbyterian government, and purged its episcopacy. After which it sent commissioners to London to demand that the king subscribe to the Covenant. Hardly in the spirit of a happy union.

Laud expressed his horror, and Charles priced up a war. The estimate was something just shy of £1 million. As a gesture, Charles pawned some of his jewellery, and took out a couple of City loans. A sort of start. A small force of around 20,000, mainly levies, untrained and ill-equipped, ventured up to Kelso, before scurrying back to Berwick. Sir Edmund Verney had never seen such a rubbish army; 'so raw, so unskilful, so unwilling'.[105] Charles negotiated a 'Pacification', a temporary cessation. Laud worried the impact of the Scottish 'violence' on English 'impressions'. Charles worried about his honour, and lack of money. The possibility of another prerogative tax was ventured, but not with much confidence. Which left the obvious: parliamentary subsidy.

But that would require a Parliament. Charles consulted his newly returned Lord Deputy of Ireland, Sir Thomas Wentworth. Who, having cowed the Irish Parliament, was pretty sure he could do the same with the English. Charles recalled his Parliament in February 1640. It opened on 13 April. Lord Keeper Finch articulated His Majesty's wish for a 'happy' Parliament, and a large amount of money. Sadly, though, it was unable to help; with either aspiration. Too many 'ills and distempers', Pym confirmed. Before subsidies, there must be 'grievances'. There was also a plot, to 'reduce our land to the pope'. It was rumoured that Pym rather liked the idea of sending his king to war without a 'shilling'.[106] Charles dissolved his 'Short' Parliament on 5 May. Long enough for moan, but not much else.

Meanwhile, emboldened by the chaos at Westminster, and bored of 'Pacification', the Scottish Covenanter army moved south, making a pre-emptive strike for Newcastle and routing a small English army at Newburn on 27 August. The civil wars had begun. With a first defeat for the king, who was left with no alternative but to sue for peace. Under the terms of the Treaty of Ripon, the Scots were to receive £25,000 a month. Protection money, in effect. Cheaper than keeping his army going though, at £40,000 a month. Charles asked the City for further support. Hardly much of an investment, the request was politely declined. Unable to fund an army, and unable to fund its defeat, Charles was left with the same unpalatable solution. Parliament was recalled.

The more optimistic reiterated their hope that this really would be a 'happy' parliament. Where, Sir Henry Slingsby assured himself, everyone's 'grievances' would be 'settled'. The 'Long' Parliament opened, on 3 November. It would cover the cost of the Treaty of Ripon, or at least some of it. But there was a price to be paid. And a list. Of evil counsellors who must be removed. Various judges, including those who had got *Hampden's Case* wrong. An especial animus towards Sir John Berkeley, 'for what we have suffered'.[107] Lots of prelates, too, including

Laud. And the returning Lord Deputy, the man who had supposed that Parliament might be cowed. 'Black Tom' Wentworth, to his limited array of friends, and rather more enemies. Not an easy man to like, as Sir Philip Warwick confirmed, 'sour and haughty'.[108]

We might understand the meteoric fall of 'Black Tom' if we properly appreciate his meteoric rise. The younger Tom had, in fact, aligned himself with the emergent opposition during the parliaments of the later 1620s, even expressing support for Coke's *Petition*. But then moved over to Charles during the 1630s. Appointed Lord Deputy in 1634, it was Tom who also recommended a policy of 'thorough' government. Meaning tighter concentration of power in central institutions, better run. 'The authority of a king is a keystone which closeth up the arch of order and government.' A peerage arrived in January 1640: Earl of Strafford. An elevation which coincided with a very generous donation to the royal Exchequer, of £20,000. Not, in truth, that much of a stretch. Tom was a very wealthy man, owning vast tracts of south and west Yorkshire.

And well-worth a couple of van Dykes. A first painted around 1635, looking very saturnine, and martial, as might befit a Lord Deputy, armoured, with marshal's baton and obedient mastiff by his side. And very familiar, at least to any who knew their Titian, especially *Charles V with a Hound*. And then a second Tom, painted sometime in late 1639 or early 1640. Just as saturnine, but rather less martial, trusted dog replaced by trusted secretary. A different Titian for inspiration this time, *George d'Armagnac with Guillaume Philandrier*.[109] Looking a lot more weary too. But then it had been an exhausting few years. For when it had all started to go wrong, it was Tom who got the blame; for prerogative taxation, for Laudian Church reforms, for the marauding Scots, for the prospectively marauding Irish.

Four days into the new Parliament, Pym rose to relate a terrifying tale on a familiar theme, of closet popery and plots to ship over an army of Irish barbarians. A 'design' no less, 'to alter the kingdom in both religion and government'.[110] Four days after that, he moved a motion to commence proceedings for Tom's impeachment. Essential, 'diseases of the brain' being the 'most dangerous'.[111] Tom could consider himself a little unlucky, for the reasons we noted earlier in Steenie's case. Impeachment was of the moment. Charles had managed to save Steenie by the simple expedient of shutting Parliament. Not this time though. Charles was broke, which meant that there would have to be sacrifices; other people's.

On hearing of Pym's intentions, Tom tried to attend Parliament in person but was ordered to withdraw. By the end of the day he was in the Tower.[112] Pym kept things nicely on the bubble through December. The *Root and Branch Petition* arrived on the 11th, demanding that the Church be torn up from its 'roots' and its 'branches' cut off. Signed by fifteen thousand. Drafted, it was rumoured, by Oliver St John. A busy man, St John was also helping to write the impeachment articles. Another long list, as became apparent when the articles were finally presented at the end of January; seven principles, and twenty-eight in particular. In effect, a 'cumulative' treason.[113] Conveyed back to the Tower to await his trial, Tom seemed relatively relaxed. In correspondence home, he assured his wife that 'his Majesty' would anyway 'pardon all'.[114]

The trial opened at Westminster on 22 March. On 10 April it collapsed. Few of the charges seemed convincing. Suggestions that the earl had incited the Scots to invade the year before, and then betrayed army dispositions at Newburn, were barely credible; not least because it was the Scots who had pressed so hard for his indictment. More feasible was the charge that he had, whilst Lord Deputy, subverted the authority of the Crown by declaring martial law and seeking to 'rule by proclamation'. An accusation that was immediately resonant with the kinds of abuse against which Coke had railed; not simply 'subverting' the Crown but subverting the common law too.[115] The most incendiary charge, however, was that he had assured the king that 'You have an army in Ireland you may employ here to reduce this kingdom'.[116] Pym promised 'five or six witnesses' who would attest to the charge. The law demanded that there should be at least two. In the end there was just Sir Henry Vane, who conceded a critical ambiguity; 'this kingdom' might just as readily have referred to Scotland as England.[117] All rather flaky.

The underlying problem was semantic, incisive and becoming familiar; how to prosecute a charge of treason against someone who had carried out the orders of his king. A variant of the argument that would trouble prosecutors at Charles's trial in January 1649; just how might the king be supposed to have committed treason against himself? The only solution lay in the fiction of the king's 'two bodies', that one of the bodies might commit treason against the other. The 'subversion of the King and state', as Sir John Glynne put it, in his closing address.[118] Something to keep the jurists entertained. But no-one else. A tarnished spectacle, and a humiliating reversal, Pym was obliged to abandon the impeachment proceedings. There could, though, be no question of Tom just walking away from Westminster, dropping in on the king at Windsor for a quick chat and then, for all anyone knew, sailing to Ireland and raising an army. He must be 'knocked on the head', St John confirmed, however it was done. Andrew Honyman ventured an alternative metaphor; 'dead dogs bark none'.[119]

Two days later, Haselrige presented a Bill of Attainder in the House of Commons. Passed with minimal fuss; by 204 votes to 59. Greater doubts in the House of Lords. Strafford had few friends. But the justice was evidently rough, the precedent concerning. Digby articulated a representative discomfort. We 'must not piece up want of legality with matter of conveniences'.[120] Time for a bit more skulduggery. An army 'plot' was discovered in early May. The king, Pym informed a hushed House, was actively contemplating the use of military force to retrieve Strafford from the Tower.[121] Their Lordships fell into line. But it still needed the royal assent. Only months earlier Charles had assured his trusted adviser that 'upon the word of a king, you shall not suffer in life, honour or fortune'. It ought to have been enough; if Charles Stuart had been resolute, and a man of his word.

Sadly, for Tom, Charles was neither. Supposing, reasonably enough, that resolving moral dilemmas might be part of their peculiar skill-set, Charles had approached his senior bishops for some counsel. Spiritual guidance, though, proved to be frustratingly inconsistent. The archbishop of Armagh thought that Charles was bound in all conscience by his oath. The bishop of Lincoln thought the converse. The archbishop of York urged the king 'even for conscience sake, to pass the act', and save himself; an 'ignominious' argument, which earned Hyde's contempt.[122] 'I never met with a more unhappy conjuncture', Charles later recalled, when faced with the demand that he should sign Strafford's death warrant. Forced to 'chuse rather what was safe, then what seemed just, preferring the outward peace of my Kingdoms with men, before that inward exactness of Conscience before God'.[123] Not that it would elicit much sympathy from John Milton. If Charles really did scruple to 'sentence that for Treason which he thought not Treasonable', it did not say much for his strength of character.[124]

In the end, Strafford made the king's decision easier, in a sense at least, by releasing him from his promise. 'I do most humbly beseech you, for the preventing of such massacres as may happen by your refusal, to pass the bill; by this means to remove' the 'unfortunate thing forth of the way towards the blessed agreement which God, I trust, shall for ever establish between you and your subjects'. It was the ultimate sacrifice. On 10 May Charles gave his assent. 'My Lord Strafford's condition is happier than mine', he was reported to have said. Not by much. Strafford's response is a matter of contention. Some reported that the earl was stoical in the face of his misfortune. Others recorded a rather bitterer repost; 'Put not your trust in Princes'. The poet Thomas Stanley suggested that the 'compliant sin' would stay with the king for the rest of his days.[125] Tom made his final walk to the 'accustomed place' on 12 May 1641. Along the way receiving a final blessing from Archbishop Laud, waving out of a window. A poignant moment that Shakespeare would surely have written into his 'Tragedy of King Charles I'.

And a point made. Parliament had arrested the two men who were most associated with the 'personal' rule. It had executed one, and imprisoned the other. An estimated seven thousand turned up to watch Tom's execution. In his *Memoirs*, Sir Phillip Warwick recorded that 'many' departed 'waving their Hatts' and 'crying his Head is off, his Head is off'. Very 'brutish'.[126] Amongst those present was John Lilburne. Asked what might transpire, he had apparently replied 'If we do not have the Lieutenant's life, we will have the King's'.[127] Perhaps. For now, the reality was plain enough. An impotent king and an uncompromising Parliament. In late November the Commons approved a *Grand Remonstrance*, containing 'all the present evils and grievances of the kingdom'. Reflective and prospective. And long. The 'multiplied evils and corruption of fifteen years' brought to account.[128] Two hundred and four in total, the most thrilling devoted to yet another pending Catholic insurrection, the most abrupt being a demand that the king purge his episcopacy. Amongst the particular 'evils' attached, discovered in Article 26, was the usurpation of matters 'determinable of right at Common Law'. Coke would have been proud. Hyde was appalled. A 'bitter' document. Presented to the king on 1 December, rejected three weeks later; 'very sensible of the disrespect'.[129] And we know what happened next. A stroll down Whitehall, a couple of weeks later, accompanied by a guard of inebriate 'swordsmen', and a very awkward half an hour in the House of Commons.

The triumphs of Charles Stuart

Followed by a hasty departure from London, to Windsor and then onto Oxford. Early spring was spent drifting around the kingdom, squabbling with parliamentary commissioners and assorted garrison commanders. April found Charles at the gates of Hull, hoping to seize its arsenal.[130] But the governor, Sir John Hotham, refused to open the city gates. Impressed, it seems, by the terms of the Militia Ordinance, which Parliament had passed a few weeks earlier. 'Acts of justice and protection', the Ordinance had confirmed, were vested in the 'ministers' of the Crown, not the 'person' of the king. Hostilities had commenced, even if the war had not quite started.[131] Selden likened it to 'Gamesters' falling to a 'scuffling'.[132] Negotiations limped along through the summer. Until we arrive at Nottingham, on 22 August.

An afternoon for a kingdom

Where Charles has just raised his Standard on a newly painted flagpole, a small detail to which we will return, and was reading a short speech in which he declared war on his Parliament. Another moment which might again have gone better. For being England, in summer, it was raining, and windy. A 'very stormy and tempestuous day', Hyde later recalled, a 'general sadness covered the town'.[133] The Standard blew down, the paper upon which the speech was written disintegrated. 'Please God to open the eyes of our people', Charles muttered, peering through the mizzle. By then most of the three dozen who had bothered to pitch up had started to wander home.

An irresistible metaphor; an uncomprehending nation falling apart before the eyes of an uncomprehending king, reading a barely comprehensible speech. The Earl of Berkshire would later wonder 'what we have fought about all this while'.[134] Not that the earl fought very hard. Digby expressed a similar bewilderment, in the moment. An England, on the one part, 'in a state of the greatest quiet and security', but on the other 'groaning' under the rule of tyranny, the 'liberty of the Subject fundamentally subverted, ravished away by the violence of a pretended necessity', with 'men of the best Conscience ready to fly into the wildernesse for Religion'.[135]

Hyde, who blamed Digby for much that had gone wrong, would intimate the same in his *History of the Rebellion*. Recalling, more particularly, a conversation with Sir Edmund Verney. As knight-marshal, it was Sir Edmund who raised the Standard at Nottingham. Out of duty, not sense. Sir Edmund did not 'like the quarrel', and wondered quite how they had all gotten into such a mess. Two months later, he was killed at Edgehill.[136] If more of the king's subjects had thought like Verney, Hyde surmised, that battle need 'never have been fought'.[137]

Plenty of seeming bewilderment amongst Parliamentarians too. 'With what perfect hatred I detest this war without an enemy', Sir William Waller famously confided.[138] Perhaps. But 'the Conqueror', as he was known to his men, was amongst the first to raise forces for Parliament. His enemies were clear enough. We will discover Bulstrode Whitelock saying something similar in a later chapter. He blamed all the 'paper combats'. And things that everyone else had said. But Bulstrode knew precisely what was coming in late summer 1642, and the consequence; 'he that draws his sword against his prince, must throw away the scabbard'. Perplexed perhaps, but hardly surprised. Back at the beginning of June, Parliament had sent the king its *Nineteen Propositions*. Which, in effect, demanded his surrender. Whitelock helped with the drafting.

Whilst the Commons resolved to preserve the king's 'honour', they would also presume to reform his Church. They would also assume sole authority to choose his counsellors and raise armed forces. And his wife would need to convert to Protestantism. Charles could not accept. The 'propositions' threatened a 'chaos of confusion', and would make him nothing more than the 'sign of a king'.[139] Hyde, who drafted the king's *Answer to the Nineteen Propositions*, referred to them as 'articles of deposition', and ventured a maxim which would resonate six and a half years later. *Nolumus Leges Angliae mutari*; 'we do not wish the laws of England to be changed'. The king stood for continuity and the common law. At the same time, though, Hyde appreciated the greater political import. The moment for compromise passing, the 'whole business of the matter was whether the King was above Parliament, or Parliament, in ruling, above the King'.[140] Time to find out.

An inconclusive autumn, with an inconclusive first engagement at Edgehill. Charles might still have marched on London. And did, in a half-hearted fashion, only to turn back when faced by Skippon's Trained Bands drawn up at Turnham Green. Another fatal moment of 'lukewarm temper', as Sir Philip Warwick put it.[141] 1643 though started brightly, for the king at least. A series of victories at Adwalton Moor in the north, Chalgrove, Landsdowne and Roundway in the south. Followed in early 1644 by the defeat of William 'the Conqueror' at Cropredy Bridge, and then in the autumn further victories at Lostwithiel and the second battle of Newbury. Away in London, the mood was sombre. The stunning success at Marston Moor, in early July, had provided some consolation. But if it assured Cromwell of anything, it was that Parliament needed an army that was properly God-fearing. Better trained and paid too.

The following April, Westminster passed a Self-Denying Ordinance, purging the senior officer corps, and presaging a 'new modelled' army. Out went all the corpulent earls. In came an assortment of 'Brewers, Taylors, Goldsmiths, Shoemakers and the like', according to a sneering Denzil Holles.[142] The army that Cromwell wanted, though, each troop led by a 'plain, russet-coated Captain, who knows what he fights for, and loves what he knows'. An Army of God purposed for crusade. Each trooper enrolled in the New Model received a copy of the so-called 'Soldier's Bible', replete with choice excerpts from the testaments intended to stiffen resolve, 'to fight the Lords Battels, both before the fight, in the fight, and after the fight'.[143]

We will join the New Model on the morning of 14 June 1645, on the outskirts of the village of Naseby in Northamptonshire. Somewhere between eight thousand and ten thousand royalist troops had drawn up on high ground, to the north, overlooking an open landscape 'partly corn and partly heath'.[144] About a mile away could be dimly discerned a parliamentarian army. It was not entirely clear how big it was because its commander, Sir Thomas Fairfax, had deliberately hidden much of it behind a hill. It was in fact about twice the size. Numbers do not always determine the victor. Cromwell would famously defeat a vastly larger Scottish army at the battle of Dunbar in 1650. But more often than not, they do. If Charles had known how seriously he was outnumbered, he might have retreated. It was certainly what his old friend Tom Wentworth recommended, his spirit reportedly visiting Charles a couple of evenings before at the Wheatsheaf Tavern in Daventry.

A caution aired a month earlier, too, at a Royalist Council of War held at Stow-in-the-Wold on 8 May. An afternoon of heated conversation and a fateful decision. Lord Goring was despatched, with some of the best cavalry units, to lay siege to Taunton. Whilst the king and Prince Rupert would move towards Chester, to raise the siege of the city, and hopefully join up with Montrose's Scottish forces. Only to change their minds, on hearing that Fairfax had laid siege to Oxford. Returning south, the king marched towards Leicester, which his forces stormed on the evening of 30 May. The event would be revisited in January 1649, an eye-witness testifying that the king had ridden through the burning city in 'bright armour' encouraging his troops to 'cut down' his 'enemies' without mercy. A war crime, it would be alleged.

And a delusion. Blood up, and spirits, Charles decided to draw Fairfax and his 'New Noddle' into battle. The astrologers were supportive too, on balance. William Lilly surmised that June was a parliamentarian month.[145] The Court astrologer, Sir George Wharton, however, disagreed. The heavens did 'generally render his Majesty and his whole army unexpectedly victorious and successful in all designs'. The king was on his way to win 'the battle of all for all'. More of Wharton shortly. Digby, a bit of an amateur astrologer himself, agreed. As did the Cavalier poet Robert Herrick: 'The Day is Yours Great Charles! And in the War / Your Fate, and Ours, alike Victorious are.'[146] Charles always preferred poetry to prose, and he was usually persuadable. My 'affairs were never in so fair and hopeful a way', he sought to assure his wife in far-away Paris.[147] In truth, by now he had very little choice. Report arrived, late on 13 June, that Fairfax was only six miles away, and fast approaching.

The following morning, as dawn mist gave way to bright sunlight, the command was given for the royalist army to advance, infantry in the centre, cavalry on the wings.[148] It is, at this point, possible to paint a romantic picture of Naseby field, of 'floating colours and glinting arms', of Charles riding out on his Flemish steed, drums beating and generals crying 'March on boys'. After all, as one jubilant parliamentarian pamphlet subsequently 'related', it was an 'afternoon for a Kingdome'.[149] But once the fighting began, the romance gave way to a more predictable horror, the deafening shrieks of agony, nostrils filled with the stench of blood and musket-smoke. Amidst the carnage, fortune seemed to sway back and forth. The parliamentarian left, under the command of Cromwell's soon to be son-in-law Henry Ireton, gave ground to Prince Rupert's cavalry, whilst the veteran Royalist commander, Lord Astley, pushed back Skippon's infantry in the centre.

On the royalist left, however, Langdale's much-vaunted, but seriously outnumbered 'Northern Horse' was overcome by Cromwell's cavalry. It was at this point that months of incessant drill paid off. Whereas Rupert's triumphant Cavaliers carried on charging into the far distance, Cromwell managed to halt his cavalry, wheel around and tear into Astley's infantry. Fairfax brought up his reserve and joined the assault on the royalist centre. As the army's secretary John Rushworth later confirmed, what 'made our horse so terrible to them was the thickness of our reserves and their orderly and timely coming on'.[150] By the time Rupert returned to the field it was all but over, the royalist cavalry was scattered, its infantry in desperate 'distresse'. According to Hyde, the king had apparently countenanced the possibility of making a counter-attack with his life guards. Caesar might have given it a go. But the Earl of Carnwath intervened and 'swearing two or three full-mouthed Scots oaths' seized the king's bridle and turned his horse. 'Will you go upon your death?' he had inquired.[151] Charles would not.

It had, in the end, taken little more than a couple of hours. And, as had become customary in an increasingly vicious war, the denouement was unpleasant. New Model cavalry cut down swathes of fleeing royalists.[152] Quarter would be asked, sometimes given, mostly not. There was to be no quarter when detachments of Fairfax's infantry came across the royalist baggage train in the early afternoon, complete with what appeared to be a number of Irish 'whores and camp-sluts' of 'cruel countenance'. A year earlier Parliament had approved an ordinance of 'no quarter' for 'any Papist whatsoever born in Ireland who shall be taken in hostility against Parliament'. And any officer who was 'negligent' in its enforcement would be 'reputed in favour of that bloody rebellion'.[153] There was some medieval jurisprudence which held that non-combatant servants might be regarded as legitimate targets. Shakespeare famously treated the subject in *Henry*

V, condemning the killing of English camp-followers at Agincourt as 'expressly against the law of arms', but defending the reciprocal murder of French prisoners in terms of necessity (4.7.1–2).[154]

But early afternoon on 14 June 1645 was not a time for poets, or jurists. Only a week before, parliamentarian journals had confirmed that a thousand Irish women had been brought over to service Charles's army. Unable to comprehend the language in which the captured were pleading for their lives, the troopers assumed they must be Irish. A hundred were slaughtered, the rest mutilated. In fact they were more probably Welsh, and according to one royalist account 'some' of 'Quality' even.[155] But the distinction would likely have made little difference. Slaughtering whores and papists was God's work, and now was not the moment to 'anxiously look about'.[156]

The destruction was as complete as it was savage. Five thousand royalist soldiers captured, another thousand lay dead on the field. Charles retreated across the Midlands to Wales, in the hope of raising a new army. Bristol remained in royalist hands, and there were various other strongholds scattered around the West Country. There was hope, if not much. In public Charles remained upbeat, advising the Earl of Glamorgan that the likely arrival of an Irish army would reverse his 'late Misfortune'. More doubtful in private, writing in secret to his eldest son to urge him never to accept 'dishonourable terms' should his father be 'taken'.[157] His 'position', he wrote to Ormonde, was 'at so low an ebb as to be a perfect trial of all men's integrities to me'.[158] He could, he confided in his nephew Prince Rupert, conceive 'no probability but of my ruin'.[159] In the meantime he stayed at Raglan castle, in south Wales, playing bowls with his host the Marquis of Worcester.

Hocus pocus

Away in London there was a palpable sense of relief. The City hosted a celebratory banquet for Parliament at the Grocer's Hall, after which everyone joined in singing the 46th Psalm: 'God is our refuge and strength, a very present help in trouble'. And a day of Thanksgiving, as Fairfax had urged there should be, in his report sent to Parliament later that evening; 'That the honour of this great, never to be forgotten mercy, may be given to God, in an extraordinary day of Thanksgiving, and that it may be improved to the good of his Church'.[160] An attribution commonly made. Colonel Okey urged Parliament to 'magnifie the name of our God, that did remember a poore handfull of despised men'. Cromwell likewise, in his report to Speaker Lenthall, 'Sir, this is none other but the hand of God; and to Him alone belongs the glory, wherein none are to share with Him'.[161] An already familiar refrain that would only become more so; as miraculous victory followed on miraculous victory. There could be no other explanation.

Reason, then, for celebration. And a triumphal procession. A week after Naseby, the New Model paraded through London, with three thousand prisoners and fifty-five captured standards. Not quite on the scale imagined in Mantegna's *Triumphs*; hundreds of chariots leading tens of thousands of captured Gauls, not to mention all the elephants. But a decent effort all the same; for a God-fearing people that was never entirely comfortable with the margin that was supposed to distinguish the heroic Roman from the popish. Moreover, that was not all that had been captured. There was a still bigger prize. Charles lost an army on 14 June and, hindsight confirms, a war.[162] He had also, in his haste to depart the battlefield, neglected to secure his Cabinet and, with it, all his personal correspondence. Discovered along with the unfortunate camp-followers and the rest of the baggage train. The contents were devastating.

As Lucy Hutchinson confirmed in her husband's *Memoirs*: 'which letters being carried to London were printed, and manifested his falsehood when, contrary to his professions, he had endeavoured to bring in Danes and Lorrainers and Irish rebels to subdue the good people here, and given himself up to be governed by the Queen in all affairs both of state and religion'.[163] Milton would later attest the same. Evidence of continued negotiations with the 'Papists and Irish Rebels', along with the 'French, Dutch, Lorrainers and our old invaders the Danes'. Even worse, they also 'shewd him govern'd by a Woman'. Something long suspected but now 'visible to all men'.[164] The letters did indeed confirm a series of desperate and deluded attempts to bring over various continental armies. The King of Sweden was offered the Orkneys and Shetlands. The Prince of Wales was touted to various prospective fathers-in-law. A promise, conveyed to the Pope, that Charles would 'take away all the penal laws against the Roman Catholicks in England'.[165] In return for an army. His Holiness sent a nuncio. The best hope, as ever, seemed to be Ormonde in Ireland. The long-anticipated army of marauding papists. Exciting for all concerned, albeit differently.

Parliament had quickly appreciated the importance of the discovery, establishing a Joint Committee to consider how the correspondence might be most effectively edited and made public. Assistance, in the former regard, would be provided by the parliamentarian propagandist Henry Parker, along with the dramatist Thomas May and Marchamont Nedham, editor of *Mercurius Britanicus*. A man of fluid political allegiance, Nedham would later become Cromwell's press secretary. Though we will next encounter him in autumn 1648, in the pay of the Presbyterians, casting aspersions against the idea of putting the king on trial. The age of the popular press, of 'scribbling' for money, was dawning. Along with that of the professional journalist. Nedham was a pioneer of the hired pen, the 'King's Cabinet' a brilliant scoop.

By the first week of July, a selection of the letters was on view at the Common Hall in the City of London. An edited version, entitled *The King's Cabinet Opened*, was printed and sold 'by special order of Parliament'. The introduction confirmed the purpose; to reveal 'what affection the King beares to his People', to permit its readers to 'consider with sorrow' what 'comes from a Prince seduced out of his proper sphear', who 'walked in the counsels of the ungodly'.[166] A selection of thirty-nine letters, together with fourteen pages of annotation. Confirming that Charles Stuart was vain and deceitful, and a loser. Nedham had been fashioning the caricature since the summer of 1644.[167] A year on, the rhetoric had assumed a tone both contemptuous and foreboding. Charles was 'a wilful King, which hath gone astray these four years from his Parliament, with a guilty conscience, bloody hands, a heart full of broken vows and protestations'.[168] The Naseby Cabinet was then reprinted in all its grisly detail in Nedham's *Mercurius*, over an eight-week period during early autumn. 'I will shew you more *Tricks* here than ever *Hocus-Pocus* did', its editor gleefully announced.[169]

Charles would later term the publication of his private 'letters' a 'barbarous' act of incivility.[170] But it was more than that. It had been possible hitherto to accept, as Lord Saye pretended, that Charles was a gentle prince 'misled by the evil counsel of sycophants'.[171] Not anymore, and not just hapless. The evidence seemed incontrovertible. Charles Stuart was a habitual liar. It was, as Milton later confirmed, of the 'greatest importance to let the people see what faith there was in all his promises'.[172] On reading the published correspondence, Sir Trevor Williams, a leading Welsh royalist, went over to Parliament. The Presbyterian Robert Baillie was horrified by the 'shameful secrets' uncovered. It confirmed Hugh Peter's belief that the king could never again be trusted. Edmund Ludlow would later record his particular exception to news that Charles had sought the aid of the Danes, promoting civil war between protestant states.[173]

A fateful day then. A battle lost, and a war. And something else, every bit as important. The last vestige of trust. Many in the army concluded that further negotiation with the king was 'hopeless'.[174] There was still another six months to go, until the war was finally lost. Another three and half years until Charles Stuart would find himself in Westminster Hall accused of treason. But we can venture this surmise; if he had taken a little more care with his correspondence Charles might never have lost his throne, or his head. Later in the autumn another 'cabinet' was captured. The correspondence, this time, of Sir Kenelm Digby, acting on behalf of the queen. Trying once again to elicit papal support, and more importantly some money to fund an Irish army.[175] Meanwhile further correspondence, captured in Sligo, confirmed that negotiations with Ormonde were still ongoing. London printing-houses gleefully conveyed all the dreadful details to their reading public. Charles Stuart was deluded and duplicitous; just in case there was any lingering doubt. Quite prepared to make a pact with the Pope and his Irish minions in order to contest the will of God. It might as well have been with the Devil himself.

The slaughter of Digbeth Street

Not that they ever came. Ormonde never crossed the Irish Sea, nor Uncle Christian the North. Neither did the Duke of Lorraine venture across the Channel. The war drifted on to its inexorable conclusion. Goring's western army was routed at Langport, a few weeks after Naseby. Rupert surrendered Bristol in September, earning his uncle's bitter reproach. Montrose's Scottish army was destroyed at Philliphaugh that same month. The remnants of Langdale's 'Northern Horse' were routed at Sherburn a few weeks later; more of them shortly, a last hurrah. Basing House fell on 13 October, after a long siege. Within its walls could be found the Marquess of Winchester, the architect Inigo Jones and a number of papists. Jones and the Marquess survived. The papists did not. A few weeks later Goring suffered another crushing defeat at the battle of Torrington.

It all came to an end in the pretty Cotswold village of Stow-in-the-Wold. All cream-teas and antique shops today. Hard to imagine anywhere more idyllic. Not though on 21 March 1646. The bodies of around two hundred royalists lying in the surrounding streets, the ducks bathing in their blood. The main road into the market would be named in grisly honour of the moment; 'Digbeth'. Around fifteen hundred more, many bearing horrific injuries, crammed into St Edmund's Church. Likely wondering their future, if they had one. Likewise, perhaps, their commander, Lord Astley. Sat on a drum in the market square, chatting with Sir George Wharton. If anyone knew what was coming, it was surely the king's astrologer. A predictable locale too. The area between the king's headquarters at Oxford and the Parliamentarian garrison-ports of Bristol and Gloucester had seen plenty of action over the previous three years. Back in 1643, the Royalists had won significant victories nearby, at Lansdowne and Roundway. The location for the fateful Council of War held a month before Naseby too.

Early 1646 found Astley wandering about the south Welsh marches with a rag-bag army of around two thousand five hundred; seven hundred cavalrymen, the rest infantry. A few veterans, including some from the once-vaunted Cornish infantry regiments. But most were raw recruits; levies from the Marches, and local farm-hands who accidently found themselves volunteered for service. Astley had decided that the best course was to return to Oxford, in the hope of joining what scattered forces remained in the city. He got as far as Stow. But then found his way blocked by Parliamentarian forces under the command of Major General William Brereton, who had moved south following the surrender of Chester. A fervent puritan, later named amongst the commissioners at the trial of the king, Brereton had earned a reputation as a brilliant cavalry commander.[176] Further reinforcement was supplied by Colonels Thomas Morgan and John Birch, respective governors of Gloucester and Hereford.[177] In sum, Brereton had an army roughly twice the size of Astley's. Numbers again.

Royalist field commanders were, by now, well used to being outnumbered. Along with being seriously under-provisioned, and losing. On 20 March, Astley arrived on the outskirts of Stow, and drew up his forces on a low hill. Camp was struck and they bedded down. The royalist password was 'Patrick and George'. A quirky choice, later interpreted by the Parliamentarians as evidence of Irish soldiers amongst Astley's ranks. Brereton went with 'God Is Our Guide'. Any fitful slumber in the Royalist camp was ended shortly before dawn, with news that the Parliamentarians were attacking. Brereton's cavalry hurtling up the slopes on the right, two hundred of Birch's musketeers behind. Whilst Morgan's infantry was marching up through the middle. More cavalry, drawn from Colonel Rous's Gloucestershire regiment, to the left. Astley's forces held for a while, and then broke. Some fled along the country lanes to the east; where they would come across yet another Parliamentarian army, under the command of Colonel Charles Fleetwood, approaching from Oxford. For the remainder there was nowhere really to go, except back into Stow. Astley ordered a fighting retreat. A last stand in the market square. A parley and then surrender.

The terms permitted those held in the church to go home. The officers under parole; on condition that they would not again take up arms against Parliament. Amongst their number were Sir Charles Lucas and Sir George Lisle. More of them a little later; two very dashing, but very silly, cavaliers. Astley, meanwhile, chatted to his captors. He might have lost the last battle of the war, but he still had the best lines. As he often did. His battle-prayer before Edgehill is renowned: 'Oh Lord! Thou knowest how busy I must be this day. If I forget Thee, do not forget me.' And he had another decent line now, every bit as prescient: 'Gentlemen, ye may now sit down and play, for your have done all your work, if you fall not out amongst yourselves.' Prophetic, and quite possibly apocryphal. But too good a line to be dismissed for simple reason of provenance. The next three years would be as difficult as the last three, as the contentions of war gave way to the contentions of peace. We will shortly see just how difficult.

Once we have located the king. News of Astley's defeat had reached Oxford within a day. Charles apparently contemplated a last stand. But then characteristically changed his mind. And his coat. And his name. He also had his beard trimmed and his lovelocks cut off. Harry, a servant, dressed in a very dreary cloak, slipped out of Oxford shortly after tea-time on 27 April 1645. Accompanied by a couple of gentlemen. The first was Michael Hudson, a personal chaplain, who just so happened to be a military scout; a handy companion for scurrying about the countryside. The second was John Ashburnham, a trusted companion who had frequently served as a negotiator for the king over the previous few years; a similarly useful skill-set. Needless to say, no-one was entirely sure where they should go. France was attractive, Newark nearer, where the Scots army was in camp. After a bit of dithering, they opted for Newark.

Ashburnham had already made preliminary advances. Indeed, the idea that the king might seek succour with the Scots, in return for accepting the Covenant, had been revisited during the previous winter; negotiations conducted through the offices of the French ambassador to Scotland. The cunning lay in the possibility of splitting the Presbyterians from the army. The basis of Charles's strategy for the next three years. It would, of course, have been easier if he had started negotiating a little earlier; rather than dreaming of non-existent Irish armies. As Prince Rupert had advised in the weeks after Naseby. To sue for 'a happy peace'. In truth Hyde had been arguing the case since the summer of 1643. But once again Charles had made the wrong call. God, the king had replied, 'will not suffer rebels or traitors to prosper'.[178] But He did.

Which is why a chastened Charles found himself at Southwell on 5 May, discussing the terms of his surrender with the commander of the Covenanters, David Leslie.[179] The king was apparently willing to 'be instructed' in the virtues of Presbyterian governance. But not prepared to make a firm commitment to the Covenant, at least not yet. A few weeks later he was taken up to Newcastle. Lodged in the castle, a few miles along the Tyne from Newburn; scene of the crushing defeat inflicted by an earlier Covenanter army in 1639. It can be a small world. Consolations though. Golf on the town common, a day-trip to Tynemouth on a barge and some decent dinners, 'fifteen dishes of English diet every meale', it was reported. And some instruction, of the spiritual kind. Courtesy of Andrew Cant, appointed to the role by the Kirk. 'Thou piece of clay', Cant intoned in one sermon, given in early July, 'where thou sittest, think of thy death, resurrection, judgement, eternity', and place all hope in 'mercy upon repentance'.[180] True enough, if hardly cheering.

Visitors too. Commissioners sent from Westminster, bringing with them a document which became known as the *Newcastle Propositions*. Charles was customarily polite and evasive; it would take him fifteen months to say no. Procrastination had become policy. The politics of the 'negatif', as Charles admitted to his closest advisers in late 1646.[181] Not that he had much alternative. Various commissioners went back and forth. A developing pattern. There was, though, a risk in strategic indecision. Others would do the deciding. Which is what happened in January, when the Scots decided to trade in their asset. Negotiations had commenced the previous autumn, Parliament voting to offer £100,000 to cover the costs of the Scottish Army securing the north. The Scots countered with the suggestion that £2 million would be nearer the mark. In the end they settled for £400,000. And the king was transferred into the custody of the English Parliament. As the Scots left Newcastle they were treated to chorus of 'Judas'. The bartered king, acute to the resonance, chided his captors that they had sold him at 'too cheap a rate'.[182]

Charles was escorted to Holdenby House in Northamptonshire. Another bit of the world that could seem very small. Naseby was just half a day's ride away. Spring coming, it might have been a nice trip out. Likely to be a bit chilly though, and a bit sad. Charles never went. There were though some lovely parks in which to stroll, whilst he waited to see if his enemies would indeed 'fall out' amongst themselves. Reason to hope. A couple of weeks after purchasing the king, Parliament set about dismantling its army. Issuing a declaration regarding the 'distempered condition' of a number of regiments, warning that 'those' who continued to agitate would be 'proceeded against as enemies of the state'.[183] A cursory offer of six weeks' pay was made. And rejected. Thus giving Parliament the excuse to disband a number of the offending regiments. Or at least try. Fairfax moved to Newmarket, and drew up some fresh battle lines.

And someone sent a junior cavalry officer named George Joyce to Holdenby.[184] Joyce, an apprentice tailor in his former life, arrived early on the morning of 3 June. Meeting the king shortly after breakfast, the Cornet confirmed that he was there to take custody. When Charles asked his commission, Joyce took him to a window and gestured to the five hundred cavalrymen waiting in the courtyard below. 'These sir, are my instructions.' It was, the king replied, 'as fair a commission, and as well written as he had seen a commission in his life'.[185] A dignified response, in a remarkably undignified circumstance. A trafficked king, now stolen at gunpoint.

After which, Charles was taken on an extended perambulation around the home counties, towards London. Via Childerley House, where he met Fairfax and Cromwell. Fairfax, it was reported, bowed and kissed the royal hand. Cromwell just stared. A different kind of customary hand-kissing was irritating him. As he wandered the by-ways of the east Midlands, Charles had continued the practice of 'touching' for the 'King's evil'.[186] Cromwell had tried to have it stopped; but the crowds had kept coming. Charles was still curing lucky subjects on the Isle of White a year later, as John Taylor recorded; a cripple whose 'lameness ceased in three days', a child with a 'closed' eye which magically opened as soon as Charles stroked it with his 'spittle'. Just the sort of things which divinely ordained kings do. There would be another audience with Fairfax and Cromwell, a few weeks later, at Caversham. Along with some 'walks full of pleasure' at Hatfield, tea with the Earl of Northumberland at Sion and an evening at Stoke Poges. More touching, of course. And lots of negotiating. Including a famous exchange with Henry Ireton at Woburn. 'You will fall to ruin if I do not sustain you', Charles proclaimed.[187] The generals, he surmised, were bluffing.

Another wrong call. On 6 August, the army occupied London. Its General Council recommended a purge of Parliament, and Ireton presented a fresh document entitled *Heads of Proposals*. Charles again procrastinated, tempted now by the possibility of fresh negotiations with the Scots. Ireton despaired. Another portent. Charles would spend much of 1648 making the same mistakes which had been made in 1647, and 1646, and pretty much every year since 1640. A percipient monarch might have spotted the pattern. Not Charles. By now ensconced at Hampton Court. Closer confinement, but comfortable still, with some cracking art to admire. Not least all the Mantegna hanging on the palace walls. Reason to worry though, as Sir Thomas Herbert intimated. The 'fairest day is seldom without a cloud'.[188] Not least, rumour of a remarkable conversation taking place twenty miles to the east, in a church hall in Putney. About what England might look like, if it got rid of Caesar altogether.

3 THE TRIAL OF CHARLES STUART

FIGURE 3 Eikon Basilike.

The morning of 30 January 1649. Chilly, light snow, frost on the ground. A temporary scaffold erected outside Whitehall Palace, abutting the first floor of the Banqueting House. Another stage, in the performance of the 'Tragedy of Charles I'. In a sense, the last; in another, just the beginning. We might, before we join the throng milling around outside, pause to note the date. A curious coincidence. The second lesson appointed for that day, in the Common Prayer Book, was *St Matthew* 27:1. The trial and crucifixion of Christ: 'When the morning was come, all the chief priests and elders of the people took counsel against Jesus to put him to death.' The best that might be said of choosing 30 January as the appointed day for the execution of Charles Stuart is that it was careless.

Charles had woken early, and spent the first couple of hours in prayer with his chaplain William Juxon; still, for a few weeks more, bishop of London. Faith provided a consolation. The last few days had been spent re-reading George Herbert's *Devotions*, and contemplating other martyred kings. The possibility seemed to appeal; to 'dye patiently like a Martyr'.[1] And had indeed been foretold. On being invited to give a sermon to the king, on his succession, John Donne had chosen the text: 'The last thing Christ bequeathed to thee was his blood, refuse not to go to him but the same way too, if His Glory require that sacrifice.' The bishop of Carlisle had taken a similar line at the coronation. A bit eerie. Back to the morning of the 30th. Charles dressed in preparation, a second shirt against the cold. He did not want to be seen to shiver. After a light breakfast, Colonel Hacker arrived to escort him across St James Park to Whitehall. A 'bit of bread' and 'a glass of claret' taken in his old bedroom, after which Charles was removed to the Banqueting Hall.[2]

Where he was asked to wait, and then wait some more.[3] Another glass of claret. He might have cast his mind back to another prescient sermon, again chosen for his coronation a quarter of a century earlier. Taken from *Revelations* 2:11:

> Fear none of those things that thou shalt suffer: behold, the devil shall cast some of you into prison, that ye may be tried … be thou faithful unto death, and I will give thee a crown of life.

He may also have taken the time to survey the décor. More especially the famed ceiling. Commissioned by Charles back in 1629. In memory of his father. Happier days. Painted by Peter Paul Rubens, installed, finally, in 1636.[4] Three main canvasses, entitled *The Union of Crowns*, *The Peaceful Reign of James I* and *The Apotheosis of James I*. There is no evidence that Charles was given to irony. But he might have been forgiven a wry smile. It was the wretched idea of a Union of Crowns which had precipitated the civil war. It was the Scots who had sold him to Parliament. As for the *Apotheosis*, it might have provided some kind of consolation. Derived from classical Greek, it means to deify, to rise.[5] A motif for the morning.

Along with waiting and carelessness. A 'better Kingdome' awaited, as Juxon had kept reminding his master over the last few days, which 'God hath prepared'.[6]

It would wait a little longer. Time for some more prayer, maybe another glass. It had occurred to someone, rather belatedly, that killing the person of the king did not abrogate the office of the Crown. The two 'persons' again. There would need to be a statute, rendering the proclamation of a successor unlawful. But it would take a while, at least a couple of hours. *An Act Prohibiting the Proclaiming of Any Person to be King of England* rushed through a couple of readings, and the report stage, late morning, and a third reading shortly after lunch. No need for an assent.

Finally, around 2.00 p.m., everyone was ready. The king was taken out, through a window, onto the scaffold, draped in black. Unsure as to how he might react, iron staples had been driven into the wooden floor. If necessary, Charles could be restrained. But there was no need. A final scene. And a final few words, which would calibrate political conversation for weeks, months, centuries to come. Confirming his 'innocency', condemning the 'great robbery' of his Kingdom and 'His Church', and then making a confession. Not to any crimes of which he had been convicted, a few days earlier, in Westminster Hall. But to his complicity in the 'unjust sentence' suffered by the earl of Strafford seven years earlier. The ghost of Black Tom again. An 'unjust sentence that I suffered for to take effect is punished by an unjust sentence on me'. Some further jurisprudential aspersions in closing. A first gesturing to a familiar controversy, that a 'subject and a sovereign are clean different things'. A second, no less familiar, warning of the consequence when the 'laws of the land' are 'changed according the power of the sword'.[7] The foundations of an appeal laid.

Scaffold speeches were part of the custom; sometimes treated with respect, sometimes not. This was one of the latter occasions. Cromwell's troopers had been instructed to clap loudly to drown out the king's voice. The crowd was held back a distance anyway. Juxon though heard, and remembered. He had anyway helped with the draft, and also had some final words of consolation. 'There is but one stage more', he had told his king as he knelt, 'This stage is turbulent and troublesome. It is a short one. But you may consider it, it will soon carry you a very great way. It will carry you from earth to heaven, and there you shall find your great joy the prize. You haste to a crown of glory.' To which Charles had replied 'I go from a corruptible to an incorruptible crown, where no disturbance can be.'[8] A willing 'martyr to the people', he concluded.[9] So Juxon recorded; which is all that matters. A brilliant script, acted brilliantly.

A performance of 'true magnanimity and Christian patience', Bulstrode Whitelock would later recall.[10] The 'first act of that tragicall woe which is to be presented upon the Theater of this Kingdome', the royalist preacher Robert Browne averred, 'likely to continue longer then the now living spectators'.[11] A still eerier prescience in Robert Herrick *Good Friday: Rex Tragicus*, composed just a couple of years earlier:

> Put off Thy Robe of Purple, then go on
> To the sad place of execution …

The Crosse shall be Thy Stage; and Thou shalt there
The spacious field have for Thy Theatre …
Why then begin, great King! ascend Thy Throne,
And thence proceed, to Act Thy Passion. (1–2, 17–20)[12]

The Passion of Christ. And everyone knows what happens next. After the crucifixion comes the Resurrection.

Speeches over, Charles had taken off his cloak, and his Order of the Garter, and asked Juxon to ensure that his hair was tucked into his white cap; in the hope that it might help the executioner to avoid the kind of hideously botched decapitation suffered by his grandma, Mary Queen of Scots. A last prayer, after which the king laid down his head and spread his arms, as in crucifixion, to signal that he was ready. No-one ever discovered the identity of the executioner. The official hangman, Richard Brandon, declined to serve; or so he said. Royalist propagandists would later venture that it might even have been Cromwell himself, or maybe Hugh Peter. Or a woman, some surmised; wearing a very improbable beard. If so, she got lucky. A clinical piece of butchery, one blow and the head cleanly severed. At a later post-mortem supposed, the second and third vertebrae.

'Behold the head of a traitor.' Raised to the crowd, eliciting, it was reported, a 'Grone by the Thousands present, as I have never heard before & desire I may never hear again.'[13] Audience participation. A 'People' drowning in a 'flood of teares', as another royalist news-sheet reported, 'with Hands wringing each other to express the anguish of their Hearts'.[14] Not, though, the hands of a young Samuel Pepys, who skipped school to watch. And later recounted the moment to his friends, with the rider that if he had to preach a sermon on what he had seen, he would have chosen: 'The memory of the wicked shall rot.'[15] He might have got himself a souvenir. Handkerchiefs dipped in blood were always popular. The guard would have held them all back of course. Not because it was considered unseemly. But because there were proprieties of a more financial kind.

Attendance at the execution of Charles I was not cheap. There was a charge to get into the scaffold area, and then further charges for the souvenirs. A handkerchief brought by a patron was treated as a kind of corkage. For those who had forgotten to bring anything, there was all manner of blood-stained bits and bobs for purchase; not just fragments of cloth but scraps of scaffold-board too. Such was the demand, it seems, that the soldiers resorted to a kind of auction. 'I would we could have two or three such Majesties to behead', one is reported to have remarked, 'if we could but make such use of them.'[16] After which the body was removed to St James Palace, where the head was stitched back on, and then displayed to the public; paying, of course.

Unless you went after hours, as Cromwell apparently did. On the night of the 30th, the king's body lay in rest in St George's Chapel at Windsor, attended by the earl of Southampton. At some point around midnight, the earl was roused from an understandably fitful doze by the arrival of a heavily cloaked figure, who muttered the words 'cruel necessity'. Southampton thought it sounded like Cromwell. Maybe. The story, originally recorded by the antiquarian Joseph Spence, was reiterated by the eighteenth-century poet Alexander Pope. Testament to a continuing fascination. Now, though, back to June 1645. A familiar moment, and a familiar place.

Prologue

Two days after it had secured its 'blessed' victory at Naseby, the Presbyterian divine Richard Baxter decided to visit the Army of God in camp. Not what he expected. In fact, Baxter was appalled. Sectaries and 'agitators' everywhere, evincing a frightening independency of 'spirit'. Precisely why 'popularity' was such a bad idea. Ordinary rank-and-file troopers elected by their peers to convey their aspirations, and their discontent, to senior officers. Organized moaning. Radical pamphlets too, 'abundantly dispersed'.[17] Cromwell alluded to the tensions in his Naseby report, urging Parliament not to 'discourage' those who had ventured their lives 'for the liberty of his country'.[18] The customary refrain, customarily ignored.

A week in Putney

Forward again, to summer 1647. We have already tracked the fortunes of the fallen king. Surrendered, sold, then stolen. His person, like his sovereignty, 'contended for, as in a game of cards', as Thomas Hobbes put it.[19] A wander about the home counties and then, finally, arrival at Hampton Court. The inevitable consequence of a strategy which amounted to not doing much. The world still turned; but Charles no longer did the turning. A metaphor famously deployed by John Taylor, in a pamphlet published in August 1647, *The World Turn'd Upside Down*. So it must have seemed. A captive king, the New Model Army marching into the City of London, watched in stunned silence. Fairfax visited the Tower, and took a look at *Magna Carta*, stored there for safety. 'That is what we have fought for,' he was reported to have said, 'and by God's help we must maintain.'[20]

Shortly after, Sir Thomas was invited to peruse another text. It was entitled *The Case of the Army Truly Stated*, presented on behalf of the 'poor oppressed people of this nation' in whom 'all power is originally' held. Similar, and different. The author was a radical young lawyer named John Wildman. Just the kind of radical Baxter feared the most: clever, articulate, liked a drink. And connected. Friends in the City, friends in the army, a leading figure in an emergent, and worryingly organized, group which had taken to calling themselves Levellers. Progenitors of English socialism, it is sometimes surmised. Which, if so, makes the Saracen's Head, located next to St Sepulchre's in Newgate 'without', a place of peculiar significance. It is where Wildman lodged, and drafted his *Case*. And where, just possibly, the idea of putting the king on trial was first ventured. Or maybe that was at the Star Tavern in Holborn, where the senior officer corps preferred to go. Ireton's local. The charges against the king would be thrashed out at the Star. Easier perhaps to comprehend regicide, after a stiff drink or three.

And oddly English; a new Jerusalem designed down the pub. Other Leveller haunts included the Windmill in Old Jewry and the Nags Head, next to Blackwell Hall, where John Lilburne held court. We have come across Lilburne before, scrapping with Lunsford's cavaliers in Westminster yard in January 1641, and watching Strafford get his head cut off a few months earlier. By then already familiar to the authorities, hauled before Star Chamber in 1638 for distributing 'factious and scandalous books'. Where he faced-off with Laud, apparently reducing the Archbishop to a seething 'rage'; or so Lilburne claimed.[21] Duly fined £500, whipped and thrown into the Gatehouse. From where, a few months later, he would smuggle out a pamphlet entitled *Cry for Justice*, written whilst his 'hands were fettered with Irons'. Addressed to the 'courageous and valiant apprentices of the honourable City of London', it incited them to rid England of its most 'guilty Traitors'.

We might briefly track Lilburne's career. An eventful war. John liked fighting. Present at Edgehill and Marston Moor, captured during a skirmish at Brentford, charged with treason in Oxford, then released as part of a prisoner exchange. Back in London most of his energies were re-directed against Presbyterian peace initiatives. John liked writing almost as much as he liked fighting.[22] Hauled before the Commons Committee for Examination, in May 1645, having accused the earl of Manchester of being a closet royalist, there is record of a minor confrontation with a familiar figure. On his way to the Committee, William Prynne had caught Lilburne's sleeve, intending to admonish the 'obscure apprentice' with 'forgetting his duty to Parliament'. A gesture which was met with a predictable response: 'A turd in your teeth; if you were outside of the Hall I would teach you to lay your hand on mine.'[23] Enough said. A few weeks later, Prynne identified Lilburne as 'the Ringleader of this New Regiment of Firebrands' and accused him of being behind the *Marpriest* pamphlets. More of them in due course.

Later the following summer Lilburne would stand trial for his 'many libels' against the earl; and be represented by an upcoming young barrister named John Bradshaw. A pamphlet would appear, in early 1646, entitled *A Remonstrance of Many Thousand Citizens*. Berating the Commons over its treatment of 'Free-born' John, and casting a few wider aspersions. Not least towards the hallowed *Magna Carta*, a 'beggarly thing, containing many markes of intolerable bondage'. Not everyone was as enamoured as the commander-in-chief. And the Presbyterians, who 'love their Kings more than all this Nation' overturning all the hard-won victories of the last four years.[24] Lilburne alluded to precisely the same metaphor in his *Copie of a Letter*. The Presbyterian 'Blacke-Coats' bringing the 'chosen' people back 'into Egyptian bonds'.[25] A revolution still in need of completion. And a suggestion, bluntly stated in another of Lilburne's 1646 tracts, *Regal Tyrannie discovered*. Charles Stuart 'ought to be executed'.[26] Something to ponder.

The immediate problem, though, was more prosaic. Resolving army grievances, back-pay in particular. On hearing rumour that Parliament's preferred solution was disbandment, Fairfax had called a rendezvous at Newmarket race-track for the first week of June. A *Solemn Engagement of the Army* read out and assented by each regiment. 'We are not a mercenary army', it began, though we do want paying. Meanwhile Cromwell despatched Joyce to Holdenby to secure the king. A week later the New Model broke camp and began a slow march towards the capital: Royston, St Albans, Windsor. We have caught up. On 4 August, advanced regiments entered the City gates. Out of Newgate came Lilburne and Overton. Into the Tower went Lord Mayor Sir John Gayer and five of his aldermen; to await impeachment.[27] Another purge. And a resolution to call a General Council of the Army, to meet at St Mary's church hall in Putney. A time to air grievances, and silence them.

The Council convened on 28 October, for twelve days. Not least remarkable is the fact that a record remains of much of what was discussed; courtesy of an army secretary named Clarke. The focus was supposed to be Wildman's *Case* and its possible implications. More broadly it was the familiar conjunction, or disjunction, of faith and constitution. Toned in the prospective. For they were, after all, sketching out a template for the new Jerusalem. With, broadly, three sets of discussants. Army agitators and civilian Levellers, such as Wildman and Lilburne. Senior officers, or 'grandees', most notably Cromwell and Ireton. And the devoted. Like Colonel Goffe, 'Praying William' to his men, there to impress a very simple premise. Nothing really mattered, other than doing His Work.

The initiative was immediately seized by the radicals. Who, on the very first morning, presented another document entitled an *Agreement of the People*. With four particular demands, designed to 'avoid both the danger of returning into a slavish condition and the chargeable remedy of another war'; for parliamentary representation on an equal basis; the dissolution of the current Parliament in a year's time, biennial Parliaments thereafter; and more broadly so that the power of the representatives should be considered 'inferior only to those who choose them'.[28] The rhetoric of 'birthright', and reinvestment. Bringing the English back to their God, and their 'ancient' constitution.

The product of a legal mind for sure, most likely Wildman again. Articulating grievances that had been crystallizing for at least a generation. Echoes of Coke's *Petition*, taken too far, of course. Echoes of Overton's *Remonstrance* too. And the refrain of so many army petitions. Such as that of Colonel Hewson's regiment, complaining of 'Oppression by Foraign un-English'd Laws'. And the officers of the

Hull garrison, who cast a collateral aspersion, against the lawyers who made a 'nose of wax' out of their 'barbarous Dialect'. English law must be rewritten 'in the home-spun language of our native Nation, that every man might in some sort be able to understand and plead his own Cause'. The 'Great Charter' rewritten, radically. 'Tyrannous Laws now forfeited' by the victories which 'God hath given his people, on purpose to make them free'.[29] The 'yoke' cast aside, once and for all; the Red Sea finally crossed. Marston Moor, Naseby, Stow, Putney; it all led to this moment. And the next.

The broader sentiment was not in dispute. The imputation was. Pretty much all of the first day was given over to debating whether the *Agreement* should be considered at all. Cromwell wondered the 'very great alterations' it proposed.[30] But he could hardly deny Sexby's famous opening, that 'God hath been with us, and yet we have found little fruit of our endeavours'.[31] Goffe likewise, wondering if God 'be departed from us'. Time for 'expedition'. Captain Audley put it pithily. If 'we tarry long the king will come and say who will be hanged first'. Ireton though, a lawyer of the more pedantic variety, was concerned with temporal considerations; most especially the nature of their continuing 'engagement' with the king.[32] Such engagements were 'the foundation of justice between men and men', for which reason 'covenants freely made, freely entered into, must be kept'.[33] Colonel Rainsborough, darling of the army radicals, was unpersuaded. If they were thus 'engaged' to the king, why had they gone to war in the first place?

The morning of the 29th opened with a couple of hours of prayer, to calm the nerves and ensure that there was, as Cromwell put it, no 'doubleness of heart'. After which the Council considered the principle of representation on an 'equal' basis. Rainsborough's contribution is renowned:

> For really I think the poorest he that is in England hath a life to live, as the greatest he; and therefore truly, sir, I think its clear, that every man that is to live under government ought first by his own consent to put himself under that government; and I do think that the poorest man in England is not at all bound in a strict sense to that government that he hath not had a voice to put himself under.[34]

The same was repeated by Wildman and Sexby. Ireton's response was blunt. Only those with sufficient 'interest' should expect to partake of government, and by interest he meant property: 'No person hath a right to this, that hath not a permanent fixed interest in this kingdom.' Rainsborough was just as blunt. The idea that politics should be founded on property was contrary to God, whilst property law was the 'most tyrannical law under heaven'. Moreover, if they were not intending to redistribute property he would 'fain know what we have fought for'. Ireton sensed an anarchist before his time. The 'constitution', he replied, 'founds property'.[35]

The 30th was again spent bickering over the terms of the *Agreement*, the 31st in prayer. Next day Cromwell opened proceedings by wondering if God had spoken to any of them. Goffe reported that God had told him to be careful about 'tampering' too much with their enemies. Captain Bishop however had received different instruction. It was time they tampered rather more. He even intimated that there might be a case for bringing the 'man of blood' to account. Cromwell tried to reconcile the barely reconcilable. God did seem to want them to act, but it was not clear how. The Council would continue to meet for another week during which time the mood appears to have turned more hostile against both king and Parliament.

It is possible that the idea of a trial was aired. In the end, absent a clearer record, we can only surmise.[36] Possibly, probably. After all, God had given them victory for a reason. As Captain Bishop surmised. Why were they labouring to preserve a 'man of blood' when the judgement of God was plain?[37] Nedham cast an aspersion, in a pamphlet entitled *The Leveller Levell'd*, published a few weeks later: 'No King, the Levellers do crie, / Let Charles impeached be … Bring for the King, chop off his Head.'[38] Ireton, though, counselled caution against any 'desire to set up the King'. Cromwell too. The king was still 'King by contract'.

And then the Council dissolved, with not much decided perhaps, but plenty learned. Rainsborough called a rendezvous at Ware. Agitators waved copies of the *Agreement*. Cromwell had the ring-leaders rounded up, and one, drawn by lot, shot. God, it seemed, had decided against the Levellers, for now. The winter was spent in quarters. The presses continued to roll though. January found Lilburne in the Commons, along with Wildman, answering charges of sedition and brandishing copies of Coke's *Institutes*. A *Petition of Many thousands of Freeborn people of England* followed. Later would come *An Impeachment for High Treason against Oliver Cromwell and Henry Ireton*, and a new version of the *Agreement*, in autumn 1648. By then, of course, much had happened. As we will now see. Starting back in November 1647. With the discovery that the king had disappeared.

The case of the dashing cavaliers and the broken promise

We left Charles wandering the corridors of Hampton Court, admiring the Mantegna. He would not have known everything that was being discussed twenty miles to the east. But he evidently knew something. And had, most likely, heard rumours of Leveller assassination squads. Fearing for his life, he made a bid for freedom, breaching in the process the terms of his parole.[39] And blighted, of course, by the usual lack of direction, literally. Getting out of Hampton Court was easy enough; fifteen hundred rooms to flit about in. But then what? Charles sent for advice from the astrologer William Lilly. Who suggested Essex, which was a bit dull. France was more attractive, where Henrietta Maria had established an exile Court, at St. Germain-en-Laye. But it was nearly winter, the idea of taking a boat across the Channel somewhat daunting. So instead Charles made the slightly less perilous trip across the Solent, assured that the governor of Carisbrooke castle was 'not very averse to his Majesty'.[40] A bare recommendation. Colonel Hammond was, though, relatively gracious. Parliament was informed, and the Colonel advised to 'seek to know the mind of God', and keep a sharp eye on his new guest.[41] Not that Charles had to stop his bowling, though, or his golf, or reading his Shakespeare.[42]

Or receiving more guests. Rival sets of commissioners rolled up within weeks, armed with various draft 'engagements'. Charles preferred the Scots. The English wittered on about constitutional monarchy, the Scots offered to bring an army and restore him to his 'original' authority. On 26 December, Charles signed an 'Engagement' with representatives of the Scottish parliament by which he agreed to the confirmation of the Covenant in both kingdoms. A copy was buried in a lead casket in the castle garden, necessary paperwork smuggled out in the shoes of trusted servants. Of all Charles's rotten decisions, this might have been his worst. Not least because, up in Edinburgh, the Kirk was far from convinced about the wisdom of invading England. Partly because it no longer trusted the king, but more prosaically because it lacked the money to equip a credible army. Charles tried to assure the commissioners that thousands of English royalists were ready to rise up too. But doubts remained; with good reason.

After much debate, the Kirk declined to sanction the campaign, a decision which robbed the 'Engager' army of the services of its most experienced officers. Leaving the duke of Hamilton to venture south with a rag-bag army of levies, amounting to roughly a third of the thirty thousand promised. Crossing the border in early July and making its way down into Lancashire, a month later it had arrived in the Ribble valley. Where it had been raining, for weeks. Something which made the lack of tents an issue, as well as the failure to properly wad their powder-barrels. Not that there was anything like enough muskets anyway. Whilst Hamilton had pottered his way down to the Ribble, Cromwell had marched up from Pembroke, where he had just received the surrender of the castle. Stopping at Nottingham to pick up fresh provisions, tents, boots and stockings. Then Doncaster where he awaited armoury from Hull. And then onto to Otley, where he joined up with Lambert's cavalry. In numbers the armies were pretty well matched. Not, though, in anything else.

On 16 August Cromwell entered the Ribble. Hamilton's army was all over the place, literally. Next morning, the veteran royalist commander Sir Marmaduke Langdale collected together around thirty-five hundred, including five hundred of his 'Northern Horse', and began marching up to the top of Preston Moor. Where they ran into advanced units of Lambert's cavalry. Four hours later, what remained of Langdale's 'Horse' was careering back down the hill. Crashing through the camp below, scattering hundreds of terrified Lowland conscripts. The battle of Preston was already decided. A couple of days of casual slaughter, followed by formal surrender on the 25th. Two thousand 'Engagers' were dead, another nine thousand in custody, most of whom would be sold into slavery. The Hand of God once more, Cromwell reported back to London. Together with the rotten weather, and the interminable squabbling that characterized Kirk politics.

Still some work to be done though. Back down south, Fairfax was laying siege to Colchester, wherein could be found around four thousand royalists. The city was completely encircled by 2 July, the river Colne blockaded. The siege lasted through until 28 August, ending when the royalist commanders received news of events in the Ribble. It had already proved to be peculiarly savage engagement. The torture of a captured royalist messenger-boy was notorious. Surrender terms granted the soldiery quarter, though, and the city was spared plunder, on payment of £14,000 in cash. The officers, as was the custom, surrendered 'on mercy'. Which, by the same custom, would ordinarily mean on parole terms; an oath to desist from any further taking up of arms against Parliament. But this was not an ordinary moment.

As seven officers were about to discover. Three were members of the nobility, Lord Goring, now earl of Norwich, the Lords Loughborough and Capel, and for this reason despatched to London, for Parliament's consideration. In due course, Norwich and Loughborough would be exiled. Capel, who evinced a peculiar determination to continue plotting, would be executed in March 1649. Along with the duke of Hamilton, who had been captured in the aftermath of Preston. The remaining four were Sir Charles Lucas, Sir George Lisle, Sir Bernard Gascoigne and Colonel Farre. Their fates were already determined. Summary execution. No question of a trial, even a court martial; for those who so blatantly defied the Will of God.[43] And no time to be wasted. An impression enhanced by the fact that Farre managed to escape later that afternoon. Gascoigne's sentence was commuted, on discovery that he was a foreign national. But there would be no reprieve for Lucas and Lisle. Taken to the walls of the castle on the evening of 28th and shot to death. A most 'bloody' act, as Hyde would later recall.[44]

In many ways Lucas and Lisle were cut from similar cloth. Both close to Prince Rupert, which made them cavaliers of the more dashing kind. Lisle's dashing had been curtailed in June 1645, badly injured at Naseby, after which he was appointed Master of the Royal Household. Lucas, though, had carried on dashing until the bitter end, captured at Stow the following spring; ending five years of distinguished service for the king, including starred appearances at Marston Moor and Lostwithiel. Hyde later accounted Lucas 'very brave in his person, and in a day of battle a gallant man to look upon and follow'.[45] Brave undoubtedly, and reckless, as befitted a dashing cavalier. And also stupid, and untrustworthy. As part of the terms of his surrender at Stow, Lucas had taken an oath not to raise arms again. It was the breaking of this oath which gave Ireton the excuse he needed. As for

Lisle, the very fact that he had continued fighting so long after God had given His Judgement was reason enough. Fairfax would later justify proceedings on simple terms. To 'avenge for the innocent Blood they have caused to be spilt'.[46]

We might just pause to imagine the moment. The walls of Colchester still smouldering, the smoke adding to the haziness of the coming dusk. Bodies lying about, New Model troopers hissing their contempt. Fairfax and Ireton sat on horseback, stony-faced. A firing squad stood ready, a few yards away. A few too many in Lisle's opinion. Lucas was the first to be marched out and shot. Lisle followed, stopping on the way to kiss the body of his friend lying on the ground. Taken to the same spot under the walls. At which point he wandered off script, literally. Walking towards the firing squad, smiling and opening up his shirt as he went, or so royalist presses later reported. The squad commander had asked him to stop, with the assurance 'Sir, I warrant we will hit you'. To which Lisle had cheerily replied 'Friends, I have been nearer you, when you have missed me'.[47] A bit of dash left. And a lot of loathing. There could be no conciliation with men like Charles Lucas and George Lisle. Or Charles Stuart. No longer just fighting Parliament, but defying Providence.

The time for overturning

The time is 'come amongst you', the self-proclaimed 'true' Leveller Gerard Winstanley liked to say, for 'overturning, overturning, overturning'.[48] It had indeed. A different kind of 'overturning' though. At the point of the sword, rather than the pitchfork. A revolution of free 'love' and free digging was not what Cromwell or Ireton had in mind. For which reason the Promised Land would not, in fact, be discovered at St George's Hill in Surrey, where Winstanley and his disciples arrived in early 1649 to start 'enjoying the fruits and benefits of the earth'.[49] And then, shortly after, be turfed off by a couple of troops of the New Model. By then there had been quite enough overturning, for now.

Which brings us back to the previous autumn, and the most spectacular overturning of all. Effected, in prosaic terms, by a military coup. A 'juncto of army blades', as one very early historian put it.[50] Up in Pontefract, Cromwell signalled his approval. Down in London, Ireton started to put the wheels in motion. Arguably, in that moment, the most powerful man in England. The 'Armie's Alpha and Omega', as Lilburne described him, begrudgingly.[51] The Moses leading the English out of their slavery, for those who preferred the more Hebraic, and fawning, analogy.[52] In the context of what was about to occur, just a few months later in Westminster Hall, perhaps the most apposite descriptor is that of executive producer.

Whose first task was trying to measure audience expectations. Conducive, but distinctly over-wrought. A Leveller petition arrived in the Commons on 11 September. Forty thousand signatories wondering the delay. Assuming that 'you would have done justice upon the Capital Authors or Promoters of the former or late Wars', and reminding the dilatory parliamentarians of the 'abundance of innocent bloud that hath bin spilt, and the infinite spoil and havock that hath been made of peaceable harmlesse people, by express Commission from the King'.[53] There was no doubt as to the identity of the most 'capital' of the 'authors', and it really was time to be getting on with it. Two days later, it was reported that the petitioners had returned 'to clamour at the very Doors' of Westminster, demanding, in effect, a purge.

Dozens of similarly tempered petitions arrived through early autumn. From Oxfordshire, demanding 'That Justice may be executed upon the Capitall offenders in the first and this last Rebellion'. From Berkshire too, and Leicestershire. From Ireton's regiment, pointedly observing that the king was responsible, 'by his own confession', for 'all the blood-shed in these intestine wars'.[54] From Yorkshire, in like terms, requesting

> the Impartial and speedy execution of Justice upon offenders, especially such as are guilty of polluting our land with blood, and our own sad experience that told us, that the neglect thereof had a special Influence into these later revived calamities ... That God may be glorified, the cause and honour of the Parliament asserted and vindicated, the land cleansed of blood, and rendered Capable of some happie establishment.[55]

And Newcastle. A first petition signed by over eighty 'merchants' and 'members of the lesser trades', a second casting a more pointed aspersion, wondering if there was much difference in bending the 'knee to Baall at the King's command' and bending it on the steps of Westminster. *The Army Scout* expressed the same contempt for the Presbyterian 'cheats' sat in Parliament.[56]

The Newcastle petition concluded by rebuking Parliament for selling the liberties of the people 'for a Messe of Pottage, so that they may enjoy a slavish Peace'. A workable metaphor. Hugh Peter warned in like terms that the English had 'not yet' crossed 'over the Red Sea'. So too John Price, another preacher of the distinctly fiery variety. The army had brought the people to the 'very edge of Canaan', only for the Presbyterians to conspire, once again, to bring them back 'to the bondage of Pharaoh'.[57] *The Moderate*, which had been campaigning to have the king brought to trial since late summer, insinuated the same. 'The Reader may observe hence, that all the people of this Nation are yet slaves by and from the Conquest, being under the laws and government of William the Conqueror', it observed, concluding, rather pointedly, that 'all the Laws of this Land' are 'Tyrannical and Arbitrary, being made and maintained by the sword'.[58]

And then news of another unfortunate tavern-related incident. Doncaster this time, the White Hart in the marketplace. Where, on 29 October, the 'gallant' Rainsborough had been assassinated, having dodged his bodyguard to visit the landlord's daughter; or so rumour had it. Vengeance, royalist news-sheets proclaimed, for the execution of Lucas and Lisle. A 'butchery' which must be 'doubly avenged', the *Army Scout* responded. *Exodus* 21:24: 'eye for eye, tooth for tooth'. Against the 'original cause', Charles Stuart 'that man of blood'. Rainsborough's funeral took place on 14 November. An estimated fifteen hundred marching through the City behind the hearse. Ending up at St John's in Wapping, where an *Elegie* was circulated, advising any who continued to seek 'peace' with the king that the consequence would be their 'own dearest blood'. The army, the *Moderate* averred, could be 'silent' no more.

The issue, for Ireton, was temperature control. Keeping everything nicely on the bubble, without letting it 'o'errun the stew'.[59] On 9 November, he attended a meeting of the Army Council at Windsor, summoned to consider a 'thing of importance'. A couple of days earlier he had received a note from a group of officers headed by Colonel Whalley. A 'call from God' demanding action. Two days later, Ireton presented Council with a *Remonstrance of the Army*. Owing something, undoubtedly, to the furore surrounding Rainsborough's assassination, as well as Whalley's note. And some likely conversations with closer allies, including Thomas Harrison and Hugh Peter. The hard core, according to Nedham, amongst those 'very hot for justice'.[60]

In effect, the *Remonstrance* served as the indictment. Prefiguring many of the arguments which would be ventured, two months later in Westminster Hall. Most obviously, the idea that kings were 'elected' upon 'trust', which Charles had broken, as 'the Author and Continuer of a most unjust warre' and by 'the spilling of much blood and desolation and spoyl'.[61] The theme of blood-guilt; the animating charge. The *Remonstrance* did not demand the king's death, not quite; but it did demand 'atonement according to righteousness', and 'exemplary justice'. A trial at least. After all, God had 'brought' the king into their 'hands' for a purpose.[62] Whitelock certainly recognized a 'design against the King's person'.[63] As did the editor of *Mercurius Elencticus*; a plan to 'depose and then murder' the king.[64] The Presbyterian MP Sir Roger Burgoyne too. Rather 'tedious', Sir Roger concluded of Ireton's script, but the 'drift' was plain enough.[65] As it would have been to anyone who attended a meeting of army and civilian Levellers at the Nag's Head, Blackwall, on the afternoon of 15 November. Where the topic of conversation, according to Lilburne, was simply conceived; whether or not they should 'cut off the King's head' and 'thoroughly purge' Parliament, and in which order.[66]

A sentiment which chimed with Ireton's demand that Parliament must 'forbear any further proceedings' with the king.[67] Not that the so-called Newport 'treaty' negotiations appeared to be getting anywhere. The king possessed, as Sir William Temple confirmed, of a 'strange conceit of my Lord of Ormonde working for him in Ireland'. The 'twig' to which he clung.[68] And still pondering the possibility of a last-minute escape. Various plots had been hatched over the summer; most half-baked. A futile attempt, the previous spring, to squeeze through the bars of the window of the king's chamber was perhaps the most notorious; the account left by his butler Firebrace hovering at the edge of dark comedy.[69] Ireton's request had its desired effect. Negotiations were finally abandoned on the 18th, as news arrived that Charles was to be moved to more secure accommodation at Hurst castle on the Solent. A 'dolorous place', Sir Thomas Herbert recalled, of 'unwholsom vapours' and 'fogs'.[70] To await escort to Windsor.

Meantime, Fairfax could occupy himself with the dozens of regimental petitions which were continuing to land on his desk. All supporting the *Remonstrance*. He might have noted, in particular, the petition despatched by the 'well-affected' of the Isle of Wight, enjoining the local garrison in petitioning for 'speedy justice' against their recently departed guest.[71] Suggestive for a number of reasons, aside from geography. Most obviously, the coincidence of anxiety, of the particular 'well-affected', with whichever regiment or garrison was presently camped on their doorstep. Thus Colonel Hewson's regiment and the 'well-affected' of Kent, Colonel Horton's regiment in South Wales, Sir Hardress Waller's Western Brigade, expressing a shared frustration with the gentlemen of Devon and Somerset. And the 'well-affected' of West Yorkshire, writing to confirm their support for Major General Lambert's Brigade. And the Major General, should he decide that enough was enough. Which it pretty much was.

On 26 November, the Council of Officers gathered at Windsor to resolve the 'great business now in hand'. Minds cast back to April, and a previous prayer-meeting at Windsor, held as news broke of the king's 'engagement' with Scots. They had then resolved 'that it was our duty, if ever the Lord brought us back again in peace, to call Charles Stuart, that man of blood, to an account for the blood that he has shed'.[72] He had brought them back, victories at Preston and Colchester, across Wales, and elsewhere. It could not be clearer. They were indeed the 'instruments' of His justice. How 'wonderfully God appears in stirring up and uniting every man's heart as one in the prosecution of this business'.[73]

It was certainly crystal clear to John Goodwin. The 'Army are truly the people of England'.[74] And to Cromwell, who added to Fairfax's in-tray with a letter, sent on 20 November, affirming his belief that there must now be 'impartial justice done upon all offenders'. The king was 'a man against whom the Lord hath witnessed'.[75] The *Remonstrance* was presented to Parliament. A trap laid; and sprung. On 1 December, the Commons duly rejected it, and, four days later, denounced the removal of the king from Newport. Further approving a motion to continue negotiations. As Ireton surely expected. The following morning, his ally Colonel Thomas Pride stationed himself at the top of the steps leading into Westminster Hall, with a detachment of troops, and a list.

Upon which were the names of those who would not, that day, be allowed to enter. Next to him stood Lord Grey of Groby.[76] To put faces to the names. Forty-five were considered sufficiently malignant to be taken into custody, another hundred and eighty-six turned away. Mainly Presbyterian. The 'wolves and foxes in sheep's clothing', Henry Marten termed them. Along with a scattering of Levellers. Around eighty more excluded themselves. The remaining 154 became known as the 'Rump'. On arriving, later that day, Cromwell informed Ludlow that whilst he had not 'been acquainted with this design; yet, since it was done, he was glad of it, and would endeavour to maintain it'.[77] Barely credible. A few days before, his personal secretary had written to a friend at army headquarters, expressing himself very 'glad' to 'hear of a beginning of action with you', starting with 'that great idol the Parliament'.[78] The evening was spent in the Star Tavern with the rest of the senior officers, catching up and sketching out.[79] The detained MPs were placed in protective custody, in a different pub; to wait and see. An evening in *Hell*.[80] Back in early 1643, Lord Brooke had justified taking up arms against his king on the grounds that 'the laws of the land (being but mans invention) must not check God's children in doing the work of their heavenlie father'.[81] The essence of puritan revolution. Judgement came early for Brooke, shot to death whilst trying to capture Lichfield cathedral a few weeks later. Now it was coming for Charles Stuart.

The dreams of Lizzie Poole

More petitions. The 'well-affected' of Tavistock assured that the time for 'terrible judgements' had arrived.[82] And the 'council of officers' still camped outside Pontefract, unable to 'hide our great rejoicing' at news of the purge. And the 'godly people' of Norfolk, equally approving. For 'How can there be a Kingdom of Saints, when the ungodly are electors, and elected to Govern?' An insinuation here, and a prophecy. Colonel Pride had made a beginning. Over the following months, corporations up and down the country would be similarly purged. The City of London Council in early February 1649, its Presbyterian Lord Mayor replaced by the prominent Baptist Sir Thomas Andrews.[83] Two weeks earlier, Sir Thomas had signed the king's death warrant. Overturning.

   Back to 15 December. Nine days after the purge, the Council of Officers reconvened at Whitehall. In principle, to debate a new *Agreement of the People*. More broadly though to take cognizance of a remarkable responsibility. As the now Captain Joyce proclaimed, 'called unto the greatest worke of Righteousnesse that ever was amongst men'.[84] To bring justice upon the king, and work out what to do next. Something which, according to the 'seeker' William Erbury, demanded a closer reading of the 'Word of God' rather than another discussion about 'agreements'.[85] A sentiment shared by Colonel Harrison. The 'word of God doth take notice that the powers of this world shall be given unto the hands of the Lord and his Saints, that this is the day, God's own day, wherein he was coming forth in glory in the world'. There might be a prosaic value to documents such as the *Agreement*, but 'our Agreement shall bee from God'.[86] The reason of governance has purpose, but only the Word can bring assurance. It would tell them what to do with Charles Stuart.

Starting with fetching him to Windsor; an order despatched from Council on the first day; 'in order to the bringing of him speedily to justice'. With the added instruction that there would be no more waiting 'on the knee'. Nor, it transpired, would there be any 'plum pies' to celebrate the coming Christmas. Nor indeed Christmas. Whether the accompanying resolutions were amongst the 'horrid villainies' that so appalled John Evelyn, who attended the 'debates' on the 18th, we can only conjecture.[87] Either way, matters were progressing. A couple of caveats though, in Ireton's mind. First, there would still need to be some kind of constitution, when all was done, 'the necessity of it for preserving peace'. Thus the need to take the draft *Agreement* seriously. And then there was the question of being completely sure what He wanted. The same anxieties which had pervaded Putney; no less urgent now. To 'call upon His name, seek His face, and to know His mind'.[88]

Scriptural exegesis was the obvious recourse. Hugh Peter, the 'carnall prophet' of the regicide, as Prynne would later term him, strove mightily to the purpose.[89] A stream of sermons over the closing weeks of December and January, given at Whitehall and Westminster, designed to stiffen resolve. All the usual Old Testament suspects. Oreb and Zeeb in *Judges* 7:25, Joash in 2 *Chronicles* 2:24, Eglon in *Judges* 3:15, 20–21. Myriad Pharaonic references. Ahab in 1 *Kings* 16–22. It was the story of Ahab which the similarly 'carnall' George Cockayne revisited in his Commons sermon on 29 November: 'If God do not lead you to do Justice upon those that have been the great Actors in shedding innocent Blood, never think to gain their love by sparing them.'[90] Plenty more suggestive bits of scripture. *Deuteronomy* 19:13: 'thine eyes shall not pity him, but thou shalt put away the guilt of innocent blood from Israel'. *Psalm* 149, an especial favourite: 'To bind their kings with chains, and their nobles with fetters of iron; / To execute upon them the judgement written: this honour have all the saints.'

Still, ambiguities lurked. The alternative was to seek a more direct guidance, a 'messenger' of God perhaps. Someone suggested Lizzie Poole, the famed Abingdon mystic. Arriving on 29 December, Lizzie described a recent 'vision' in which she had seen an ailing woman supported by a man. The latter being a 'member of the Army', the former representing the 'distressed State' of England. Reassuring. An 'impression' of the 'Testimony' of God, Colonel Rich enthused, who was indeed with 'the army'.[91] Ireton was similarly impressed, clearly 'the Spiritt of God'. At least with this bit of Lizzie's vision. The further supposition, that it confirmed His liking for the 'liberty' of conscience, was more troubling; the suggestion that 'any thinge' might be called 'Religion'.[92] But that was for another day.

Lizzie's second vision, related on 5 January, was less helpful. Be wary of 'Temptations' and do not 'betray your Trusts'. Which apparently meant that putting the king on trial was fine, 'that he may be convicted in his conscience'. But 'touch not his person'. An awkward bit of scripture too. *Romans* 12:19: 'Vengeance is mine; I will repay, saith the Lord'. Colonel Whalley was appalled. That Charles Stuart, plainly guilty of so many 'filthy things' and 'great crimes', should get away with it.[93] Had Lizzie not read the first book of *Samuel*, was she unaware of what happened to Saul when, against the express Will of God, he spared the king of the Amalekites? Evidently not. Ireton wondered if this second 'vision' really was 'delivered from God'; or just made up.[94] Lizzie was sent back to her herb-patch. Hugh Peter had seen enough though. He was 'not in the mind we should put our hands in our pockets and wait what will come'.[95] The 'Spirit of God' was clear enough to Sir Hardress Waller too. 'Ten thousands of men are senseless', Sir Hardress observed.[96] Their sacrifices must not be wasted. Lizzie might have wobbled, but they could not.

Except that they did. The days passed. On the 14th, a visibly agitated Joyce opened proceedings with a tirade against those seemingly possessed by the 'spirit of feare'. Spleen vented, it was back to chatting about the *Agreement*. Which was, finally, presented to the Commons on the morning of the 20th. Proposing a constitutional monarchy, with the *Agreement* serving as a kind of coronation oath. The sort of compromise that, in the end, satisfied no-one. A maudlin tone. They had done their best:

> Now as nothing did in our own hearts more justifie our late undertakings ... then the necessity thereof in order to sound Settlement in the Kingdom, and the integrity of our intentions to make use of it only to that end ... that neither that extraordinary course we have taken, nor any other proceedings of ours, have been intended for the setting up of any particular Party or Interest ... but that it was and is the desire of our hearts, in all we have done ... to make way for the settlement of a Peace and Government of the Kingdom upon Grounds of common Freedom and Safety.[97]

A statement intended to 'prevent misunderstandings'. The Council was thanked for its efforts, the Commons promising to take the matter into consideration 'when the necessity of affairs will permit'. It never did. Understandable, though, if everyone was a bit distracted.

Production

Earlier that morning, the king had been brought up the Thames on a barge. Late, of course. A bit of mist on the morning breeze. 'He is come! He is come!' Cromwell exclaimed as the barge finally heaved into view. Nervous apprehension; again understandable. The 'great day of judgement' had arrived, as the prosecutor, John Cook, put it, 'when the saints shall judge all wordly powers'.[98] And a tacit admission. Cromwell was the support, in the wings, watching on. The lead, for the next couple of weeks, would be the man sat on the barge. Who would, shortly, take a different seat in the middle of Westminster Hall, to listen to the charges being laid against him. No-one could be sure quite how he might react. Maybe disorientated, apprehensive. Ashamed perhaps. 'There is nothing more contemptible,' Charles was reported as saying on his arrival at Windsor, 'than a despised prince.'[99] Most likely something of each. Everything to play for, though. Except of course the ending.

Stage and cast

The Lord had set His people a peculiar task, in demanding that Charles Stuart be brought to judgement. Plenty of English monarchs had been usurped, deposed and murdered. A list that included Richard II, together with William II, very probably, Edward II very definitely, Henry VI quite possibly. The various 'sad stories of the deaths of kings'.[100] But none had been hauled before a court of law and prosecuted on charges of treason. There was no precedent for that.

As the realization dawned, that the king was likely to stand trial, the November edition of *Mercurius Pragmaticus* presented its readers with a few questions:

> What court shall the King be tried in? Who shall be his Peers? Who shall give sentence? What eyes dare be so impious to behold the execution? What Arm be outstretched to give the stroke against the Lord's Anointed, and shall not wither like that of Jeroboam, when he lifted it against an anointed prophet?[101]

A Presbyterian journal. So loaded questions. And some scarcely veiled insinuations too. Judgement had already been reached. The jury would be stacked, any trial a show, probably an abomination. Oddly enough both sides craved the spectacle. The king wanted martyrdom, and martyrs need to be noticed. The army wanted a public atonement. It must not be some 'thing', as Colonel Harrison would famously declare, 'done in a corner'.[102]

A tone, and an aspiration, enjoined by Cook in his opening address. Anticipating 'the most comprehensive, impartial and glorious piece of justice that ever was acted and executed upon the theatre of England'.[103] Samuel Butler spotted the necessary irony, writing a little later in 1682. Noting the closure of the theatres during the 1650s,

> We perceive, at last why plays went down; to wit, that murders might be acted in earnest. Stages must submit to scaffolds, and personated tragedies to real ones ... No need of heightening revels; these Herods can behead without the allurements of a dance. These tragedians have outvied invention.[104]

An ascetic age heralded by a spectacular moment. Which meant some challenges familiar to the producers of any show; the need to identify the right stage, set it, recruit a credible cast and write a convincing script.

Stage first. A matter of determining what and where. Questions intimately related. The law of treason was well-enough established, but it was not fitted for trying monarchs. Nothing really fitted. Royal miscreants had, in the past, been prosecuted and convicted by the Privy Council. But it had been suppressed back in 1641. The Army Council might have served. But there were two problems here. The first was that such a proceeding might have smacked of martial law, and that was expressly disapproved by Coke out of 'time of peace'.[105] But, more importantly, it would hardly have made for much of a show. It was conceivable that Charles could be impeached by his 'peers'. Except that he was not supposed to have any. And anyway, the House of Lords had already declined to approve a Commons Ordinance establishing a High Court. It was certainly not going to sit in judgement on the king. Related doubts militated against the use of an Attainder Bill, which would also have required the assent of the Lords, and indeed the king. The prosecution would, in the end, lay charges of impeachment. Albeit with a necessary jurisdictional adjustment. More of that shortly.

Meanwhile, on 4 January, the Commons issued a statement confirming that it was 'supreme power in this nation', by virtue of being the 'chosen' representative of the 'people' who are, under God, 'the original of all just power'. A declaration repeated two days later in an Ordinance designed to complement an *Act for Erecting of an High Court of Justice for the Trying and Judging of Charles Stuart*. The preamble to the Act spoke of a nation 'miserably wasted', and a king deserving of 'exemplary and condign punishment'.[106] Some hints for the committee presently drafting the charge. Rushworth termed it 'an Ordinance of Attainder', a legislative condemnation rather than a procedural facility.[107] Three days later, the Sergeant of Arms, Sir Edward Dendy, opened the more ceremonial part of proceedings, entering Westminster Hall 'attended by six trumpets, and a guard of two troops of horse, himself with them on horseback, bearing the mace'.[108] After which he was despatched about the city, replete with his trumpets and his guard, to do some marketing.

As to the question of 'where', that was something remitted to a committee comprised chiefly of senior New Model officers.[109] Established on the 12th, for 'considering of the circumstances' of the pending trial. Westminster Hall seemed obvious, the customary venue down the ages for high-profile treason cases. An alternative, mooted alongside the idea of a trial before the Army Council, was Windsor. But again hardly lending much to spectacle, or provenance. So Westminster it would be. Despite the evident concerns. At nearly 17,000 square feet it was difficult to secure. The assassination of the king was a possibility; more likely the assassination of his prosecutors. A 'Guard of Court', comprising two hundred 'foot soldiers', would be deployed about the palace. To be camped in the gardens of the Cotton House, adjacent to the palace. Where the king would be lodged during the trial. Ireton took particular care in regard to the conditions under which Charles would be held. Not just reiterating his instruction that there must be 'nothing done upon the knee', but ordering that the door to the king's chamber should be locked 'in time of night'.[110] No more escapes. As to Westminster Hall, mindful of what had occurred in 1605 there would be daily inspections of the palace under-vault, as well as 'rails' set up half-way down the hall, to keep the spectators at least 'forty-foot distance'. All of which took up a fair chunk of the £1,000 voted by the Commons to cover 'incident charges'.

The rest to go on interior design, and decoration. Something else remitted to the committee of 'circumstances'. The nominated commissioners, serving as the jury, would be arrayed at the west end of the Hall, on raised seating. The Lord President of the Court would sit in the middle of the front row, on a raised chair swathed in crimson velvet, in front of which was placed a desk with a crimson velvet cushion. To match his crimson velvet-lined gown, extra-padded against any knife-wielding assassin. The committee invested heavily in crimson velvet. Appearance was everything. The benches on which the commissioners would be seated were also decked out in crimson. Heralds too, maces and swords of state. And smart new kit for the 'guards' stationed around the hall perimeter, holding 'rich javelins with velvet and fringe', crimson again. The king would be sat opposite the commissioners, in the middle of the Hall. His chair, of course, covered in crimson velvet. Splendid isolation. A gamble of course. Staging can make or break a production. Charles might feel horribly alone and exposed. Or, he might feel magisterial and magnificent. Only time would tell.

And it would tell the latter. Charles played a blinder, stole the moment and most of the scenes. But before we take a closer look at the performance, we need to finish the casting. The support. It had been hoped that Oliver St John, Chief Justice and close friend of Cromwell, might serve as Lord President. But he declined. In the end, the position was taken by John Bradshaw, a forty-seven-year-old lawyer from the north-west. Royalists would later make much of Bradshaw's relative obscurity. 'Meanly qualified' according to Sir Philip Warwick, 'bold and seditious'.[111] Hyde agreed. A man 'not much known' but of 'great insolence and ambition'. In fact, Bradshaw was a more than competent lawyer, with a very particular client-list. 'Much employed by the factious and discontented', Hyde recalled.[112] Two years earlier he had defended Lilburne against treason charges. No 'English gentleman', Bradshaw had closed his argument in Lilburne's defence, should ever 'be made slave to satisfie the malicious and virulent humors of a tyrannicall Court'.[113] Food for thought. Earlier in 1648, Bradshaw had been appointed Chief Justice of Cheshire and North Wales. So some judicial experience too. Hardly preparation for what was about to happen, though. Probably nothing was.

The prosecution was to have been led by the Attorney General, William Steele. But he too pulled out at the last minute, afflicted, as luck would have it, by a dodgy tummy. Not, he was at pains to add, out of 'dissatisfaction to the proceedings'.[114] Bulstrode Whitelock was unconvinced. One of the many to 'purposely avoid this business'; like indeed Bulstrode.[115] Sir Thomas Widdrington, another commissioner of the Seal, made himself scarce. As did Serjeant Nicholas, who had prosecuted Archbishop Laud. Shortly to be appointed a justice in the renamed Court of Upper Bench; but otherwise detained in January 1649. The responsibility was shared, in the end, by Cook, a Gray's Inn barrister who had also represented Lilburne, along with the Dutch jurist Isaac Dorislaus, who did much of the drafting of charges.[116] 'Eminent only for their obscurity', Hyde sneered of the pair.[117] A bit much perhaps. But neither were, in truth, established stars of the courtroom. A fact that was not much changed by the time that the trial of the king was complete. Dorislaus preferred to stay in the wings, Cook buried in his brief.

The jury would comprise the 135 commissioners. Plenty of familiar names from amongst the senior officer corps, unsurprisingly. Cromwell, Fairfax, Ireton, Skippon, Fleetwood, the 'hard core' of Cromwellian Colonels, Ludlow, Okey, Goffe, Harrison, Hewson, Whalley. Thomas Pride too, the master-purger. Around fifty in sum. Men of 'mean worth', royalist news-sheets proclaimed. Again true in some cases. Pride, a drayman, Okey, a brewery stoker, Hewson, a cobbler, Goffe, a salter. But nonsense in others. Ireton, Fleetwood and Ludlow all educated at the Inns of Court. Skippon at Cambridge. The names of Fairfax and Lord Grey, son of the earl of Stamford, even leant a certain aristocratic tone to proceedings. Lord Lisle likewise, son of the earl of Leicester. A scattering of knights and baronets, a few again familiar. Sir William Brereton, victor of Digbeth Street. And the Wallers, Sir William and Sir Hardress, both senior parliamentary commanders.[118] There were even some former courtiers. Sir John Danvers, great-grandson of Catherine Parr, and Gentleman to the Bedchamber, in more 'halcyon days'. And Sir Henry Mildmay, one-time Master of the king's Jewel House.[119]

Some civilian commissioners too, effectively pre-selected on 6 December. Five City Aldermen, including the coming Lord Mayor, and Sir Isaac Pennington, host to the five MPs who escaped the king in January 1642. Other Rumpers of the more enthusiastic variety included the firebrand Henry Marten, who had been agitating for a trial for years. Marten attended every day. Not many others did. Fifty-seven would turn up on the first day. Thereafter numbers hovered around the same. So quorate, but hardly a convincing vote of confidence. No English peers, of course; a consequence of the Lords rejecting the trial ordinance. The list of absentees said something too. Not just Fairfax, but Lambert and Skippon, and Brereton and Sir William Waller. Various reasons, or excuses. Lambert would later claim a crisis of conscience. Waller was a Presbyterian, who opposed the trial in principle. Brereton busy chasing down royalists in Cheshire. Fairfax, another with a dodgy tummy. Jurisprudence worried a couple, including Sir Henry Vane. And Colonel Algernon Sidney, who later recalled a heated conversation with Cromwell, in which he had questioned the legality of what was proposed. Earning a famous retort. They would 'cut off his head with the crown upon it'.[120] The edge was hard, the nerves frayed.

Finally, the Chorus. Made up of various kinds of spectators: clerks, guards, journalists, the otherwise curious. The named clerks were Andrew Boughton and John Phelps. Both of whom left formal record of proceedings.[121] Boughton wrote out the death warrant. Amongst the various tasks assumed by the 'Court of Guards', along with security and cheerleading, was ushering. Dealing with barrackers. Like Lady Fairfax. Eschewing the opportunity to join her husband on retreat at his Yorkshire estate, Lady Anne stayed in London, to take in the show. And indulge a spot of heckling. Most famously when Sir Thomas's name was read out as a nominated commissioner. He had more 'wit than to be here', a voice rang out from the gallery. Parliamentarian presses had it put about that those responsible were a couple of 'malignant' whores. But enough knew different.[122] Sir Thomas might have been a Parliamentarian hero, but Lady Anne was a royalist. A couple of days later she was back, to shout some more abuse.

Scripting

An instructive experience, for all concerned. Stages set might be set, lead and support selected with the greatest of care. But no-one can ever be sure how the audience will react. A tight script can help. Starting with the right brief, suitably toned. Difficult here though, for the reasons we have already noted. Blighted by the lack of precedent, and the fact that neither of the established procedures, impeachment or attainder, seemed to quite fit. Which left the script-writers looking at drafting some kind of mutant treason charge. Not easy. When the trial Ordinance was placed before the House of Lords for their consideration, at the beginning of January, the earl of Northumberland articulated a broader doubt, which crushed any lingering thought of an impeachment trial.[123] 'There is not one in twenty of the people in England' who were 'yet satisfied' that the king was responsible for the war, still less that there was a 'law extant that can be produced to make a treason in him to do so'.[124]

The matter of drawing up the charge was remitted to another committee. Largely civilian this time, albeit steered by Ireton and Harrison.[125] In essence, it was a matter of finding a credible position between the esoteric and the pragmatic. In the former regard there were a couple of options, more or less compatible. The first was the theory of kingship discovered in the common law, and the attendant fiction of the king's 'two bodies'. It was, after all, why they had gone to war in the first place. To defend the principles of the 'ancient' constitution, and the 'liberties' of people, against the 'person' of a tyrannical king. By no coincidence, the Huguenot tract, *Vindiciae Contra Tyrannos*, was republished at the end of 1648; 'although kings die, the people meanwhile, just like any other corporation, never dies'.[126]

All, we can safely assume, familiar to the author of the November *Remonstrance*. The spirit of Edward Coke walked in the person of Henry Ireton, barrister of the Middle Temple.

A second theory, rather more of the moment, was covenanted kingship. The logic of Reformation, according to Henry Burton, supposing that 'innovations' in religion had corrupted the 'indissoluble bond' of heritable kingship,[127] Not a logic that appealed much to King James if we recall. To plenty of others though. All 'power which princes have is but derivative and secondary', a parliamentary pamphlet declared a couple of weeks before Charles had raised his Standard back in summer 1642, 'the foundation and efficient cause is the people'. Kings, another had confirmed a few weeks later, 'come lawfully in with the choice and consent of their people'.[128] Later still, in 1647, a petition from Colonel Robert Overton's regiment urged that 'all future kings be hereafter elected by the People's Representatives upon conditional trust'.[129] And most pertinently, perhaps, the principle written into the Ordinance of 6 January. Bradshaw would venture the idea that English kingship was 'elective' during the trial; with, as we shall see, mixed results. Dorislaus was keen on the idea too, schooled in continental theories of covenanted sovereignty.

Familiar from scripture, of course. Where it could assume an almost literal meaning. Moses covenanted with God. *Deuteronomy* 32:26: 'Take this book of the law, and put it in the side of the ark of the covenant of the Lord.' We will, in due course, encounter Milton recommending it in his defences of regicide. Ireton also used the language of covenant in his *Remonstrance*. And in the *Heads of the Charge Against the King*, which appeared on 24 December. A king 'trusted with a limited power to rule according to Law, and by expresse Covenant and Oath'.[130] The variant idea, of contractual sovereignty, shortly to find famous expression in Thomas Hobbes's *Leviathan*, may have appealed rather more to the common lawyer. But that hardly detracted. Quite the opposite. The scriptures of God and the common law, mutually sustaining.

If beset by some similarly familiar perplexities, of the kind which commonly attend legal 'fictions'. The formation of the contract for a start. The coronation oath perhaps, in which Charles had sworn to defend the 'laws, customs, and franchises of the people'. A 'compact' wherein the king was 'trusted with a limited power to govern', so the indictment read. Which had been broken when he 'traitorously and maliciously levied war against the present Parliament'. Cook could ratchet up the rhetoric, in his opening address confirming that it was, as a consequence, the 'highest Treason' that 'was ever wrought'.[131] But the argument was still shaky. Witches might 'compact' with the Devil, merchants with their clients, but no-one was sure that kings ever contracted with their subjects. Not really. No less contentious was the matter of consequence. What might happen if a party was deemed to be in breach of their obligations? Easy enough if it was a subject in breach. Less easy if it was a sovereign. Hobbes dodged the issue of consequence altogether.

Others, though, were prepared to take it on. Milton, as we will see in the next chapter. A century earlier, John Knox had wondered 'Whether obedience is to be rendered to a magistrate who enforces idolatry and condemns true religion'.[132] And answered in the negative. The binding relation of God, sovereign and people was the kernel of covenant. Which made the deposing of kings for reason of theological error, or indeed constitutional impropriety, not just a right but a duty. God-given, in a literal, scriptural, sense. The jurisprudential arguments would be fleshed out in the months and years to come. In texts, indeed, such as *Leviathan*, and plenty more. No-one, royalist or other, ever thought quite the same about English kingship after January 1649.

For now, though, while gesturing to associated ideas of common law and 'elective' kingship, the charge brought against Charles Stuart sought safer ground in more prosaic matters, of blood-guilt and alleged war crimes. The 'crying sin', a treason that everyone could comprehend. A war 'traiterously and maliciously levied' against Parliament and the people, 'carried on for the advancement and upholding of a personal interest of will, power and pretended prerogative'. The treason originally affirmed by the House of Commons, in its declarations of the 1st and then the 4th of January; to 'levy war against the Parliament and Kingdom of England'. All the battles and sieges at which the king had been present. Specific mention for Leicester and 'Naseby field', where many 'thousands of the free people of this nation' had been 'slain', and pointed reference to the 'renewing of war' in 1648. Futile and 'wicked'. The 'said Charles Stuart' was, in conclusion, 'the occasioner, author, and continuer of the said unnatural cruel and bloody wars; and therein guilty of all the treasons, murders, rapines, burnings, spoils, desolations, damages and mischiefs to this nation, acted and committed in the said wars, or occasioned thereby'. Plenty enough to 'impeach' a 'tyrant, traitor, murderer' and 'implacable enemy' of the people; maybe even a king.[133]

This was the charge which Cook would flesh out in his prosecution brief. And then reaffirm in his own narrative of the trial, which appeared a few weeks after, entitled *King Charles His Case*. A 'man of blood', held to account for waging a war against his own subjects, a 'stranger to the work of grace and the spirit of God'. Gestures to the God-given duty too, lots of familiar scriptural referents to bulk up the brief. Like the dreadful King Ahab, another prince short of cash, who was tempted to use his 'pretended prerogative' so that 'he might have any man's estate that he liked, without paying for it'. Agag, the godless king of the Amalekites who Saul neglected to slaughter. Nimrod, the 'first Tyrant and Conqueror who had no title'. The 'Pharaoh', of course.[134] A litany of despots, none legitimate, being not 'elected', and each deaf to the 'prayers and tears' of his people. And each removed on His instruction.

The *Case* against Charles Stuart was written in this key. In part to persuade fellow jurists. But in part also to engage the appeal process, already well-underway by the time that Cook sat down to re-edit his 'defence' in February 1649. Rewriting the past to make better sense of the present. Laud's redrafted coronation oath proving, from the 'very first day', a 'design to alter and subvert the fundamental laws and to introduce an arbitrary and tyrannical government'.[135] And to chart the future, however dimly. In the next chapter, we will encounter Milton doing the same, repeatedly. Re-scripting. Not just because the audience had changed; from those who had sat in judgement in Westminster Hall, to those who now sat in judgement across the rest of the country. But also because the trial was over, the production ended. And it had not quite gone to plan. The perils of production, and a lead that went rogue.

The king's gambit

We will pick up the narrative on the morning of 20 January.[136] Charles sat on his chair in the middle of the Hall. Hardly surprising, perhaps, if he felt some trepidation. Being the centre of attention was not unfamiliar of course. Princes are trained to the role. Forever upon the 'stage', as Shakespeare put it. Personality matters though, and Charles was naturally reticent. A tendency exacerbated by a less than imposing physique and a pronounced stammer.[137] And an unhappy childhood; a mother who made little effort to hide her disappointment, and a father who just made little effort. Laud noted the disjuncture. A 'mild and gracious prince, who knew not how to be, or be made great'.[138] A kinder spin. A 'miracle of clemency and patience', Thomas Morton, bishop of Durham, confirmed.[139] Another cleric with all the right words.

And probably true enough. There is no evidence of viciousness in the character of Charles Stuart. But there is of vacillation. Plenty. The king who momentarily fancied playing Caesar at Naseby, but then thought again. A 'tractable and counsellable disposition', the earl of Dorset confirmed.[140] It drove the queen to despair. As events began to run alarmingly out of control in spring 1642, Henrietta Maria tried to bolster her husband's resolve. A 'want of perseverance in your designs hath ruined you,' she wrote, 'you are beginning again your old game of yielding everything.'[141] A brute honesty justified by the moment. Charles was on his way to Hull; to prove her right. 'Fitter to stand in a shop with a white apron, than to be king of England', the schoolmaster Alexander Gill recorded in his diary. Discreet at least. Unlike Joan Sherrard, hauled before the justices of St Dunston, for having loudly dismissed God's anointed as nothing more than a 'stuttering fool'.[142] In sum, just the kind of prince who might, with a bit of luck, go to pieces in a courtroom. So Cromwell and Ireton hoped.

But also a man who loved theatre, who had been preparing for this role for months, probably years. A man who craved martyrdom, who sensed that this might be his moment. Who would, it was reported to Cardinal Mazarin, 'rather lose his crown than his soul'.[143] A man, certainly, who knew how to dress. Making decisions, and friends, may not have been his thing, but fashion was an entirely different matter. Charles was in his element. Meticulously apparelled each day, wearing the insignia of the Order of the Garter, the jewelled 'Great George' round his neck, his favourite ostrich-feathered hat on his head, where it stayed, despite the request that it might be removed as a mark of respect to the court.[144] A similar instruction, that he might stand when the officers of the court entered each day, was met with equivalent disdain. And, given that he was seated in the middle of the Hall, with no-one in attendance, there was not much that could be done to make him either stand up, or take his hat off. A strategic insolence, designed to impress. In his reworked narrative of the trial, Nalson would describe a king possessed of a 'majestic and unmoved countenance'.[145] Sir Philip Warwick likewise; 'majestic and steady'.[146] Prejudiced perhaps. But still, there are no accounts of Charles looking anything other.

Most importantly, of course, none of this was scripted. The hat-wearing, the refusal to stand, the chuckling whenever the prosecutors tried to make a serious point. A famous moment, from the opening day, set a tone. Cook opened his case, extrapolating the charge. Stood just in front of the seated king. Charles tapped on his shoulder with his silver-topped cane, asking him to 'hold a little'. Cook looked fleetingly irritated. It was his moment, and he needed to get it right. So he pressed on. Charles tapped him again. This time the silver-top came off, and dropped onto the floor. A sudden silence, everyone waiting; Charles, not used to picking stuff up, amongst them. When it became apparent that no-one, least of all Cook, was going to retrieve his silver-top, Charles stood up, bent over and picked it up. And then, very slowly, returned to his seat. At which point he had the temerity to nod to Cook, as if to suggest that he might now continue. Another scene stolen. It quickly became apparent that, given the chance, Charles would act them all offstage.

Leaving the prosecution to try to cut through the drama with the colder certainty of legal argument. But this, on closer inspection, was hardly compelling either, for reasons we have already considered. Charles was not himself a jurist, though he had been well-schooled on the precepts of Stuart kingship. 'I am no lawyer professed,' he confessed, 'but I know as much law as gentleman of England.'[147] And neither, as an alleged traitor, was he allowed representation in court. For the reason that Coke confirmed in his *Institutes*; that 'the testimonies and the proofs of the offence ought to be so clear and manifest, as there can be no defence of it'. But he was allowed defence counsel in private. And chose well. A later Attorney General, Geoffrey Palmer, and a couple of Restoration Chief Justices, John Vaughan and Orlando Bridgman. We will encounter Orlando again in a later chapter exacting a brutal revenge on those responsible for the execution of his client. A credible team, quite capable of spotting the flaws in the prosecution brief. But still, it was Charles who would have to present his defence. And did; possibly brilliantly, possibly to excess, probably both.

Two central arguments, both advanced from the start. The first was jurisdiction. 'I would know by what power I am called hither,' Charles inquired,

'I would know by what authority, I mean lawful.' There were plenty of 'unlawful authorities in the world', he continued, 'thieves and robbers by the highway'.[148] A biblical echo, of course; Jesus refusing to recognize the pretended jurisdictions of Herod and Pilate. But also speaking to a more familiar ambivalence in English constitutional theory. Predictable, so Bradshaw had an answer; of a kind. They were sat as the 'High Court of Parliament'. Henry Marten had tried to get ahead of the argument, confirming that they were sat 'in the name of the Commons'. But that rather conceded the point. As Charles responded. The Commons alone was 'never a court of judicature'; where were the peers? The question hung in the air. Later, at the close of the first day, an exasperated Bradshaw simply replied that 'we are satisfied that are your judges'. But it was not for the judges to satisfy their own 'apprehension', Charles shot back. It was a matter of satisfying constitutional 'precedent'.[149] 'Show me a precedent' he kept asking. Bradshaw had none. For the next four days, Charles refused to acknowledge the legality of the court on precisely the same terms. And all Bradshaw could do was keep repeating himself.

The second defence was to challenge the substantive charge; that he had been bound by a covenant which he had traitorously broken. Charles was certainly aware of the implications of covenant. Spelled out, clearly enough, in his father's *Trew Law*. A decade earlier he had written to Hamilton expressing his distaste. So 'long as this Covenant is in force', he observed, 'I have no more Power in Scotland than as a Duke of Venice, which I will rather die than suffer'.[150] A tragic prescience. Cook set off with the breach of covenant argument on the morning of the 20th. That the king had declared war on Parliament with the intent to impose a 'tyrannical power' on his people. Thus all the battles listed in the charge; each a testament to the king's treason, and its consequence. There could be no clearer evidence of a broken trust. Except, of course, that the same argument might just as easily run the other way. Here the events which took place on 22 August 1642 assumed a pivotal importance. A declaration of war. In due course, evidence would be produced from various people who had stood about in the Nottingham drizzle that afternoon. More of the witness depositions shortly; another part of the production that proved less than straightforward.

Here again Charles had a simple, and compelling, counter. There might be lots of clever treatises on 'elective' kingship, but there was no precedent in English law for assuming that a king held his office under the terms of some kind of contract. As he kept telling the Lord President. To distraction. In their testy exchange at the end of the first day, Bradshaw again tried to cut Charles short with the simple affirmation that he was on trial 'in the name of the people of England, of which you are elected king'. Nonsense, Charles responded. 'England was never an elective kingdom, but an hereditary kingdom for near these thousand years.' His was a 'trust committed to me by God, by old and lawful descent'. The other bit of the coronation oath. If Bradshaw could show 'authority' to the contrary, 'warranted by the Word of God, the Scriptures, or warranted by the constitutions of the Kingdom', he continued, 'I will answer'.[151] Again, Bradshaw had nothing.

Proceedings were brought to a swift conclusion, the king escorted out of the hall. The Guard began shouting 'Justice', as the script, and their commander, Colonel Axtell, demanded. But louder still, it was reported, were cries of 'God Save the King'. As he was hustled out of the Hall, Charles pointed 'with his staff' towards the axe, set on display. 'I do not fear that.'[152] Another scene stolen. It has been surmised that, having won the jurisprudential argument, or at least having scuppered Bradshaw's, Charles then overplayed his hand. In his *Remonstrance*, Ireton accused Charles of being a compulsive gambler, always seeking the 'surest play'. He might have changed tack at this point, saved his life, even his crown; an argument that gathers credence if the trial can be reconfigured as part of a broader negotiation strategy being pressed by the army 'junto'. Perhaps. The counter-argument is that Ireton knew his man. That Charles was a gambler, and that he was prepared to take his chances. Reconciled anyway to the prospect of martyrdom, should the gambit fail. Either way, the day was his. Later than evening, Hugh Peter tried to stiffen resolve amongst the commissioners, declaring it to have been 'a most glorious beginning of the work'. In truth, it could hardly have gone worse.

Farewell sovereignty

And it was not about to get any better. The 21st, a Sunday, was spent in prayer and anxious conversation. The 'frighted junto', properly frighted.[153] The lead sermon was given by Fairfax's chaplain, Joshua Sprigge, who chose the text 'He that sheds blood, by man shall his blood be shed.' At best it was ambivalent. The 22nd began with a meeting of the commissioners in the Painted Chamber, to discuss what might be done about the king's 'carriage'. Not much really, aside from keep trying. Which made for a predictable afternoon, when the court reconvened. Charles 'still insisted' that the court had no legality, in either scripture or law. Quoting a handy passage from *Ecclesiastes* 8:4 in regard to the former: 'Where the word of a king is, there is power: and who may say unto him, What doest though?' And then challenging Bradshaw, yet again, to 'show' any precedents for calling kings to account in English law.[154] Knowing, of course, that there were none.

Something else too. Charles was growing into his role. Sensing perhaps that the prosecution was floundering. And that his jury might be starting to have doubts too. If not about their duty, or the verdict, certainly about the conduct of the trial. It was reported that the king 'spoke very much against the court, as no true judicature, and that he did not believe the major part of the commissioners were of that opinion'. A fair assumption, as we will shortly see. Something more too. When Bradshaw pressed again for a plea, Charles declined on the basis that doing so would betray the very 'trust' which was being contested. It was not 'only my own particular case' but the 'freedom and liberty of the people of England'. And 'do you pretend what you will, I stand more for their liberties'. For 'if power without law may make laws, may alter the fundamental laws of the kingdom, I do not know what subject he is in England that can be sure of his life or anything that he calls his own'. Not only did the king sound suitably magisterial, but so too was he sounding increasingly like a martyr. You are 'before a court of law', an increasing irate Bradshaw responded. No, Charles replied calmly, 'I am before a power'.[155] He was certainly that. Another day brought to a hasty conclusion.

Not what the producers had hoped. The fact that the king was proving to be something of a 'hostile' witness was hardly surprising. And neither should have been his arguments. The fact that he was proving to be so adept at all the 'improv' might have been less easy to anticipate. Back they came on the 23rd. The same happened. 'For the charge, I value it not a rush,' Charles declared, 'it is the liberty of the people of England that I stand for.'[156] He would not plead. Bradshaw and Cook were baffled. The law permitted them to enter a plea *pro confesso* 'by default', and Cook had worked the rhetoric of public 'notoriety' throughout the trial; a treason as 'clear as crystal'.[157] But presumption was not proof, and moving direct to sentence would ruin what was left of the increasingly tarnished spectacle. Cook wanted his day in court, most particularly the opportunity to examine all his witnesses. Cromwell, though, was running out of patience. Another day spent in heated deliberation. They would push on, but there would be no more bickering over jurisdiction. A plea of *pro confesso* was entered.

And the witnesses, thirty-three in total, would be examined over the next two days. Most simply confirming that Charles was present at various battles. Plus a few who could testify to events at Nottingham on 22 August, including one Robert Lacey, who had painted the flagpole upon which the Royal Standard had been raised, and had seen the king 'divers times' riding about the town. And a spy who had been trying to keep an eye on the king at Carisbrooke, and who could testify to his various subterfuges. Another witness, a London scrivener named Richard Price who acted as a kind of double-agent, provided similar evidence of the king's 'tampering' back in 1644, trying to 'turn' some 'Independents' away from the 'cause'. Price was further able to confirm that the king was, at that time, trying to lure an army over from Ireland.[158] The ideal moment for the court to be reminded of the Naseby 'cabinet', from which choice excerpts were then read out.

The 26th was spent drafting the verdict and sentence. The next morning, as was customary, they all assembled in the Painted Chamber, to plot the day. Then, after lunch, off to the Hall. Where the king would be given a last opportunity to acknowledge the jurisdiction of the court, in return for which he would be granted the opportunity to be 'heard'. An offer predictably declined. A short recess, before the court returned to confirm that it would proceed to sentence. Silence proclaimed, an expectant hush descended. Not for long though. As Bradshaw began, reiterating that the charge had been laid 'in the name of the people of England', a familiar voice in the gallery shouted out 'tis a lye, not a tenth of the people are concerned in it', before adding 'but all's done by the Machinations of that Traitor Cromwell'.[159] Lady Fairfax again. Axtell offered to have his soldiers fire into the gallery; an offer perhaps wisely declined. In the end, he settled for hurling some abuse back. 'Down with the whores', he screamed at the wife of his commander-in-chief. Commotion downstairs too, not least amongst the commissioners, some thinking that the king should, even now, be permitted to address the court.[160] When Colonel Downes supposed that it would be at least polite, a furious Cromwell swung round and hissed at him to be quiet. The court recessed once again, so that Downes might be reminded, in no uncertain terms, that they were doing His work.

A sort of calm restored, Bradshaw set off once again, on a nervy forty-minute speech. Fashioning an awkward parallel between Charles and Caligula, recommending a quick glance at how things were done in Aragon, and by King Fergus of Scotland, and then revisiting some selected precedents from English history, most pertinently the usurpations of Edward II and Richard II, neither of whom had come close to the 'height and capitalness of crimes that are laid at your charge, nothing near'.[161] Before moving on to reassert the jurisprudential integrity of proceedings. As confirmed in the 'old law' of England. First, that Parliament was indeed a 'high court' of justice. And second, that an English king held his power on 'trust' from the 'people of England', represented in that same Parliament; the 'great bulwark of the liberties of the people'. A 'contract and a bargain made', with 'reciprocal' duties, 'for as you are their liege Lord, so are they your liege subjects'. The 'one tie' of mutual obligation; the 'bond of protection that is due from the sovereign' and 'the bond of subjection that is due from the subject'. And 'if this bond be once broken farewell sovereignty!'[162]

A moment of rhetorical splendour ruined by the king laughing again. After which, a visibly annoyed Bradshaw wandered back into the Old Testament. *Genesis* 9, to confirm how dreadful were 'all the bloody murders'. *Daniel* to revisit Nebuchadnezzar and his 'golden' idols. And finally *Samuel 2* and the repentance of King David, for having 'given cause to the enemies of God'. More heckling in the Hall. Still, they had got there, finally. Treason proved, and murder, for which there could only be one sentence.[163] Determined in law and scripture, prefigured in Ireton's *Remonstrance*. That 'Charles Stuart, as a tyrant, traitor, murderer and public enemy, shall be put to death by the severing of his head from his body'. Charles was removed from the court.

Royalist news-sheets making much of his 'heroic patience', as he was led past jeering soldiers.[164] Another nice line too, as he went: 'Poor souls, for a piece of money they would do so for their commanders.' Familiar enough to anyone who knew their *Matthew* 26:15. Judas and his 'thirty pieces of silver'. Meanwhile some more stiffening of resolves needed in the Painted Chamber, where the commissioners gathered to sign the death warrant. At least those who had not already absented themselves. Fifty-nine signatures in the end, after two days of not-so-gentle cajoling. There is an account, perhaps apocryphal, that Cromwell started flicking ink about to relieve tensions. More likely is another account, of him stood grimly by the table steadying hands; there are a lot of shaky-looking signatures.[165]

Reprise

The courts of Europe seemed stunned. The possibility of putting a king on trial was 'inconceivable', according to Mazarin.[166] The Scots sent down some commissioners to convey their discomfort. Some more turned up on the 26th, from the Dutch Estates-General, proposing that the trial might be adjourned to some kind of court of arbitration. A little late. Granted an audience on the 29th, they adjusted their request to a delay in execution of sentence. Too late. It has been wondered if Charles might, even now, have done something to save himself. If, that is, he was inclined. Some kind of 'mission' headed by the earl of Denbigh at the very end of December had been waved away.[167] No more 'twigs'. Stubborn to the end, but now heroically so. Sir Philip Warwick, Charles's personal secretary, would later report a king both resilient and tearful during these last days. Conscious, perhaps, of an appeal already underway, and a final performance that beckoned.

The king's book

An anonymous pamphlet entitled *Monumentum Regale*, which appeared a few weeks after the regicide, spoke to both. Charles 'the best of Kings, best of Divines … / Mirrour of Princes'.[168] A familiar metaphor too. In truth, royalist presses had started templating 'King Charles the Martyr' long before he walked out through the upstairs window at the Banqueting House on the afternoon of 30 January. Crucifixion shortly after lunch, resurrection by tea-time. The 'passion' of his 'Saviour's person'.[169] *A True Relation of the King's Speech to the Lady Elizabeth and the Duke of Gloucester, the day before his death*, was in circulation within hours. An 'abundance of tears' from the Lady Elizabeth, and some fighting talk from the young duke, promising to be 'torn in pieces' before he agreed to become king, ahead of his exiled brothers Charles and James.[170] Meantime, Rushworth's account of the scaffold speeches was already rolling off the presses. *A Handerkerchief for Loyal Mourners*, attributed to the later Dean of Worcester, Thomas Walmstry, was likewise available by 2 February.[171] A literary complement to the familiar custom. And an opportunity, indeed, for those unable to attend on the 30th to still feel part of the experience. A few weeks later appeared *A Deepe Groan Fetch'd at the Funerall of that Incomparable and Glorious Monarch, K.Charles I*, written by Henry King, bishop of Chichester; serving much the same purpose. An elegy, with some recommended reading: 'Then look / Upon his resurrection, his book: / In this he lives to us.'[172]

By which King meant the *Eikon Basilike: the Portraiture of His Sacred Majesty in His Solitudes and Sufferings*. Or the 'King's Book', as it became more popularly known.[173] Precisely when the *Eikon* hit the streets remains uncertain. Some have supposed that it was circulating later on the 30th; possibly in the hours before the execution.[174] First editions were printed and distributed by Richard Royston, of 'Ivie Lane'. Royston had form, having been charged with printing 'scandalous' books in 1645, and duly sent to the Fleet prison. He would be again, a few months later in 1649; on this occasion bound over 'not to print or sell any unlicensed or scandalous books and pamphlets'. Royston later claimed to have received the manuscript of the *Eikon* on 23 December; having been alerted to its existence as early as October. Which would have given him plenty of time; despite the obvious need for discretion. It seems probable that any version circulating on the 30th was an advance copy. To be followed by the revised, sold on the streets by hawkers. Royston later confirmed that this second issue, which sold out in a couple of days, ran to two thousand copies. A third issue was then distributed, most probably to trusted booksellers. George Thomason annotated a copy of this third issue for his collection, dated 9 February.

Authorship remains a matter of some controversy. At the Restoration, the newly appointed bishop of Exeter, John Gauden, was quick to assert a claim, suggesting that he had begun drafting the work as early as summer 1647. Hyde leant some credence. So too Dr Walker, in his *True Account of the Author of a Book, entitled Eikon Basilike*, published in 1692. Later editors of the *Eikon* have expressed greater caution. Christopher Wordsworth, younger brother of William, became mildly obsessed with the question of authenticity. In 1825 he published a text entitled *Who Wrote the Eikon Basilike?* Concluding that it was probably Charles, but with Gauden assuming editorial responsibilities.[175] Altogether more sceptical was Edward Almack, who edited an edition in 1904; dismissing Gauden's claim as nothing more than 'sycophancy'.[176] The quality of prose has led some to suspect the involvement of another Restoration Bishop, Jeremy Taylor. A protégé of Archbishop Laud and chaplain in ordinary to the king, Taylor is known to have been in London in autumn 1648.[177]

All of which leaves us to conjecture the extent of Charles's involvement. The later bishop of Winchester, Peter Mews, suggested that the king had already begun dictating reflections to Sir Edward Nicholas and his secretaries as early as summer 1645. He was certainly contemplating some kind of martyrdom. 'I have alreddy cast up what I am lyke to suffer,' he confided in early 1646, 'which I shall meete (by the grace of God) with the constancy that befits me.'[178] Mews, who was present at Naseby, suggested that early drafts of the *Eikon* had been seized with the king's Cabinet. One of the king's personal chaplains, Dr Gorge, attested the same; and that Charles was especially perturbed at the loss of the manuscript. It became commonplace to suppose that Charles had willed away his spare hours at Carisbrooke working on his testament. Colonel Hammond later confirmed that it was 'writ when he was my prisoner', having apparently discovered draft pages scattered about the king's chamber. William Levet, a groom of the bedchamber, likewise, having recovered a draft with the annotation 'Writ with his Majesty's own hand'.[179] The testaments came later of course, as did the conjectures regarding authenticity. Back in spring 1649, the inference was plain enough. The *Eikon* articulated the 'personal reflections' of the martyred king.

A perception reinforced by the famous frontispiece to the first edition. An engraving by William Marshall, inspired by Titian's *Saint Catherine of Alexandria*.[180] The king is seen kneeling in prayer, with three crowns; an earthly at his feet, a crown of thorns in his hand and his eyes fixed reverently on a heavenly crown which awaits.[181] Other versions of the *Eikon* would incorporate different images. But it is Marshall's engraving which inscribed itself on the memory of royalist England. Thereafter follow twenty-eight chapters; from the 'calling' of the king's 'last Parliament' in 1641 through to successive captivities at Holdenby and Carisbrooke. The final two chapters comprise a long letter to his son, Prince Charles, on how best to govern his kingdom, and some maudlin 'meditations' written in anticipation of his 'violent, sodaine and barbarous death'.[182] Above all, he advises the prince, be 'settled in your Religion', avoid 'exasperating any factions' and guard against the 'pretensions' of Reformation.[183] Well indeed.

Each chapter follows a similar pattern. A moment is recalled, a 'misery' or a 'misfortune', a betrayal perhaps, then a prayer offered in atonement. Plenty from which to choose. Chapter 2 revisits the execution of the 'unfortunate' Strafford, explained by the 'necessities of the time and the Temper of that People'. But still an act of 'sinful compliance', for which Charles offers up a suitably repentant prayer, and himself. A patent inference. Charles Stuart must atone for his own sins, and for those of 'his people'. 'Impute not me with the blood of my subjects', Charles prays, as he reflects on those who lost their lives in the 'unhappy war', but 'wash me with that precious blood which hath been shed for me by my great peacemaker, Jesus Christ'.[184] Not just a simple defence of the divine right of kings; though it is certainly that. For 'yet hath He graven such characters of divine authority and sacred power upon king as none may without sin seek to blot out'.[185] But a personal divinity. 'Thy Priest, Thy sacrifice'. Necessary for the redemption of a 'chosen' people momentarily astray. Charles as the martyred Christ. A 'parricide so heinous, so horrible, that it cannot be paralleled by all the murthers that ever were committed since the world began, but onely in the murther of Christ'.[186]

An irresistible parallel, to be refined for generations to come. Four months after the regicide, the bishop of Down and Connor published a sermon entitled *The Martyrdom of King Charles or, His Conformity with Christ in His Sufferings*. Trials so similar that 'it may seeme but … the Stage onely changed and new actors entered upon it'. 'Farre worse than Pilate', the bishop continued, are 'the Priests, Scribes and

Pharisees, who have lately murthered' their king. Men who 'thought fit to adde the mockery of justice, to the cruelty of malice (as they who crucified Christ) that so they might destroy him with the greater pompe'. All of which Charles suffered, as did Christ; 'so like his Saviour, when he was reviled he reviled not again; but was led like a sheep unto the slaughter, and opened not his mouth'.[187] A couple of years later the rabidly royalist Owen Feltham would make the same explicit in his *Epitaph to the Eternal Memory of Charles I*: 'Here Charles the First and Christ the Second lies'.[188]

The *Eikon* was not, then, written as a piece of early-day revisionism. Certainly it rewrote some of the past. But the greater purpose was to write the future. More particularly still to inspire a genre of Christological testament; to the trials of 'Charles the Martyr'. Gauden would later claim that 'In a word, it was an army, and did vanquish more than any sword could'.[189] Gauden had reason to oversell himself. But it is also clear that the authorities, back in early 1649, had reason to worry. A first print-run of the *Eikon* sold out in two days; a third within ten. And kept selling; thirty-five editions in circulation by the end of the year. And getting bigger. An edition published by William Dugard in March added some further accounts of the king's final days. Plus, four handy prayers which had been 'Delivered to Doctor Juxton, Bishop of London, immediately before His Death'. Not just a testament but a devotional manual for bereft royalists.[190]

And so it would continue throughout the 1650s, and beyond. Ever longer, ever saintlier, ever more lachrymose. And selling and selling. In time there would be editions in Dutch, Danish, French, German and Latin. Even a version put to music, another to verse.[191] Needless to say, it did better still at the Restoration. Royston produced a revised edition in 1681, with a new poem attributed to Charles entitled 'Majesty in Misery'. In time the *Eikon* and its various accretions would become the centrepiece of a grand folio edition of *The Works of King Charles the Martyr*, published in 1687. There would be rebuttals of course. Cook's *Case* was a pre-emptive strike. Too much jurisprudence though, and far too dull. The *Eikon* was a treatise on the aesthetics of kingship. We will, in the next chapter, take a closer look at how the authorities, in the person of one particular civil servant, tried to engage the *Eikon* on these terms. For now, though, we will close this chapter with a brief trip up to Yorkshire.

A comely head

To the relative tranquillity of Nun Appleton, nine miles south of the city of York, and just ten miles from Marston Moor; scene of the great parliamentarian victory in July 1644. The seat of the Fairfax family. It was to Nun Appleton that Sir Thomas retreated in late 1648, and then again eighteen months later. To recuperate and spend more time with his twelve-year-old daughter Mary. Ready now for the next stage in her education. Sir Thomas hired a young scholar with a rising reputation named Andrew Marvell. At the time putting the final touches to what has been appraised as the 'greatest political poem' in the English language.[192] Entitled *An Horatian Ode Upon Cromwell's Return from Ireland*, it was the first in a series of what are commonly termed Marvell's 'Cromwell poems'. Alongside which can be placed another set, written during his sojourn at Nun Appleton, the 'Fairfax poems'. A composite poem of life in republican England. And a lament. Before we take a closer look, we should pause to contemplate the context; of moment and author.

It became quickly apparent that no-one had really planned for a republic. The spring of 1649 had seen the rather haphazard passage of various statutes intended to regularize the situation. Mostly abolishing stuff, and rebranding what remained. Here again, we will take a closer look in the next chapter. Suffice to say that an awful lot of Englishmen and women felt thoroughly unsettled. Sir Thomas certainly. The trial and execution of a king, which he refused to sanction, the purging of a Parliament that he found 'horrible'. A country now 'languishing'. Much like him, 'distracted in his mind', as Burnet would later confirm.[193] Remaining in post for a while, as 'Captain-General', to lend the new regime some kind of credibility, but playing no active part. A nominal member of the newly established Council of State too. The Council, the members of which were approved by Parliament, was designed to fill the considerable gap in the constitution where the Crown used to be.[194]

Finally, in summer 1650, Fairfax gave up, declining to subscribe to the newly devised Oath of Engagement. The problem was not the declaration of fidelity to the Commonwealth. It was the presence of 'some particulars that looked back', as the similarly troubled earl of Denbigh put it.[195] Namely an affirmation of the 'Commonwealth of England, as it is now established without King or House of Lords'. An implicit approval of the regicide, which was especially concerning to those who had, only a few years before, subscribed to the Solemn League and Covenant. It had bound subscribers to do all in their power to secure the 'Honour and Happiness of the King'. The Engagement was not quite mandatory, but it was required of all those who aspired to hold public office. Or indeed go to court. The moment had come. In his resignation letter to Speaker Lenthall, Fairfax alluded to 'debilities both in body and mind'.[196]

Time to reflect, to tend to the roses, and his horses, and his daughter. Indulge some consoling poetry perhaps. Which is where Marvell also came in. Not an easy poet to read; for a reason. By his own admission 'naturally ... inclined to keep my thoughts private'.[197] Raised in a Calvinist family, educated at Cambridge, the young Marvell had spent the war abroad. Developing a love of the classics and a liking for cavalier poetry, Lovelace, Cowley. Fashionable, romantic, above all melancholy. In late 1648 he published *An Elegy Upon the Death of My Lord Francis Villiers*. Villiers had been killed during Lord Holland's fated uprising in Kent earlier that summer.

Entirely suited to poetic lament. Less heroic was the death of the nineteen-year-old Lord Hastings in summer 1650. Smallpox. But propitious all the same. Another scion struck down. Marvell contributed to a memorial collection entitled *Lachrymae Musarum*, published by Richard Broome.[198] Lament for a generation, and a creed.

Marvell probably felt the loss. But still there was a career to build, and alternatives. Which is why he ended 1650 at Nun Appleton, helping Mary conjugate her Latin verbs. And reflecting perhaps on the final drafts of his *Horation Ode*. Some context again. Cromwell's Ireland campaign, ventured on the pretext of suppressing a Confederate army raised by the earl of Ormonde. Not an immediate threat to the English republic, but it gave the New Model something to do. It also joined the longer regicide narrative. His Work, expiating blood-guilt. Most notorious were massacres at Drogheda and Wexford.[199] Reporting back to Parliament, Cromwell provided a simple, and familiar, reason. The 'righteous judgement of God, on these barbarous wretches, who have imbued their hands with so much blood'.[200]

And Marvell, it seems, more or less agreed. There is certainly nothing in the *Horatian Ode* which betrays much sympathy for the Irish: 'ashamed / To see themselves in one year tamed' (73–4).[201] And there is much that intones the same scriptural menace: ''Tis Madness to resist or blame / The force of angry Heaven's flame' (25–6). But there was a further inspiration. Rome. Not the Rome of the papists of course, but that of Horace and Virgil and Lucan, classical, republican, heroic, mostly.[202] Milton, as we will see, was similarly inspired; his 'Defences' of the English Republic littered with Roman generals. Contemplating the Roman republic necessitated some selective reading of course. It did not end well. The same was true of republican writings of more recent vintage. Machiavelli's *The Prince* for example. It too required a certain discretion.

They did, though, confirm something which pretty much everyone knew. The new Republic needed a strong leader, heroic ideally. And the mighty Cromwell slaughtering the Irish was something. Drawn from 'his private gardens, where / He lived reserved and austere' (29–30). Imbued with all the requisite republican virtues. Not least fidelity. A devoted servant to his country:

> How good he is, how just,
> And fit for highest trust.
> Nor yet grown stiffer with command,
> But still in the Republic's hand:
> How fit he is to sway
> That can so well obey. (79–84)

Victorious, he returns, and 'to the Commons' feet presents / A Kingdom for his first year's rents … / And has his sword and spoils ungirt, / To lay them at the Public's skirt' (87–90). Only to assume them once more, almost immediately. At that very moment, as Marvell is pouring over his scansion, Cromwell is assuming his position as the new commander-in-chief, and preparing to invade 'the Pict'. A miraculous victory at Dunbar will shortly follow. God's Englishman indeed. And yet. The ambiguities lurk; a 'Caesar' on the outside, a Machiavellian prince on the in?[203]

And the spectres. Back to autumn 1648. Charles Stuart at Carisbrooke. From:

> thence the royal actor borne
> The tragic scaffold might adorn:
> > While round the armed bands
> > Did clap their bloody hands.
> He nothing common did or mean
> Upon that memorable scene:
> > But with keener eye
> > The axe's edge did try:
> Nor called the gods with vulgar spite
> To vindicate his helpless right,
> > But bowed his comely head
> > Down as upon a bed.
> This was the that memorable hour
> Which first assured the forced power. (53–66)

A moving account, conspicuously so. Fully consonant with the dominant metaphor in contemporary royalist hagiographies; Charles as actor as well as martyr, the lead in the Passion recast. In his 'passion and manner of death' resembling nothing less than 'his great Master'.[204] Almost certainly inspired by the passage in Horace's 'Actium' *Ode*, in which the audience is drawn away from Octavian's brilliance to the tragedy of the defeated Cleopatra. And, very probably, by contemporary accounts of another beheading. That of the Marquis of Montrose, up in Edinburgh. The Marquis, it was reported, had carried himself with a 'comely' dignity.[205] Another lament.

Whether Marvell's verse betokens more than sympathy must be left to conjecture. Regret perhaps? The theatre consumes the moment; almost. The *Ode* does not touch directly on the legality of the king's trial. But it does cast an aspersion; a 'right' rendered 'helpless' before a 'forced power'. The same point made a few lines earlier:

> Though Justice Against Fate complain,
> And plead the ancient Rights in vain:
> > But those do hold or break
> > As Men are strong and weak. (37–40)

A dose of reality; Machiavelli again. Tears might be shed, but history moves on: 'To ruin the great work of time, / And cast the kingdom old / Into another mould' (34–6). A new state will be constructed, 'A bleeding head where they begun' (69).

The prickling leaf

And a lesson learned. In the months following the regicide Nedham published an essay entitled the *Case of the Commonwealth of England*. Not, as we have already noted, the most consistent of writers. But experience had taught him something. That the 'power of the sword is, and ever hath been, the foundation of all titles of government'.[206] Away in Paris, Thomas Hobbes was completing one of the most influential books in the history of modern political thought. And reaching pretty much the same conclusion. 'Covenants, without the Sword', readers of his *Leviathan* would discover, 'are but Words, and of no strength to secure a man at all'.[207] A sentiment, and a text, we will revisit. And a lesson for princes and prosecutors alike. No amount of 'divine right' theory was going to be much use against the 'force' of 'angry Heaven', properly equipped, well-shod, with muskets that fired in the rain. Neither were any metaphorical contracts.

Sadder and wiser, like, we can assume, most of his compatriots, Marvell moved on to quieter contemplations. The 'Fairfax poems', at first glance pastoral muses with an elevating theme, *Upon the Hill and Grove at Bilborough*, *Upon Appleton House*. Lots of foliage and reminiscing; 'oracles in oak' (*UHGB*, l.74). And some insinuations. *Appleton House* closes with a pointed allusion. The garden was neat enough. Outside though, a 'rude heap together hurl'd; / All negligently overthrown, / Gulfes, Deserts, Precipices, Stone' (772–4). Completed in 1651. Another year had passed, and England was still a mess. In his *Horation Ode*, Marvell had wondered the need of 'architects' to rebuild Jerusalem (69–70). Men indeed, like Sir Thomas. *Appleton House* has long been acclaimed as a defining expression of 'Protestant historiography'. Reaching back to the Reformation to emphasize the continuity of English history; despite all present appearances. And the stability lent by families such as the Fairfaxes. But maybe also to chide a little? Only half a day's ride away, the New Model is in camp at Ripon, preparing to invade Scotland. But Fairfax is pottering about his garden.[208] Which begs a pregnant question.

To which the simplest answer is weariness. The more interesting, though, is the 'prickling leaf' of 'conscience … /which shrinks at ev'ry touch' (357–8). An immediate allusion to the Oath of Engagement, perhaps. But maybe something more. Later that summer the anguished Fairfax, a bit of a poet himself, wrote a few lines in his commonplace book: 'Oh Lett that Day from time be blotted quit / … But if the Power devine permitted this / His Will's the Law and we must acquiesce'.[209] A terrible deed demanded by an irresistible God. As Marvell had surmised. Something for the pair to chat about, after a hard day pricking out. Along with early drafts of verses 69 and 70 of *Appleton House*. Which describe the felling of the 'tallest oak', made weak by a 'traitor-worm, within it bred' (551–2, 554). Not just an irresistible God then.

At some point in late 1652 Marvell departed Nun Appleton. Cromwell needed a new tutor for his ward William Dutton. The Duttons were monied and Cavalier, and young William was rumoured to be a prospective suitor to Frances, Cromwell's ninth and youngest daughter. Plenty of reasons for Marvell to accept. Back in London, Marvell wrote *To His Coy Mistress*, and met John Milton; an incongruous coincidence. They would become friends, Marvell taking up an appointment as Milton's personal secretary, working at the heart of government; both under the nominal authority of John Thurloe, secretary to the Council, in effect Cromwell's spymaster. The mildly satirical poem *The Character of Holland*, published in spring 1653, served as a kind of job application. After which Marvell proceeded to write a set of songs for the marriage of another of Cromwell's daughters, Mary. By then he was firmly part of the Cromwellian 'court', an unofficial laureate.[210]

In early 1655, Marvell would dutifully produce a cloying poem to celebrate a first year of Protectoral rule, entitled rather unimaginatively the *First Anniversary*. Six years now since the 'fertile Storm' of autumn 1648, which had culminated in the execution of Charles I. A metaphor of replenishment; of 'Waters' to 'Heal' England's devastated 'Commonweal'. Sprinkled with the successive despatch of the Rump and the 'Barebones' Assembly, and the establishment of the first Protectorate; events we will revisit very shortly. Not such a starring role for Charles in the *First Anniversary*. His brutal decapitation wound into the same metaphor. The 'storm' did 'wet the King' (237–8, 401–2).[211] Just a bit. We will leave Marvell now. A natural survivor, we will next encounter him carrying a piece of wood down Whitehall in late autumn 1658. And then again in the Restoration, rewriting history, and having a go at Sir Edward Hyde.

And revert to Nun Appleton. To which Lady Anne returned in 1650, when the theatres shut down and London started to get seriously dull. As for Mary Fairfax, her mind turned to matters of the heart. Or at least to wondering who her parents might have in mind as her intended. Ideally someone she quite liked.[212] But most importantly someone who might help to settle the fortunes of the family, financial and otherwise. Someone like George Villiers, 2nd Duke of Buckingham; Steenie's son. George and Mary married in 1657. It might seem a strange affinity, for the daughter of a revered parliamentarian general. It did to both Cromwell and Hyde. But not for the daughter of Lady Anne Fairfax, formerly de Vere.[213] There was something else too. Sir Thomas had acquired the sequestered Villiers estates. An acquisition which might now be future-proofed. A marriage of convenience, in every sense.

But also, it transpired, love. At least on Mary's part. Horace Walpole would later describe her as 'hopelessly in love'. And him as having the 'genius of Alcibiades'. Slippery, in other words. Dryden would later pay a sort of compliment to a 'man so various'.[214] Apparently very handsome, though, which might explain Mary's infatuation. Not that Lely managed to capture it. A podgy, rather worn duke peers out of the canvass, painted in 1675. Well past his best. Perhaps it was all the drinking and the whoring, and the endless squabbling. A predictably volatile political career awaited George in 1660. In the meantime, though, he did at least take the trouble of saying a few helpful things about his father-in-law when the authorities started to look about for some sacrificial 'regicides'. Though what mattered most perhaps, in that moment, was the fact that Fairfax had not actually signed the death warrant. Other prominent Parliamentarians had, as we will now see, been rather less circumspect. For them Restoration England would prove to be a rather more trying experience, in every sense.

4 MILTON'S WAR

FIGURE 4 Milton at his desk.

Oliver Cromwell died on 3 September 1658. An auspicious day. The anniversary of so many 'Triumphs', as *Mercurius Politicus* dutifully noted; the battle of Dunbar in 1650, Worcester the year after. Providence for sure. Though in case anyone was not paying close calendrical attention, the Lord visited a storm upon his 'chosen' people.[1] It was an age of portents, and prophecies. Not easy, though, on 3 September, to predict what might happen next. Oliver had been in his second spell as Lord Protector, his terms of office refined in the *Humble Petition and Advice* of May 1657. Amongst which was the responsibility of identifying a successor.[2] Something which, Hobbes would later suppose, made him an 'absolute monarch'.[3] Unlike the *Instrument of Government*, which had ushered in the first Protectorate in late 1653. It had declared that the office would be 'elective', a successor to be chosen by the Council of State.[4] Rather more redolent of January 1649.

Much though had happened over the intervening decade, and September 1658 was not a moment for constitutional nuance. There would be no 'election', by Parliament or anyone else. Neither would there be any kind of magisterial 'rotation', as recommended in texts such as Sir James Harrington's *Oceana*. Instead, eyes looked where they usually looked, down the bloodline. To the person of Richard Cromwell. Chosen, it was rumoured, by the dying Oliver. If so, an odd choice. Not just because it was the kind of things which kings did, and Oliver had decried the idea of being a king. But because he knew him. Richard was a pleasant chap, by all accounts close to his dad. But hardly kingly, in manner or inclination. He tried to sell himself as the 'Golden Mediocrity'; less pejorative then perhaps, but hardly stirring.[5] A 'peasant in his nature', Lucy Hutchinson concluded.[6] The royalist press took to calling him 'Tumbledown Dick'.[7] Dick lasted six messy months. The 'meer contingencie of a begetting', as John Milton termed it; precisely why magistracy should not be heritable.[8]

Back to September 1658, and the similarly pressing question of what to do about a funeral. The English Republic, in its various guises, had wrestled with related questions of ceremony and theatre ever since spring 1649. Puritan temper militated against both. But it was plain that the Republic, if it was to survive, would need to perform; a bit at least. It would need to carve out an aesthetic too. We will see what they came up with shortly. First, though, a more prosaic bit of carving. The funeral ceremonies for the now departed Oliver were based on those accorded King James I. Beginning with three weeks of lying-in-state at Somerset House. An opportunity for the paying public to come and pay their respects. The men at least. A darkened room, guarded by some suitably glum-looking Life Guards, with a coffin mounted in the centre. Upon which could be spied an effigy of the Lord Protector, wooden body, waxen face. Apparently a very good likeness.[9]

Matters of décor more generally were left to Mr Kinnersley, the Master of the Wardrobe. Who, as far as possible, stuck to the familiar template. The wooden Oliver was duly dressed in his robes of state, sceptre in one hand, orb in the other, an 'imperial crown' hovering above the head, on a golden chair. After a few days, the effigy was raised from prone to propped, and the crown placed on the head. The same elevation as that accorded to James I, intended to represent the passage of the body from Purgatory to Heaven. A bit Catholic though, as Ludlow observed. If hardly surprising, given that Kinnersley 'inclined to popery'.[10]

And then, on 23 November, a funeral procession. The 'joyfullest' that John Evelyn had ever seen, 'for there were none that cried but dogs'.[11] A seven-hour meander from Somerset House to Westminster. Where the effigy was propped up again. A final opportunity to pay some respects; and 2s 6d for a ticket. A chilly day. Sombre crowds carefully corralled by lines of New Model troopers, arms dipped. A bit of a to-do with the order of mourning. Custom suggested that plebs went to the front, followed by the servants of 'quality' and then the 'quality'. Needless to say everyone wanted to get as far to the back as they could. At the very back were the 'grandees'. The effigy was carried in an open chariot. Just behind which trooped Cromwell's favourite musicians and singers, intoning some appropriately mournful verse. Then came the versifiers. To include Andrew Marvell, John Dryden, Edmund Waller and Thomas Sprat. And John Milton. We can only wonder what Milton felt as he wandered along. More than likely, he shared the Quaker Edward Burrough's doubts; few more 'foolish' idolatries than sublimating before a wooden king. He might also have wondered the cost. The Venetian ambassador hazarded £100,000; which, if true, was twice the amount splashed on the funeral of James I.

As befitted the moment, the poets duly set about composing some appropriately earnest elegies. Waller and Sprat adopted a martial theme; all the battles. A more reflective tone could be discerned in those produced by Dryden and Marvell. A troubled, doubting Cromwell in Dryden's *Heroique Stanzas*. A troubled, doubting Marvell in *A Poem upon the Death of His Late Highness the Lord Protector*. 'I saw him dead', the mourning Marvell concludes, 'How much another thing, no more that man?' But also a 'Monarch', of the seas at least (247, 254).[12] Doubting perhaps, but at least Marvell gave it a go. Unlike Milton. Moved enough to join the others in their seven-hour stroll, but not in composing an elegy. This chapter is about Milton, and his resistance; to circumstance, and to temptation.

Back in 1652, he had written a suitably fawning sonnet *To the Lord General Cromwell*. Concerned by proposals for the tighter regulation of worship being presently considered by the Committee for the Propagation of the Gospel. Cromwell had saved England in the past: 'Guided by faith and matchless fortitude / To peace and truth thy glorious way has ploughed.' And must now do so again. Despatch the 'hireling wolves whose gospel is their maw' (3–4, 14).[13] And then continue the revolution. There was much to 'conquer still' (10). A hopeful tone. More difficult six years on. Cromwell as Lord Protector. A 'paper king', a disdainful Lucy Hutchinson called it. The 'ape of a king' which Milton's friend Robert Overton had anticipated back in early 1649. Hardly what, to borrow the Putney refrain, they had all 'fought for'.

It is the fact that Milton played along with the charade on the 23rd which intrigues. Not just for what it said about him, or indeed what it said about England in autumn 1658. But because of what it said about the enduring fictions of kingship and authority. The private body of Oliver Cromwell had been buried a month or so earlier, space found in a corner of the Chapel of Henry VII. Milton carried the 'public'. Wooden kings, like paper kings, had 'two bodies'. At least. For if the events of 23 November confirmed anything it was the possibility of a third, flitting about in the public imagination. The hardest of all to depose. The physical body of a king might be dismembered, the office abolished. But purging this imaginary king was much the more difficult. Milton spent much of his professional life in the endeavour, as polemicist and poet. And failed.

We will, in due course, encounter Milton in the service of the Republic, struggling with precisely this responsibility. We will also revisit the later Milton, in retreat, trying to make sense of the failure. In doing so we will encounter some of the most brilliant poetry in the English language. *Paradise Lost*, *Paradise Regained* and *Samson Agonistes*; an epic chronicle of a cause betrayed. The testament of a disappointed poet, and a disappointed God. Still resisting. We will start though with the younger Milton. Writing in the 1640s. The 'scribbling' age, as Prince Rupert famously termed it.[14] Hardly natural allies, but on this they agreed. Never had the moment for nurturing a revolution been quite so conducive.

A scribbling age

The English Reformation was supposed to achieve many things; not least the salvation of a 'chosen' people. It was not though supposed to stimulate violent revolution. Neither was it supposed to make more people write more; and certainly not tracts recommending the decapitation of the governor of the Church. But it did. We need, when considering the tragedy of Charles Stuart, to contemplate a coincidence of three revolutions: in Church, in state and in print technology. Martin Luther famously acclaimed the latter as a gift from God, the 'highest and extremist act of grace'.[15] Milton would say much the same, as we will shortly see. Not everyone was so sure though. Including, we might reasonably infer, Charles Stuart.

Paper combats

We might recall Charles stood on his hillock next to Nottingham castle in August 1642, clutching his sodden speech. Shakespeare would have noted the poignancy. He had placed uncomprehending princes in such places before. Richard Plantagenet on the battlements of Flint castle, wondering why providential intercession was so long in coming: 'For well we know no hand of blood and bone / Can gripe the sacred handle of our sceptre, / Unless he do profane, steal, or usurp' (3.3.79–81). God will shortly strike. Meantime, as Aumerle advises, he must 'fight with gentle words' (3.3.131). God never did strike, of course; at least not in the way that Richard might have hoped. And anyway, as Hobbes would famously confirm, words are never enough without the 'sword'. The bitter experience of civil war taught him this much. Words never end a war.

But they can start one. A couple of weeks after Charles's declaration in August 1642, Bulstrode Whitelock wrote home in tones which we might term revisionist:

> It is strange to note how we have insensibly slid into the beginnings of a civil war, by one unexpected accident after another, as waves from the sea, which have brought us this far, and scarce we know how, but from paper combats, by declarations, remonstrances, protestations, votes, messages, answers and replies, we are now come to the raising of forces.[16]

We might note a couple of things in Whitelock's letter. First the disingenuousness. Whitelock was not alone in trying to absolve himself of responsibility in summer 1642. We might recall Sir William Waller saying something similar; wondering who were his enemies. We also noted that Sir William knew exactly who they were. Just as Whitelock knew exactly why they had 'slid' into war. It was because of men like him, incessantly 'stirring'. Bulstrode was very much a man of 'words'. Fully attuned to living in a 'scribbling age'. If not always comfortable with the conversation.

Which could be variously prosaic and strange, exhilarating and terrifying. Millenarians anxiously awaiting the Second Coming. The Muggletonians had already spotted Him; in the person of Ludowick Muggleton. Guerilla gardeners too. Winstanley and his Diggers, shortly to be found wandering deepest Surrey, tearing down fences and planting in tubers. And telling people about it; 'drawn forth by the Spirit to write'.[17] 'True' Levellers, they called themselves. As distinguished from the other Levellers with their weird ideas of parliamentary democracy and voting rights. We might also recall Richard Baxter wandering the New Model camp after Naseby, noting with dismay all the radical pamphlets so 'abundantly dispersed' amongst the soldiery. Left 'to read when they had none to contradict them'. Thomas Edwards likewise, in his *Gangraena*, published in late 1646. The 'divers Pamphlets and some Sermons' of the sectaries, written to 'bring in Anarchy and confusion', and worse still 'Democracie'.[18] Even those who found it all wonderfully exhilarating, such as William Walwyn, admitted that there was a need to read cautiously in such 'warping times'.[19]

Much to discuss then. And a conversation which it had never been so easy to facilitate. Some statistics for emphasis. There were three newspapers in London 1641. Twelve months later there were fifty-nine. Nine hundred printed titles in

1640. Two thousand in 1641. Over three thousand five hundred in 1642.[20] So much to read. And so many readers. By 1640 the national literacy rate was upwards of 30 per cent. In London it was nearer 75 per cent. Parliament would act in 1643, issuing a new ordinance intended to address a 'want of politick regulation', and reinforce the regulatory powers of the Stationer's Company. Including the right to seize papers to be burned and presses to be 'defaced and made unserviceable'. Plenty of paper though, and easy enough to build another press. Technology militated against censorship, as did the moment. Pamphlets flew about, as Cuthbert Sydenham put it, like 'atomes in the air'.[21]

Which brings us to *Areopagitica*. Published in 1644, by a young scholar with a growing reputation for radical anti-prelatical writings. The title alluded to the Areopagus, a rocky outcrop in Athens, and a place where free expression was deemed sacrosanct, literally.[22] The author was, of course, John Milton. And his essay, in defence of the 'love of truth', has assumed a foundational place in the history of modern liberalism. The closer context was the establishment of the regulatory regime just noted, in 1643. The *Ordinance for the Regulation of Printing*, which granted the Stationer's Company reinvested licencing powers, along with the quasi-judicial authority to destroy presses and arrest unlawful distributors. Something which could only inhibit the spread of the Word. Milton thought as Luther thought. The printing press was the 'trumpet of reformation to all Europe'.[23] Liberty and godliness, hand in hand. Plenty of similarly pithy lines, to similar purpose. None perhaps more renowned than 'He who destroys a good book, kills reason itself, kills the image of God'.[24] Another to follow. The attempt to suppress free expression, and conscience, likened to 'the exploit of the gallant man who thought to pound up crows by shutting his park-gate'.[25]

It was never, of course, a licence to print anything. Even Milton drew a line. More precisely at 'popery, and open suspicion'.[26] Milton's uncompromising hostility towards Catholicism might seem odd today, almost unthinking. But it was not. He thought very hard, appreciating that liberty needs to be secured.[27] And identified the greatest threat in the Catholic 'inquisition'. Even if the immediate threat was closer to home, in the shape of the Presbyterian 'peace' party in the Commons, and their *Ordinance*. Purposed not just to quieten civil unrest and political opposition, but to regulate consciences. And to stop people like Milton from publishing strange essays. Such as those which he was presently publishing on the subject of divorce. We will take a closer look at these very shortly; for within them can be discerned the seeding of a regicide brief.

In August 1644, Milton found himself hauled before a Commons committee. To answer some challenging questions. Not just about his essays on divorce but about some equally strange essays on the subject of Church governance. More on them too very shortly. For now, we might notice who else was brought before the same committee. On his part, to explain quite what he meant by a text entitled *Man's Mortality*; which seemed to contest the existence of the soul.[28]

The author of this text was Richard Overton. Amongst his later works could be counted the *Remonstrance of Many Thousand Citizens*, written in support of his close friend John Lilburne in 1647. But perhaps the most notorious of Overton's writings, in that near-moment, were the *Martin Marpriest* pamphlets. A series of vicious anti-Presbyterian satires, which appeared a year earlier. Amongst which could be found *The Arraignment of Mr Persecution*, a dramatized trial of all things Presbyterian. Chief amongst charges laid against 'Mr Persecution' is his determination to censor 'the mouthes of all good men'.[29] Written from bitter experience.

The extent of Overton's creative contribution to the *Marpriest* pamphlets, as opposed to the editorial, remains uncertain. As indeed does his relation with Milton. Different in many ways. Overton a paid-up member of the Windmill 'tribe'; as Prynne sneeringly termed it. Quill on one hand, mug of ale in the other. Milton preferring quiet evenings at home immersed in Livy and Lucan. What they had in common mattered more though. A belief in liberty of conscience. 'Stand fast therefore in the liberty wherewith Christ hath made us free, and be not entangled again with the yoke of bondage.' *Galatians* 5:1; a shared favourite. In time, this passion would mutate, aligning religious liberty with civil; the 'quarrel' which, as Cromwell would aver, 'was at the first'.[30] We have already come across some remarkable expressions. In myriad Leveller tracts, at the Putney and Whitehall Councils, in Westminster Hall in January 1649. A king impeached for breaching the 'liberties' of his subjects.

We might recall another name, another scribbler. Who likewise found himself embroiled in the *Marpriest* affair. Marchamont Nedham, the original hack for hire.[31] We come across Marchamont editing the Naseby 'Cabinet' in summer 1645. A year later writing for the royalist *Mercurious Elencticus*, working alongside George Wither. A couple of years on, back in the pay of Parliament, editing *Mercurius Politicus*. And promising its readers something a little different. The

> design of this pamphlet being to undeceive the people, it must be written in a jocular way, or else it will never be cried up: for those truths which the multitude regard not in a serious dress, being represented in pleasing popular airs, make music to the common sense, and others the fancy, which ever sways the sceptre in vulgar judgement, much more than reason.

Why, Nedham wondered, 'should not the Commonwealth have a Fool as well as the King had?'[32] Different ways to tell the truth. In 1655, Marchamont would be formally recruited into the Protectoral civil service, working for Thurloe, his skills at swaying 'vulgar judgement' properly appreciated. Working alongside Milton indeed. They became friends apparently. We might imagine a few serious conversations on the subject of authorial integrity. Now, though, back to the early 1640s and the younger Milton, venting his spleen against all things 'popish'.

Casting down imaginations

A fierce set of anti-Laudian tracts, published in 1641 and 1642; *Of Reformation, Of Prelatical Episcopacy, Animadversions, Reason of Church Government* and *Apology for Spectymnus*. Reinvesting the familiar image of a nation on crusade, entrusted with a divine 'Precedencie' to 'be the first Restorer of Buried Truth'. God 'hath ever had this island under the special indulgent eye of his providence'.[33] More closely, Milton confuted the writings of Joseph Hall, bishop of Norwich, whose *Episcopacy by Divine Right Assured* we encountered in an earlier chapter, and James Ussher, archbishop of Armagh. 'Imposters' both, representative of 'universall rottenness' in the Church.[34] Two particular themes. First, the corruption of Church and state, as evidenced not just in the events of the 1630s, or indeed the kind of stuff that Hall and Ussher were writing, but in a century of frustrated Reformation. And second, the defence of the 'Word' against those who would have it silenced or corrupted. The 'fierce encounter', as Milton termed it, 'of truth and falsehood'.[35]

Which demanded a dual strategy; of casting down and building up. We have come across this 'encounter' before, in the mind of William Prynne. The extent to which Prynne's 'case' turned Milton towards godliness remains a matter of conjecture. It is certainly possible to read allusions into his 1637 poem *Lycidas*. Milton would become a very different kind of puritan, of course. But they did share an abiding passion. For England, the 'Nation, chos'n before any other', and its Reformation.[36] Which meant, also, a common strategy: the casting down. Here again we have already come across physical manifestations. Lady Davies and her kettle, Henry Sherfield and his stick. Hall recorded similar, when parliamentary commissioners turned up at Norwich Cathedral in late 1641: 'Lord, what work was here! What clattering of glasses and beating down of walls! What tearing up of monuments! What pulling down of seats!' Hall was appalled. Not Milton though. The 'damned blast' of an angry God.[37] 'Tearing up' was not just a preference. It was a duty. Like many puritan window-smashers, Milton liked to cite 2 *Corinthians* 10:5. For the 'Casting down imaginations, and every high thing that exalteth itself against the knowledge of God'.

Where the factional differences became evident was in the manner of reconstruction. For Prynne it meant a Presbyterian reformation of the English Church. For Milton, it meant getting rid of the word 'the'. In the place of the Church, there would be myriad churches and congregations. Limits of course. There could be no freedom of conscience for papists, as we have already noted. But the principle was otherwise defining. And not simply for spiritual reasons. Liberty of conscience could not be sensibly distinguished from liberty of political expression. A cause commonly held amongst independent congregations of various theological and political hue. For Lilburne, a member of John Duppa's East End Baptist congregation, it meant simply this; the 'voluntary profession of faith'.[38]

And the liberty to publish weird stuff. Nothing perhaps weirder than the subject of Milton's next set of essays, on the subject of marriage.

Four in sum, published between August 1643 and early 1645; in sequence, the *Doctrine and Discipline of Divorce*, the *Judgement of Martin Bucer*, *Tetrachordon* and *Colasterion*. All bad, the first being probably the most shocking.[39] Partly because it was about divorce, but mainly because it was about doctrine and discipline, addressed to the recently established, and Presbyterian-dominated, Westminster Assembly of Divines. In simple terms, Milton recommended what would become known as 'companionate' marriage, with 'no-fault' divorce. At least a couple of centuries before his time.[40] An idea born, it is commonly surmised, of bitter experience. Milton had married his first wife, Mary Powell, in June 1642. Aged just sixteen, Mary was nine years younger than her new husband. And had left the marital home in London after just a month; not given, it was later surmised, to a 'philosophical life'. And not given to return either, at least not anytime soon.[41]

A spur for sure. But not the only reason why Milton decided to publish his thoughts on matrimonial law. The divorce tracts were also a strategic intervention in the same critical conversation, about the reach of Church 'discipline'; albeit from a rather more particular, and peculiar, direction. And a strategic reflection on something else, too. A legal instrument which would, a few years later, assume still greater import in a very different circumstance. Marriage as a contractual relationship, a 'private Covenant'. Which might, in particular circumstances, be breached and voided.[42] And which, most importantly, was governed by laws designed by human hand. We might ponder the sub-title of the *Doctrine and Discipline of Divorce* which continued: *Restor'd to the Good of Both Sexes, From the Bondage of Canon Law, and other mistakes, to Christian freedom, guided by the Rule of Charity, Wherein also many places of Scripture, have recover'd their long-lost meaning: Seasonable to be now thought on in the Reformation intended*. Anti-prelatical politics in the home.

And not much approved. The Commons ordered their seizure and destruction, at Prynne's urging. Precisely what the new *Ordinance* was for. In another moment, Milton might have found himself pilloried, imprisoned perhaps. Not in this though. Reputation intact, enhanced even, he carried on writing. A short essay entitled *Of Education*, composed as an open letter to his friend Samuel Hartlib. A primer for future puritans, those especially who will 'assume the offices both private and publicke of peace and war'.[43] Lots of Latin being the key. Back in 1638, the young Milton had embarked on a tour of Italy, dining with cardinals and assorted men of letters in the Umbrian sun. Rome had not always been the seat of the Anti-Christ. It had, in more distant times, been the 'lodge of humanity and of all polite learning'.[44] Milton lost lots of things over the coming three decades, but not his love of the classics. Following his essay on education came a collection of 'republican' poems published in 1645. An intensification of hostilities against a familiar foe: 'New Presbyter is but old Priest writ large.'[45]

A theme for the nearer future. Finding expression, a little later, in a sonnet to Fairfax, probably written in the aftermath of Colchester. A 'nobler task awaites thy hand', the Lord General is advised, to purge the land of 'Avarice & Rapine' and restore 'Public Faith'; against the 'Public Fraud' of the parliamentary Presbyterians.[46] It would not, though, be the wearying Fairfax. Someone else would do the purging. The restoration of 'public faith' likewise. A coming clerisy of republican intellectuals, versed in the classics, speaking its languages. Literally. Which brings us to the next stage in the career of John Milton.

Chosen

In early 1649, the new Republic found itself in need of a secretary for Foreign Tongues. In effect, a kind of permanent secretary to the Foreign Office.[47] A particular job-spec, requiring a proven polemicist of unimpeachable political credentials, also fluent in Latin, Italian and Spanish, the languages of the gentleman scholar and diplomat. There were other candidates. It is thought that Selden might have been approached. But Milton was the stand-out, his candidature likely supported by both Bradshaw and Whitelock. Acquaintances both, Milton would later eulogize Bradshaw as a name 'commended' by 'liberty herself'.[48] Appointed in April, the position came with a nice set of rooms in Whitehall, a decent stipend, of £288 13 6 pa, and an oddly imbalanced in-tray. Some diplomacy. Milton was charged with 'settling of amity and good correspondence with foreign kingdoms and states'.[49] And a lot of marketing. Somehow explaining away the 'woeful bloody spectacle' of the king's execution.[50] Selling the idea of an English Republic, home and abroad.

Milton's brief

The Republic had arrived, as we have already noted, in a bit of a muddle. These were 'doubtfull, staggering times', as one Leveller petition put it.[51] Congratulatory missives lent some reassurance. They had executed a 'desperate ignorant Roman', the 'well-affected' of Newcastle confirmed.[52] Whilst, at the same time, adding to the sense of spiralling excitement. Whitelock would recall inviting Ireton and Cromwell to supper in the weeks after the regicide, where they 'discoursed together' until midnight, and 'told many wonderful observations of God's providence'.[53] Major Francis White likewise detected a 'shaking the heavens', the 'throwing downe the Thrones and Dominions of the wicked powers of the world, to make way for the Kingdome and Dominion which shall have no end'. Less sure about the execution of the king though. Hardly in the 'Christian spirit', the Major observed. Unconvinced, moreover, that there was any 'legal authority' that 'can justly do it'. The 'military power is exalted above the regal and legislative power, and is now come to the throne of God, and under no other legal judgement'.[54] The rule of law bothered Major White.

It bothered Lilburne too. The absence of a 'balancing power … against the Army'. 'All legal authority in England now broken', a murderous king deposed by a murderous junto.[55] Not obvious how it might end. John Owen had an indication though. Invited to preach to the Commons the day after the regicide, Cromwell's favourite chaplain concentrated on matters of planning:

> As the days approach for the delivery of the decree, so the shaking of Heaven and Earth, and all the powers of the World, to make way for the establishment of that Kingdom which shall not be given to another people … must certainly grow.[56]

The execution of the king was merely the prelude to something so much greater. A week later Joseph Salmon preached to the army in similar tones. Theirs was a 'Commission from the Lord', and they must act 'fully, hotly, sharply'. The 'time draws near that is allotted'.[57] The Lord was Coming, and He would not wait.

Much to be done then, and quickly. Starting with some more throwing down of the wicked. On 3 February, the High Court was reconvened to try the duke of Hamilton, the earls of Holland and Norwich, Lord Capel and Sir John Owen; all implicated in the rebellions of the previous year. Norwich and Owen were reprieved, the others executed on 9 March. A 'new piece of butchery', Hyde recorded.[58] A messy start. Meanwhile the 'King's Book' was rolling off the presses. And pilgrims started turning up at the king's burial site at Windsor; which nobody had thought to shut. And praying before portraits of the king; which nobody had thought to make illegal.

As spring unfolded, there would be some necessary statutory reforms, designed to affirm the legitimacy of the new regime.[59] An *Act for the Abolishing of Kingly Office*, passed on 17 March. Being 'unnecessary, burdensome and dangerous to the liberty, safety and public interest of the people'. Evelyn was prosaic: 'Un-kingship proclaimed.'[60] Followed, two days later, by an Act establishing a 'Commonwealth and Free State' in its stead. And an Act declaring the House of Peers to be likewise 'useless and dangerous', and abolishing it. No immediate need to do anything about the Church, the roots of which had already been hacked away. The High Commission abolished in 1641, the Common Prayer Book replaced by a Directory of Worship in 1645. The episcopacy long since purged, church buildings repurposed. St Paul's converted to cavalry barracks, Lichfield Cathedral into a prison, St Asaph's a wine outlet. What remained of the established Church would, to stretch the metaphor, be allowed to wither on the vine. A calculated neglect. Replicated in regard to various mooted legal reforms. Nearly all of which could be politely ignored.

It fast became apparent that the Rump was disinclined to do anything particularly fast. Partly out of fear. Sir Henry Vane reported that his parliamentary colleagues were 'now in a far worse state than ever yet they had been', most living in daily apprehension 'that the whole kingdom would rise and cut their throats upon the first occasion; and that they knew not any place to go unto to be safe'.[61] The Levellers were an ongoing concern. Lilburne railed against the 'factious' company sat in Westminster, and insinuated that the time might have come for another revolution. *England's New Chains Discovered* was in circulation by the end of February, *The Second Part of England's New Chains Discovered* a month later. The king might be gone but not 'the old arbitrary and tyrannical' laws. The 'designes' of 'this Faction of Officers' had become only too apparent. Duly arrested and brought before the Council of State to answer charges of sedition, Lilburne arrived in time to hear Cromwell prepping those inside:

> If you do not break them, they will break you; yea, and bring all the guilt of the blood and treasure shed and spent in this Kingdom upon your heads and shoulders; and frustrate and make voide all that worke, and with so many yeares industry, toile and paines you have done, and so render you to all rationall men in the world, as the most contemptiblest generation, of silly, low spirited men in the earth, to be broken and routed by such a despicable contemptible generation of men as they are.[62]

Lilburne was duly carted off to await yet another treason trial, later in the summer, at the Guildhall.

And enjoy a spectacular acquittal. Brandishing his trusty copy of Coke's *Institutes*, Free-born John would stand in the dock and appeal to the 'righteous God of heaven and earth against you'. At just the moment a large part of the courtroom collapsed in. The jury was impressed.[63] As, presumably, were the five hundred women who descended on Westminster on 23 April, with a petition in support of Lilburne and other imprisoned Levellers. When one MP remarked that it was strange to see women petitioning, he was met with the rejoinder, that 'it was strange that you cut off the King's head, yet I suppose you will justify it'. They returned on 5 May, claiming an 'equal interest in the Kingdome, with the men of this nation in those liberties and securities contained in the *Petition of Right*'.[64] Probably not what Coke had in mind.

Small wonder, then, if the Rump was a little anxious. Accosted by gangs of uppity women, terrified by rumours of royalist hit-squads wandering the streets, radical regiments on the edge of mutiny and Him likely to arrive any day.[65] Whilst not much could be done about Him, or it seemed the women, there was a something that could be done about the New Model. Despatched on an extended crusade across the British Isles. Starting at the Promised Land of St George's Hill in Surrey, with the swift despatch of Winstanley and his 'diggers', caught planting 'parsenipps, carretts and beanes'. Then off to Ireland to wreak some divine vengeance along the south-east coast, before marching up to Scotland and destroying another Covenanter army at Dunbar in 3 September 1650.

In a *Declaration* issued a few weeks earlier, the 'English Army now in Scotland' attested itself 'powerfully convinced' that it was still working to the 'Lord's purpose'. A year earlier it had 'carried forth … justice upon the King, that man of blood'.[66] Now it would do the same to the Scots. A year to the day later came the battle of Worcester. There could be no greater 'testimony', republican England was surely blessed. Except that it still seemed to need some convincing. Which brings us back spring 1649, Milton and marketing. An official *Declaration of the Parliament of England* appeared in early February, playing heavily on the theme of a trust broken. Cook's *Case* appeared at much the same time; the 'work of God upon my own spirit'.[67] And then, on 13 February, an essay entitled *The Tenure of Kings and Magistrates*.

Conceived in the frenetic weeks which preceded the trial of the king, the *Tenure* was Milton's first 'defence' of the coming Republic. And, despite the heat of the moment, perhaps his calmest. A draft of the *Tenure* was in private circulation as the trial of the king unfolded. Whilst Milton had no direct role in the proceedings, it is reasonable to suppose that his essay would have been received as a kind of *amicus* brief. Set against a backdrop of increasingly frenetic appeals to save the king. Whether the *Tenure* was written in response to any more particular event remains a matter of conjecture. The appearance of William Prynne's *A brief memento to the present unparliamentary junto* in early January possibly. Milton cannot resist a disdainful comment on his old adversary's 'barking monitaries and mementos'.[68] As is the appearance, at much the same time, of Gauden's *Religious and Loyal Protestation*. It is quite possible that he was also aware of a draft version of the *Eikon Basilike*, shortly to take the publishing world by storm. Milton knew what was pending; an appeal in the case of 'King Charles the Martyr'.

Which would require something more than the prosaic reason provided, a little later, in his *History of Britain*; regicide being 'the only effectual cure of ambition that I have ever read'.[69] There would need to be deeper foundations, in scripture and jurisprudence. Expediency alone could not determine the 'tenure' of a king or a magistrate. Still less their execution. There had to be principle, and precedent. Which meant a repeat appearance for plenty of familiar tyrants, biblical and classical. And plenty of familiar historians. Such as Seneca, the great defender of depositions, in whose opinion 'no sacrifice to God was more acceptable' than that of a tyrant king.[70] And George Buchanan, author of *De Jure Regni apud Scotus*, a piece of 'mirror' literature written to impress upon young princes of the necessity of ruling within the law. We came across Buchanan before, tutor to the young James Stuart. Milton was a fan, probably more so than James.[71] And John Knox. A little trickier. Not because of the blunt misogyny discovered in Knox's *The first blast of the trumpet against the monstrous regiment of women*. Milton was no keener on princesses than he was princes. The problem with Knox was the militant Presbyterianism. The *Tenure* opened with a pointed assault on those 'dancing divines' who had voiced their opposition to the trial of the king. Who had 'juggl'd and palter'd' to the bitter end.[72]

As to the narrative flow of the *Tenure*. First a commentary on monarchy, and its misunderstandings. The idea that a king might be chosen by 'divine right' is treated with contempt. Dependent upon unthinking 'blind affections'.[73] If 'men within themselves would be govern'd by reason', and knew their Old Testament, they would also know that 'all men naturally were born free, being the image and resemblance of God himself'. And that an 'autoritie and power of self-defence and preservation' was 'originally and naturally in every one of them'.[74] It might then be covenanted away, but never entirely. Rather it would be placed in the 'trust' of a sovereign, who must govern in accordance with the law. Held in 'tenure'. In effect, Milton's foundation myth. He would say much the same a few months later in a second essay on the regicide, *Eikonoclastes*. It is 'absurd to think that the Anointment of God, should be as it were a charme against Law'.[75] The place of the king 'under' the law is confirmed in the 'ancient Books' of the common law. In Bracton and Fortescue and then, more recently, in texts such as Sir Thomas Smith's *Commonwealth of England* and Coke's *Institutes* and *Reports*.

And, at a variant, in Aristotle. Whose idea of a 'commonwealth' chimed readily with that of a 'common law'. Milton strove mightily to make Aristotle an early-day contractarian. Whose writings might, if read correctly, justify the trials of tyrant kings:

> It being thus manifest that the power of Kings and Magistrates is nothing else, but what is only derivative, transferr'd and committed to them in trust from the People, to the Common good of them all, in whom the power yet remaines fundamentally, and cannot be tak'n from them, without a violation of thir natural birthright.[76]

Otherwise a subject is nothing more than the 'King's slave, his chattel'. The reference to 'trust' is definitive. A contract might have allowed parties to adjust terms and conditions. A cunning king might even persuade his subjects to contract away certain rights. But this cannot be. Power can only be held on 'trust', bound by oaths of engagement. Which led neatly back to matter of deposition; the consequence of breaching 'trust'. As both scripture and the common law again confirm, 'if the King or Magistrate prov'd unfaithfull to his trust, the people would be disingag'd'.[77]

Which, Milton reassures his readers, is precisely what happened in the case of Charles Stuart. His guilt proved by the 'Victory' given by 'the Sword of God'. A 'precedent' moreover for all protestant peoples, of what can be justly done with an 'unbridl'd Potentate or Tyrant'.[78] Milton ventures a little further. And so, it 'follows' that 'since the King or Magistrate holds his authoritie of the people, both originaly and naturally for their good in the first place, and not his own, then may the people as oft as they shall judge it the best, either choose him or reject him, retaine him or depose him'. Even indeed, if he be 'no Tyrant, merely by the liberty and right of free born Men, to be govern'd as seems to them best'.[79] Resonances, not just of covenants and 'elective' magistracy, but Putney and 'liberty', and incipient democracy. Milton was hardly a democrat, but there was a logic.

The *Tenure* appeared a fortnight after the execution of Charles Stuart. An opening rebuttal in what would be a long engagement.[80] Suggestive, too, of the vying intellectual pressures which would eventually shape the emergent Republic; appeals to classical and Venetian models, along with remembrances of a 'good old cause' and a 'chosen' people directed by the Hand of God. Precisely the same tensions could be found in Marvell's poetry, in treatises such as Harrington's *Oceana*, which would appear in 1656, and Nedham's various editorials. It was not going to be easy to bring all this together, along with all the practicalities of governing England without a king. In the end it would prove impossible.

Meantime, more enemies to engage, on all sides. Within weeks of taking office as the secretary of Foreign Tongues, Milton was instructed to compose a rebuttal to Lilburne's *New Chains*. He never did. A few months later, Lilburne published another tract with a similarly pointed title, *An Impeachment of High Treason Against Oliver Cromwell*. Still Milton declined to engage. Distractions, maybe scruples too.[81] Instead he focused his attention on completing a defence of the pending Irish campaign, *Observations upon the Articles of Peace Made and Concluded with the Rebels*. Lots of dreadful 'papists' deserving of divine vengeance, and the fury of the New Model. And then, as summer wound on, rumours of a text about to be published entitled *Defensio Regia pro Carolo I*, authored by a French scholar named Claudius Salmasius. Commissioned by the exile court, for a fee of £100. It would need a response. And there was still something to be done about the *Eikon Basilike*, edition after edition of which was rolling off royalist presses. Plenty to keep the new secretary usefully busy.

Subtle dissimulation

The authorities had quickly recognized the threat that the *Eikon* posed. Cromwell summoned the printer Royston to the Whitehall, for some not-so-gentle persuasion; hoping that he would disavow the idea that the *Eikon* was 'written' by the martyred king. Royston apparently refused and was imprisoned for his impertinence. Meantime hawkers could be chased around the streets, shops raided. New ordinances, too, prohibiting the printing and distribution of 'unlicensed, scandalous and seditious books'. In September, the Council issued one against 'spreaders of false and seditions news, lyes and rumours', replete with the customary powers to issue fines, and even arrest and imprison persistent offenders.[82] Not just authors and printers but also readers. Fines of 20 shillings for any found in possession, magistrates authorized to 'grant warrants for searching of Packs and Packets'. Bullying and harrying, though, could only do so much.

Combat would need to be renewed. Of the 'paper' variety; print against print. Or, more precisely, the Word against the word. A measured presence in jurisprudential texts, such as Cook's *Case* and Milton's *Tenure*. More manic in the printed sermons of fiery millenarians, predicating the Second Coming and the ready despatch of the 'horned Beast'. Chapter 11 of the *Book of Revelations* proved a predictably popular recourse: 'The kingdoms of this world have become the kingdoms of our Lord, and of his Christ' (11:15). Useful, unless of course Charles was Christ. In which case Parliament started to look like the 'horned' Beast. And anyway rather limiting. Preaching to the converted, literally. Catching the attention of a broader audience would require something different, and more nuanced.

Nedham's *Mercurius Politicus* embarked on a crash-course in the virtues of republicanism. Alighting, like many, on the apparent success of the Venetian republic. George Wither joined the chorus of appreciation. Noting more especially that the Venetians had 'by long experiment / Found' that their 'great Body never want a Head / That's visible'.[83] A twist here, though. Not easy casting that head, 'visible' or other; fashioning an ascetic aesthetic. Lilburne would later confess the difficulty of engaging the 'Craftsmen', without doing a bit of crafting. The 'wicked art of flattery'.[84] So would Milton, as we will shortly see, endeavouring to write 'dramatick' histories with all the usual 'mummeries' and 'gay shewes' stripped out.[85] A prosaic truth here. The citizens of the newly minted Republic needed some 'shewes'. The only question was how 'gay'.

A few baubles might be a start. So a new coat of arms, St George's cross alongside the Harp of Erin. Some necessary re-labelling too. Thus the Court of King's Bench became the Court of Upper Bench. A new Great Seal, re-inscribed to read 'In the First Year of Freedom by God's Blessing Restored 1648'.[86] The image of the king replaced, rather optimistically it might be thought, with that of the Rump in animated debate. And nothing wrong with a few military parades, when the opportunity arose. Celebrations of God's work. Such as the slaughter of the Irish in summer 1649, worth an *Horatian Ode* and some serious cannonade. And the battle of Worcester, celebrated in some style a year after. Two days of New Model regiments marching up and down Hyde Park and Piccadilly, with a subdued chorus of manacled Scottish prisoners bringing up the rear. Presented, in the words of *The Weekly Intelligencer*, 'to shew the Cavaliers a true copy of their Kings countenance, in his gallant designe to over-runn the Nation at once with Barbarism and Tyranny'.[87] The triumphs of another Caesar; demanding though, of a discerning eye. And some discerning poetry.

Less discerning perhaps was Wither's *British Appeals*, which arrived that same summer. A rather brusquer defence of 'Publick Justice; in a Publick place'. Which might now, Wither surmised, be smartened up a bit. A palace 'new model'd out' and 'duly beautifi'd / With Gardens, walks, and with what els, beside'. Open to a discriminating public. Which meant 'No little children in the garden sprawling', no 'bakers boy' and no milkmen leaving their 'milk pails' lying about, nor anything else 'To offend the eye, / Or smell, no dung, or sinks'.[88] The Rump, predictably, never got around to it. But Cromwell did. A spruced-up Whitehall became his official residence in late 1653. Fit for a king, John Evelyn grudgingly admitted, if only England had one.

Back in 1649, though, the priority was the *Eikon*. A first rebuttal appeared at the end of August. Entitled *Eikon Alethine*, or 'truthful image', it promised its readers an alternative 'portraiture' of the events of the previous winter 'wherein the false colours are washed off'. The 'King's Book' was not in fact written by Charles at all. But by a 'presumptuous priest', in tones of 'effeminate Rhetorick'. The identity of the author of the *Eikon Alethine* remains a matter of conjecture. The Council had again approached Selden to write something. But he declined. So, instead, it had turned to Milton. More obliging; though not the author of the *Alethine*. Milton's repost would take a little longer. *Eikonoclastes* appeared in September. His second, and very different, defence of the Republic. Same brief, written to persuade those still coming to terms with the execution of Charles Stuart that there was a 'safer interest in the common friendship of England, than in the ruins of one ejected Family'.[89] But a very different strategy. And tone. The *Tenure* was tempered, written in aid of a Republic under construction. *Eikonoclastes* was personal and vicious, written to destroy an enemy who simply refused to die.

We will start at the beginning. With Milton alluding to the events of the previous January:

> And he who at the Barr stood excepting against the form and manner of his Judicature, and complain'd that he was not heard; neither he nor his Friends shall have that cause now to find fault; being met and debated with in this op'n and monumental Court of his own erecting; and not onely heard uttering his whole mind at large, but answer'd.[90]

A prescient metaphor. Presaging a painstaking counter-narrative of the events depicted in the 'King's Book'. There was room for aspersion of course, not least in regard to the authenticity of the *Eikon Basilike*. And some familiar arguments about the justification for removing unwanted kings. The usual suspects, Ahab, Nimrod, Herod, Nero, Caligula. The message was plain enough, proved by scripture. Kings had been deposed before, rightly and with God's blessing. Here again, though, the tone was sharper. In seeking to sanctify the person of his 'sacred' majesty, the *Eikon Basilike* had committed an abomination.

Thus the linguistic violence.[91] Charles Stuart was not just misguided or badly counselled. He was a bloodthirsty, papist zealot, a 'Tyrant' whose 'deepest policy' had 'bin ever to counterfeit Religion'. The reader is reminded of Charles's fraught embassy to Spain in 1623, in the hope of securing marriage to the Infanta; a shameful 'madding'. And then there is the princess he did eventually marry, Henrietta Maria. Rather than convert his wife to Protestantism, Charles preferred to make his subjects 'half-way Papists'.[92] But perhaps worst of all, Charles seemed to like the Irish, 'ever friendly', and ever pleading with them to send over an army.[93] The 'Popish Plot' writ large; raising memories of the Armada and the Powder Plot, and so many other incidents of 'Romish' malignancy.[94] And Charles Stuart was personally responsible. Not just for marrying a papist and inviting more papists to invade his kingdom, but for perpetuating a hellish war against 'his faithfull subjects'.[95] There could be no quarter.

The stakes were of the highest. Of 'truth', and who got to write it.[96] The truth nurtured by the 'Christian conscience of libertie', which would lay bare the 'papistical' politics of counterfeit and 'suttle dissimulation'.[97] Easy enough in some cases. The 'knowing Christian' was satiated by the simple 'truth' of the Word. But what of the unknowing, the 'blaspheming Cavaliers', and the 'inconstant, irrational, and image-doting rabble'?[98] All those who craved the 'quaint emblems' and 'devices' of 'Romish guilded Portrature'. All those too easily seduced by 'some Twelfth-nights entertainment'.[99] All those who passed their Sundays as recommended in the Stuart *Book of Lawful Sports*, dancing 'Jiggs' and cavorting about 'May-poles'.[100] A decade earlier Milton had trusted the 'capacity of the plain artisan' to come to the right decision. Not anymore.[101] But what to do? A dilemma indeed. How to counter the collected delusions of 'fansie' and 'imagination' without resorting to the same.[102]

To which the answer was, in fact, to do exactly the same; but more cunningly. To make a 'fansie' out of simplicity. Discovered in the same two places. In the 'spirituall words of holy censure' and the lessons of Reformation history. 2 *Corinthians* 10:5, once again; for the 'casting down of imaginations, and every high thing that exalteth itself against the knowledge of God'. And the casting down of those who join 'their armies with the Beast'. The admonition of *Revelations*. All played out in the history of Charles Stuart. Simply told. A tyrannical king conspiring to subvert the true protestant church, to place it under the 'servile yoak of Liturgie', and to distract its congregation with 'fantastik dresses' and 'gaudy Copes', and 'painted Windows, Miters, Rochets, Altars'.[103] A king now despatched as a 'speciall mark of favour'.[104] And a people saved. Along with their constitution. Their liberties no longer given 'by meer gift, as when the Conduit pisses Wine at Coronations'.[105] Their laws now 'ingrav'd' as they were 'in the hearts of our Ancestors, and by them so constantly enjoy'd and claim'd, as it needed not enrouling'.[106] The union of church and constitution, the very pith of the English Reformation.

Eikonoclastes was painstaking; each chapter rebutting an equivalent chapter in the 'King's Book'. A close rebuttal skilfully vouched in a rhetoric of measured anger. Which no-one seemed that interested in reading. The *Eikon Basilike* went through thirty-five editions in a year. *Eikonoclastes* managed just three, all subsidized. An impossible brief perhaps; writing cold contempt hotly.[107] Easier for the royalist hagiographers, writing about love and devotion and sacrifice. A series of responses to *Eikonoclastes* appeared through the late autumn, all working the Christology theme. *King Charles, His Imitation of Christ, Or the Parallel Lives of Our Saviour and King's Sufferings drawn through forty-six texts of Scripture* did well. Thomason acquired a copy in early December. So too *The Life and Death of King Charles the Martyr Parall'd with our Saviour*. The most pointed was *The Princely Pelican: Royall Resolves Extracted from His Majestie's Divine Meditations, with satisfying reasons that his Sacred Person was the only author of them*. In effect a sequel, written in familiar tones. Lots of meditations, lots of prayer. 'As for princely policy; I hold none better than sincere piety', and so on.[108] The voice beyond the grave again. Shortly after came Salmasius's *Defensio*.

And Milton's rebuttal. Eventually. *A Defence of the People of England* appeared in February 1651.[109] All the familiar arguments, together with a few choice comments regarding the sexual proprieties of the 'bold-faced' Salmasius.[110] Written in the main for a continental audience. But not only. The merits of kingship, and by implication the regicide, were presently under consideration in Parliament; a sort of internal review. Thus the sideswipes at the 'lukewarm' men, the 'Laodicians'. Those who seemed willing to give up already, to abandon the 'cause' and countenance another Stuart. Charles I had been executed, not on the whim of men but under direction of God. The same God who expects his people to purge Parliaments too, where necessary. The test of their 'wisdom'.[111] Even Moses, the 'best of kings', recognized that law is given under God; 'since all things are done by God, and through God'.[112] As did the great 'philosophers', Seneca, Cicero and Aristotle. Each appreciating that a 'commonwealth' is properly governed when it 'agrees' with the 'law of God'.[113] And some of England's better kings. Alfred and Athelstan, and Edwin of Northumbria and Ina, king of the West Saxons, disinterred from a very misty past, and Edward the Confessor. Even William the Conqueror, apparently. Each recognized that their coronation 'oath' obliged them to rule in accordance with the 'common' law and the 'wisdom' of their counsel. Salmasius had not read his Bracton properly, or his Coke. A 'king of England cannot make any law of himself; for he was not appointed to make laws but to guard those made by the people'.[114]

The *Defence* did rather better, running to a dozen editions, plus a Dutch translation. Liking a disputation, especially about the merits of establishing Republics, humanist Europe was intrigued. Catholic Europe less so. Burned in France and across the Holy Roman Empire. A useful notoriety. The debate bubbled along. Milton would publish a *Second Defence* in early 1654. Stimulated on this occasion by the publication of another royalist tract entitled *Regni Sanguinis Clamor* which had appeared in late 1652. Author unknown. Some thought it was Salmasius again.[115] Familiar rhetoric certainly. The execution of Charles Stuart was a 'heinous parricide' and a 'horrendous sacrilege'. Some sage advice too on the importance of avoiding 'factions, hatreds, superstitions'.[116] Milton countered in predictable terms. The 'English people' casting out 'malevolent demons', the execution of the king, their 'one heroic achievement' still.[117] Arguments entrenched. Unlike the republic, which was anything but.

The ape of a king

Understandable, perhaps, if the Rump was shuffling a little anxiously in spring 1649. But then came news of Drogheda and Wexford, and Dunbar. And then Worcester, in September 1651. Providence, again and again. Exhausting though. Certainly the Rump seemed exhausted. Time to settle and take stock. The Laodician moment. Minds drifted back, to the possibility of reinvesting the principles of the 'ancient' constitution, entrenching its own prerogatives, maybe even finding another king. At the very end of 1651, Speaker Lenthall hosted a conference to discuss the 'settlement of the nation'. The idea of a 'mixed monarchical government' had been again ventured, the assembled contemplating the possibility of inviting the ten-year-old Prince Henry, still stuck in the Tower. A long 1652, spent doing not much. The calm before the coming 'storm', Marvell would later report in his *First Anniversary*. Recalling a parliament of 'tedious Statesmen' who 'many years did hack, / Framing a Liberty that still went back' (69–70).[118] That storm assuming a familiar shape.

On the morning of 20 April 1653, Cromwell arrived at the Commons and took his customary seat. A few minutes of glowering, and then a gesture to Colonel Harrison waiting at the door with a troop of musketeers. The Speaker held in his chair, an eerie echo of the indignity inflicted upon Sir John Finch a quarter of a century earlier, whilst, according to Algernon Sidney, Cromwell proceeded to 'chid them' all 'soundly'. A Parliament in 'spirit not according to God', and full of 'whoremongers', he added, staring pointedly at Henry Marten.[119] After which he picked up the mace, that 'bauble' as he described it, and tossed it on the floor. Parliament was dissolved. 'Ye have sat long enough, in the name of God go', he concluded.[120] Which, at the point of a musket, they did. Later that evening a wit chalked on the doors: 'This House to be let, now unfurnished.' The doors were locked, for the next six years. Some were appalled. Ludlow denounced an act 'treacherous and impious'.[121]

Not Milton though. A place of 'unprincipled peculations' and 'corrupt gratifications'.[122] Less convinced, though, by what followed. An Assembly of 'saints', selected variously by congregations of true believers. Like 'the forming of God as ever people were', Cromwell exulted, 'called by God to rule with Him and for Him'. The millenarian moment; 'overturning days', the 'erecting of the Kingdom of Jesus Christ'.[123] Made possible by the 'spirit of Moses'. In the corporeal shape of Oliver Cromwell, 'the great Deliverer of his people (through God's grace) out of the house of Aegypt'.[124] *Exodus* 18:21: 'Moreover thou shalt provide out of all the people able men, such as fear God, men of truth, hating covetousness.'

Energetic at first. But lacking in resolution, and far too easily distracted. Like their predecessors, the 'saints' were intrigued by the possibility of legal reform, even contemplating the abolition of Chancery.[125] Only to be frightened off by the same lawyers painting dreadful pictures of the likely consequence. The wrong sort of apocalypse. So instead, they turned their attention to matters of spiritual edification, more particularly tithe-reform and proceedings for ejecting ministers. A summer of dither turned into an autumn. Finally, on the morning of 8 December, a group of moderates arrived slightly earlier in the Chamber, took a quick vote and dissolved themselves. No great fuss this time. No need for a harangue.

Cromwell would later reflect on his 'folly'.[126] 'God's Englishman' had never exhibited much faith in models of governance. 'Dross and dung in comparison with Christ', he liked to say.[127] Perhaps. But still, there had to be something. A country 'rent and torn in spirit and principle', yearning for 'healing and settling'. A 'fundamental'.[128] And one possibility, above all others, suggested itself. A king. It would require some more statutory drafting, and some judicious rewriting of history too. Something for the lawyers, and the poets. The execution of Charles I would become a familiar contingency rather than a moment of constitutional revolution. Kings had been deposed in the past. And then replaced by new kings. Cromwell was though unpersuaded. The possibility of installing a puppet-king, such as Prince Henry, would be a 'business of more than ordinary difficulty'.[129]

And there was, as the Venetian envoy Paulucci noted, a rather obvious alternative. A king that would be anything but a puppet. A man of 'lofty spirit', though not 'loved by all'.[130] The extent to which Cromwell seriously considered the crown in late 1653 remains a matter of conjecture. The Fifth Monarchist John Carew suspected that he might 'King it'. Whitelock recorded a passing conversation. Cromwell asking his advice, 'what if a man should take upon him to be a king?' To which Bulstrode sagely responded that the 'remedy would be worse than the disease'.[131] And Ludlow would later report Hugh Peter supposing that Cromwell might have been tempted; seeing in his victory at Worcester a greater 'elevation'.[132] Not, it seems, great enough. Instead, on 16 December 1653, Cromwell put on a sober black suit and proceeded to Whitehall to be invested with the powers of Lord Protector.

In his inaugural address, the new Protector made familiar reference; assuming a responsibility to guide England through the 'wilderness, many signs and wonders towards a place of rest; I say, towards it'.[133] A plain enough insinuation. The 'chosen' people were still a bit lost. After which came a 'noble banquet' at Grocers' Hall, and a short ride-about, but otherwise all very 'solemn', as James Fraser reported. *Mercurius Politicus* was impressed by the sobriety. A 'good example to the rest of the Nation'. Paulucci less so, surmising that the people were more 'dashed than glad'.[134] And probably a fair bit bemused. There was a vague familiarity to the institution; a 'government by a single person and a Parliament', as the new Protector would resolve.[135] There had been Protectors in the past, generally assuming regency powers for monarchs who were too young or too mad. None, though, who had assumed office in quite such a circumstance. And the precedents were hardly convincing. Most protectorates had ended messily.

The office came with a new constitution, entitled the *Instrument of Government*. To which Cromwell 'contracted' himself, by oath, in 'public'. Remarkable certainly for its clarity; though hardly written for revolution. The converse indeed. No more 'rooting and striking at fundamentals', as Nedham put it.[136] Legislative authority rested in Parliament, executive authority in the office of the Lord Protector, advised by the Council of State. Ancillary provisions addressed the length of parliamentary sittings, who might vote, the funding of a permanent army and so on.[137] The keynote was balance. Cromwell would later suppose that his only powers, as Protector, were those of a 'coordinate'; there to keep everything in harmonious operation.[138] Articles 35 to 37 addressed the vexed matter of conscience, and said pretty much what Milton, already drafting his *Second Defence*, would have hoped. Any who 'profess faith in God by Jesus Christ' should be 'protected' in the manner of their worship. There would be no 'penalties' levied, except against those who espoused 'Popery or Prelacy'. Just 'sound doctrine and the example of good conversation'. The philosophy of a man 'known for nothing so much as his devotion to the Puritan religion and his upright life', as Milton described the new Protector.[139] And himself. Cromwell had 'spurned' the 'name of King', and 'rightly so'.[140] For now, Milton remained on board.

Supporting words from Nedham too, and a familiar metaphor. A 'better Caesar is approaching', he supposed, 'like a new star to light up the world'. And from Marvell, whose *The First Anniversary* appeared in early 1655. A second coming for 'angry heaven's flame', now recast as a composite Old Testament prophet guiding a 'headstrong' people, part Moses, part Elijah, part Gideon, famed scourge of 'kings grown great'. And law-giver; 'our Amphion' tuning his 'ruling Instrument' (67–8, 73, 234).[141] Metaphors aside, though, the defining question remained. Marvell made recourse to a familiar office, even as he sought to distinguish it: 'For to be Cromwell was a greater thing, / Than ought below, or yet above a King' (225–6).[142] A few months later, Edmund Waller published a *Panegyrick to My Lord Protector*. A closer resonance still. Cromwell as Augustus Caesar, 'rais'd above the rest', bringing peace to a shattered 'empire': 'Your never-failing sword made war to cease; / And now you heal us with the arts of peace.'[143] Kingship by poetic inference.

The Council of State meanwhile commissioned Peter Lely to paint the Protector's portrait. Armoured, wistful and blotchy; the consequence of a renowned injunction, to 'paint my picture truly like me and not flatter me at all … pimples, warts and everything'.[144] Much like the 'King Noll' ridiculed in royalist pamphlets; the alter ego of the other Cromwell commonly discovered in the same literature, the scheming 'Stage Machiavel'. Royalist cavils were to be expected, the Machiavellian insinuation predictable. The fact that former allies expressed similar suspicions was more concerning. 'Carried on and huddled up by two or three persons', Edmund Ludlow concluded of the process by which the *Instrument* was drafted, a 'work of darkness'.[145] The huddlers were, of course, happy enough. According to Whitelock, the *Instrument* quickly earned a 'very general acceptance, especially amongst the lawyers, the ministers and merchants'.[146] England back in business, literally. And run by lawyers. A flattered Bulstrode agreed to be a commissioner of the Great Seal.

It was principle, as much as process, which bothered Lucy Hutchinson. 'This Caesar found in our dissembling Age', she mockingly dismissed the Augustan imagery, a paper king with a 'paper crown', presiding over a 'court full of sin and vanity'.[147] Amongst the most strident opponents were Quakers and Fifth Monarchists. Anna Trapnel pitied the falling Gideon. Vavasor Powell suggested that they all 'go home and pray, and say unto the Lord wilt though have Oliver Cromwell or Jesus Christ to reign over us'.[148] Old-school Levellers too. Back in 1649, Overton had warned that Cromwell might 'aspire' towards a 'new regality'. A 'Stately thing / That confesseth itselfe but the Ape of a King'.[149] Resonant, and well-worth a reprint. When hauled in front of the Council in 1654, Overton compared himself with 'Cremutius in Tacitus'; an aspersion which cast Cromwell as the Emperor Tiberius. His 'sweet' friend Milton would not have missed the allusion.[150] Another familiar name from a more hopeful past was moved to write a short tract with a pointed title. *Killing No Murder*, by Edward Sexby. Who 'made thee a prince and a judge over us?' A simple enough inference based on consistency. They had killed one tyrant in January 1649; they could kill another.[151]

And there were plenty more sat in the first Protectorate Parliament who seemed unconvinced by much of what was written into the *Instrument*. A line was crossed with the tabling of a motion intended to restore parliamentary authority for raising militia. Parliament was dissolved on 22 January 1655, just as Marvell's *First Anniversary* appeared. Where there should have been 'mercy and truth', a disappointed Lord Protector informed the departing Members, there were 'briars and thorns'.[152] Back to the drawing-board. Another experiment in governance. This time a radical devolution of power. England divided into eleven 'cantons', each governed by a Major General, variously assisted by the local godly and variously loathed. Twelve months on, the Major Generals were thanked for the efforts and retired. Patience and money had run out on the 'silly, mean fellows', as Lucy Hutchinson concluded.[153] Time for another Parliament.

And another constitution. Stimulated as much by the looming question of succession. Back in November 1654, Cromwell had narrowly avoided serious injury in a reported riding accident. Saved by a 'higher Force', as Marvell observed in his *First Anniversary*. But still. The newly reinvested Protector was in his fifty-seventh year, and looked it; as anyone who glanced at Lely's portrait might have concluded. Malaria, endless bowel and urinary infections. A Somerset

MP named John Ashe, set the tone in a debate in early January 1657, rising to propose that Cromwell should 'take upon him the government according to our ancient constitution'. A few weeks later, Parliament approved a *Humble Petition and Advice*, to be presented to the Lord Protector at the end of March in the Banqueting House. Under the watchful gaze of King James, still rising. At its heart was the offer of the crown, monarchy being the institution 'most agreeable' to 'the temper of the people'. Cromwell, typically, chose to dither. He would 'ask counsel of God'.[154]

Meanwhile crack a few slightly awkward jokes. When Colonel Jephson appealed in person for Cromwell to take the Crown, he was gently chided. 'Get thee gone for a mad fellow, as thou art.'[155] Smilingly though. The 'kinglings' had reason to hope. The lawyers were keen too. Whitelock had certainly come round to the idea, helping to draft the *Petition*, along with the Lord Chief Justice, Sir John Glynne. A king is 'known in the law of England', it has 'certainty'.[156] Edmund Waller supplied some supportive verse, and had an idea to help with financing. Melt down some plate recently captured from a Spanish treasure fleet: 'A royal sceptre, made of Spanish gold!'[157] Surely, this time, Cromwell would accept. Ludlow suspected that he was 'vehemently desirous to be king'.[158] The Swedish ambassador likewise. Nothing else fitted the constitution, or the poetry. Moreover, everything else about the Protectorship resembled a monarchy. A polished-up palace, to house a 'court' full of 'liveries, lackeys and yeoman of the guard'.[159] A House of Peers on the horizon too.[160] To include the earl, lots of lawyers and all the 'silly mean fellows'.

Who still called the shots. As Cromwell discovered on the afternoon of 6 May, the day before his planned coronation. Taking his customary stroll around St James Park, and joined by his old friend Major General Desborough. Not the 'counsel of God' perhaps, but cautionary enough. If Cromwell took the crown, he would resign his commission, as would Fleetwood, Lambert and Pride.[161] The 'kinglings' were confounded. Cromwell recoiled. 'I would not seek to set up that which Providence hath destroyed and laid in the dust', he advised Parliament, 'and I would not build Jericho again'. He 'loved not the title' and would continue instead as 'a good constable to keep the peace of the parish'.[162] A second Protectorate.

A slightly grander investiture this time. In Westminster Hall, on a throne under which was placed the Stone of Scone. All the accoutrements; a velvet-draped table, upon which was placed an embossed Bible, a huge golden sceptre and the sword of state. A 'rich and costly robe of purple velvet', for the Protector himself, 'lined with ermines, being the habit anciently used at the investiture of princes'. Seated behind was an entourage of 'divers of the nobility and other persons of great quality'. Cromwell took an oath to 'maintain the true Reformed protestant church' and to protect the 'three nations'. After which, according to *Mercurius Politicus*, came the formal proclamation and then 'several great Acclamations' of 'God save the Lord Protector'.[163] So nearly a king. And so nearly a coronation. Except for the bit that mattered most, the crown.

Fallen

And the bit that mattered next most. We have already visited autumn 1658, when the question of succession assumed a pressing importance. The fancies of 'elective' kingship giving way to the more familiar glance along the bloodline. 'Your father Julius was', Thomas Pecke urged Richard Cromwell, 'Augustus be'.[164] A little hopeful. By early 1659 the 'Golden Mediocrity' was in the custody of the army, a puppet Protector. In April he was finally removed, submitting, he declared, to the 'hand of God'. A chip off the block, in that sense at least. Not in any other. The third and final Protectorate Parliament was dissolved. To be replaced by a restored Long Parliament on 7 May. The Rumpers plus a few chosen guests. Not that the future seemed any the clearer, nor the present. Which left plenty of room for speculation.

The fall of Babel

'Jesus Christ has come to reign', the Quaker George Fox assured himself.[165] Richard Baxter set his sights a bit lower. In early 1659 he published *A Holy Commonwealth*, in a failing expression of support for 'Tumbledown Dick'. Dick gone, Baxter adjusted his sights again. If the previous decade had proved anything it was this; monarchy was the 'best' form of government 'under God'. Baxter could conceive another Stuart. So rather obviously could Sir George Booth, who mounted a precipitate rebellion in Lancashire. Easily crushed by Lambert. The whiff of gunpowder again. Others preferred a different aroma. That of caffeine and sherbet. The age of the London coffee-house was dawning. A first established in 1652, a second in 1656. By 1663, there were eighty-two within the walls of the City. A little more temperate, perhaps, than the beery taverns in which inebriate Levellers had first contemplated butchering their king. But constituted for much the purpose. We might briefly drop in on the Turk's Head coffee-house in New Palace Yard, the home of the Rota Club.

So named in honour of its founder James Harrington, the author of *The Commonwealth of Oceana*. The system of 'rotation' being the mainspring of governance recommended in Harrington's treatise, a way of refreshing sovereigns and senators, and pretty much everything else. A resonance, once again, with the idea of 'elective' kingship; albeit without a king. And not entirely novel. The Council of State had operated by means of 'rotation', members elected each year. *Oceana* was published in 1656, replete with strategic dedication to the Lord Protector. The author's rather confusing past had stymied an initial attempt to secure a licence to publish. The one-time gentleman to the royal bedchamber who might even have been present on the scaffold in January 1649, or so it was rumoured, but whose 'melancholy' had been since dispelled by close study of the Venetian republic.[166]

When it did finally emerge, *Oceana* quickly became, as Aubrey confirmed, the toast of the 'coffee-houses'.[167]

The Rota met through most of the second part of 1659 and into early 1660. Membership was broad. Amongst the more regular attenders were Aubrey, and the former Leveller John Wildman. Amongst the less was Samuel Pepys and possibly Andrew Marvell.[168] Amongst the never, it seems, was Milton. Not by nature a clubbable man. The topic of conversation at the Rota would have interested though. Mainly politics, more pertinently the chaos of the moment and how it might be overcome. *Oceana* served as a template, against which the caffeine-addicts of the Turk's Head could contemplate Harrington's overarching question; whether or not the principles of republicanism were 'so well sowen and rooted'. Harrington was hardly sure, confiding that the 'people of England' were 'twenty to one for monarchy'.[169]

Milton probably suspected the same. For now, though, he clung to the possibility that a republic might still be saved. A series of essays published not in Latin this time, but in the vernacular. The exigencies of the moment. First came a *Treatise on Civil Power*. Familiar arguments; liberty of conscience, the egregiousness of tithes. Published in mid-February 1659, just as the last Protectorate Parliament was mulling over a motion condemning 'heresies'. A few months later came *The Likeliest Means to Remove Hirelings from the Church*; a pointed title. Freedom of conscience again. And then, in mid-February 1660, a final fling. An essay entitled *The Ready and Easy Way to Establish a Free Commonwealth*. The first edition appeared just as the restored Parliament began its final session. Three weeks later the Rump dissolved itself. The Rota gave up too. The aroma of coffee momentarily replaced by that of burning brisket. The 'Roasting of the Rump' in the streets of London.[170] Harrington was right. England was ready for a party, and a king.

Still Milton resisted. In March, he composed a 'letter' to General Monk in Scotland, entitled *The Present Means, and brief Delineation of a Free Commonwealth*. Whether it was ever sent remains unknown; or whether it was read. A briefing note on the *Ready and Easy Way*. A revised second edition of which appeared in April, addressed more closely to those about to elect a new Parliament. The 'face of things hath had some change', the threat of a new 'bondage' appearing now all the greater. But still, the people of England might save themselves. The *Ready and Easy Way* reflects the competing sentiment. Passages of constructive political discourse vying with expressions of resignation and despair. Testament to a moment of critical disjuncture; in the history of England and the history of John Milton. The constructive commentary comes in arguing the case for a 'settled' commonwealth. Established with the overarching purpose of securing the 'best part of our liberty, which is our religion'.[171] A reset, to January 1649. No king, no state church. And no rotation either. Difficult, Milton argues, to settle a commonwealth that is constantly 'jarring' its governance, or at least its governors.[172] Instead, a settled commonwealth of the godly, governed by the 'reason' of liberty.[173]

Finally, though, the despair consumes. Milton as Jeremiah, with 'none to cry save the stones and the trees', the once 'chosen people' returning to the 'gilded yoke' of Egypt, the 'thraldom' of another Stuart king.[174] Popery restored under the guise of the 'Presbyter'. A passing allusion to the 'charge' of the 'father' written into the closing passages of the *Eikon Basilike*.[175] And its prophecy. Realized in a history of 'ingrateful backsliding' and 'new-disgorg'd atheisms'. What, Milton asks, 'will they say of us, but scoffingly as of that foolish builder mentioned by our Saviour, who began to build a Tower, and was not able to finish it: where is the goodly tower of a Common-wealth which the English boasted they would build, to overshadow kings and be another Rome in the west?' A 'foundation indeed they laid gallantly'. But then 'fell into worse confusion, not of tongues, but of factions', then those building the tower of Babel'. A people now 'insensible and unworthy' of God's mercy. Their only 'memorial', the 'common laughter of Europe'.[176] A complaint and a first lament; for a people who had, in the end, disappointed.

Milton had been disappointed for a while, the optimism of the 1652 sonnet long dissipated. He had retained his position as secretary of Foreign Tongues throughout the 1650s, and had continued to write the party line in his successive 'defences' of the Republic. A tiring argument, though. At least as much time spent defending his own reputation as that of the Republic, or indeed Cromwell, reference to whom tended to be retrospective. A great man still, but largely because of what he had done, past 'deeds' which 'far outstripped not only the achievements of our kings, but even the legends of our heroes'.[177] Rather than what he was now doing. No real surprise that there was no fawning elegy in autumn 1658. Milton had barely written a word, political or poetic, in three years. A toe dipped into the water at the end of 1658, a short essay entitled *The Cabinet-Council*. Another edition of the second *Defence*. And then the plunge. The *Ready and Easy Way*, and the rounding aspersion; that the tyranny of 'one imperious lord' looks much like any other.[178] Milton was done with 'God's Englishman'.

And he was not alone. The royalists, of course, had exulted in the death of the hated Machiavel. Star-turn in Gauden's *Cromwell's Bloody Slaughter-House* which appeared in early 1660, and in William Winstanley's strange series of potted biographies, *England's Worthies*; even worse than 'the Florentine' for having hid behind the 'vizard of Religion'.[179] Milton did not go that far. But neither was he inclined to join the chorus of Augustan elegists. Nor did he find a place for his former hero in the *Ready and Easy Way*. History, and its poets, can be unforgiving. Nedham was. Looking back on the previous half decade, he concluded that it had been 'a great Chasma, a praeternatural vacuity', in which every constitutional experiment had become 'legally defunct as they were done, coming into the world still-born'.[180] A plain enough inference. Ludlow would reinvest the more familiar metaphor a few years later, in his *Voyce from the Watchtower*: 'Instead of building the howse, and doing the worke of God', they had built a 'Babell'.[181] Too much chatter. In one of his final addresses to Parliament, in January 1658, the

Lord Protector had surmised the same. A people, it seemed, constantly 'making wounds, and rending and rending and tearing, and making then wider'.[182] Not the first sovereign to have approached his deathbed blaming everyone else; and not the last.

The 'easiest way' was, in fact, backwards. The new Convention Parliament assembled on 25 April 1660, and immediately began preparing for the arrival of the next Charles Stuart. Sir Matthew Hale, outgoing Cromwellian Justice of the Common Pleas, moved the formal address. Appointed Chief Baron of the Exchequer a few months later, Hale knew how to 'trim'. The essential art-form of Restoration England, as we will discover. Parliament duly approved the *Declaration of Breda*, published back in early February. A process eased by Hyde's willingness to say all the right things. We will encounter a very judicious passage shortly, confirming a 'free and general pardon' to all but a handful of 'excepted persons', along with the confirmation of all sales of Royalist land made since the war, the immediate payment of army arrears and a 'liberty to tender consciences'. The *Declaration* further confirmed a willingness to govern 'according to the ancient and fundamental laws of this kingdom', which 'is, and ought to be, by Kings, Lords and Commons'. What, Hyde inferred, should have been resolved back in 1641. A 'happy' Parliament despatched some commissioners to go and retrieve their king. Amongst their number was Pepys. A 'very joyful business', with a 'little too much' drinking of the 'King's health'.[183]

Charles arrived at Dover on 25 May.[184] Four days later he was welcomed into London. His thirtieth birthday. Oak Apple Day, as it was henceforth to be known, in remembrance of the prince's miraculous escape after the battle of Worcester. John Evelyn described the scene; of 'streets strewn with flowers, the bells ringing, the streets hung with tapestry, fountains running with wine', dignitaries laden with 'chains of gold and velvet', balconies laden with 'ladies', and 'trumpets' everywhere.[185] 'Joy on all sides', Hyde confirmed, 'with the greatest excess'.[186] Charles liked all of it; probably the wine and women the most. A man of 'enjoyment', the Venetian envoy noted perceptively, evidently at ease in 'public'. Evelyn likewise; 'easy of access', down to the 'little spaniels' who 'would lie in his bedchamber'.[187] Not entirely approving, in truth. And access to the king's bedchamber would become a matter of some contention in years to come. For now, though, England could count its blessings; literally so, according to *Exultationis Carmen*. Graced with a 'milde Caesar, born of Heavn'ly Race', the 'living Image of our Martyr'd King'.[188]

The mark of Cain

Different though, where it mattered. A flashy coronation would come a year later. By which time Milton had long departed his rooms in Petty France and gone into hiding; where he would stay for sixteen weeks. Not a regicide, but reason to be concerned. No-one, over the previous decade, had worked harder to justify the killing of 'our Martyr'd King'. In late August, the Commons resolved that copies of *Eikonoclastes* and the first *Defence* should be burned by the common hangman, whilst the Attorney General was instructed to draw up an indictment against the former secretary of Foreign Tongues. Meanwhile, other poets were switching sides at breakneck speed. Dryden hastily distanced himself from the 'lawless savage Libertie' of the previous decade in *Astraea Redux*.[189] Waller's *To the King upon his Majesties Happy Return* was out by early June. The *Panegyrick to My Lord Protector* reworked as a collective confession, with some necessarily gnomic advice: 'If your Grace incline that we should live, / You must not Sir too hastily forgive'.[190] Whether the sentiment or the rhyme would have earned Milton's greater contempt is a matter of conjecture.

In the end, Milton would survive. Pragmatics in the main, and a touch of irony. Despite the indictment, Milton was no longer much of a threat to anyone. He might even be 'turned', like Dryden and Waller.[191] Which explains, perhaps, why Sir Thomas Morrice, newly appointed Secretary of State, appears to have interceded on his behalf. And Sir Thomas Clarges, another member of the repopulated Council of State, who was usefully close to Monk. Marvell likewise spoke up on behalf of his old friend. As for the irony, benevolence was prescribed in the closing passages of the *Eikon*. The martyred king dying for the sins of his most acerbic critic. 'He sowed in teares what we are now reaping with joy', as another lucky preacher put it in early 1660.[192] We can only speculate whether Milton felt especially lucky in spring 1660.

The portents, for everyone, were hardly clear. Hyde's *Declaration* supposed that retribution would indeed be measured:

> To the end that fear of punishment may not engage any, conscious to themselves of what is past, to a perseverance in guilt for the future, by opposing the quiet and happiness of their country, in the restoration of King, Peers, and people to their just, ancient and fundamental rights, we do, by these presents, declare, that we do grant a free and general pardon.[193]

Passed 'under our Great Seal of England', with a forty-day period of 'grace and favour'. There was, though, a further clause, which read 'excepting only such persons as shall hereafter be excepted by Parliament, those only to be excepted'. Sobering and suggestive. Someone was drawing up a list.[194]

The length of which would become apparent in June, with the passage of the *Act of Indemnity and Oblivion*. A general pardon for all except fifty-two named 'enemies' of the king, comprised mainly of those regicides still alive. Plus a few others who were deserving of despatch; who had taken part in the trial proceedings or the subsequent execution of sentence. The rationale would be confirmed a couple of months later, in a Royal Proclamation which accompanied the *Act for a Perpetuall Anniversary Thanksgiving on the Ninth and Twentieth Day of May*. The regicide had been the work of a 'Fanatick rage of a few miscreants'.[195] Punishment would stretch that far, but no further. And not, fortunately, as far as Milton. Even now, though, there was reason for caution. Indictment, and brief period of arrest in the Tower, persuaded Milton to secure a personal pardon under Seal. As did Whitelock, who managed to secure an audience with the king, and the supportive presence of Sir Edward Hyde. For a bribe of £250. Plus, he noted rather pedantically, £32 18 8, for the actual pardon.[196]

Those who did make it onto the list were ordered by Royal Proclamation to surrender themselves to the authorities. A few were already gone. To 'wander to and fro about the world with the mark of Cain upon them', as Sir Heneage Finch, the newly appointed Solicitor General put it.[197] Into the Wilderness once more; various wildernesses in fact. John Hewson, former cobbler turned Parliamentary Colonel added master-of-disguise to his career profile, and disappeared completely, last seen somewhere near Rouen. Cromwell's brother-in-law, Valentine Walton, got himself to Germany. Major Generals Goffe and Whalley pitched up in Connecticut, along with John Dixwell.[198] Ludlow fled to the Swiss canton of Vevey, a £300 reward on his head. Safer, if not entirely secure, he would spend the rest of his life dodging royalist assassins and writing tendentious 'memoirs'; more of which later. A few others ended up nearby, including the two clerks, Boughton and Phelps.

The rest were taken into custody. There was an implication, in the *Declaration*, that all who surrendered themselves might at least escape capital punishment. It convinced Henry Marten. In 'no great danger', he reassured one of his mistresses.[199] Wrong. There was, though, a brief moment during which the Commons seemed susceptible to a suitably contrite petition. Colonel Ingoldsby seized it. A first airing for the story that Cromwell had forcibly made some regicides sign the warrant. The Commons approved the petition, and Ingoldsby got off.[200] Likewise Colonel Hutchinson, repenting being 'involved in so horrid a crime as merits no indulgence'. His kinsman Lord Byron put in a helpful word too, as did Sir Allen Apsley, one of the new king's drinking chums. The Colonel's petition was also accepted. Just in time. For this the particular charade was about to come to an end. The next to try his luck, a few days later, was Colonel Scrope. But when challenged as to whether it was 'well done to murder the King?' Scrope fluffed his lines.[201] There would be no more petitioning to the Commons in the hope of dodging trial. The rest of the tardier regicides would have to take their chances in court.

It was a passing frustration that many of those most deserving of punishment had passed on. There could still be a sort of retribution. The property of all regicides, dead or alive, was seized under the terms of an *Act of Attainder of severall persons guilty of the horrid murther of his late Sacred Majesty King Charles the First* which was passed in December. The Commons further ordered the exhumation of the bodies of Cromwell, Ireton, Pride and Bradshaw, presently interred in

Westminster Abbey. To be taken, on 30 January 1661, to Tyburn to be hanged in chains.[202] A discomforting 'dishonour', according to a percipient Pepys.[203] Not alone in wondering if the nation's mind might have been better concentrated, at that particular moment, in remembrance of its martyred king.

Colonel Harrison's case

As for the living, at least those in custody, legal proceedings commenced in October. With the trial of Colonel Thomas Harrison. A 'miscreant' of the undoubtedly more 'fanatick' kind. Veteran of Marston Moor and Naseby, fervent Fifth Monarchist, unrepentant regicide, we have come across Harrison before, plenty of times. Cromwell's right-hand man. And God's. A man of intense piety, and unassuageable confidence. Traits that would come in very useful in summer 1660. Harrison made no effort to escape, preferring to spend his last days of freedom at home, 'looking for the immediate reign of our Saviour upon earth'.[204]

Various accounts of his trial remain. That written up by the Solicitor General comes closest to being the authorized version. Ludlow left a rather different report.[205] Hardly a fine-grained exercise in criminal jurisprudence. Harrison's chances were about as good as those faced by Charles Stuart eleven years earlier. Specially constituted for the occasion, the regicide court was housed at the Sessions House in Clerkenwell. A Grand Jury of twenty, headed by Sir Orlando Bridgman, now appointed Chief Baron of the Exchequer, and shortly to become Chief Justice of Common Pleas. Amongst those keeping Bridgman company could be discovered a mixture of ardent royalists and apologetic parliamentarians. Denzil Holles, the earls of Manchester and Sandwich, Monk of course. And the public hangman, invited along to sit next to the accused, halter in hand. A touch of the macabre, to add to the tone.

Impressed by Bridgman in his opening address on 9 October. 'No story that ever was, I do not think any Romance, any Fabulous Tragedy, can produce the like' of what they were about to hear. As for the jurisprudence, a few helpful pointers. A king 'is immediate from God', and no-one, not even Parliament, has 'any coercive power over the King of England'. This is not to say that an English king rules 'absolutely'. But it is to affirm that he cannot be judged in court, still less be 'put to death'. The most heinous, and dangerous, of treasons. To 'cutt off' the 'head of the commonwealth, leaving just the trunk, an inanimate lump'. The patent metaphor. 'You are', the Chief Baron reminded his fellow jurymen, by way of conclusion, 'now to enquire of Blood, of Royal Blood, of Sacred Blood; Blood like that of the Saints under the Altar ... This blood cries for vengeance and it will not be appeased without a bloody sacrifice'.[206]

The matter of guilt was hardly in question, for any of the twenty-nine indicted 'murderers of a king'. 'They all seem to be dismayed', Pepys observed at the end of the preliminary session, 'and will all be condemned without question'.[207] The likes of Thomas Harrison certainly knew what was coming. Up first, with Sir Hardress Waller and William Heveningham, an otherwise obscure East Anglican gentleman who, aside from serving as a commissioner at the king's trial, had made no greater contribution to the 'cause' than serving as Vice Admiral of the Suffolk coast for a few months in 1651. Sir Hardress had a sharper profile, former New Model colonel, who had momentarily seized Dublin castle in February 1660. But the star-turn, in this first instalment, was Harrison.

Various witnesses, all confirming Harrison's presence as a commissioner at the king's trial, and serving as his gaoler. Particular evidence that Harrison had, whilst helping to draw up the charges against the king, tried to 'blacken' his name.[208] At this, Finch recalled, there was 'humming' in court. Something which earned a reproof from the Chief Baron; 'more fitting for a stage-play than for a court of justice'. A seeming disapproval. And a metaphor joined by Harrison, reiterating his renowned injunction, that the trial of the king had not been 'done in a corner'. The 'things I have done, have been done upon the stage, in sight of the sun'.[209] Some suitably incriminating documentation, including the death warrant. And some eerily familiar argumentation too. Challenging the constitution of the court. Not his 'business', Bridgeman responded. A squabble in regard to Harrison's plea, and whether he should be allowed to address the court. And some ghosts. Not just the 'blessed' Charles, but Richard II and Edward II again. Their murderers so 'modest' in their aspirations, at least when compared to the consummate 'villainies' of Harrison and his friends.

Against all of this, Harrison's simple defence, that 'what I did' was 'out of conscience to the Lord', was never likely to cut much ice. Nor the suggestion that the trial of the king had been the 'revealed will of God'. A brief assay into constitutional jurisprudence, suggesting that the king had been lawfully tried before the 'High Court' of Parliament met with still shorter shrift. Holles obliged the court, and himself, with some contrary evidence. It was not Parliament that tried the king, but the 'power of the sword'. As 'clear as noon day', an appreciative Chief Baron confirmed.[210] And certainly more welcome than Harrison's preceding aspersion, that 'divers of those that sit upon the bench' had been 'formerly as active' in the prosecution of the king.[211] Some awkward shuffling no doubt. Time to move on, if not far. 'I think you need not go out', the jury was advised by a visible enraged Chief Baron; the 'evidence is so clear and pregnant'.[212]

A few moments, and the verdict was confirmed. And then the inevitable sentence. That the prisoner be 'drawn upon a hurdle to the place of execution' and there:

you shall be hanged by the neck, and being alive shall be cut down, and your privy members to be cut off, your entrails to be taken out of your body, and (you living) the same to be burnt before your eyes, and your head to be cut off, your body to be divided into four quarters, and your head, and quarters, to be disposed of at the pleasure of the King's Majesty: and the Lord have mercy upon your soul.[213]

We do not need to recount each grisly execution. The 'bloody theatre', as Ludlow would call it.[214] There would be eight more, in the shorter term, each despatched to 'God's tribunal'. Five warrant-signatories, including the unfortunate Scrope.[215] And three others deemed sufficiently 'malignant': Axtell, Cook and Hugh Peter.

Any differences were a consequence of performance rather than script. Some might climb the scaffold in a state of gibbering madness. Or drunk. Peter was both.[216] Others with quiet dignity, such as Cook. Others still would seize the moment and embrace their fate with an unnerving, and magnificent, courage. Harrison was one of these, stone cold sober, sustained in his faith, eager to meet his Day of Judgement. 'By God', Harrison was said to have declared on the scaffold, 'I have leaped over a wall; by God, I have run through a troop; and by God I will go through this death, and He will make it easy for me.'[217] Harrison went down with a fight, literally; reaching out and punching the hangman whilst his innards were being burned in front of him. Samuel Pepys, typically, had dropped by to watch. And was impressed:

He looking as cheerful as any man could do in that condition. He was presently cut down, and his head and his heart shown to the people, at which there was great shouts of joy. It is said that he was sure to come shortly at the right hand of Christ to judge them that now had judged him. And that his wife did expect his coming again.[218]

Quite a performance.

Albeit smelly. The locals, living near the site of execution, at Charing Cross, started complaining. Sentences were, as a consequence, commuted. Colonel Hacker was hanged instead. A particular disappointment for Mrs Hacker, who had somehow persuaded herself that producing the original death warrant might help to secure a commutation of sentence. A couple of years later, three recaptured regicides, Colonels Barkstead, Okey and Miles Corbet, were also hanged.[219] This time at Tyburn. A marginally more elevated fate awaited Sir Henry Vane. Beheaded, on Tower Hill, on the anniversary of Naseby, also in 1662. Not a regicide. But in the opinion of the king 'too dangerous to let live if we can honestly put him out of the way'.[220] The meaning of 'honesty' being a variable. The jury in Sir Henry's case were denied food and drink until they returned the correct verdict.[221]

Otherwise, it was incarceration. Or, for the luckier still, a fine and prohibition from public office. Speaker Lenthall was one of these, his case helped further by a timely 'gift' of £3000 to the king, and an eager willingness to provide evidence against other 'regicides'.[222] Amongst those destined to end their lives behind bars was Colonel John Downes, his rather half-hearted protestation during the trial now proving invaluable. 'I did my best; I could do no more', Downes protested.[223] A bare excuse, but enough to save his neck when it mattered. Likewise, Colonel Hutchinson, rearrested in 1663 and despatched to Sandown castle in Kent. And Henry Marten, who ended up in Chepstow. Interestingly, during his trial, Marten was prepared to concede that the court established to try the king had been very 'irregular', putting him in a 'worse condition than the meanest Englishman'. A bit of contrition too. Even so, Marten could count himself lucky. As could the extravagantly named Colonel Hercules Huncks, who was 'turned' during the protracted investigation into who might have been the executioner on 30 January.[224] He suggested Axtell or more likely Hacker. This particular question had been raised during Hugh Peter's trial, in the hope he might confess it. He did not. He did though admit to having given his notorious sermon during the trial, urging the commissioners to 'Bind your King in chains'. And saying plenty more that was similarly dreadful. Nothing was going to save Peter.

Unlike the two who had stood beside Harrison on the first morning of the trials, Sir Hardress Waller and William Heveningham. Both similarly fortunate in having the right friends. And the right relatives in Heveningham's case, saved 'out of respect' for his grandfather-in-law, the royalist earl of Dover. The fact had he not signed the death warrant was similarly propitious. Waller had, and might count himself especially fortunate. The rest of his life would be spent in Jersey. In Mont Orgueil castle, in the company of another former comrade-in-arms, Robert Overton. Again not a warrant-signatory, but still a former Major General in the New Model who had said plenty of unpleasant things about the dead king. The 'apostle of revolutionary integrity', according to his old friend John Milton. Consoled by the thought that He 'was pulling all downe again, leading our strength into captivity'.[225] A metaphor that would have struck a resonance with anyone who knew their *Book of Judges*.

Eyeless in Gaza

Milton remained in London until 1665. Keeping a sensibly low profile. 1661 had opened with the discovery of a Fifth Monarchist plot, hatched by an East End cooper named Thomas Venner, and ended with the passage of the first acts of what would comprise the Clarendon 'Code'. 1662 saw the further tightening of measures against people who kept doing, and saying, the wrong things, including a revised *Licensing of the Press Act*. Expressly designed to shut up the crows. In 1663 Milton got married again, for the third time. In 1664 came the *Conventicle Act*, of which more in due course. More shutting up. In 1665 came the plague. Confirmation, undoubtedly, of divine displeasure. And a good reason to seek the tranquillity, and fresher air, of the countryside. Milton moved, with his new family, to Chalfont St Giles in Buckinghamshire, renting a cottage from the duke of York.[226]

Found for him by his Quaker friend, Thomas Ellwood. Along, indeed, with a new set of Quaker friends, presently living in the area, including Isaac Pennington, Edward Burrough and James Nayler. All escaping the provisions of the 1662 *Quaker Act*, passed in the aftermath of the Venner plot. It was later supposed that Ellwood inspired Milton to write *Paradise Regained*. 'What has thou to say of Paradise Found', he had apparently remarked on returning a draft of *Paradise Lost*.[227] Perhaps; it is a nice story. And fits the intellectual narrative. Milton in the 'wilderness', writing differently. Partly circumstance, partly preference. The moment for fiery polemic had passed. That of spiritual reflection, composed in allusive verse, made far more sense.

A few years later, John Bunyan would famously set his 'pilgrim' on a journey in search of personal salvation. Milton despatched his on a journey no less arduous. Three brilliant, complicated, poems; *Paradise Lost, Paradise Regained* and *Samson Agonistes*. A 'dramatick' lament to a lost 'cause' and a lost people. The first edition of *Paradise Lost* would appear in 1667.[228] An intriguing moment in Restoration politics, for reasons we will discover in the next chapter. God seemed unhappy. And not much happier three years later, when *Paradise Regained* and *Samson Agonistes* were published, together. The regicide and its consequence is most closely contemplated in the latter. But Milton did not expect his pilgrims to arrive at *Samson Agonistes* having stepped around *Paradise Lost* and *Regained*. Neither should we.

Much of *Paradise Lost* was already in refined form by 1665. Certainly Marvell appears to have read a more or less complete draft around this point. It is possible that some passages had been conceived a decade earlier, maybe more.[229] Very likely changing tone, as well as substance. It had been quite a decade. So many ambiguities to be accounted. Not least in the author, conjuring bitter disappointment and diminishing hope.[230] Now 'fallen on evil days/ ... In darkness, and with dangers compassed round,/ And solitude' (7.27).[231] Clear enough allusion to the Clarendon 'Code' too, 'heavie persecution shall arise / On all who in the worship persevere / Of Spirit and Truth' (12.532–3). More of the Code shortly. The history is, though, much longer. Back to the very beginning, to the 'happy state', long before the Normans and the papists and the 'grievous wolves' of prelacy (12.508). To Adam, the first puritan.

Paradise Lost is, throughout, a political, as well as theological, testament. Evidently guised to get past the censors. If not John Beale, in whose opinion the poem was a shameless attempt to articulate 'horrible Blasphemyes' through 'the Mouth of Satan'.[232] It is critical commonplace to suppose the brilliance of the poem is found here. It famously led William Blake to wonder if Milton was 'of the Devil's party without knowing it'. Percy Shelley similarly. Tempted by Satan into rebellion, and then shamed. Satan as Cromwell, the causative symbol of a failed revolution?

Or maybe the trickster king, the 'Author of all ill', tempting the 'godly' into rebelling against the Word (2.381)? Or maybe Satan as the dissimulating Presbyterian; the 'lewd Hirelings' who can never be trusted (4.183–7)? Satan is everywhere, the consummate actor. And the voice of reason? The consequence of the fall, and the saving.[233] Maybe. It is the Son who advises that salvation lies within. In place of 'fabled' history, God has 'left free the will, for what obeys / reason is free, and reason is made right' (9.352). The conversation of 'rational delight' is God's concession, a glimmer (8.391). The blessing, and the bane, of free will.

Played out in the drama of political theology. Most immediately in the aesthetics of Satanic majesty, 'hell's dread emperor with pomp supreme / And Godlike imitated state' (2.510–11). As to which emperor? Any, all. Charles I undoubtedly. A close parallel found in *Eikonoclastes*, the tyrant king both 'human and fiendish', possessed of the 'conscience' of 'Lucifer'.[234] Seeking to rule by means of 'mistie' rhetoric, Satan is cast down as a 'Rebel to all Law' (10.83). Charles II too, perhaps. Master of ceremonies in the now godless England. The inconstant 'herd', all 'now turned to jollity and game / To luxury and riot, feast and dance' (11.714–15). We do not know if Milton attended the coronation of the second Charles Stuart in April 1661. We do know that he attended the faux-coronations of Oliver Cromwell. An experience which might have lain behind the following lines: 'the tedious pomp that waits / On princes, when their rich retinue long / Of horses led, and grooms besmeared with gold / Dazzles the crowd, and sets them all agape' (5.354–6). The 'imitated state' of the Lord Protector, Milton's Satan as Lucan's Caesar, the republican hero who fell prey to the temptations of tyranny? Possibly, probably.

The idea of *Paradise Regained* was born amidst the barely reducible ambiguities of *Paradise Lost*. Birthed, almost certainly, by Milton's growing affinity with Quakerism. The pilgrim-reader progresses. Through the great 'Temptations and Tryals' of the political world, as Burroughs termed them.[235] To 'travel in patience', guided by the Word, equipped with reason and liberty, towards a 'state' in which the 'pomp and sacrifice' of false 'Temples' is dispelled, in which each man is king for 'on his shoulders each man's burden lies: / For therein stands the office of a king'. And 'he who reigns within himself, and rules / Passions, desires, and fears, is more a king' (2.462–3, 466–7).[236] The tone, moving from endurance to assurance, ascribed to moment and place. The reflective tranquillity of Chalfont St Giles, perhaps, in contrast to deathly chaos of a plague-ridden Babel. The biblical inferences which consumed the second half of the 1660s. Milton could not have missed them. Leaving Satan to his own destruction, guided by an 'inward oracle', the pilgrim approaches a life of humble sincerity, 'Close in a cottage low together got' (2.27–8, 460).

Which brings us to the final part of the pilgrimage; *Samson Agonistes*. A still more personal testament; the pilgrim-poet bearing the burdens of a fallen people. Conceived, very probably, in 1660; as Milton railed despairingly against the 'confusions' into which the collapsing Republic had sunk. A longer history of course, of 'notorious whores' and 'disgorg'd atheisms'. And a more recent, of religious suppression, intellectual darkness and courtly dissolution. The 'Idolatries of Heathen round' identified in *Paradise Regained*, the 'abandoned rout' of which John Evelyn despaired (3.417). And Marvell, in his *Last Instructions to a Painter*; a text which we will revisit in the next chapter. The England indeed foretold in the *Ready and Easy Way*. The moment when Milton most probably conceived the idea of reworking the familiar story found in the *Book of Judges*; the fallen hero who redeems himself in an act of apocalyptic sacrifice.[237] God's Leveller.

We might start here. A brilliant scene, recounted by a breathless Messenger:

> ... such other trial
> I mean to show you of my strength, yet greater;
> As with amaze shall strike all who behold.
> This uttered, straining all his nerves he bowed,
> As with force of winds and waters pent,
> When mountains tremble, those two massy Pillars
> With horrible convulsion to and fro
> He tugg'd, he shook, till down they came, and drew
> The whole roof after them with burst of thunder
> Upon the heads of all who sat beneath. (1643–52)[238]

After which, the reader is assured, came 'calm of mind all passion spent' (1758). Much as his Quaker friends would have recommended; the place of 'patience' reached.

And William Juxon too perhaps. Recalling his final words of assurance as Charles Stuart knelt down to lay his 'comely head' on the scaffold at Whitehall. Different mood, same 'trial'. Probably not the parallel that Milton intended to conjure. But present nonetheless. The spectre of Charles Stuart haunts *Samson Agonistes*, just as it did Marvell's *Ode*.[239] Importing all the same discomforting insinuations. It might be the prophesy of the pending fall of the Restoration Court. Samson strikes the Philistines whilst they are 'Drunk with idolatry, drunk with wine' (1670). Or it might be a reflection in the 'convulsion' of a Republic, the fate of which was sealed on that same January day. Or both, the cycles of 'frenzy' and 'lamentation' (1675, 1708).

Again, though, Milton would not have his pilgrim begin at the end. There is a Wilderness to get through. The path for which is laid out in the preface. This is a tragedy, of the kind familiar from the ancients, purposed to raise feelings of 'pity and fear, or terror'.[240] An appreciation, concession perhaps, that the 'dramatick' can move in ways that prose cannot. But also a condemnation of the 'wonted arts' of theatre. The familiar contention, still defying conciliation. A poetic of godly progress, through the same 'temptations and tryals'. Another guide here, the Chorus. And a guiding metaphor, familiar enough in the literature, as we have already noted, and of especial poignancy in Milton's case. The journey from darkness to light, out of Egypt. The pilgrim-reader finds the formerly 'invincible' Samson now 'Eyeless in Gaza, at the mill with slaves' (41). Weary and despairing, 'O dark, dark, dark, amid the blaze of noon', now living 'a life half dead', a living death, a 'Life in captivity / Among inhuman foes' (80, 100, 108–9). The metaphors of confinement come thick and fast; a 'Prison within a prison', the 'Dungeon of thyself' (153, 156). Pertinent to Samson's condition, of course. But also casting a wider aspersion.

To the failure of 'Israel's governors', to 'nations grown corrupt, / And by their vices brought to servitude, / Than to love bondage more than liberty' (242, 268–70). A longer contempt, reaching into the 1650s, and beyond. Here the metaphors are those of secrecy and sorcery, of a 'sacred trust' betrayed (1001). Attaching to Delilah, of course, who now 'striv'st to cover shame with shame' (841). Delilah the Presbyterian apologist, yielding her 'Private respects' to the 'public good' (867–8). And then, when thwarted by Samson's refusal to accept her feigned apology, revealing her true colours: 'Nor shall I count it heinous to enjoy / The public marks of honour and reward / Conferred upon me, for the piety / Which to my country I was judged to have shown' (991–4). A 'manifest serpent by her sting', the Chorus concludes as she departs the poem, 'Discovered in the end, till now concealed' (997–8).

Metaphors of law, and injustice too. Written into the fissures that open up between the 'universal' laws of God and the corruptible laws of 'men' (293–4). Not just invocations of 'trial' and 'judgement', of God the 'mighty leveller'.[241] But more distant echoes of the divorce tracts, in the 'wedlock-treachery' that eases Samson's fall, the 'Spousal embraces, vitiated with gold' (389, 1008–9). And more recent. The resonances of regicide. Contemplating the fall of those once 'solemnly elected' and deserving of the 'highest favours past' (678, 685). But now:

Not only dost degrade them, or remit
To life obscured, which were a fair dismission,
But throw'st them lower than thou didst exalt them high,
Unseemly falls in human eye,
Too grievous for the trespass or omission,
Oft leav'st them to the hostile sword
Of heathen and profane, their carcases
To dogs and fowls a prey, or else captived:
Or to the unjust tribunals, under change of times,
And condemnation of the ingrateful multitude. (687–96)

An encompassing vengeance. Those brought before tribunals and slaughtered. Latter-day 'saints' embracing, like Samson, the 'trial of their fortitude' (1288). Those despatched to different island prisons. And those already dead, whose rotting carcases would be disinterred for public delectation.

Milton died three years after the publication of *Samson*. In November 1674. A few months earlier a second edition of *Paradise Lost* had rolled off the presses, with Milton's name bolded on the front. And containing a critical verse-commentary by Marvell. Marvell read a poem of resignation and lament. But what interested him most was the poet. He had just completed his last great satire, *The Rehearsal Transpros'd*. A bitter reflection on the politics of poetry and poets, which we will shortly revisit. Many had sold their pens, if not their souls. Marvell had Dryden more especially in mind. Not Milton though. The 'poet blind, yet bold'.[242] Still a hero, still a republican, still a regicide. Marvell imagined him as Samson.

5 THE HISTORIES OF EDWARD HYDE

FIGURE 5 Sir Edward Hyde.

We will start on 23 April 1661. Samuel Pepys had been up since 4.00 a.m., determined to get a good seat in Westminster Abbey. For the coronation of the new king. The culmination of a week of festivities, planned and managed, in the main, by the Lord Chancellor, Sir Edward Hyde. Commencing with an investiture service for some new Knights of the Garter at Windsor, and some old. Such as Prince Rupert, invested in 1646, but denied his nice day out, until now. The Dukes of York and Ormonde similarly. Lots of trinkets to be handed around, and lots of titles. Sixty-eight new Knights of the Order of the Bath, created ten days earlier. And six new earls, and six barons. Hyde gave himself one of the former. Henceforth, to be known as the Earl of Clarendon.[1]

A busy few days for the decorators too, getting everything 'spick and span' for the 'cavalcade' which was to take place on the 22nd. Literally so; cracks nailed over, bronze buffed up.[2] The defining metaphor of Restoration England, and its historians. Resplendent in gold and crimson velvet, a natty pair of studded-sandals on his feet, Charles had tottered off at 8.00 a.m. sharp from the Tower, escorted by a detachment of Monk's Regiment of Foot Guards, various gentlemen of his bedchamber and his 'herb woman'.[3] Four hours later he arrived at Whitehall, where he would spend the night in Cromwell's old rooms. He might have taken a moment to contemplate Rubens's ceiling. He might also have taken a moment to admire the fine horse which he had ridden that day. Loaned by Fairfax; its mum had been at Naseby.

And a busy week for Pepys. The theatre on the 20th, for a rather dull play, brightened up by the presence of 'many great beauties', along with the king. Raining on the 21st. And a tiresome walk home, the roads 'thronged with people to see the Triumphal Arches' which marked the route of the 'cavalcade'. Four in fact, stationed at convenient intervals. The first, positioned at the entrance to the City, depicted Monarchy triumphing over Rebellion. Dressed in a crimson robe, bloody sword in hand, the latter announced herself as 'Hell's daughter, Satan's eldest child'. Her sidekick Confusion wore her clothes back to front and carried a broken sceptre in each hand. Easily despatched. It was Monarchy that invited Charles to enter on the 22nd, declaring that she represented the best form of government. So it seemed. God-given, perhaps. But the script was written by experience. Next came the arch of 'glittering Plenty'. Just the thing.

Pepys got his seat, and described the great day. Monk, now Duke of Albemarle, carried the sceptre. The Earl of Shrewsbury got the sword of state, the Duke of Buckingham the orb. We might conjecture a tense moment, which tells us something about Restoration England. Steenie's son, recently married, we might recall, to Mary Fairfax. And about to embark on a high-profile affair with Lady Shrewsbury. Which led, eight years later, to a duel. Pepys would wonder what the 'world' might 'think' of a country in which 'the greatest man about', the king, 'is a fellow of no more sobriety than to fight about a whore'.[4] But that was then; and much, as we will see, had changed. This was now. Back to the coronation. And another familiar name. The Duke of Ormonde, who got to carry the crown. Newly forged by the renowned goldsmith Robert Vyner; duly knighted for his efforts. At a cost of £30,000.[5] More of Vyner too in due course. The newly appointed Archbishop of Canterbury, confirmed in his position the previous September, officiated. Another ghost from the past. William Juxon, now nearly eighty. The customary anointment, followed by the crowning. After which there was recorded a 'great shout'. The assembled nobility then swore oaths of fealty, promising to defend their new king.

Next on stage was the Lord Chancellor, shining like a 'diamond', it was reported, and covered in ostrich feathers.[6] He read out a proclamation of general pardon. After which coronation medals were thrown in the air; an oak tree, symbolic of Charles's famous escape following the battle of Worcester, lucky and providential, bursting into life, with the motto *Iam Florescit*, 'Now it Flourishes'. A nice way to end part one. A short break. And then they all moved next door, into the Hall, for the coronation feast. His dad was surely present, in spirit. It all kicked off with the arrival of Sir Edward Dymocke, on his horse. With his page, who read out a solemn declaration 'That if any dare deny Charles Stewart to be the lawful King of England, here was a Champion that would fight with him'. A 'brave sight', Pepys observed of the Quixotic Sir Edward.[7]

A splendid day, as Dryden confirmed in a predictably simpering *Panegyric on his Coronation*:

All eyes you draw, and with the eyes your heart;
Of your pomp yourself the greatest part:
Loud shouts this nation's happiness proclaim
And heaven this day is feasted with your name. (33–6)[8]

The evening festivities were though rather dampened. The rain came back, and the firework display had to be cancelled. Nothing to stop the partying though. Pepys recorded 'a light like a glory round about it with bonfires'. Back home in Axe Yard, he was accosted by 'gallants' who 'would have us drink the King's health upon our knee'. A 'strange frolique'. Not that Pepys ever refused a drink. Later that evening he would visit Mr Thornbury, who happened to be the yeoman of the royal wine-cellars and a personal friend. And then to bed, where his 'head began to hum, and I to vomit'. And to sleep, until he awoke to find 'myself wet with my spewing'.[9] Quite a night.

We might track back a couple of months to a calmer moment. The afternoon of 27 January 1661. A Sunday, Pepys had gone, as was customary, to church. In fact, he went twice. A 'poor dull sermon' in the morning, given by a 'stranger'. Better in the evening. A 'good sermon' given by the resident curate at St. Olave's, Seething Lane, Mr Mills. To which was appended a 'proclamacion' for 'the keeping of Wednesday next, the 30th January, a fast for the murther of the late King'. It was Convocation which had, the previous May, decided to enter 30 January in its *Calendar of Saints*. Many royalists had already adopted the habit. John Evelyn had kept the 'day of martyrdom' since 1650.[10] The Fast Day approved by Convocation would commemorate 'Charles, King and Martyr'. The title of service read:

> Being the Day of the Martyrdom of the Blessed King Charles the First; to implore the Mercy of God, that neither the Guilt of that sacred and Innocent Blood, nor those other sins, by which God was provoked to deliver up both us and our King into the hands of cruel and unreasonable men, may at any time hereafter be visited upon us or our posterity.

So back to church the following Wednesday, to hear a 'most excellent sermon', from Mills again, 'upon "Lord forgive us our former iniquities"'. Pepys had already been forgiven his; by now, appointed Clerk of the Navy Board. The *Diary* entry continues: 'Speaking excellently of the justice of God in punishing man for the sins of his ancestors.'[11] So Pepys passed judgement on the English Republic, and his former self. Brushed over, we might say. 'Now our sad ruins are removed from sight', Dryden attested in similar vein.[12] Someone else with a bit of explaining to do.

Not everyone was quite so lucky as Pepys, and Dryden, as we discovered in the previous chapter. There had to be a measure of atonement. But no more. Much easier to secure a Restoration if the future looked bright rather than blood-soaked. Absent 'animosities', as the new king advised his Parliament. In the words of his Lord Chancellor. Who had, just a few months earlier, intimated the same in the document that elevated the Restoration from a possibility to a probability. The *Declaration of Breda*, written to reassure one Englishman in particular. George Monk, presently venturing south with his Army from Edinburgh, arriving in London in early February 1660. Having ordered the Rump to dissolve itself on the 11th, it was far from clear what Monk then intended. Thus the despatch of a draft copy of the *Declaration*, along with some very accommodating letters from the king, and some serious bribes. Very wise, given that it was up to Monk whether Charles got his throne back. And a happy ending. Charles did get his crown. Whilst Monk got a dukedom, a fair chunk of Devon, and a large pile of cash.[13] An extraordinary few weeks, Pepys concluded, 'past imagination'.[14]

This chapter begins in Restoration England. We have just been here, of course, in the company of John Milton. A different companion this time, though. Arguably the most important man in England in summer 1660. A tendentious judgement. Some might suppose that it was the new king, or maybe Monk. But, in terms of settling the Restoration, making it stick, no-one mattered more than Edward Hyde. In due course we are going to take a look at Sir Edward in retirement, in the sun-kissed south of France. Where he polished up his *History of the Rebellion*. An 'eloquent and interesting' account, Sir Philip Warwick confirmed, rather faintly.[15] Before we revisit the *History* though, we need to spend some time with its author.

Merry once more

History tends to paint a 'merry' picture of Restoration England. A sense of release, and indulgence. A 'company of comedians', Trevelyan would later suppose, replacing a troop of weary 'tragedians'.[16] With a suitably 'merry monarch', albeit 'scandalous and poor'.[17] An England of partying and poetry and puking. The England of Samuel Pepys in large part. Of Andrew Marvell too, and Daniel Defoe, neither of whom were entirely impressed. We will catch up with Marvell very shortly. Defoe would later recall a 'lazy, long, lascivious reign'.[18] Which had, in fairly short order, begun to lose its charm. A 'great' plague in 1665, a 'great' fire the following summer, which left a sixth of Londoners homeless. In between, a freakishly cold winter. Tens of thousands dying of something or the other. And then, the following summer, an invasion of Dutch warships. Not locusts, but still all rather biblical. As John Bell, clerk to the London Company of Parish Clerks, noted, 'May not then this Nation justly expect Gods greatest judgements to fall on the people of it, for shedding the blood of their lawful sovereign?'[19] Indeed. In due course, there would have to be another sacrifice.

Clarendon's law

We will get to that shortly. But first we need to tread back, all the way to spring 1640. And the arrival in Parliament of the new Member for Wootton Bassett. Just turned thirty-one, and inclined, it seemed, towards the opposition 'junto'. The Hydes were a lawyering family. Uncle Nicholas had been Lord Chief Justice. And Edward had spent much of the 1630s developing a practice in Common Pleas. A brilliant lawyer, even if he said so himself, 'used with more countenance by all the judges in Westminster Hall' than 'was usually given to men of his years'.[20] Pepys would later admit to being 'mad in love' with Hyde, 'for he doth comprehend and speak so well, and with the greatest easiness and authority'.[21] Skills enhanced, no doubt, by youthful evenings passed in conversation at the Oxfordshire home of Lucius Cary, 2nd Viscount Falkland.[22] The so-called Tew 'Circle'.[23] We have come across Lucius before. A very dashing cavalier who lost his life in 1643 at the first battle of Newbury. Hyde would write a devoted testament into his *History*. A man of such 'inimitable sweetness and delight in conversation, of so flowing and obliging a humanity and goodness to mankind'. A 'lover of justice', and 'wit, and fancy', devoted to king and Church.[24] Everything that the testator wanted to be. Save for the suicidal heroism. Edward Hyde was a survivor.

On arrival in the Commons, Edward had sought to refine a conciliatory position which would, in time, evolve into what has become known as constitutional royalism. The first word matters more than the second. Hyde thought as Coke had thought. The authority of the Crown was rooted in, and defined by, the common law. As was the prerogative. There could be no 'diminution of the King's authority'; but neither should it ever be allowed to exceed 'its just limits'.[25] It was for this reason that Hyde opposed Ship Money; as 'something evil in its own right'. A king defined by his prerogative. And by his responsibilities as governor of the Church. The classic statement could be found in the *Answer to the Nineteen Propositions*, which Hyde drafted in June 1642, a 'happy, well-poised' constitution.[26] By then though it was too late, to stop a revolution at least.

Forced to choose, Hyde went with his king, and his Church. Personal loyalty, along with the sense that, in apportioning blame for 'this unnatural war', most of it lay with the puritan hot-heads. Hyde would though continue to seek accommodation, constantly leading negotiations, drafting terms, as much time spent battling the queen and her 'cavalier' supporters. Until it became clear that he had failed, again. At which point, he fled to the Scilly Isles, with his ward, the Prince of Wales, and then on to Jersey. It was here that he started to draft bits and pieces of a 'history'. Then to Madrid, appointed ambassador to the Spanish Court. Time spent studying the *Psalms*. Fascinated by the biblical David, his patience especially. There was, he advised his charge from a distance, much to be said for leaving God to sort things out. The 'resurrection of the English affection and loyalty' would surely follow.[27]

Not for the first time, though, no-one listened. Hyde skipped Worcester, not one for clambering trees, or making futile gestures. The rest of the 1650s were spent trying to deter his prince from doing anything else quite so daft.[28] In 1658 he was made Lord Chancellor; the 'highest place' in government he would later proudly proclaim, and the most 'trusted'.[29] In late 1661, Dryden would compose a sonnet *To My Lord Chancellor*, to celebrate his work in securing the Restoration. Hyde as the 'Earth' to his monarch's 'Heaven'. Chosen by Charles, and God, to 'dispose the Laws and Guide the State' (26, 33, 36).[30] A fair inference. It was to Hyde that Charles had turned, not just to draft the *Declaration of Breda* and the *Act of Oblivion* but much of the statutory settlement which followed. Rolled out across 1660 and 1661. The triumph of constitutional royalism, at long last. The 'excellent temper and harmony of affections' nurtured by the 'government's firm commitment to the laws of the country and the settled ways of the constitution'.[31]

Albeit not to last that long; as we will see. Conciliatory, at first glance, restorative. Much confirmatory too. Such as the abolition of Star Chamber and High Commission, and the backdating of the reign of King Charles II to 30 January 1649. Symbolic, in essence. Elsewhere more prosaic, to do with money. A statute to raise some much needed finance, granting the Crown £1.2 million a year, funded by tax and restored estate revenue. Another designed to make longer-term savings. An *Act for the Speedy Disbanding of the Army*. At a cost of £835,819, 8 shillings and 10 pence, but worth every last penny. For so long as a restless, unpaid army 'continued there would be perpetual trembling in the nation'.[32] Lessons learned.

The greatest legislative energy was, though, invested in the Church. The Supremacy was taken to be continuing. But there was a particular need, it was felt, to tighten Church discipline. The 1661 *Corporation Act* was the first of four statutes passed to that purpose. Excluding from public office anyone who refused to take communion in the Church, or swear the oath of allegiance. The following year came a reinvested *Act of Uniformity*. In effect formalizing a series of measures introduced over the previous eighteen months; abrogating the Solemn League and Covenant, re-adopting Anglican liturgy and restoring the bishops to the House of Lords. At much the same time, Parliament approved a *Conventicle Act*, which forbade religious meetings of more than five people, with fines ratcheted from £5 for a first offence, to transportation for habitual offenders. Finally, in 1665, came the *Five Mile Act*, which barred nonconformist preachers from going within five miles of their former ministries or towns.[33] In sum, a regulatory regime aimed at those whose 'tender consciences' had in the recent past, quite literally, run riot. Milton and friends. To become known, collectively, as the Clarendon 'Code'.

A testament to its author. And to the harsher pragmatics of restoration. The *Declaration of Breda* had promised 'liberty' to precisely these 'consciences'. Not, though, licence. The king put it succinctly. 'If the power of interpreting the scriptures be in every man's brain, what need we have of a church?'[34] By 1664, Hyde was urging that the *Conventicle Act* should be enforced with 'utmost rigour'.[35] Two thousand ministers would be ejected as a consequence. Not that it seemed to make settlement any easier. 'That which hath been the great Occasion of our Trouble, and is still of our Fears,' Edward Stillingfleet would declare in 1678, 'is Religion.'[36] That and money. A running deficit of £300,000 pa according to a Treasury account. Charles could just have spent less. But decided instead to sell Dunkirk to King Louis XIV, for £320,000. The City was appalled.[37] The Commons, Hyde recalled, 'morose and obstinate'.[38] Later, Hyde would suggest that an 'unhappy temper' had undermined his efforts from the very start. Cavalier 'jealousies' on one side, puritan 'perplexities' on the other.[39] And about to get a lot worse.

The finger of God

A minor uprising in Yorkshire in 1664, followed by a snowstorm in London in August. The following summer, conversely, was unusually hot and humid, ideal for incubating a bubonic plague. The authorities tried to enforce a sort of lockdown, and the College of Physicians busied itself recommending herbal tinctures. But nothing seemed to help. In the end something between 80,000 and 100,000 Londoners are likely to have died over a gruesome fifteen-month period. Until, eventually, the 'finger of God' intervened.[40] And brought some sun. A lot of sun. Summer 1666, the 'driest that ever man knew', according to Baxter.[41] A tinder-box, literally. A city still built of 'sticks'. A 'Great' Fire destroyed two-thirds of the City in the first week of September, including St Paul's Cathedral, another eighty-seven churches and approximately 13,200 houses.

'God's Terrible Voice', John Vincent declared, another who suspected that the formerly 'chosen people' had still not been forgiven the dreadful sins of 1649. Like Edward Chamberlayne. 'God's just anger' for 'abetting and instigating the shedding of the precious innocent Blood' of their former king.[42] Helped by a freshening breeze, and the absence of a functioning fire service. The problem, the following year, was the absence of a functioning Navy. The Dutch Admiral de Ruyter sailed up the Medway to Chatham dock, where he destroyed three ships of the line, and towed away the *Royal Charles*, by a 'sorry boat and six men' it was reported.[43] The ships had been laid up with a skeleton crew, the Admiralty having run out of money. All, it was generally agreed, Hyde's fault.

Dryden tried to put a positive spin on it all, sort-of, in his *Annus Mirabilis*. Celebrating some earlier victories over the perfidious Dutch, and pointing out that even more of London might have burned down, had God not answered the 'King's prayer'. John Evelyn read the situation rather differently. The 'late dreadful Conflagration, added to the Plague and Warre' bore the 'resemblance of Sodom', and was incontrovertible evidence of 'the most dismal judgement'. Nothing 'but what we highly deserved for, our prodigious ingratitude, burnings lusts, profane and abominable lives'.[44] Hyde surmised the same, afterwards; 'scandalous debauches' and 'liberty of vice' which had, in the end, 'corrupted' Court and country.[45] Parliament acted in October, ordering that there should be a day of 'fasting and humiliation', to atone for the 'crying sins of the nation'. Which seemed to work. A couple of days later, the weather finally broke, and it poured.

Still, the feeling that things were starting to go wrong again was growing, long before de Ruyter sauntered up the Medway. Pepys recounted a dinner in February 1667, at which 'we talked of Cromwell, all saying he was a brave fellow and did own his crown he got to himself as any man that got one'. And then again, a couple of months later, musing how 'strange' it was that

> everybody doth nowadays reflect upon Oliver and commend him, so brave things he did and made all the neighbour princes fear him; while here a prince, come in with all the love and prayers and good liking of his people, and have given greater signs of loyalty and willingness to serve him with their estates that ever was done by any people, hath lost all so soon.[46]

De Ruyter would never have dared take such liberties with 'King' Oliver.

James Harrington would have nodded. Back in 1660, he had suggested that it would be seven years before all the 'cavaliers' turned 'Commonwealth men' again.[47] Not quite, at least not yet. He was twenty-two short. What they did turn, though, was vindictive. The Lord Chancellor had always seemed a bit of a drag in the eyes of more excitable cavaliers. Hardly a wit, and nothing like tough enough on sectaries or papists. His close association with the king's brother, the Duke of York, fashioning more envy than admiration. The Duke had married Hyde's daughter, Anne, in January 1660. The two had been lovers in exile, and when Anne was discovered to be pregnant, Charles had insisted that they must marry. Against the advice of many, including it seems Hyde; or so he would later intimate, having the 'least jealousy or apprehension of it'.[48] A disapproving Pepys supposed that the marriage had, in one moment, 'undone the kingdom, by making the Chancellor so great above reach, who otherwise would have been but an ordinary man, to have been dealt with by other people'.[49] Prescient, but differently. It was the conversion of the Duke to Catholicism which would, in time, undo the kingdom. And it was Anne who set him off on his spiritual journey. She would not, though, see it completed. Dying, at the age of just thirty-four, in 1671. More of Anne shortly, and her daughters.

By then, Hyde had gone. Victim to a rather familiar kind of history. A riven Court, a Duke of Buckingham winding people up, and Parliament looking for an evil counsellor to blame; the irony of ironies. Time to be 'king himself', Buckingham whispered in the royal ear. A view probably shared by Charles, who was tiring of his Chancellor's periodic lectures on the 'excess of pleasures' and their consequences. And by the Duchess of Castlemaine, Barbara Villiers, with whom Charles presently enjoyed a fair bit of excess. Hyde would later blame Barbara for his fall; she hated him 'mortally'.[50] Pepys reported the story of his final audience with the king at Whitehall, on 28 August 1667. As he left the palace, Barbara rushed onto her balcony, in her nightgown, 'joying herself'. Hyde surrendered his seals of office the following day.[51] Thus, it might be surmised, ended the Restoration.

So the Duke of York later intimated. The 'most fatal blow' that his brother ever 'gave himself to his power and prerogative'.[52] Buckingham encouraged Parliament to ponder the possibility of impeachment. On a couple of grounds.[53] First, the attempted suspension of habeas corpus the year before, on the pretext of national emergency; very distant memories might have harked back to 1637. Second, rumour that Hyde had committed treason in betraying secrets to France. The former charge had some credibility, the latter none. Needless to say the impeachment process took a customary course, and got stuck in the Lords.[54] An alternative bill, for Hyde's banishment, was drafted. Hyde read the runes, a Falstaff no longer loved by his Hal.[55] A boat to France on the last day of November 1667. We will catch up shortly. Now, though, for another perspective.

The art of trimming

The term 'trimmer' did not enter the Restoration lexicon until the 1680s. Lord Halifax famously recommended the idea in his *Character of a Trimmer*, published in 1685. A politics that lay between 'Monarchy, a thing that leaveth men no liberty, and a Commonwealth, such a one as alloweth them no Quiet'. Whether Hyde might have recognized something of himself in Halifax's caricature is moot. Sharper Tory critics would turn the appellation into a pejorative. But the idea that a constitution is 'blessed' where 'dominion and liberty are so happyly reconciled' would surely have appealed to the incoming Lord Chancellor.[56] An apposite metaphor too. Carrying a range of connotations. In its original expression, nautical. Hyde might have noted his captain trimming sail as he bobbed about in the Channel in late November 1667. Shifting direction, to catch the breeze. But also something that an artist might do. To tidy up a painting or a sculpture, or a piece of writing. To make it presentable, a better fit to fashion. And then, finally, in the vernacular, to give someone a good beating. Each serves our purpose.

We will start with the tidying-up. More accurately, some brushing up. Few brushed harder in Restoration England than Sir Peter Lely. Lely had arrived from the Low Countries back in 1643, two years after the death of van Dyck. The young Lely had painted for Charles I. And then for Cromwell, 'warts and all'. And then for Charles II. Art rising above the tawdry politics of the age, whilst also shaping it. Appointed 'principal painter in ordinary' in 1661, at £200 a year, 'as formerly' paid to van Dyke. Just as prolific too. A new generation of cavaliers to paint, as well as a new king. And his wife. Lely managed to capture a rather blank-looking Catherine of Braganza sometime around 1664. And all the royal mistresses, far more engaging. Many recorded in the celebrated 'Windsor Beauties' series.

Including Anne Hyde. Not that Anne was a mistress of the king, of course. She had, though, been mistress of his brother James. The 'Windsor Beauties' were in fact commissioned by Anne, keen to be associated with the coolest girl-gang of the age, even if they were mostly high-class prostitutes. Or lower, as in the case of the celebrated actresses Nell Gwynn and Margaret Hughes, both painted by Lely a few years later, in the early 1670s.[57] A sly glance each, and a naked breast; somehow definitive of the 'lascivious' moment. As for Anne, not by common account a beauty, Pepys struggled to see the attraction; 'not only the proudest woman in the world, but the most expensefull'.[58] Too silly to be a queen, and nothing like pretty enough. The French ambassador commended her 'courage, cleverness and energy'. Not bad attributes. But hardly enough for Anne, or Lely. So, instead, it is a knowing smile, another daring breast and a teasing play of the hair.

Hyde did not much like Lely. No-one much liked Lely. A 'mighty proud man and full of state', according to Pepys.[59] Still, a visit to Lely's studio was pretty much a rite of passage for anyone who wanted to matter in Restoration England. Royal mistress or Lord Chancellor. Lely painted Sir Edward sometime around 1665, resplendent in his robes of office. And a little heavy; the port and the fatty diet taking their toll. The 'Windsor Beauties' were installed in the Duke of York's private chambers. Alongside another set, which would play a supporting role in the life and career of Edward Hyde. The so-called 'Lowestoft Flagmen'. All the naval heroes who had taken part in the great victory over the Dutch at the battle of Lowestoft in 1665. To include, of course, the duke himself; Lord High Admiral of the Fleet. A few other familiar names too. The newly ennobled Duke of Albemarle, Deputy Lord High Admiral. Prince Rupert, who would be Lord High Admiral in 1668. The Earl of Sandwich, Lieutenant Admiral and Pepys's boss at the Navy Board, and a man of some experience, having served as Fleet Admiral during the Cromwellian Protectorate. Nothing that a little discretion could not brush away. Less said about what happened after Lowestoft the better. Rather than pressing home the victory and securing the sea-lines for a generation, the 'flagmen' retreated to Lely's studio, to pose. The Dutch, meanwhile, refitted their fleet.

Posing, painting. Remoulding too. Lots of corporation-maces to be recast. The 'middling' of Congleton had theirs redone, to read 'The freedome of England by God's blessing restored to CR 1661.' A good year to be a blacksmith or a bronze-caster, particularly if you were good at inscribing oak-trees and acorns. The new king's escapade following Worcester became iconic. Statues garlanded in oak apple, medallions minted to celebrate the coronation, and then the king's birthday, Oak Apple Day as it was now called. John Aubrey worried that the acorn had, previously, been 'abused by the Druids to superstition'. No-one else did. In 1664, the king announced himself especially pleased by a brand new 100-gun ship-of-the-line, christened *Royal Oak*. Less pleased three years on, when de Ruyter left it burning in the Medway. The liking for all things oak continued though. In 1681, Charles established a military hospital at Chelsea, for 412 'pensioners'. All to wear the same arboreal insignia on their lapels and hat badges.

Every king needs a cult; or at least every Stuart king felt the need. Which brings us back to Charles the Martyr, and a certain sense of dilatoriness. Not forgotten, of course, not quite. New editions of the *Eikon* would keep trundling off the presses, as we have already noted. Some pictorial remembrances as well. A painting depicting Charles as Christ, holding a crown of thorns, displayed at Covent Garden. And a statue, eventually, a little further along at Charing Cross. We will take a closer look at the history of that Charles very shortly. The Fast Days, of course. Even some church dedications. There could be no St Charles, at least not in the Anglican Church; but there could be the next best thing. A first at Falmouth, dedicated to King Charles the Martyr in 1664. Near to Pendennis Castle, where the young Prince Charles had fled England after Naseby. Three more by the end of the century, at Shelland, Newtown-in-Wem and Tunbridge Wells. And the Chapel at Kilmainham Royal Hospital, dedicated in 1680. An architectural gem. That was it though; no more until the later eighteenth century.

Brushed over, bronzed over and written over. Which brings us to another familiar name. We left Andrew Marvell as he left Nun Appleton. On his way to become laureate at the court of 'King' Oliver. And then pall-bearer at his funeral, alongside Milton. All of which might have given Marvell some pause in 1660. Not for long though. Marvell was a natural 'trimmer'. Inclined to shun the 'extremities', the 'truth for the most part lies in the middle'. Happy to reshape his own history too. A reluctant revolutionary, it transpired, which is probably true. Caught by circumstance: 'I think the Cause was too good to have been fought for. Men ought to have trusted God; they ought and might have trusted the King with the whole matter.'[60] Not exactly a cavalier, but not exactly a puritan. Marvell was careful to be not exactly anything.

A strategy which fitted the moment. The age of 'wit writing', as Dryden termed it.[61] Variously subtle, and not. John Wilmot, Earl of Rochester, provided an alternative reading of the 'Windsor Beauties' in his *Signor Dildo*. The 'ladies all of merry England', and their 'rabble of pricks' (1, 81).[62] Fun, of course. But not only. At much the same time as he was touching-up the 'Beauties', sometime in 1673, Wilmot was also musing on the nature of majesty. Just one 'prick' in *On King Charles*. Famously 'of a length' with 'his sceptre'. Wilmot did not have a problem with a king who 'loves fucking much'. He and Charles got on pretty well, most of the time. But there was a worry if 'she that plays with one may sway the other' (11–12). A sentiment which the exiled Sir Edward might have shared. And Marvell. Not that they shared much else.

Hyde is the subject of two of Marvell's most renowned pieces of 'wit writing'. Both composed in 1667, as the net began to close around the beleaguered Lord Chancellor. On the theme of touching-up. The first is *Clarendon's Housewarming*. Hyde had started building his grand house, at the north side of Piccadilly, in 1664. A vanity project which appeared somewhat incongruous, with all the 'deluges threatening our land', the plagues, the fires, the Dutch (3).[63] Though hardly incongruous to anyone who knew Hyde, the 'old Volpone', as Ludlow called him.[64] Burnet reported a great 'outcry' across the City, with a fair bit of localized vandalism around the perimeter of the house. At one point, a mock gibbet was erected outside the gates.[65] The Chancellor was though undaunted, and pushed on. Marvell's poem hurled some more elevated brickbats. Lots of classical allusions, to vanity and corruption, to get the reader underway. Before arriving at a bitter close. A personal assault on the man who was, more than any, responsible for what had gone wrong.

Hyde on the 'terrace' of his palace: 'A lantern like Fawkes' surveys the burnt town / And shows on the top, by the regal gilt ball, / Where you are to expect the sceptre and crown' (90–2). Loaded imagery, of plotters and over-mighty subjects, and emperors watching their cities burn. An 'idol of state' sitting 'adorned and accursed', looking around for others to 'blame' (98, 102). But justice will come, when Parliament opens again, and the Chancellor is 'roasted'. And there is, at least, a parting 'convenience', in that the house should be situated so near to 'Tyburn'. It will 'spare the Tower barge' (108, 112).

Last instructions

The second of Marvell's summer 1667 satires is *Last Instructions to a Painter*. A response to Waller's cloying *Instructions to a Painter, for the Drawing of the Posture and Progress of his Majesties Forces at Sea*, which appeared in 1666. Celebrating the same victory which inspired the 'Lowestoft Flagmen'. Not so easy in 1667, though. A nation collapsing into 'mindless chaos', its capital in ruins, its navy shamed. A Restoration, it might be said, in need of restoration. But, as with the raising of Sir Edward's new house, the final attempts at touching-up the canvas serve only to emphasize the incongruities. As the painter's attention is drawn through the various characters and incidents of the supposed 'Golden Age', he finds nothing but 'great debauch' (8, 47).[66] Inevitably so. For, on closer inspection, the 'Lady State' of England is nothing but a painted whore (1).

The poem opens at the Court of King Charles II, with the various characters who prostitute themselves to its rapacious appetites. Starting with the Lord Chamberlain, Henry Jermyn, Earl of St Albans. Responsible for the governance of the Court, but too busy trying to pimp England to the French. Master of the whores, who come next. The fading of Lely's 'Beauties'. Pride of place given to the Duchess of York. Her marriage an 'experiment upon the Crown', secured by a strategic pregnancy. Painted to resemble her father, with the 'Chancellor's belly and so large a rump'. A plain woman desperately trying to escape her plain-ness. Like her husband, 'nightly' escaping the palace to chase other 'prey' (52, 63, 78). After Anne comes Barbara Villiers, another fading 'beauty', with an apparently insatiable sexual appetite, encompassing various grooms and younger courtiers. Not a pretty picture, of Barbara, or her Court.

The painter then turns his attention to 'affairs of state', pausing more closely at the events of the previous February, and the prorogation of Parliament. A moment to 'survey / With what small arts the public game they play' (117–18). A variant on the theme; the whoring of Whitehall. A sequence of dismal caricatures working the metaphor. The 'close Cabal' letting loose the 'monster' of excise, to stalk 'all day in streets concealed from sight' (139, 150). The English 'senate', this 'new whore of state', its 'wittols' sat in the Commons (149–51).[67] The 'troop of Clarendon'; once there was none 'better clad, nor so well paid' (176–7). Not now though. The prorogation saves the Chancellor, but not for long. With spring comes 'fresh news', of the 'Isle of Candy, Dutch and ships!' (397–8)

A city terrified, Parliament recalled by the Lord Chancellor's 'pen'; irony of ironies. 'Never old lecher more repugnance felt / Consenting with his rupture to be gelt' (473–4). Marvell might have deployed a variety of metaphors; a thirst for power, an addiction. But he went with lust, and castration. Then more news, of the 'Medway chase ravished' by de Ruyter (744). In time, Parliament would find a scapegoat in a Navy Commissioner named Pett. Marvell smelt a cover-up. Defending Pett in the

Commons, and pouring scorn on his accusers in *Last Instructions*. Interestingly, Marvell remained chary as to the wisdom of pressing the impeachment charges against the real culprit. Probably because he knew that they would never get through the Lords. The 'old lecher' shamed and exiled was good enough.

There were anyway further 'instructions'. 'Paint last the King, and a dead shade of night' (884). A picture of 'calm horror all alone / He wakes, and muses of the uneasy throne' (889–90). Visited in his fitful dreams by two 'pale ghosts'; 'grandsire Harry and of Charles his sire' (918).[68] More Macbeth than the 'merry monarch'. Harry 'reveals' the 'grisly wound' where he was stabbed to death by his assassin. Whilst 'ghastly Charles, turning his collar low, / The purple thread about his neck does show' (922–3). And 'then whispering to his son in words unheard' disappears through 'the locked door' (924). We can surmise what was said. For the 'pensive King revolves / And rising straight on Hyde's disgrace resolves' (925–6). Remember 1642. A point affirmed in the apologia which ends the poem. The very 'last' instruction, 'To the King'. And a last metaphor, of 'vermin' and 'scratching courtiers'. Who, unchecked, will bring England to 'waste', again (978, 981).

And did; as Marvell knew they would. In 1672 appeared the first part of what Burnet would later suppose the 'wittiest book that ever appeared in this age'.[69] *The Rehearsal Transpros'd*, written against the increasingly stringent regulations governing conformity of worship.[70] A few more ghosts. Of previous prelates who were prepared to decorate the country into war. Laud most obviously, his 'Arminian jangles' and dreams of 'absolute government'.[71] A few months before his death, in August 1678, Marvell would publish a final substantial piece of prose, *An Account of the Growth of Popery and Arbitrary Government*. Anonymous, this time though. Such were the tensions of the moment, rumours of 'popish plots' swirling about. The authorities offered £100 for the identity of the author.

Finally, a scattering of bitter satires. On the familiar themes of trimming, and lack of money. And statues. The first being that of King Charles II, erected at the Stocks Market in 1672; famous for its butchery. Purchased by the same Sir Robert Vyner who had furnished the new mace in 1660. By now, the king's banker and, by no coincidence, shortly to be elected Lord Mayor. On hearing report that there was a nearly complete statute of the Polish King John Sobieski going cheap, Vyner made an offer, got it and then paid to have it polished up and erected.[72] John became Charles II, and the Turk, cowering under the hooves of his magnificent steed, became Cromwell. Still, apparently, wearing a turban.[73] In his *Critical Review of the Public Buildings of London*, James Ralph would later dismiss the statue as 'ridiculous and absurd'.[74] Marvell was another predictably unimpressed. A king recast in the City: 'Say his Majesty himself is bought too and sold' (24).[75] Resembling 'a monster more like than a king' (12). The wrong kind of restoration.

The second statue popped up a couple of years later, at Charing Cross. The idea that there might be a statue commemorating the martyrdom of the first Charles had bounced around since 1660. Following Vyner's lead, the Earl of Portland volunteered information as to an earlier statue which his dad had commissioned for his flower-garden, back in 1633. Depicting Charles on horseback carrying a marshal's baton. The statue had, in the end, been placed at the Exchange. Where it somehow survived until 1648, at which point it was vandalized by some classical scholars, the words *Exit Tyrannous Ultimus* scrawled on its base. Then removed, and sold to a blacksmith named Rivett, in the expectation that he would melt it down. Instead Rivett hid it and then, rather impertinently, put it up for sale at the Restoration. In the end, the Sheriff of London was instructed to issue a writ of replevin, and the statue was retrieved. To be erected, finally, at Charing Cross in 1674. On a nice new plinth, carved by Grinling Gibbons. A sort of apotheosis, if only by a couple of feet.

Some were impressed. Edmund Waller adopted the pertinent metaphor in his celebratory poem *On the Statue of King Charles at Charing Cross*; 'kings so killed rise conquerors again'. Others less so. Ralph appreciated the plinth, but not much else; 'tamely executed' with a king strangely devoid of 'expression'.[76] And Marvell, in his *Statue at Charing Cross*. A piece of 'Theatre', commissioned by the Lord High Treasurer, the Earl of Danby, done on the cheap (7).[77] The 'old King on Horseback is but an Halfecrown', a 'monarch of Gingerbread would doe as well' (28, 48). The poem is as much about Danby, the Strafford of his moment, just as corrupt, just as dangerous. History repeats, or threatens to: 'And 'tis forty to one if he Play the old Game / Hee'l shortly reduce us to fourty and eight' (23–4). Back, in other words, to 1648. The final stanza bites:

So the Statue will up after all this delay,
But to turn the face to Whitehall you must Shun;
Tho of Brass, yet with grief it would melt him away.
To behold every day Such a Court, such a son. (53–6)

The latter theme, of the disappointed father, would be revisited a couple of years later, in a poem entitled *A Dialogue Between the Two Horses*. Almost certainly Marvell's work again, written most likely in 1675. Corruption everywhere, financial and moral: 'The King on thy back is a lamentable tool' (124).[78] It is, notably, the Stocks Market 'horse' that reaches back to a still-recent past, in order to venture what would prove to be a prescient warning:

Tho Father and Sonne are different Rodds,
Between the two Scourges wee find little odds ...
I freely declare it, I am for old Noll.
Tho' his Government did a Tyrants resemble. (127–8, 138–9)

The 'Gods', the poem concludes, 'have repented the Kings Restoration' (162). And so it would prove.

Other aspects of the Charing Cross statue bothered Marvell too. Not least the site, where Harrison had been butchered a decade and a half earlier. Since used, most commonly, for hosting fairs and pillorying dissenters.[79] Hardly auspicious. But it was the dilatoriness that was most obvious, reinforcing the sense that Restoration England was, to put it bluntly, all flash and no substance. Lacking the money, lacking the dignity. And the will. For all his saintliness, Charles the Martyr was not a comfortable fit. Too sad for 'merry' England, and dull. A better fit, ironically, in the 1650s, when everyone was sad and dull. Which brings us to a last statue, almost.

And a funeral. That of the Duke of Albemarle, in 1670. A first state funeral for a non-member of the royal family; unless Cromwell counts. A lying-in-state at Somerset House, a vast procession through the City, catafalque by Inigo Jones. Followed by an august ceremony at the Abbey, presided over by the temporarily homeless Bishop of London, and then interment in the Chapel of Henry VII. All suitably splendid, as befitted the man who allowed the king to get his throne back. But which also threw into sharper relief the fact that no-one seemed so bothered about the same king's father; including, it seemed, the same king. To be fair, Charles had wondered the possibility that his dad's remains might be retrieved from their present 'obscure place', somewhere in St George's Chapel at Windsor, and reburied them at Westminster Abbey. But he had not wondered hard. And there was a ready excuse. No-one actually knew where Charles the Martyr was buried. A lost king, literally. The remains had, in fact, been placed in the vault of Henry VIII and Jane Seymour. Marvell might have enjoyed the irony; the martyred Charles destined to spend eternity in the close company of the man who first decided that a 'reformation' of the English Church might be a good idea.

Absent the remains of the king, the idea of his reburial had to be abandoned; for 'reasons of state'. And so, in its stead, minds turned to the possibility of building a magnificent mausoleum. A different kind of locational problem here; finding the money. Finally, in 1678, Parliament agreed to levy a special tax. To raise £70,000. Enough, not just for the mausoleum but for a funeral, and maybe another statue. Sir Christopher Wren was set to work. And came back with a suitably splendid design. Of King Charles I 'in modern armour', standing on a shield borne by four cardinal Virtues, and being offered a crown by angels up above; reminiscent, again, of Rubens's ceiling. Sadly, though, it never came to pass. 'Incidents of the Times', Sir Christopher ruefully concluded, and 'Motives unknown to the public'.[80] Marvell might have guessed; someone had creamed off the money. Best to move on.

A life in history

The year 1702 is not a year which excites the historian's heart. The War of Spanish Succession trundled along. Defoe published a satirical tract entitled *The Shortest*

Way with Dissenters, and got himself pilloried. The death of Pepys and the birth of John Wesley worthy of passing note, and Isaac Newton became president of the Royal Society. Hardly surprising if England was ready for a rest. An armchair and a good book perhaps. Defoe and Swift for the lighter-hearted, and the darker. The latter's *Tale of the Tub* would come out in early 1704. And, for the historian, the publication of the first volumes of Sir Edward Hyde's *History of the Rebellion*.

The history of Edward Hyde

Of course, the other thing that happened in 1702 was the succession of Queen Anne. The last Stuart monarch, as it would transpire. A consequence not of revolution but of dodgy prenatal care and high infant mortality rates.[81] A couple of things to note about Anne. First, she was less interested in politics than friends, which tended her towards politicians of the less contentious, more 'trimming' kind. And second, she was a solid Anglican; just like her maternal granddad. 'Entirely firm to the interests' of the Church.[82] Both factors giving rise to the suspicion that the moment might be conducive to publishing a few Tory histories. So, for example, the *Memoirs of Sir Philip Warwick*. Sir Philip had been the martyred king's personal secretary. And those of Sir Thomas Herbert, who pretended to have been his best mate.

And the *History* of Sir Edward Hyde. The moving force here was Sir Edward's second son, Laurence. Created Earl of Rochester in 1682, Laurence had held high office in the reigns of both Charles II and James II.[83] A Tory in his father's mould and, of course, uncle to the Queen. Not that they got on particularly well. Both possessed difficult tempers. The tipping point arrived, indeed, with the publication of Sir Edward's *History*. Laurence decided to compose a preface. It should be remembered in an 'an age when so many memoirs, narratives, and pieces of history come out as it were on purpose to justify the taking of arms against the King, and to belittle, revile and ridicule the sacred majesty of an anointed head' that only half a century ago a dreadful 'murder' had been 'committed on a pious prince'.[84] Innocent enough at first glance; and we will take a look at some of these belittling 'narratives' in due course. But not at second. A couple of difficult insinuations. The first was that made by Marvell; that the martyred Charles was not, in fact, being much remembered at all. The second, that unless the new Queen paid closer attention to the state of her Church, and her country, the same thing might easily happen to her. England was still in a 'perplexed condition', blighted by the 'like root of animosity and discontent'.[85] Anne was not impressed. A 'ridiculous' example of editorial 'vanity'.

Another fallen Hyde. Laurence was relieved of his duties as Lord Lieutenant of Ireland, and exiled from Court. Which brings us back to his father. Left, if we recall, on his way to France in late 1667. Montpellier, in the end. Where he would spend the next four years of his life, much of it writing. Before he moved to Moulin, and then finally Rouen, where he died, in 1674. It was hardly surprising if he wanted to reflect upon the history of the previous three decades, and his place in it. It had been a remarkable life. Neither is it surprising that he wanted to present himself in a positive light. Which is why he decided to incorporate material from another book which he had been drafting, provisionally entitled *A Life, by Himself.* The first parts of the *History* had been drafted during the later 1640s.[86] So it was a matter of updating, and bringing all the constituent parts together. In this way, it might be said that Sir Edward covered all the bases. Providing his readers with a chronicle of what had happened, a 'full and clear narration', along with a personal testament of how he had tried to help.[87]

Enhanced by two particular attributes. First that he had been 'present' at so many of the incidents. The 'greatest' of parliamentarians indeed, trusted by all. Not least by the king, who was keen, on many an occasion, to proffer his personal 'thanks' for all his many 'good services'. And second that he was a man 'whose integrity was ever without blemish, and believed to be above temptation'. Esteemed for the 'innate goodness and justice of his nature', as well as the 'wonderful tenderness' of his character, and for his loyalty to the constitution, the Church and the Crown, motivated at all times by a desire to 'maintain the government and preserve the law'.[88] No-one was better placed to write a history of the 'great rebellion'. Purposed to entertain, of course, but also to educate and to counsel. As Laurence rather tactlessly emphasized. So 'that posterity may not be deceived'. To make 'visible' how easily 'all foundations of law and liberty' might be destroyed.[89] All of which makes for a slightly compromised history. Tory in its politics, Whig in its aspiration.

And prejudiced to its root. The politics written into the *History* is thoroughly personal. A manifesto for the kind of settlement that Hyde urged during the 1640s, which he had written into his *Answers to the Nineteen Propositions* in summer 1641. A constitution founded on Church and Crown, and everything in moderation. Held by Hyde in 'zealous esteem and reverence'.[90] Despite the bitterest of experiences, Hyde never doubted the essential stability of this constitutional 'settlement': Church, Crown and Parliament ruling in an 'exact' harmony. Hooker's constitution, in essence. And, most particularly, the role of the Privy Council in securing the exercise of a 'just prerogative'. The institution, the 'lustre whereof always reflects upon the king himself'.[91] Just so long as he picks the right counsellors.

There again, if he picks too many of the wrong kind, consumed by their own 'pride' and 'envy', the 'root and the spring of all calamities' is discovered.[92] The failure of the early 1640s was a consequence, not of fundamental instability but of human error, and 'great malice'. Men 'disposed' to 'compass confusion' in Parliament, such as Pym, Hampden and Holles.[93] Puritan zealots such as Lilburne and Prynne, heading their 'lunatic rabble'. And Cromwell, the 'greatest dissembler living', possessed of 'all the wickedness against which damnation is denounced and hell-fire prepared'.[94] But also the egregious errors of venal counsellors such as Strafford, in whose impeachment Hyde had been instrumental. A man 'notorious' in his 'pride'.[95] And Digby, responsible in Hyde's opinion for so much that went wrong in late 1641 and early 1642. And Laud, like so many clergymen the 'least' able to understand political pragmatics. Hyde did not doubt Laud's piety, nor his fervency in regard to matters of Church reform. But there was nothing in church 'ornaments' that was 'worth the charge' of a civil war.[96]

A familiar motif, then. A prince too easily 'prevailed' upon. Stretching back past Laud and Strafford, to Portland and Buckingham. No family, Hyde surmised, had done more damage to the English throne than the Villiers. All pretty, all venal; starting with Steenie and finishing with Barbara. Of course, a more percipient prince might have been expected to spot the charlatans, and the whores. But Charles was not the first Stuart to be too readily flattered, nor the last. And not the first to be tempted to rule at the margins of law. Or to misunderstand the reach of prerogative. The successive dissolutions of Parliament in the late 1620s, as often as not to save Steenie, were 'ungracious' and unwise. As was the decade of 'personal rule' which followed. Ten years of 'cheerfulness' lost. The 'ill-husbandry' of Ship Money. We have already noted Hyde's disapproving account of *Hampden's Case*, and the 'damage and mischief' it brought. Quoting Thucydides: "That men are much more passionate for injustice than for violence'.[97] The road to Naseby started here, in the Court of Exchequer in 1637.

A pattern which continues into the 'history' of the 1640s. Listening to the wrong people, making the wrong calls. It was not that Charles did not listen to Hyde. But when push came to shove, at the critical moments, he tended to pay greatest heed to the wrong counsellors. And his wife. The longer Hyde reflected on the 'calamity' of war, the more he was inclined to blame Henrietta Maria. The peremptory dissolution of the Short Parliament, the dithering over Strafford's fate, the attempt to arrest the Five Members in January 1642, the consequential flight from London, the stubborn refusal through 1643 to take negotiations seriously and 1644. Hyde is keen to distance himself from all of this. An 'absolute stranger' to a series of mistakes, most of which he 'perfectly detested'.[98] The king's fault perhaps, the queen's for sure. But certainly not his.

That all said, the king was still the king. And, moreover, a king of genuine piety and personal kindness; quite simply 'the best Christian in the world'. A close reading of the *History* might raise questions about the nature of Hyde's 'royalism'. But not the integrity of his 'loyalism', his 'devotion and passion for the person' of Charles Stuart.[99] It is impossible, on reading the *History*, to imagine Hyde going anywhere in summer 1642, other than to join his king. Hyde envelops a predictably glowing testament into his account of the 'lamentable tragedy' of the king's trial and subsequent execution. Derivative of course. If Hyde had been present in London, he would likely have been part of the defence team. But he was not. So, having little to add in regard to the jurisprudence of the event, the 'particular so well known', Hyde focuses on the characters.[100] And most especially the lead. Who, of course, rose to the moment magnificently. Displaying a 'Christian courage and patience' which was nothing short of 'saint-like'. The Charles of the *Eikon Basilike*. But not just. In regard to the saintliness of the martyred king, Hyde could speak to personal experience. The 'worthiest gentleman, the best master, the best friend, the best husband, the best father, and the best Christian that the age in which he lived produced'.[101]

The *History* did not, of course, finish in 1649. Even if, as subsequent historians have supposed, the best bits did. The history of the 1650s is consumed by the tyranny of Oliver Cromwell. Hyde was amongst those who feared that Cromwell would take the Crown. Nothing in English history suggested that a Republic might last; but nothing suggested that a usurpation could not. So reason to be worried. Interestingly, in his description of Cromwell's character, written into a commentary on his death, Hyde is prepared to concede certain qualities. Entirely devoid of 'moral honesty', perhaps, but also a man of 'admirable circumspection and sagacity, and a most magnanimous resolution'.[102] The Cromwell that Pepys would recall in February 1667. Charles Stuart in the negative.

On to 1660. A moment of vindication. Of patience, not least. Providence has led the 'chosen people' through the 'Red Sea'.[103] Almost Miltonic. But then, new temptations; or rather old. Seven years of struggle against the voices of vanity and 'prejudice', and the Villiers family, followed by dismissal. All terribly unfair. 'Folly and neglect'; but, again, not his.[104] So far was Sir Edward 'from an immoderate appetite to be rich' or desirous of 'any other extent of power than was agreeable to the great office he held'.[105] A moment to stress, once again, the difference between his fall and that of earlier over-mighty counsellors. Such as Laud and 'Black Tom'. The former 'too proud', the latter too easy in his abuse of 'the law'. There was no such 'blemish' on Hyde's record.[106]

Suffice also to say the *History* would live on, long past the death of its author. Not least because nothing that happened in 1689 appeared to detract from the acuity of Hyde's account, or the essentials of constitutional settlement which it appeared to recommend. Favoured by nascent Tories of course. Pepys lived long enough to read the first volume, and sent his compliments to the editor.[107] There would be a lot of Hyde in eighteenth-century Tory histories. Lauded in the mid-century *Biographia Britannica*. A more hedged Hyde in David Hume's *History of England*. Recommending a history which 'pleases us at the same time that we disapprove it', written in style that is 'prolix and redundant' but which also evinces 'imagination and sentiment'. In sum the product of a historian who inclines to be 'entertaining' rather than 'accomplished'. Hardly purring. But Hume's sharpest observation is surely this; that Hyde's *History* was 'more partial in appearance than reality'.[108] A prologue to the 'glorious' revolution, coated in Tory gloss.

But not so thickly that it might put off the more trimming Whig. Such as Lord John Hervey, Lord Privy Seal in Walpole's 1740 administration. In whose opinion Hyde was a 'true patriot', who had saved the English from being reduced to 'absolute slaves'. And John Granger, who adopted the same line in his 1779 biographical dictionary. Declaring Hyde to be, above all, an 'honest' historian who resisted the re-imposition of Stuart tyranny in 1660. Possessed of 'all the virtues of Cato' indeed.[109] It might have been supposed that Catharine Macaulay would have struggled to be quite so generous in her appraisal. But not so. There was no more 'faithful account' of the civil wars, and their aftermath.[110] Precisely what Hyde had hoped. A history written in such a way that it seemed to rise above narrower political prejudice. There would be later critics, of course, as we will shortly see. But few doubting the perception of the *History*, or much questioning its integrity. The doyenne of seventeenth-century history, and historians. Back, though, to some of the others.

Voices

The *History*, as Laurence's preface intimated, was published as a rebuttal to a wave of republican 'memoirs' which had appeared in recent years. All of which recalled a rather different revolution. And a different Sir Edward Hyde. A fleeting appearance in Lucy Hutchinson's *Memoirs of the Life of Colonel Hutchinson*. Just enough to lay bare his vindictiveness, so 'cruelly' determined to exact vengeance on the sainted Colonel. A man who managed everything in the 'most oppressive and illegal ways'.[111] Not that Lucy was any more impressed by Charles. Shifty, malevolent, 'secretly grudging of his people' and 'bent upon' tyranny.[112] At his trial, conspicuously unrepentant of his many sins. Treating every charge with 'disdainful smiles', and leaving the court with no alternative. Possessed of a 'disposition so bent to the ruin of all that had opposed him and all the righteous and just things that they had contended for' that the execution of 'justice upon him' was demanded by God. For which reason the Colonel had signed the warrant, 'according to the dictates of a conscience which he had sought the Lord to guide'.[113]

Lucy's *Memoirs* were not, in fact, amongst those which appeared in the final years of the century. Printed, instead, for private circulation.[114] Unlike John Rushworth's *Historical Collections*. An assiduous chronicler, with a rotten sense of timing. A first volume of *Collections* appeared in 1659, articulating a few acerbic observations as to the perspicacity of Charles Stuart; a king too 'excessively in love with his darling prerogative'. Not the best moment. A second volume came out in 1680, at the height of the Exclusion crisis. Shortly after, Rushworth arrived at King's Bench prison, short of money and very short of friends.[115] He never left, dying there in 1690. Two further volumes would appear in 1692 and 1701. Better then. By which time republican memoirs had become positively fashionable. *The*

Short Memorials of Thomas Lord Fairfax, the *Memoirs of Denzil Holles*, a revised edition of Harrington's *Oceana*, all appearing in 1698.

Along with Algernon Sidney's *Discourses Concerning Government*.[116] We might recall Algernon squabbling with Cromwell over the mooted trial of the king. Algernon had, very sensibly, skipped abroad in 1660. But then returned in 1677; in order to resolve an inheritance dispute.[117] For a man who had subsequently appraised the regicide as 'the justest and bravest act' that 'ever was in England', and the Restoration as a 'pernicious mischief', it was a risky move.[118] So when the Rye House 'plot' was foiled, in autumn 1683, Algernon found himself high on the list of suspects. Hard evidence of involvement proved elusive. Not though a draft copy of the *Discourses*. Wherein could be found a passionate defence of elective magistracy and civil disobedience. A 'king is under law', and 'swords were given to men, that none might be slaves'.[119] Remember Caligula and Nero, the *Discourses* suggested, before moving on to cast some aspersions regarding the 'bawds, whores, thieves' and other 'vile wretches' who could be found lounging around the second Caroline Court.[120] More than enough to prosecute a trial, according to Lord Justice Jeffreys. Who, in the absence of much else by way of compelling evidence, allowed the manuscript to be produced as one of the two necessary 'witnesses' to treason. To 'write is to act'.[121] An unrepentant Algernon was executed in December 1683. His scaffold-speech, in print a couple of days later, cried 'vengeance' for 'righteousness sake'.[122]

Another republican testament to appear in 1698 would prove, over time, more notorious still. It purported to be the *Memoirs of Edmund Ludlow*. Ludlow, we might recall, ended up in Vevey, where he was visited by his old friend Slingsby Bethel in 1692.[123] Bethel returned with a draft text entitled *The Voyce from the Watchtower*. Very big, and it is the big-ness which intrigues. For when the *Memoirs of Edmund Ludlow* appeared a little later, they were a lot less big. In fact, around three-quarters of a million words had been edited out. Possibly Bethel's work. More likely John Toland. Already giving Harrington a make-over, and Holles and Sidney, and writing up a *Life of Milton*.[124] Each emerging from the experience a little less puritan-zealot and a lot more patriot-Whig.

Not that it made so much difference to Ludlow's Charles Stuart, or his Edward Hyde. Ludlow's Charles is much the same as Lucy Hutchinson's. 'Impudent' at his trial, 'as if he had not been guilty of the blood that hath been shed in this war'. And mendacious and deceitful. His manifest 'duplicity' evidenced by the king in his various 'negotiations' during the closing years of the war. The Naseby 'cabinet' stuck in Ludlow's mind. A principled objection, too, to the idea of monarchy, 'no way conducing to the interests of this nation'. Ultimately, though, it was the tyranny that did for Charles. 'I bear no malice to the man's person,' Ludlow concluded, 'than I do to my dear father; but I hate that cursed principle of tyranny that has so long lodged and harboured within him, which has turned our waters of law into blood.'[125] Ludlow signed the death warrant on these terms. And Toland ratified.

Except that more recently discovered parts of the *Voyce*, which commence in 1660, insinuate a different prejudice. A godlier Ludlow, thinking in Vevey as Milton thought in Gaza. Charles Stuart as the 'man of blood' who broke his covenant with God. The 'blood of thousands lying at his door'. And responsible, in Ludlow's mind at least, for the blood which would continue to be shed through the 1650s, and into the early 1660s. Harrison, Carew, Peter, all the other 'poor innocent lambs of Christ' torn to pieces at Charing Cross, 'slain for the word of God, and the testimony they held'. Latter-day 'witnesses' of the Revelation.[126]

But not, again, the impression that would have first struck readers of Toland's *Memoirs*. Their Ludlow rather keener on witnessing the inscription of a 'glorious' revolution than the apocalyptic collapse of the Cromwellian. Ready to march into the 'long' eighteenth century, and beyond. A ghostly army of republican heroes braced for battle with some old foes, and some new. Alongside those raised in Thomas Gray's *Elegy in a Country Churchyard*, a generation on:

Some village Hampden, that, with dauntless breast,
    The little tyrant of his fields withstood
Some mute inglorious Milton here may rest,
    Some Cromwell guiltless of his country's blood. (57–70)[127]

Memorials literal and figurative. Muted in death, but alive in history. Steeling a new generation against some familiar tyrannies.[128] And tyrants. No need to name Charles Stuart.

And no need to name the cavalier whose memorials Defoe would pretend to disinter in 1720. A man of 'Gallantry and Honour', whose narrative is confirmed by, and drawn from, 'the Histories of the Times'. And then withdrawn. *The Memoirs* of Defoe's cavalier are written in 'Confutation' of history. And more precisely still the 'extraordinary History written by the Earl of Clarendon'. Except, not quite. That would be too simple. So instead Defoe insinuates the 'many Errors', but disdains, for reasons of good grace, from labouring them.[129] It is left to the 'Sense and Judgment' of the reader to appreciate what is true, and what is not, in Sir Edward's 'history'. As they must in the Defoe's 'memoirs'. The slipperiest of histories written by the slipperiest of historians.

And saying nothing about January 1649. The single 'complaint', as Defoe affects in his preface.[130] For reason of authenticity, the narrator being no longer an 'Actor' in the unfolding tragedy. Hyde's excuse. It will be left to the 'History of the Times' to supply those 'Particulars' of the 'deposing and murthering of their Sovereign'. Well almost. Just time for a final insinuation. That of all the mistakes made by the fated king and his 'Friends', none was more telling that the 'fruitless Risings' of 1648.[131] Contingency and consequence. Daniel Defoe was a bit of a revisionist, as well as a bit slippery. Of course, it might be supposed that his *Memoirs* are a little different from Ludlow's and Hyde's, in that they are made up. But that would depend on the meaning of fiction, and 'history'. We will shortly discover the Victorians wrestling similarly. Now, though, an excuse to revisit one of the most influential texts in the history of modern political thought. Another reflection on the demise of Charles Stuart, another kind of appeal. Or *amicus* brief, perhaps, albeit belated. Except that it was hardly very *amicissimum*.

Monsters

Written in two parts. The second of which appeared, in pirated form, in the summer of 1679. It was entitled *Behemoth*, and was written by Thomas Hobbes, rather more renowned, then as now, for another book with a monstrous title, *Leviathan*.[132] *Leviathan* was the other part. Hobbes had written *Behemoth* in 1668. But the king had refused permission to publish. Possibly to protect the author's reputation; possibly to protect his own.[133] When *Behemoth* did finally appear, Hobbes was dying. At the formidable age of ninety-one. A long life, during which he had seen a lot. Most of it dispiriting.

There is an evident affinity between the two textual monsters. *Leviathan* recommending a political philosophy founded on the historical experience recalled in *Behemoth*. The sub-title of the latter tells us which history: *Of the Long Parliament*. Logic would thus suppose that they might be read in order of composition. But, in fact, it makes greater sense to start at the end. For the same bitter experience underpinned both texts, and we will understand *Leviathan* better if we get a closer sense of what Hobbes thought of the civil war, and the fate of Charles Stuart.

Hobbes's early affinities were royalist, if hardly cavalier. For most of his working life he was in the service of the Cavendish family, spending the 1630s as tutor to the 3rd Earl of Devonshire. In summer 1640 he wrote a short treatise entitled *The Elements of Law*, in which he defended absolute prerogative power. The 'first', he would much later claim, to have 'ventured to write in the King's defence'.[134] He then departed for Paris, where he would stay for the next ten years. Whether he needed to do so is moot; given that the *Elements* was not published, and hardly anyone read it. He returned to England in 1651, shortly after publication of *Leviathan*. A more tangible urgency this time, as we will see. A quiet decade of reflection followed. Thoughts turning to the idea of writing a history.

There was certainly plenty to ponder. As the opening to *Behemoth* suggested: 'There can be nothing more instructive towards loyalty and justice, than will be the memory, while it lasts, of that war.' The didactic aspiration situates *Behemoth* in the same 'mirror' tradition of Renaissance political writing.[135] Darker reflections though. *Behemoth* is history warts and all. The question of causation animates, the 'corruption' of England. It was, in a sense, a matter of balance; of too much and too little. Too little money for a start. And too little wisdom, by which Hobbes meant political common sense; as opposed to 'craft', of which there was too much. Too much 'babbling', and too much 'Greek and Latin', too many gentlemen immersed in their books of 'policy', and the 'histories of the ancient Greeks and Romans'. The hazards of the 'scribbling age'. The 'study of the curious', the cause of so much 'mischief'.[136] As Aubrey likewise intimated. Too much 'Livy and the Roman authors'.[137] Aubrey had Milton in mind. As, quite possibly, did Hobbes. Especially critical of babbling sectaries, covering their 'horrible designs' with 'the cloak of godliness'. The thought that subjects might covenant directly with God was a design of particular 'impudence'.[138]

Most dangerous of all, though, were the lawyers. In his later *Dialogue between a Philosopher and a Student of the Common Laws of England*, Hobbes would identify Coke in particular. In *Behemoth* it is a matter of insinuation. A nation 'infected' with 'maxims and cases prejudged'.[139] And the arch-miasma of *Magna Carta*. And 'mixarchy'; the arch-miasma of Sir Edward Hyde. Sovereignty 'divided' is not, in Hobbes's opinion, sovereignty at all. And the consequence of this misunderstanding is discord: 'nothing else but pure anarchy'.[140] Evident in Parliament, advertised in pulpits across the land. Against this naturalism, Hobbes plants the seeds of legal positivism. Law as clear, enforceable command. The wisdom of which is most apparent in its absence. The second dialogue lingers long over the fate of 'Black Tom'. An exercise, not in refined jurisprudence but brute political contingency. No need to blame King Charles overtly. He blamed himself; 'amiss' in not saving his former favourite. And amiss in allowing his own authority to be so obviously compromised.

Further aspersions. A more contemplative passage assesses the 'virtues' of good kingship. By which Hobbes means effective kingship, not kingship which happens to be 'commended' by classical scholars. Amongst the defining 'virtues', history repeatedly affirms, are 'fortitude' and 'frugality'.[141] Be decisive, be constant and be prudent. Qualities evident on 30 January 1649, wherein could be seen 'what courage, patience, wisdom, and goodness was in this prince'.[142] But not so much before; January 1642 in Parliament, April at the gates of Hull, August in the Nottingham drizzle. Not a flattering picture of majesty. Nor of magisterial council. Here, at least, Hobbes and Hyde are in accord. The best kings are those who heed the best counsel. Which for Hyde, meant him.

Not, though, for Hobbes. Who has Hyde down as one of the worst. A trimmer who only went with the king in summer 1642 when it was apparent that Parliament was no longer interested in his 'mixarchy'.[143] Two very different royalists then, neither convinced of the fidelity of the other, still less by their respective theories of kingship. Different philosophies, different personalities. But not, perhaps, so different histories. Their accounts of England in the early 1640s certainly bear comparison; the same saintly if rather dithery prince, the same fractious parliament, the same stubborn episcopacy. And the 1650s; the same 'shiftings', as Hobbes called them, that would eventually lead the Republic to collapse.[144]

Regardless of personal and political preference, revolutionary England, it seems, made historians of a distinctly revisionist kind. The accounting of 'accidents', as Algernon Sidney agreed.[145]

Less history, at first glance, in *Leviathan*. But still, born of the same bitter experience. Of weak kingship, and the anarchy of fickle 'appetites', the 'natural inclination of all mankind, the perpetual and restless desire for Power after Power'.[146] In his *Elements of Law*, Hobbes had ventured the idea that government might be established on first principles. Not now. The political philosophy discovered in *Leviathan* is derived from the 'practise of men', and the 'occasions of the present time'.[147] Slaughtered camp-followers at Naseby, immolated Catholics in Basing House, the savagery of Stow. The too ready retreat into the 'state of nature'. The 'condition of man' is that 'of Warre of every one against every one'.[148] Difficult, in the context, to disagree. Nor with a still more famous aphorism; that in such a 'condition' the 'life of man' is 'solitary, poor, nasty, brutish, and short'.[149]

Whilst the civil wars provided the broader context to *Leviathan*, there was also a tighter. The Oath of Engagement, imposed in autumn 1650. The idea of subscribing an oath of fidelity to the Commonwealth stuck in the craw of many a royalist. And not only. Presbyterians too, indeed any who had subscribed to the Solemn League and Covenant a few years earlier. We might recall Fairfax and his 'prickling leaf'. But it was necessary for any who wished to hold some kind of public office, or indeed go to law. *Leviathan* suggested how, and why, they might reconcile themselves. By a theory of transferred 'Right', following 'Conquest'.[150] At the heart of *Leviathan* was the idea of mutual covenants; collectively the second 'Law of Nature'. Resonant of Milton, of course, and January 1649; but critically different. A covenant with God being an obligation of faith, those between sovereign and subject matters of secular 'duty'. To run in parallel. But the secular covenants, importantly, to be ratified sequentially. The people, wishing to elevate themselves from their 'state of nature', would covenant amongst themselves, and then 'contract' their collective 'rights' to an elective sovereign.[151]

To be understood, figuratively at least, in terms of 'common' principles of contract law; promise, performance, breach. The definition of 'injustice' is the 'not Performance of Contract'.[152] This is the third 'Law of Nature'. The only bit missing was remedy. The most important bit. Once a 'Right' is 'granted away', the subject is 'Bound' and has no power to 'make voyd that voluntary act'.[153] Experience again. If the purpose of magistracy is to check the destructive 'appetites' to which humanity is drawn by 'inclination', the best chance lies with the vesting of prerogative authority in an absolute sovereign.[154] Another famous aphorism, and a pertinent insight; 'Covenants without the Sword, are but Words, and of no strength to secure a man at all', and the conditions of civil war are set in the absence of a 'common Power to feare'.[155] The question which then arises, of course, is that of tyranny. It is here that providence intercedes. For if a sovereign breaches the terms of their covenant, God will take the necessary remedial action. Whether the logic then supposes that He might act through a 'chosen' Englishman is left to inference.

Of the various things which troubled contemporaries in Hobbes's *Leviathan*, none caused greater consternation than the apparent atheism. It was not that Hobbes denied God. But he did deny the supposition that God had much of a place in the governance of a Commonwealth. God left the governance of England to the English, to see what they could make of it. 'If the Kingdome of God,' he acidly observed, 'were not a Kingdome which God by his Lieutenants, or Vicars, who deliver his Commandments to his people, did exercise on Earth; there would not have been so much contention, and warre about who it is, by whom God speaketh to us.'[156] Another darker inference. Englishmen might pretend to fight for God; but in reality they fight for themselves. Another revisionist prophet .[157]

And an ironist. The consequence, again, of living in a 'scribbling age'. The appreciation that 'True and False are attributes of Speech, not Things'.[158] That politics is an art, of 'imagination' and 'remembrance'. An insight which adds a further, necessarily destabilizing, dimension to theories of sovereignty. Beware the 'strange Prince' who pretends to be 'God's prophet'. Who, to realize 'their own Dreams', would 'reduce all Order, Government, and Society, to the first Chaos of Violence, and Civill War'.[159] Ambiguous, necessarily. There was no shortage of strange princes, or civil wars. But some allusions were more obvious than others. The final part of *Leviathan* focused, more closely still, on the 'phantasms of the brain'. 'Priestcraft', in other words.[160] Those who wilfully misinterpret scripture, who mistake sacrament for 'conjuration', who believe in purgatory, 'fairies' and the exorcism of demons.[161] Who 'invoke' the 'images' of martyrs, sainted or princely. The 'worship' of 'finite Gods'; a most grotesque form of 'Idolatry'.[162]

Which brings us to a particular irony; the original frontispiece to *Leviathan*. Designed by the renowned Parisian engraver, Abraham Bosse, it describes a large figure with a human face and scaled body looming over the landscape, a sword in one hand, a mitre in the other, a crown on its head. The scales, on closer inspection, comprise three hundred people facing towards the figure. The 'body politic' in the figurative sense. But as to which particular body, various possibilities. It might represent Charles I, or the putative Charles II, or Cromwell. Respectively flattering, hopeful and impudent. Or, of course, it might be none of them; simply 'Artificiall Man', the representation of the state.[163] Plenty of room for speculation though, and offence. Like the text itself.

The publication of *Leviathan* caused outrage in Paris. Forty-seven chapters, none of which made for easy reading. Ended with a summative, and brutal, conclusion. In two parts. First, revolutions occur where kings 'fain to handle the Sword of Justice unconstantly'. Second, that political fidelity might be somehow re-negotiated, that 'Right' might be acquired by Conquest and then contracted anew.[164] It did make subscribing new oaths rather more palatable, for property-owning royalists. The history of the 1640s seemed to make better sense too. But at what cost? Hobbes closed, rather hopefully, with the observation that there was nothing in his 'Discourse' that was 'contrary either to the Word of God, or good manners'. Or to the 'disturbance of the Publique Tranquility'. For which reason there was nothing that could be 'condemned at this time'.[165]

Hardly. Hyde took a predictably dim view in his *Brief View and Survey of the Dangerous and Pernicious Errors to Church and State in Mr Hobbes's Book, entitled Leviathan*. Foremost of which was the accusation that a principal cause of the 'Civill warre, and Dissolution' was the counsel of Edward Hyde. The consequence of 'mixt' sovereignty and 'faction'.[166] An accusation that had to be contested, as the 'Epistle Dedicatory' affirmed. Having recently completed a 'history' composed in 'Honour of his Majesties memory', the author's next duty was to refute the 'odious opinions' discovered in *Leviathan*. The surest sign of his 'uncorrupted fidelity to your Person'. In contrast with Hobbes. Who had written his 'vile' book in order to curry favour with Cromwell. So full of 'sedition, treason and impiety'.[167]

The one bit of *Leviathan* which Hyde did admire was chapter 39, where Hobbes castigated bishops who try to distinguish matters of Church from those of state. Whereas he would have liked most of *Leviathan* to be shorter, Hyde regretted that this was not 'enlarged upon'.[168] Otherwise though, Hyde saw Hobbes as a defender of the worst kind of absolutism, his arguments 'so contrary to all the laws established in this country' that he would 'make all laws cobwebs, to be blown away by the least breath of the governor'. Closing with the observation that the doctrines discovered in *Leviathan* would 'overthrow and undermine all those principles of government which preserv'd the peace of this kingdom through so many ages'.[169] No evident sense of irony.

Hobbes returned to England shortly after publishing *Leviathan*. The Restoration brought mixed fortunes. A pension of £100 in 1661. The proscription of *Leviathan* in 1666, amidst proposals to suppress heretical writings. A panicked Hobbes burned a number of his papers. In the end, the only consequence was an effective bar on his publishing anything else in the near future. Not that it stopped him turning his mind to writing a history of the civil wars, for private circulation. Dying in 1679, we can only surmise what he would have thought of the fall of King James II and the heralding of another revolution, this time 'glorious', a decade on. Too much of a cynic to be taken in by the hype, or much surprised by the course of events, he would probably have written something. On a familiar template; a fractious Church, a rebellious Parliament and a prince lacking resolution.

Wrong but wromantic

History, as we noted at the start, is written differently. *1066 and All That*, first published in 1930, is famously different. Written to entertain, obviously, but not only. There is much that seems daft. But it is a brilliant daftness, written in a truly critical spirit, to the greater good; of making lots of other historians seem even sillier. Nowhere more so than in the reworking of the demarcation which cuts through any history of seventeenth-century England; between those who were 'wrong, but wromantic' and those who were 'right, but repulsive'. Our purpose in this final part of the chapter is to revisit some of these later histories. Starting in 1848.

A peculiar revolution

In a sense. Though actually in February 1685, with the death of King Charles II. The closing years of the reign marked with various plots, and rumours of plots; mostly animated by the question of succession. A last temptation for some familiar names. Ludlow was approached in Vevey. But declined; too old, too far. Parliament, in the meantime, had wrestled with various Exclusion bills, designed more particularly to exclude Hyde's former son-in-law from becoming king. 'Consider you do not reduce it to an Elective Monarchy', some loyalists warned.[170] Advice just about heeded, for a couple more years.

The coronation of King James II took place on 23rd April. And the 22nd. The events of the 23rd were for public consumption. Those of the 22nd were conducted in accordance with the rites of the Catholic Church, in private in Whitehall. At least it meant that the service on the 23rd was less wearying. Done by lunchtime; a slap-up feast of fifteen courses. A few portents to ponder, though. The Royal Standard blew down, again. And it was reported that Archbishop Sancroft struggled to get the crown to settle on the royal head. Hardly much of a surprise. The Church of England now governed by a Catholic. If, indeed, that was even possible; a king in immediate breach of his own *praemunire* statutes. Lots for the jurists to ponder. Lots more when James decided to re-establish the High Commission.

A more prosaic threat emerged a couple of months later. When the Duke of Monmouth mounted a rebellion in the south-west. The duke was not only romantic and protestant but also foolish and illegitimate; the eldest of Charles's many bastard sons. And his army, of a couple of thousand local peasants, was rubbish. The vengeance wreaked by Chief Justice Jeffreys, who was despatched into the region, was notorious. The so-called 'Bloody Assizes'. Two hundred and fifty peasants strung up. And a sixty-eight-year-old woman decapitated in Winchester market square. Lady Alice Lisle, wife of a former regicide, had apparently harboured fugitives. Hardly very loyal, but hardly much of a threat either. Until, that is, she had her head cut off. At which point she became another martyr to a 'cause' that was starting to assume a familiar urgency. The 'glorious' revolution celebrated in Gilbert Burnet's *History of His Own Time*, the first volume of which would appear in 1724, starts here. Easier to write a narrative of inevitability by then, of course; of another Stuart monarch brought down by an inclination to absolutism and popery, and bloody 'fury'.[171]

And pathologically incapable of distinguishing good advice from bad. Not that Sir Edward could have helped this time, having died a decade earlier. He would, though, have spotted the parallels. Alice Lisle and William Prynne. The *Five Knights* and the *Seven Bishops*. The bishops had petitioned against a second *Declaration of Indulgence* in early 1688. James intended the *Declaration* to give statutory force to the same 'dispensing' power with which he had re-established the Commission, and was now using to appoint Catholics to public office, in defiance of the Test Acts. The 'standard of rebellion', James chastised his bishops, 'I did not expect this from you'.[172] A familiar marketing disaster ensued. As the court split on the legality of the petition, and the jury acquitted on charges of seditious libel. Lord Halifax, sat in the courtroom, stood up and waved his hat, the galleries erupted in applause. A 'little rebellion', Sir John Reresby reported, 'in noise though not in fact'.[173] Not that little.

Meanwhile another seven, the 'Immortal', as the senior Whig negotiators became known, began to ponder the possibility of 'electing' a different king.[174] No Hyde amongst them. But present in the supporting cast. Sir Edward's eldest son, Henry, now 2nd Earl of Clarendon, assumed the familial position. Seeking, on behalf of the king, to fashion some kind of conciliation. He even offered to put up bail for the bishops. Burnet would later suppose that it was Henry who, a few months later, persuaded James that the game was up. And then hasten to prostrate himself before his successor. Which meant, in effect, switching his allegiance from his brother-in-law to his niece. Mary, consort to William of Orange, was a Stuart in name. But in everything else a Hyde. And pretty much exactly what the 'Immortal Seven' were looking for in a prospective queen. Sensible, credible, protestant. Like her husband.

William arrived, in Devon, in November 1688. Strategically distant. Time to win over some more hearts and minds, and allow James to properly comprehend his position. For a moment, James contemplated marching an army into the south-west. But something stopped him. The sober realization that he did not have much of an army, very possibly. Ill-health, too, perhaps; the incessant nose-bleeds, rumours of syphilis, the sheer nerve-strain. Worried, some supposed, that what had happened to his father might now happen to him. James Stuart was, by common account, a courageous man. But the fear was considerable. He decided to flee, asking Pepys to requisition him a yacht. Recognized and taken into custody at Faversham, and then released. William did not want to make another martyr; any more than James wanted to become one. Very sensible. Mary came over a couple of weeks later.

Here again we might pause for a moment, to take a look at Mary; or least take a look at Lely's Mary. Painted in 1677, to celebrate her betrothal.[175] Resplendent in orange satin. Copies would be made in Stuart blue. Sporting the 'hurly-burly' hairstyle, fashionably French.[176] Demure, intelligent, a confident gaze. Mary married William on 4 November 1677. Not, in truth, a particularly happy occasion. Reportedly on the edge of tears for much of the day, distraught by the time she clambered into the marital bed in the evening; watched, as was customary, by her dad and a few other close relatives. Including her uncle, the king, there to make a few ribald jokes.[177] Not, perhaps, the moment. Mary was fifteen. We can only surmise what Sir Edward, had he been still alive, might have thought of it. Distressed perhaps, he was reportedly fond of his granddaughter. But approving. He would probably have liked William too. A young man of 'phlegmatic serenity', Lord Macaulay would recall, of someone else recalling the prince. Something of a relief after all the febrile Stuart princes, with their fancy manners and still fancier theories of kingship. We might even go so far as to suppose that Hyde would have welcomed the 'glorious' revolution too. And not just because it brought his granddaughter back to England, and made her queen.

Which brings us to 13 February 1689, and the coronation of Mary and her husband. And to summer 1848, and the publication of the first volumes of Macaulay's *History of England*. Within the pages of which could be found a fabled account of that day. The centrepiece of which is the moment when the Clerk of the House of Lords reads 'in a loud voice' the *Declaration of Right*. After which Lord Halifax offers the crown. On terms. Accepted by William, who confirms his commitment to the 'law of England', and its Church and its Parliament. He 'should constantly recur to the advice of the Houses, and should be disposed to trust their judgment rather than his own'. Alternative accounts suppose that William sat stony-faced, only breaking pose to mutter the words 'we thankfully accept what you have offered us'. Enough, though. The Bishop of London duly proceeded to plaster anointment oil on the royal foreheads.[178] 'A shout of joy' outside, and 'thus was consummated the English revolution'. The idea of 'finality' would become definitive in Whig histories of the seventeenth century. All done. And so sensibly, in the end.

If odd. Macaulay closes with an apparent aside. Comparing the events of 1689 with those of 1649, 'we cannot but be struck by its peculiar character'.[179] Not just the oddity of two monarchs reigning together; a necessary expedient designed to mask the prosaic reality that the 'glorious' revolution was, in fact, just another baronial coup. But because it was so quiet. Providential indeed. Not the fiery Providence that excited Harrison or Cromwell or Milton. But the providence of history, of centuries of constitutional development; the kind which excited the two Sir Edwards, Coke and Hyde. A revolution in the end secured by lawyers on parchment, rather than generals on battlefields. Something which, of course, recasts the 'histories' of January 1649. A prelude to a rather greater drama.

We might briefly note the terms of the *Declaration*. Comprising a list of grievances, followed by a list of limitations on the Crown prerogative. At the end of the year, it would be enacted in a *Bill of Rights*; almost a written constitution.

The grievances were mostly familiar, from the recent past and the more distant. A dozen or more attempts to 'subvert and extirpate the protestant religion and the laws and liberties of England', including the prosecution of clergy, the attempt to raise taxes without the consent of Parliament and infringements of provisions affirmed in the 1679 *Habeas Corpus Act*. As for the limitations, mostly securing the privileges of Parliament and co-opting some of those exercised by the Crown. So, again, no extra-parliamentary taxes, no standing armies. Plus, the right for protestants to bear arms, under the law. A more comprehensive statement regarding liberty of conscience was found in the *Toleration Act*, passed the previous May. Encompassing, except for Catholics.

Coke might indeed have written it. Insofar as it drew inspiration from his *Petition of Right*, he did. Or Hyde. The constitution drafted in 1641, enacted in 1661. Or Milton. An 'elective' king at last, secured by 'compact'. An idea brought back into fashion by Algernon Sidney, and John Locke in his second *Treatise on Government*. All civil societies, Locke confirmed, were founded on 'compacts of trust' and mutual obligation. 'Nothing can make any man' subject to the laws of a particular 'commonwealth … but his actually entering into it by positive engagement and express promise and compact'.[180] To complete the picture, twelve years later Parliament passed an *Act of Settlement*, designed to exclude the Stuarts from ever returning to the throne. At least the first sixty in line, all of whom were Catholic.

We might recall poor sad Anne, the last Hyde to rule England; and by now Scotland. Dying childless in 1714. The precedent set, Parliament peered about Europe for a suitably protestant prince, who could just about make a blood-claim to the throne. And discovered one of Anne's second cousins, Georg Ludwig, Elector of Hannover. He would do. The 'Georgian' age awaited. And England's historians were left to make some choices. The more romantic would veer towards the tragic family cursed by circumstance. A couple of hapless insurrections, in 1715 and 1745, would help to build the myth; an Old 'Pretender' and a Young. Others would assume a more puritan tone. A family more cursed by viciousness and venality than by contingency. Either way the Stuarts were gone, at last.

Reflections

In the corporeal sense. Not, though, the incorporeal. Too many ghosts, as we have already noted, too easily raised. Not least on the 30th of January each year, the 'madding-day', as despairing Dissenters called it. Some madder than others. And then, flitting about a little more gracefully in the various 'histories' written out through the eighteenth century. Texts such as the mid-century *Biographica Britannica* and Hume's *History of England*, which we have already encountered, and Thomas Carte's *General History of England*. Carte was a Tory of the distinctly

Jacobite variety. Hume was not. In private correspondence, embracing a critical ambiguity; 'my views of things are most conformable to Whig principles; my representation of persons to Tory prejudices'.[181] In philosophy a rationalist, in sentiment a romantic. In sum, a man of the Enlightenment. On another occasion he described himself 'a Whig, though a very sceptical one'. Like Hyde perhaps.

Party loyalties remained, but histories were narrowing. By the mid-eighteenth century, few continued to argue against the virtues of the 'glorious' revolution; simply what it meant in the past. Tensions would surface, most commonly in matters of conscience. Otherwise differences tended to be in tone. Brusque in the case of William Blackstone. The last chapter of the fourth book of his celebrated *Commentaries* provided readers with a whistle-stop constitutional history of England. The 'despotism' of Henry VIII, the 'wisdom' of his daughter Elizabeth. And then the Stuarts. Starting with James and his 'unreasonable and imprudent exertion' of prerogative. The Whig in Blackstone detected an early warning; an 'inclination' in Parliament to 'resist'. Which his successor had missed. The 'ill-timed zeal' of Caroline Churchmen, together with various constitutional 'enormities'. Plus, Charles's own 'reputation' for insincerity. Throw in some 'military hypocrites', and you end up with 'the trial and murder' of a king.[182] Regrettable perhaps, predictable certainly. Blackstone situated himself in the tradition of Coke's *Reports*, and Sir Matthew Hale's *History of the Common Law*. The authorized version of the English Constitution, prescribed by its jurists, proved by its history. Parliament supreme, the king knowing his place. It did not make the monarch incidental, but it did reinforce the sense that the English Commonwealth was strong enough to survive the occasional usurpation. 1649, 1689; those 'accidental diseases that sometimes happen', as Hale put it.[183] Trimming histories, written by trimming jurists.

We might pay a quick visit to a rather different historian. Horace Walpole, ensconced in all the mock-Gothic strangeness of Strawberry Hill, in Twickenham. Open to the public from 1765. Plebs to wander the gardens, the more discerning invited inside. For a guinea each, to peer about in the cultivated 'gloomth'. For the most discerning, a visit to Horace's bedroom. Where they might admire some of his odder trinkets; Cardinal Wolsey's hat, Mary Queen of Scot's comb, George II's watch. And a copy of the death warrant of Charles I. With the ascription 'the least bad of all murders, that of a king'.[184] Entirely understandable if they assumed, as a consequence, that Horace was a bit of republican. Entirely mistaken if they thought it was more than that. Close friends included Princess Sophie, and the Dukes of Cumberland and Grafton. Horace was, by his own admission, a 'quiet' Whig. Much like another of his friends, Thomas Gray, whose *Elegy* he puffed around London.

And Thomas Tyers. Though not perhaps that quiet. A man of 'pleasant carelessness', as James Boswell put it, Thomas was not given to worrying too much about the occasional outbreak of civil disquiet. As news of the Gordon 'riots' spread around London in 1780, he sagely reminded everyone that if 'Charles had not lost his head', none of them would have any 'liberties at this time'. Whether Thomas would have been quite so sanguine about events a decade later, we can only surmise. He died in 1787. We can be surer of John Thellwall. Treating the jury, at his 'treason trial' in 1794, to a discourse on the relative merits of Oliver Cromwell. The 'greatest champion that liberty ever had in this country'.[185] Horace, though, had gone right off regicides by then. The execution of Louis XVI was the act of 'savages', who had 'destroyed God as well as their King'.

Like many, Horace had, for a brief moment, felt a certain thrill on first hearing of the French Revolution. 'How much the greatest event that ever was in the world', Charles James Fox advised his fellow Members in autumn 1789, 'and how much the best'. A young William Wordsworth raced over to Paris, to join the party: 'Bliss was it that dawn to be alive' (11.108).[186] Josiah Wedgwood 'rejoiced' at the prospect of a 'glorious' French Revolution, assuming that it would be much like the 'glorious' English.[187] It was not. A realization which shook a generation, some at least. Byron managed to reconcile himself. Liberty always arrives in a 'torrent' of blood. Few others were so sanguine. Coleridge later repented the 'delusion' of a generation. Distinguishing the glory of 1689 from the horror of 1649 became a touchstone. Southey made a clean break; 1689 was indeed 'glorious', 1649 unforgiveable. A chastened Wordsworth returned home from France, to begin a life-long abjuration. In 1802 he would pen a sonnet to 'The later Sidney, Marvel, Harrington, / Young Vane, and others who called Milton friend'.[188] A lot might be forgiven of someone who Milton forgave.

As for Horace, all he could do was recommend that everyone read Edmund Burke's 'wondrous', yet terrifying *Reflections on the Revolution in France*. Burke was another who had momentarily welcomed news of the revolution in Paris. But then, within weeks, turned. The *Reflections*, which appeared in autumn 1790, was the consequence. An essay on the lessons of history. Violent revolutions only end one way: with slaughtered priests and slaughtered princes. And violated wives. At the heart of *Reflections* is the notorious passage depicting the 'rape' of Marie Antoinette. It was Horace's favourite bit, in the didactic sense. A simple lesson; on how easily the plebs might run out of control, and how dreadful the things they might do. The deeper purpose of *Reflections*, of course, was to concentrate attention nearer to home. To reflect on the comparative 'delight' of the 'glorious' revolution of 1688. Which, rather than sacrificing kings and queens on the altar of 'abstract' rights, had settled a constitution in the balanced interests of Church and Crown, and subjects. And secured it in law. Small wonder that the English love their constitution with a 'generous sense of glory and emulation'.[189] Less said about 1649 the better; so Burke said nothing. Not everyone loved his *Reflections*. Tom Paine was famously acerbic. So too Mary Wollstonecraft. But plenty did. We can only surmise what Hyde might have thought of Burke and his *Reflections*. Most likely he would have agreed with Horace. And King George III; a book that 'every Englishman should read'.

Right but repulsive

The very composition of *Reflections* is a testament to memory. To the continuing hold of the past in the writing of England's present. And more especially the hold of the 'great seventeenth-century time'. Perplexing, though. A nation still divided between its cavaliers and its roundheads. Still agonizing over the fate of its tragic prince; a sin against God or a 'cruel necessity'? Still struggling to resolve Milton's agonies. And Nedham's riddle: 'Rebellion makes our nation bleed … But it is not well agreed / Who must the Rebel be.'[190] Which was, of course, the fascination.

Here again, we can only surmise how Dickens might have written the moment. He did write a novel about the Gordon riots, *Barnaby Rudge*, arguably his weakest. History did not come easy to Dickens, evidently troubled by the competing vectors; liking the cause of liberty but disliking the violence. The same tensions would be treated, at a tangent, in *Tale of Two Cities*. But the fact remains; for all the fascination of the 'great age', Dickens the novelist dodged it. Others had a go. Sir Walter Scott in *Woodstock*, published in 1826. History came easier to Scott. But again, the civil war proved a struggle. A bit part for Charles, a 'weak rider … thrown by an unruly horse', acted off the page by an enigmatic Cromwell.[191] Both Thackeray and a very young George Eliot were tempted to try, but in the end shied away. William Harrison Ainsworth, needless to say, had a couple of attempts, *Boscobel* and *The Leaguer of Lathom*.[192] Neither amongst his more successful. The Victorian poet fared little better. There was nothing that Tennyson liked better than versifying a good war; not the English civil though.

It was, instead, left to the painters. Here again the 'Wromantic' was more easily imagined. The Victorians loved a good battle scene. Landseer did a couple. *The Eve before Edge Hill* and *The Battle of Naseby*. For the latter, he chose the moment when Cromwell and Fairfax were shown the contents of the King's Cabinet. Even Cromwell's horse, taking a peek, looks disappointed. Amongst the more famous was Andrew Carrick Gow's 1886 *Battle of Dunbar*. One of 'God's most signal mercies', destined to illustrate the pages of many a children's history of the English civil wars. Gow also did *Cromwell Dissolving the Long Parliament* and *The Visit of Charles I to Kingston-upon-Hull*: intriguing choices both. No-one, though, painted quite so many civil war battles as Ernest Crofts.[193] *The Surrender of the City of York, Cromwellian Soldiers Leaving Warwick Castle, Hampden Riding away from Chalgrove Field, Cromwell at the Storming of Basing House*, a couple more of Cromwell at Marston Moor and Worcester.

Not just battles though. Crofts also painted three scenes of the regicide. *Charles I on the way to his Execution* was exhibited in 1883. Followed, seven years later, by *Whitehall, January 30th 1649*. The critic Leslie Stephen rather hoped that, after the latter effort, Charles would 'not go to execution again'; at least not on a Crofts canvas. But he did. In 1907, with *The Funeral of Charles I at St George's Chapel*. Crofts knew his market. The enduring interest in the tragic Charles is not surprising. It fitted, not least, the Victorian obsession with death. But what is perhaps more remarkable is the fact that Victorian England, like Crofts indeed, spent rather more time pondering Cromwell. Perhaps because he won all the battles. And seemed so very English. But also because, by the end of the century, it was becoming possible to reconcile the ambivalences, to regard the execution of the king as being 'repulsive' but also 'right'. The 'cruel necessity' defence.[194]

Which brings us to Thomas Carlyle, and his search for a new Tory hero. Embroiled in a struggle to reshape Victorian conservatism in the 1840s, Carlyle alighted on God's Englishman, the 'soul of the Puritan revolt'.[195] A country Tory at heart, it seems, who appreciated that the essence of Englishness was 'liberty', civil and religious. A man of sober faith and moral integrity; like Carlyle, or so he hoped. But most importantly, unlike Benjamin Disraeli. Carlyle loathed the 'Hebrew conjuror' and his faux-cavalier chums. It was against Disraeli that Carlyle raised his 'friend Oliver', as he took to calling him on his lecture tours. The consequence for Charles Stuart was familiar and predictable. Still a Tory martyr, but also a motley fool; like Disraeli. The perennially 'baffled' king, 'writhing and rustling with royal rage'.[196] The necessary support in a greater history of a much greater man. As for the events of 30 January, the 'most daring action' ever resolved by 'any body of men to be met with in history'. Charles was there, on the scaffold that afternoon. But it was not really about him. Much as Crofts intimated in his *Whitehall, January 30th*, the fated king just about discernible in the far distance.

Carlyle would later surmise that his *Letters and Speeches of Oliver Cromwell* was the 'usefullest works I shall ever get to do'.[197] Saving Cromwell for middle-class England. And English history, from the 'waste rubbish-continent of Rushworth-Nalson State-papers, of Philosophical Scepticism, Dilettantism, Dryasdust Torpedoisms'.[198] An agonizing write, finally published in 1845. The prescience would become more striking still twenty years on, as radical England turned its mind once more to the idea of a republic. The fault of Disraeli, according to Carlyle at least, who had corrupted both queen and constitution. Carlyle was not the only depressive Victorian to blame Disraeli for the passage of the 1867 Reform Act. The same inspired Walter Bagehot to write a series of essays later collected together as *The English Constitution*. Famously, Bagehot distinguished the 'dignified' part of the constitution, embodied in the office of the Crown, from the 'efficient': the cavalier and the roundhead. It was the latter that made everything tick; the former which made it all seem legitimate. Bagehot thought like Carlyle. The past was there to enchant the 'bovine masses'. The 'spectacle' of monarchy, brilliant but fragile.[199] A journalist by profession, Bagehot knew all about the darker arts.

As to the fragility, Bagehot only briefly averted to Charles Stuart in his scamper through English history; the subject of the last of his essays. Longer, interestingly, on the 'incredible and pertinacious folly' of his son James. Intimations though. Not least in the narrative drive, which assumes that the 'glorious' revolution of 1688 started in 1642. The familiar Whig feint. But also in the passing aphorisms. The 'happy accident' of bare competence, that the greater risk lies not in the 'idle' king, who does 'little good and as little harm', but in the 'active and meddling fool'. And that which closes his second essay on 'Monarchy'; the 'benefits of a good monarch are almost invaluable, but the evils of a bad monarch are almost irreparable'.[200] James for sure; his dad surely?

We might wonder where, in all this, Hyde appears. To which the shorter answer is, nowhere much. Some dutiful attributions of course. Southey would even go so far, in 1821, to proclaim that there 'is no historian, ancient or modern, with whose writings it so behoves an Englishman to be thoroughly familiar as Lord Clarendon's'.[201] Familiarity is not, though, the same as critical approval. Hyde struggled for friends in Victorian England. Too dreary for Carlyle; the architect, ultimately, of a 'Settlement of despair'. Too much the 'bigot' for Macaulay. A statesman of undoubted skill, possessed of a 'discriminating eye'. But also 'sour' in temper, and 'arrogant'; a perception Macaulay gleaned from Burnet's *History*. Trapped, in a sense, between the polarities. A royalist who was 'right but repulsive'. Matthew Ward painted him in 1847. Dressed in black departing Whitehall following his final audience with the king in 1667. Surrounded by lots of laughing cavaliers, Barbara Villiers smiling brightly from the gallery. It was entitled *The Disgrace of Lord Clarendon*. No-one else bothered to revisit the 'history' of Edward Hyde, at least not in colour.

A couple of statues, though. A first, half-way up an outside wall of the Clarendon Building in Oxford. Paid for, in part, out of the proceeds from the *History of the Rebellion*, the copyright for which had been gifted to the University by his great-grandson. Tory Oxford still remembered. A second in St Stephen's Hall in Westminster. Tasked, in 1845, with suggesting some decoration for Pugin's newly restored palace, a Commission for Fine Arts recommended Hyde, along with his old chum Viscount Falkland; to stand, in due course, opposite statues of Hampden and Selden. The *Literary Gazette* was not alone in noting the 'pairing off', royalist and roundhead. The *Eclectic* adopted a more jaundiced tone in regard to some of the choices. Including Hyde; a man of 'small pretensions'. Interestingly, Macaulay was a member of the 1845 Commission. Probably rather more enthused by Hampden, but not sufficiently disapproving, it seems, of Sir Edward.

Another sculpture to close. Another bronze, indeed. This time positioned just outside Westminster Palace. Cromwell, staring at his feet, some critics supposed, out of embarrassment. Unveiled in October 1899, to celebrate the tercentenary of his birth. The idea had been ventured a few times over previous decades. Notably in 1871, at the height of renewed republican agitation. And then again in the 1890s. At the recurring behest of Archibald Primrose, 5th Earl of Rosebery, and prime minister for a brief moment between spring 1894 and summer 1895. Archibald was mildly obsessed with Cromwell. An attempt to cajole the nation into paying for a statue by public subscription in 1895 failed. Leaving Archibald to pay for it himself; an undertaking eased by the fact that he had married the richest woman in the world.[202] Rosebery had hoped to unveil his statue on 3 September 1899, for obvious reasons. But was thwarted. So it was 14 November, in the end. A quiet ceremony, followed by a not much louder speech that evening. In which Rosebery acclaimed a 'man of action' and a 'defender of the faith'. Who was also a proto-imperialist and proto-liberal. A bit like him, the implication ran.

A final anecdote. When, during the Blitz, it was decided to retrieve some of the bronze statues outside Westminster, and put them in safe storage, that of Cromwell was left to take its chances. If anyone was capable of withstanding a bit of fire and brimstone it was surely him. Not, though, his old adversary. Far too delicate. The statue of King Charles at Charing Cross was packaged up by the Ministry of Works, and sent into the country, to the Mentmore estate in Buckinghamshire. An interesting choice, the country estate of the Rosebery family, acquired by Archibald on his marriage. Designed by Sir Joseph Paxton in the 'Jacobethan' style. Familiar architecture, nicely flashed up, Charles might have appreciated the gesture. Archibald had died in 1929. To be succeeded by his son Harry. Not much of a politician, though apparently a very good middle-order batsman, captain of Surrey CCC for a number of years. Harry served as a rather distant Commissioner for Civil Defence in Scotland during the war. Charles was installed in the garden. Not a huge risk in truth. The Luftwaffe did not bother bombing Leighton Buzzard. If they had, they might have won the war.[203] The statue was returned in 1946, complete with a new sword and badge of the Garter. All spick and span.

The retirement of Edward Hyde

Unlike, it seems, Sir Edward Hyde. Tarnished in the way he would most have dreaded; by increscent neglect. A man of unarguable power and influence, by virtue of what he did and, when that was done, by what he wrote. The 'greatest' historian of his age, it is suggested.[204] But yet, somehow 'diminished'.[205] Notably absent a modern biographer since Henry Craik's two-volume *Life* published in 1911. Scholarly attention, of course. Some new editions and 'selections' of his writings, published at decent intervals. A couple of entries in the *Dictionary of National Biography*, a century apart. Brian Wormald's revisionist account of Hyde and his *History* is a critical stand-out, carefully extracting 'Hyde the politician' from 'Hyde the historian'.[206] Other essays, of course. But still, in all, a modest return. Dullness might be an issue, as both Carlyle and Macaulay intimated. A lawyer who wrote a lawyer's history. A little self-regarding. The wrong politics too, or at least the perception. Royalist, right and repulsive. There are reasons. Nothing, though, which seems entirely sufficient.

Some ironies to contemplate. Bound up in the matter of failure. Two evident moments of the latter: 1641 and 1667. Against which might be presented some successes, 1660 being the most striking. All political lives are described in these terms, and comprise both. We might, as we come to a close, indulge a moment of whimsy. As Hyde must surely have done, sat in his garden in Montpellier, enjoying a glass of port after dinner, another day of revisions complete. Polishing up the *History*, and the historian. There was little in the *History* that admitted failure. But that does not mean it was not felt. So what, we might wonder, did the author really think of January 1649. Did he feel responsible, if only in the slightest, for the tragedy which unfolded during that hectic eight weeks minus a day which transpired between Colonel Pride's 'purge' and the decapitation of his king?

We have already encountered Hyde's depiction of the regicide; written, of necessity, from a distance. Predictably maudlin. The 'sainted' Charles brutally despatched by the 'great dissembler' and his cronies. But it is, of course, impossible to properly detach this moment from the longer history of Charles Stuart. A king brought down, not just by malice but by the 'irresolution and unsteadiness of his own counsels'.[207] By a tendency to keep making the same mistakes. Chance too. A crushing defeat, some negligent correspondence, a fated flirtation with a couple of Scottish Commissioners. Rotten luck, rotten advice, the 'vexation' of others. And a 150 years of frustrated Reformation. Something of each, and more. The appeal in the case of Charles Stuart rests here, in the balance of all of this. Plus, of course, something else. The simple fact that he should have listened more to Edward Hyde.

The same might be said of his son, the second King Charles. It was more or less said by Hyde. Who clung to the hope that he might, one day, return to England. He remained in Montpellier for three years before moving to Moulins, where he was visited by Laurence. The *History* was by then complete. A draft despatched to Charles, with a letter begging permission to return. 'I have performed a work under this mortification, which I began with the approbation and encouragement of your blessed father.' But to no avail. The past could stay where it was, and so could Hyde. A closing disappointment. Hyde died three years later, in Rouen; having moved a little nearer, still hoping. It was left to Laurence, in possession of his father's manuscript, to oversee the first stages in restoration of Sir Edward Hyde, a quarter of a century on. In truth, requiring little more than a final bit of polishing up; plus, apparently, a preface.

Hyde had already left his readers with a gleaming account of himself, and his qualities as a historian. The candour, the honesty, the generosity of spirit and all-round 'goodness'. The Hyde we have already encountered, 'without blemish'.[208] The renowned passage in which he delved into the 'duties' of a Privy Councillor told the reader everything they needed to know about Sir Edward, the epitome of those 'honest and wise men' who sacrifice everything in the service of king and country. And its remembrance. The same qualities required of the good historian. Duty-bound to record events with 'all faithfulness and ingenuity', to attest the 'faults and infirmities of both sides' and to cherish the central tenet of faith, that the 'love of truth' is the 'soul of history'. Only the historian who believes this, and does this, 'deserves to be believed'. Like Hyde. Just the man. Able to assure his readers: 'I know myself to be very free from any of those passions which naturally transport men with prejudice towards the persons whom they are obliged to mention and whose actions they are at liberty to censure.'[209]

Nothing surprising here. But this determination, of testamentary fidelity, requires Hyde to affirm something else. He can only write about what he has experienced; at least more or less. For which reason his history of the 'great rebellion' is constrained. To start at the 'beginning' of the reign of Charles I, and to end, in the first instance, at 1648. He does not say that anything prior is irrelevant; just that, as a testamentary historian, he cannot go there. Which leads, of course, to a necessary insinuation. As we have already noted; of fault personified. The 'minds' of those driven to distraction in 1642, and again in 1648, did not drift any further back than 1625. Interestingly, pretty much the same place where Sir Philip Warwick would start his *Memoirs*. Moreover, absent any grander theories of causation, his history of the 'great rebellion' will be, in essence, a history of these 'minds'. The 'weakness and folly' of certain actors, their ambitions and frustrations, their 'pride and passion'. And their dissimulations. Certain key mistakes. Pushed to identify an 'original', he supposed prerogative taxation. But there were others too. The attempt to arrest the Five Members, for example. No need to discover a more distant 'design' in the history of the rebellion.[210] Just moments.

Revisionist perhaps, ironic almost. But still somehow reading a little Whiggish. The 'ingenuity' of the historian lying in the ability to craft a dramatic narrative from the chaos of contingency. Sidney's 'accidents', Hobbes's 'shiftings'. The art of polishing up the past. And, where necessary, the polisher. Which brings us to the heart of the matter, in a sense. The particular ironies of authenticity. Any historian is a part of the history they write. But not all are part of the history about which they write. But Hyde was. More thoughts, then, to occupy Sir Edward as he sat in his garden at Montpellier sipping his port. Hopefully just the one glass; long cursed by gout, the physician's orders would have been plain.[211] Or maybe at Moulins, chatting to Laurence. About how the *History* might be best presented. And him. How best to write the 'history' of Edward Hyde.

NOTES

Introduction

1 Itzin and Trussler (1975).
2 Butterfield (1931), 11–13, 39–41, 64.
3 Carlyle (1871), 68.
4 As he did famously in *King John*, wherein there is no account of *Magna Carta*. England in the 1590s not being quite the right moment in which to write a glowing account of a baronial coup.
5 Sachse (1973), 69.
6 Sirico (1999), 52.
7 See Madison's *Notes of Debates in the Federal Convention of 1787*, reprinted in Farrand (1911), 64.
8 Klein (1997), 1.
9 Carlyle (1871), 49.

1 The casebook of Sir Edward Coke

1 Designed by the architect Cass Gilbert, and installed at the completion of the Court in 1935. Gilbert specialized in skyscrapers and state buildings. A bit of a Whig, and a lot of a classicist, Gilbert designed the Supreme Court as a Roman Temple in the Corinthian style, to represent two thousand years of jurisprudential progress.
2 Adams (1854), 9.432.
3 Loewenstein (2001), 28.
4 Brought about by the 'variety of opinions' and 'doubts' to be found in existing legal reports. Coke took his assumed didactic responsibilities very seriously. Smith (2014), 56–7, 140.
5 Gest (1909), 506.
6 Berman (1994), 1675.
7 The seminal commentary here being John Pocock's, *The Ancient Constitution and the Common Law* (1967), particularly chapters 2 and 3. For some doubts, especially in regard to the extent to which Coke might be thought paradigmatic of the common law 'mind', see Burgess (1992), 21–2, 72–8.
8 In an essay entitled *To All Ingenuous Readers*, cited in Weston (1991), 375–6.

9   Gest (1909), 510–11, questioning the veracity of the suggestion, which was first
      advanced by Lord Campbell in his *Lives of the Chief Justices*, and was based on
      similarities between some of Sir Andrew's lines and Coke's speech in the trial
      of Sir Walter Raleigh. Raleigh's trial took place in 1603, after the first recorded
      performances of *Twelfth Night*. This does not preclude, though, the possibility that
      Coke had used the same rhetorical devices in earlier high-profile treason cases.
10   Knapfla (1977), 126.
11   Jardine and Stewart (1998), 254.
12   Jardine and Stewart (1998), 190.
13   Burgess (1996), 207.
14   Gest (1909), 506.
15   Sommerville (1991a), 55–7.
16   In Knapfla (1977), 84.
17   Sharpe (1992), 216.
18   Peck (1993), 84–5.
19   See Sommerville (1986), 9–12, 23–6.
20   Sommerville (1994), 181.
21   Sommerville (1994), 64–5.
22   See Morrill (1993), 45–68 and (2011), 307–25.
23   Sommerville (1994), 81–2.
24   Sommerville (1994), 20–2.
25   Sommerville (1991b), 1.
26   Boehrer (1987), 101.
27   Sommerville (1994), 190–1.
28   Monateri (2018), 16–17, 34–7, 87–92.
29   Cressy (2015), 90.
30   Raffield (2010), 26, 200.
31   See Burgess (1996), 63–6, 70 and also Knapfla (1977), 69–73.
32   Baker (2018), 305.
33   See Coquillette (1992), 46–7, 144–6, 157–9.
34   Guy (1982), 481, 497.
35   See Smith (2014), 252, Burgess (1996), 80–5 and Brooks (2010), 119–20.
36   In Burgess (1996), 36.
37   Brooks (2010), 151.
38   Jones (1971), 29.
39   Smith (2017), 96 and Doe (2017), 116.
40   Rose (2011), 66.
41   See Lake (1988), 227, suggesting that Hooker, in effect, 'invented' the Anglican
      settlement.
42   McGrade (1989), 79–80, 87–8. For commentaries on the influence of Aristotle on
      English common law jurisprudence, see Sommerville (1986), 9–14 and Burgess
      (1992), 40–4 and 67–9.
43   Pocock (1967), 32–3.
44   Doe (2017), 126–7.
45   Polizzotto (2014), 35.
46   McGrade (1989), 146–7.
47   For those who could read French, in 1571. For those who could not, twenty-six
      years later.
48   The definitive commentary on the 'two bodies' thesis is Kantorowicz (2016).

49 See Baker (2018), 145–6 and Smith (2014), 256–7.
50 1608 6 James I, 7 Co. Rep. 10a. See Price (1997).
51 Burgess (1996), 104–5 and Barber (1998), 16.
52 Coke (2003), 40.
53 Barber (1998), 13, 19, 45, 139.
54 In Smith (2014), 266–7.
55 Blackstone (2016), 3.284.
56 Metewands were used for measuring boundaries.
57 Burgess (1996), 143.
58 McGrade (1989), 147, 217.
59 Russell (1990), 24, 158.
60 Pollock (1927), 61.
61 Smith (2014), 180.
62 Gardiner (1887–91), 1.329.
63 He had spoken in Parliament in support of the defendant in the celebrated *Bates's Case* in 1606, which had challenged the legality of an imposition on dried fruit importations. Ironically, the prosecution had been led by Coke, in his final days as Attorney General.
64 Wright (2006), 204–5.
65 Sharpe (1992), 738.
66 Wright (2006), 204, Smith (2014), 186–7 and Shapiro (2019), 45–6.
67 Named after the star-patterns on the ceiling of the room in Westminster Palace where the Chamber sat.
68 Cust (1986), 75, 87.
69 Udall was denied representation by the trial judge. But Fuller appears to have represented him unofficially.
70 A victim of timing, at least. At much the same time as Fuller was holding forth in Star Chamber, plot had been uncovered to depose Elizabeth and proclaim the deranged preacher William Hacket as the new Messiah.
71 See Smith (2014), 182–3.
72 See Wright (2006), 192–3 and Smith (2014), 194–5.
73 Wright (2006), 194 and Baker (2017), 360–1.
74 Roger Wilbraham, formerly Queen Elizabeth's Solicitor General for Ireland. Baker (2017), 362.
75 Wright (2006), 196 and Knapfla (1977), 115–16.
76 12 Co.Rep.47, Baker (2017), 363.
77 12 Co.Rep.41.
78 See here Usher (1903), 667–75.
79 12 Co.Rep.63.
80 Comments repeated in further accounts of the meeting. See Usher (1903), 669, 675.
81 See Smith (2014), 249 and Baker (2017), 367–8.
82 Perhaps. Another dramatic moment which might have been over-written. See Smith (2014), 176–7.
83 7 Co.Rep.1a.
84 Coke (1823), 1.97b.
85 The Brownists were a separatist congregation, named after Robert Browne. Subject to concerted persecution as the century turned, a number would emigrate to the Netherlands and North America. A majority of those who sailed on *The Mayflower* were Brownists.

86 The Ephori were Spartan judges, tasked with a specific responsibility to guard against monarchical tyranny.
87 Wright (2006), 198–200 and Baker (2017), 357.
88 Lockwood (1997), 17.
89 Baker (2017), 187–201.
90 In effect, the Crown took a cut of all fines levied by the Company.
91 Breward (2009), 26.
92 The nomenclature being derived from the heated steam rooms in which prostitutes commonly plied their trade.
93 Thomas (1991), 173–4.
94 Internal quotes, taken from Shakespeare (1967).
95 Stone (1967), 188, 299.
96 12 Coke Rep.74.
97 Coke (2003), 2.552–3.
98 Baker (2017), 410.
99 The extent of Coke's editorial responsibility, especially in regard to the final volumes, published posthumously, has long exercised historians.
100 Watt (2009), 67–72.
101 Cressy (2015), 35.
102 Various hard gemstones were often called 'topaz' by contemporaries. In this case, where the gem in question was pretending to be a diamond, it was probably chrysoberyl, which sparkles very nicely in the right light.
103 The sheriff was curtly advised to 'return a wiser jury' next time. Baker (2017), 419.
104 Knapfla (1977), 173–4, Smith (2014), 245–7 and Baker (2004), 261–2, 266–8.
105 Loncar (1990), 220.
106 *Colt and Glover v Bishop of Coventry and Lichfield* (1615–17) 1 Rolle Rep.451.
107 See Smith (2014), 281–2 and Jardine and Stewart (1998), 370–2.
108 Coke (2003), 3.1316, Baker (2017), 424–5.
109 Coke (2003), 3.1318–21.
110 Sommerville (1994), 206.
111 Smith (2014), 278–9.
112 And refusing to surrender his 'gold collar' to his successor, Sir Henry Montagu. Whose swearing-in ceremony had already been tarnished, according to a watching Bulstrode Whitelock, by a 'very bitter invective' launched by Ellesmere against the fallen Chief Justice. His closing advice, though undoubtedly sage, doing little to lighten the mood; 'Remember the removing and putting down of your late predecessor'. Baker (2017), 439.
113 Baker (2017), 435.
114 Baker (2017), 421, 437.
115 Henry would later marry Lady Diana Cecil, daughter of William Cecil, 2nd Earl of Exeter. A renowned beauty, carrying a dowry of £30,000. Worth the wait.
116 For accounts of the frenetic courtship, see Jardine and Stewart (1998), 400–5.
117 Sir Robert was Member of Parliament for Bishop's Castle in Shropshire.
118 In 1634, when threatened with arrest again. Robert may have joined her there. Both would return to England during the 1640s, Robert to raise a regiment for the king.
119 In Jardine and Stewart (1998), 414.
120 Cust (2007), 32–3.
121 Cust (2007), 109.
122 Cressy (2015), 85–6.

123 Warwick (1813), 13.
124 Coast (2016), 241–2.
125 Coast (2016), 248–9. Rumours that Buckingham had poisoned the ailing King James were quickly in circulation.
126 See Coast, 'Impeachment', 264, suggesting that the 1620s were a 'crucial decade in the invention of public opinion in England'.
127 Sharpe (1992), 42.
128 Clarendon (1843), 13.
129 Cust (2007), 105.
130 Sharpe (1992), 49.
131 Sir Philip Warwick recorded that the Duke's death confirmed in Charles an 'inward dislike' of Parliament. Warwick (1813), 43.
132 Willms (2006), 92.
133 Sharpe (1992), 700.
134 Smith (1994), 34.
135 Cust (1985), 222.
136 Cressy (2015), 99.
137 Cust (1985), 219.
138 Somerville (1986), 162–5.
139 Cust (1985), 225–7.
140 3 How St Tr 1 (KB 1627).
141 The Earl would spend the 1630s helping his father-in-law, Lord Saye, in shaping a Parliamentary opposition 'junto'.
142 Cust (2007), 69, quoting William Laud.
143 Ironically Darnell had, by then, withdrawn from the action.
144 Though he appears to have been amongst those courted, more particularly by Laud, with whom he had developed something of a friendship.
145 The thesis of the *History* was necessarily tendentious, and Selden was summoned to Whitehall to provide an explanation. Haivry (2017), 22–3.
146 For a commentary on the renewed interest in chapter 29, in the decades either side of 1600, see Baker (2017), chapter 7.
147 Former counsel to the Duke of Buckingham, by odd coincidence. And uncle to Edward Hyde, the hero of our final chapter. In fact, Hyde chastised both parties for the failure to bring in precedents. See Kishlansky (1999), 76.
148 Kishlansky (1999), 61, 64.
149 Kishlanksy (1999), 74.
150 Kishlansky (1999) , 73.
151 Kishlansky (1999), 74 and Morrill (1993), 289, suggesting that Charles was seeking to establish 'legal tyranny'.
152 Sharpe (1992), 23.
153 Cust (2007), 54.
154 Cust (2007), 56.
155 Cust (2007), 62.
156 Sharpe (1992), 50.
157 These three principles would later find statutory authority, in the shape of the 1679 *Habeas Corpus Act*.
158 Very likely co-authored with Selden, who spoke vigorously in its support in the Commons.
159 Baker (2017), 1, 427–8.

160 Raffield (2004), 205–6.
161 Cressy (2015), 196.
162 Sharpe (1992), 59–60.
163 Comment made in his dissolution Declaration. Smith (1994), 27.
164 Cust (2007), 118.
165 Clarendon (1843), 84.
166 Almack (1903), 1.
167 See Russell (1979), 415–19, suggesting that the events of 2 March did indeed set the country on the first steps towards revolution.
168 Haivry (2017), 49–55.
169 The icon of evil counsellors everywhere, the Roman general Sejanus had been confidante of the Emperor Tiberius, and the reputed lover of his wife.
170 After evincing some early sympathy with the moderate opposition in Parliament, Jenkins had committed himself to the royalist cause, raising a regiment on behalf of the king in South Wales. He would be threatened with treason charges in the late 1640s. But proceedings never really got going. Instead he spent much of these years, and the early 1650s, in various prisons. During which time he collected *Eight Centuries of Reports*, chiefly medieval Exchequer cases, which were published in 1661.
171 Burgess (1996), 207.
172 A few months before his death, Privy Council ordered the seizure of Coke's papers. The precaution of an increasingly neurotic king. The Long Parliament would return them to his family, in 1641, with their thanks.

2 The triumphs of King Charles I

1 Milton (1953–62), 3.343–4.
2 Royle (2005), 157.
3 Firth (1894), 1.25.
4 There was a sixth name too. That of Viscount Mandeville, son of the Earl of Manchester and a member of the House of Lords.
5 Royle (2005), 156.
6 Clarendon (1843), 230.
7 Lunsford would later raise a regiment for the king and fight at Edgehill. Where he was captured by Parliament. Released in 1644, he emigrated to Virginia in 1649, where he died four years later.
8 Rees (2016), 9.
9 Abbott (1937–47), 1.365.
10 See Rees (2016), 21–2, 104.
11 The Company was, in fact, notorious as a haven for radical officers. Amongst its number could be counted Henry Overton, Thomas Pride, George Joyce and 'Praise-God' Barebones; each destined to play a significant role in what was to come.
12 What Conrad Russell terms the 'problem of diminished majesty'; chronic by the end of 1641. Russell (1990), 23.
13 Keenan (2020), 184–92.
14 Smith (1994), 77.

15 Cust (2007), 167.
16 In fairness, when the royal collection was valued in 1649, with a view to selling off, the Gonzaga acquisition was estimated at around £25,000. So a decent investment in a radically unstable market. Very probably thanks to his employment of Daniel Nijs as his broker; a kind of super-agent of the early seventeenth-century art world.
17 Here again the 1649 sale accounts give us an intriguing glimpse of market tolerance. A Raphael went for £2000. But a bargain-hunter with a good eye could get a Rembrandt for just £6. The royal plumber was paid off with a Titian; in lieu of what was presumably a sizeable account.
18 Cressy (2015), 40.
19 Bagehot (2001), 34–7, 69–70, 185–6.
20 Cust (2007), 165.
21 Barber (1998), 137.
22 The earlier editions, in 1559 and 1563, were largely comprised of later medieval English princes. Followed by a more fanciful 1574 edition, populated by lots of made-up kings and queens, including Cordell, daughter of King Leir. The 1587 edition introduced an assortment of Roman tyrants and Scottish kings. The latter discreetly excised from the 1610 edition which reinvested a steadier cast of English heroes and anti-heroes, Arthur, Alfred, John, all the Richards, and culminating, of course, with Elizabeth I.
23 The text wherein Shakespeare discovered his hunchbacked Richard of York.
24 Whether *Richard II* is better considered a 'tragedy' or a 'history' is a hoary Shakespearian chestnut.
25 Internal reference to Shakespeare (1966).
26 More immediately inspired by Charles V's *Political Testament*, written to his son Philip. James had been sent an edition in 1592. Wormald (1991), 47.
27 Sommerville (1994), 4, 13, 43.
28 Sommerville (1994), 51–5.
29 It is surmised that Charles finally lost patience with Mytens on seeing his *Charles and Henrietta Maria*, completed at some point in late 1631 or early 1632. The two stand side-by-side holding a laurel wreath between them. Charles looking oddly alarmed, perhaps by his wife's bizarrely vacant gaze and apparently dislocated shoulder. Van Dyck would revisit precisely the same composition later in the same year. The differences subtle, but brilliant. A slight turn in the royal frame, a lean-forward, a softer eye, and a Queen who seems capable of movement. A royal couple as one, and human. Gentileschi would remain in favour, commissioned to decorate the Queen's chambers. Mytens was pensioned off, and returned to the Netherlands.
30 Van Dyck had been to England before, invited across in 1620 by a familiar figure, Coke's son-in-law, Viscount Purbeck.
31 Charles was forever gifting chains, as a kind of bonus payment, to artists and others who did him an esteemed service. The chain is prominent in *Self Portrait with a Sunflower*, one of the first paintings to be completed following van Dyck's arrival in England, completed in early 1633. Needless to say the pension payment proved to be intermittent, and invariably tardy. Van Dyck was probably not entirely surprised.
32 Lady Venetia was a renowned society-beauty, who died suddenly in 1633.
33 At least forty times, it has been estimated; the 'personalisation of power in paint'. Sharpe (2009), 19.

34 Which Charles would have seen, and very probably admired, whilst in Madrid in 1623. It is generally agreed that *King Charles in the Hunting Field* was likewise inspired, by Titian's *Adoration of the Kings*.

35 Cust (2007), 153.

36 George was the subject of another renowned van Dyck. Dressed as a shepherd with the inscription 'Love is stronger than me'. A fourth brother, Lord James, survived, to serve his king differently. And to reappear a little later in our history.

37 See Breward (2009), 31, 33.

38 An allusion to *Numbers* 11:5. Lost in the Wilderness the people of Israel recall the 'onions, and the garlick' which 'we did eat in Egypt freely'. A temptation, to be resisted. The ancient Egyptians vested considerable cultural, and religious, status in the humble onion, representative of regeneration and eternity. The dead were often sent on their way with a bulb or two. A number were discovered in the tomb of King Tut. Garlic was similarly revered, thought to be an effective charm against evil spirits.

39 J. Burroughs, *Sions Joy* (1641), in Coffey (2016), 258.

40 Amongst whose patrons could be counted Robert Carr, 1st Earl of Somerset, later embroiled in the notorious Overbury scandal, George Villiers, Sir Fulke Greville, Lord Brooke, sometime Chancellor of the Exchequer and writer of very dour Calvinist poetry, and 'Steenie'. An eclectic mix. The Lectureship was a clerical appointment.

41 Sharpe (1992), 295.

42 Breward (2009), 34.

43 'Mastix' meaning horsewhip in classical Greek, 'histrio', the teller of stories.

44 Written by Walter Montagu, staged by Inigo Jones. So flashy. Montagu was the second son of the parliamentarian Earl of Manchester, brother of Viscount Mandeville. Very different loyalties though, and faith. Having played a prominent role in the negotiations which led to the marriage of Charles and Henrietta Maria, Walter would remain close to the Queen. Going with her to France, and ending up taking Catholic orders. It was reported that Walter played a leading role in having Thomas Hobbes hounded out of Paris in 1650. We will revisit that moment in a later chapter.

45 The masque was commissioned by the Queen, as a present for her husband's birthday. The theme was devotion. The shepherd motif was very much *a la mode*. Fletcher's *Faithful Shepherdess* would be revived a year later, also performed at Court. Henrietta Maria did the costumes.

46 Raffield (2004), 191–2, Kishlansky (2013), 618–19 and Thomas (1984), 179.

47 Kishlansky (2013), 609–10, 622, 627 and Thomas (1984), 181.

48 Kishlansky (2013), 623–4.

49 Those who did not exhibit copies could be subject to a diocesan fine.

50 Cressy (2015), 261.

51 Puppet-shows were an especial bane. Especially for the inhabitants of Bridport, unable to 'keep their children and servants in their houses by reason they frequent the said shows', day and night, every day of the week. But especially on Sundays, when the puppeteers apparently liked to barrack the local preacher on his way back from service.

52 Burton was a cleric, Bastwick a doctor. Amongst Bastwick's writings could be found the fiercely anti-Catholic *Flagellum Pontificiis*. It did not take much imagination to read the *Flagellum* as being just as fiercely anti-Laudian.

53 Sharpe (1992), 760.
54 Braddick (2009), 76.
55 Sharpe (1992), 764.
56 The 1660s would be passed as Keeper of the Records in the Tower. The antiquarian Anthony Wood later paid tribute to an affable, if slightly deaf, archivist. Pepys likewise, recounting a number of 'good' conversations on various matters, including parliamentary propriety. Religion was though still a subject to be avoided. A diary entry for May 1662 describes a dinner at Trinity house, where Pepys found himself seated 'close' to Prynne. And thus subject to an extensive diatribe on the 'lust and wicked lives of the Nuns heretofore in England'. In Pepys (1993), 198.
57 Sir Philip Warwick would likewise confirm that 1637 was a peculiarly fateful year in the reign of Charles Stuart. Warwick (1813), at 132.
58 Sharpe (1992), 765, 770, 954 and Rees (2016), 29.
59 Cust (2007), 171.
60 Cressy (2015), 18–19.
61 Russell (1990), 203.
62 Cust (2007), 123.
63 Smith (2014), 103.
64 Warwick (1813), 89.
65 Clarendon (1843), 295.
66 To name just some. Montague was successively appointed bishop of Chichester in 1628 and Norwich in 1638, Bancroft Bishop of Oxford, Morton Bishop of Durham. Neile succeeded Morton at Durham, before moving to Winchester and then York. Wren was successively bishop of Hereford, Norwich and Ely. Others of similar sentiment included Brian Duppa, bishop of Chichester and then Salisbury, Richard Corbet appointed at Oxford and then Norwich, Francis White who was shunted from Carlisle to Norwich and then Ely, his replacement at Carlisle, Barnaby Potter, Francis Dee at Peterborough and John Bowle at Rochester. William Juxon too, who succeeded Laud to the bishopric of London in 1633. We will encounter Juxon again, attending the king on 30 January 1649.
67 Sharpe (1992), 328.
68 Cressy (2015), 216, 225.
69 Russell (1990), 197.
70 Cust (2007), 140.
71 Cressy (2015), 2310.
72 Comment made during the Putney 'debates' October 1647, an event we will revisit in the next chapter. Woodhouse (1986), 41.
73 Cressy (2015), 227.
74 Tyacke (1973), 134–5.
75 Russell (1990), 107.
76 Cressy (2015), 223.
77 Cressy (2015), 226, 228.
78 Smith (1995), 210.
79 Gardiner (1906), 137–44.
80 Shapiro (2019), 97.
81 In Smith (1995), 214.
82 Morrill (1993), 82.
83 Morrill (1993), 45, 54, 72.
84 Morrill (1993), 82.

85 Orr (2002), 115–16, 124, 131–3.
86 In Cressy (2015), 75.
87 The forgotten Anglo-Saxon is Alfheah, beaten to death by a gang of drunken Vikings in 1012. It was said that Becket prayed to St Alfheah in the last moments of his life. Amongst the medieval traitors can be counted Thomas Scrope, Archbishop of York, executed in 1405 for his part in the 'Northern Rising' against Henry IV. Another, of a sort, is Simon Sudbury, decapitated by irate Kentish farmers in the last days of the Peasants' Revolt.
88 In Cressy (2015), 104.
89 Sharpe (1992), 692.
90 Constables despatched to deal with non-payers were instructed to seize movable chattels. Usually livestock. Writs of replevin were issued for the recovery of wrongly distrained goods.
91 We have already encountered Sir William. One of the five MPs that Charles failed to have arrested in January 1642.
92 Clarendon (1843), 166–8.
93 Sir Edmund Hampden; one of the 'five knights'.
94 *R v Hampden* (1637) 3 State Tr. 826.
95 Whitelock (1853), 1.71–2 and Sharpe (1992), 722–3.
96 Clarendon (1843), 168.
97 Sharpe (1992), 727–8.
98 Sharpe (1992), 725.
99 Sharpe (1992), 716–17 and Cressy (2015), 110.

100 Sharpe (1992), 728. Payments would eventually pick up, to an extent.
101 Cressy (2015), 111.
102 Sharpe (1992), 496–7.
103 Russell (1990), 137.
104 A creepie-stool was a folding chair.
105 Cressy (2015), 150 and also Morrill (1993), 7, suggesting that the decision to go to war was a 'spectacular miscalculation'.
106 Sharpe (1992), 865 and Cust (2007), 254–5.
107 Jones (1971), 14, 21.
108 Warwick (1813), 119.
109 D'Armagnac was Archbishop of Avignon in the second part of the sixteenth century, Philandrier his secretary. Tom's secretary was Sir Philip Mainwaring; who was about as close a friend as Tom had. The double-portrait is commonly regarded as the model after which many similar portraits would be painted. Most famously perhaps Reynolds's *Charles Watson-Wentworth, 2nd Marquess of Rockingham with his Secretary Edmund Burke.*
110 Sharpe (1992), 921.
111 Morrill (1993), 64.
112 This part of the procedure was normal. By convention only the House of Lords could grant bail when the matter came before it.
113 Shapiro (2019), 99.
114 Royle (2005), 124.
115 See Orr (2002), 67–72, 80–4, reinforcing the argument that the charges lay within the bounds of established jurisprudence. The alternative idea, that the impeachment 'managers' were venturing a novel idea of 'accumulated' treason, is argued in Stacy (1985).

116 Cust (2007), 259–60.
117 Orr (2002), 90–2.
118 Orr (2002), 97.
119 Sharpe (1992), 945.
120 Sharpe (1992), 933.
121 Russell (1988).
122 Clarendon (1843), 144.
123 Almack (1903), 7.
124 Milton (1953–62), 3.371.
125 Royle (2005), 126.
126 Warwick (1813), 179–80.
127 An observation which was sufficiently well-reported that the king ordered an investigation. Fortunately for Lilburne the 'witnesses' were unable to corroborate. Rees (2016), 35–6.
128 In Gardiner (1906), 202–32.
129 Gardiner (1906), 233–6. The rejection was drafted by Hyde.
130 Charles was keen for it to be known that he intended to equip an army which could then go to Ireland to put down the rebels.
131 Charles immediately wrote to Parliament complaining, which elicited a predictable response. Parliament issued a declaration defending Hotham.
132 Haivry (2017), 74.
133 Clarendon (1843), 249.
134 Russell (1990), 26.
135 Norbrook (1999), 69–70.
136 The story goes that Sir Edmund's body was never recovered. Just his hand, still clutching the royal banner. All of Sir Edmund can still be seen in a Van Dyck portrait, from around 1640; the face an epitome of weary resignation.
137 Clarendon (1843), 250.
138 In the process showing off his Latin. The phrase taken from the first book of Lucan's *Pharsalia*; 'bellum, … sine hoste'. Norbrook (1999), 24.
139 Royle (2005), 165 and Cust (2007), 349–50.
140 Clarendon (1843), 256–7, 276–89 and Haivry (2017), 76.
141 Warwick (1813), 255.
142 Wilson (1985), 65.
143 Barber (1998), 96.
144 Description of the site given in Sir Henry Slingsby's account of the battle, quoted in Young (1985), 260–1.
145 Spencer (2014), 13.
146 Carlton (1995), 285–6 and Royle (2005), 325.
147 Cust (2007), 403.
148 Clarendon recorded that the battle commenced at ten. Others have supposed that it might have been slightly later.
149 Young (1985), 26, 372 and Woolrych (1991), 122–3.
150 Gentles (1992), 60.
151 Young (1985), 260, 266–7.
152 Many desperately trying to get to the royalist garrison at Leicester, twenty-five miles away.
153 In his subsequent report to Parliament on the proceedings of 14 June, Fairfax made explicit reference to the ordinance.

154 Internal reference to Shakespeare (1991). See Meron (1993), 154–71.

155 *Brief Memorials of the Unfortunate Success of His Majesty's Army and Affairs in the Year 1645*, in Young (1985), 319.

156 *Isaiah* 41:10.

157 Carlton (1995), 288.

158 Royle (2005), 369.

159 Matusiak (2017), 24–5.

160 Young (1985), 270.

161 Young (1985), 336, 339.

162 Hobbes would later conclude that the entire 'fortune' of the war was decided in that one day. Hobbes (1990), 131–2.

163 Hutchinson (2000), 200.

164 Milton (1953–62), 3.537–8.

165 Young (1985), 332.

166 An allusion to *Psalms* 1:1, 'Blessed is the man who walketh not in the counsel of the ungodly.'

167 Macadam (2011), 471–6, 486–7.

168 *Mercurius Britannicus* xcii 4 August 1645, 825.

169 *Mercurius Britannicus* xc 21 July 1645, 809.

170 Almack (1903), 199, 203.

171 Lord Say and Sele, *Vindiciae Veritatis* (1654), 34, in Macadam (2011), 485.

172 Milton (1953–62), 3 (ch. 21 at 225).

173 Firth (1894) *Memoirs*, 1.35 and 122.

174 Gardiner (1901), 2.224.

175 A remarkable man, Digby would serve as Henrietta Maria's chancellor when she established an exile Court in France in 1644. He was also a renowned alchemist, amateur astrologer and early-day celebrity chef. His renowned cookbook, *The Closet of the Eminently Learned Sir Kenelm Digby*, was published in 1669; though scurrilous report suggested that most of it was written by his cook. He also published two treatises on natural philosophy, *The Nature of Bodies* and *On the Immortality of Reasonable Souls*. Along with a *Discourse Concerning the Vegetation of Plants*, still acclaimed by historians of botanical science, in which can be found a primitive theory of photosynthesis.

176 Brereton did not attend the trial in the end. Something which probably saved his life in 1660.

177 Morgan hailed from Monmouth. A professional soldier, who cut his teeth in the Thirty Years War before returning and fighting for Parliament. He would later serve as a deputy to Monck in Scotland during the 1650s, before supporting the Restoration. In 1665 he would be appointed governor of Jersey. Birch, slightly younger, first saw action during the civil war, most notably at Cropredy Bridge in 1644. He too would support the Restoration and enjoy a long parliamentary career, first as a 'recruiter' MP in the Long Parliament, and then in successive Protectorate Parliaments, the 'Cavalier' Parliament and later Restoration parliaments up until his death in 1691.

178 Carlton (1995), 90 and Macadam (2011), 481.

179 The same David Leslie who had led to the Covenanter army into northern England in summer 1640, and inflicted the crushing defeat at Newburn. And then played a critical role at the battle of Marston Moor in 1644, taking over command of the Parliamentarian cavalry when Cromwell was momentarily wounded.

180 Matusiak (2017), 47–8.

181 Russell (1990), 206.

182 Matusiak (2017), 85.

183 Woolrych (1991), 144.

184 Most likely Cromwell. The rumour was put about by royalist presses; which, predictably enough, castigated Joyce. Joyce keeps popping up, generally doing Cromwell's bidding. In December 1648, carrying news of Pride's 'purge' to Cromwell in Pontefract. He may well have conveyed Cromwell's formal sanction in advance. It was even rumoured that he might have been the masked executioner on 30 January, though plenty were demonized on that score. In 1660 Joyce managed to escape to the Netherlands with his family, and disappear.

185 There are various accounts of what happened that morning, including Joyce's initial attempt to seek an audience with the king in the very early hours; rebuffed. But they amount to similar, and commonly pivot around the scene where Joyce gestures to his troop as his 'commission'.

186 It was thought that 'touching' might cure scrofula, a tubercular disease which attacks the lymph nodes in the neck. These days it is treated with antibiotics. Touching probably just spread the infection. Charles though was an enthusiastic 'toucher', so much so that he had a special ceremony designed and written into the 1633 Prayer Book. Queen Anne was the last monarch to 'touch'. George I thought it too 'catholic'.

187 Matusiak (2017), 112.

188 Matusiak (2017), 122.

3 The trial of Charles Stuart

1 Farr (2006), 190.

2 Whitelock (1853), 3.512 and Nalson (2016), 77.

3 Around two hours, according to Firth (1894), 1.219.

4 A year after despatch from Rubens's studio in Antwerp. On the theme of unexpected delays, when the canvasses finally arrived they were discovered to be too big. And so had to be trimmed. The Flemings, like the English, measured in feet and inches. But different feet and inches.

5 Other painted apotheoses include Carlos Brumidi's *The Apotheosis of Washington*, on the dome of the Capitol, and Ingres's *The Apotheosis of Homer*, originally commissioned for the ceiling of the Louvre.

6 Almack (1903), 263.

7 Cust (2007), 462–3.

8 Royle (2005), 500–1.

9 Cust (2007), 463.

10 Whitelock (1853), 3.516.

11 *The Subject's Sorrow: Or, Lamentations Upon the Death of Britaine's Iosiah King Charles*. In Maguire (1989), 2.

12 See Summers (1985), 165–82.

13 Lee (1882), 12.

14 *The Bloody Court: or the Fatall Tribunall*. In Maguire (1989), 3.

15 Tomalin (2003), 34–5.

16 Boehrer (1987), 97–8.

17 Baxter (1696), 53–4.
18 Young (1985), 270.
19 Hobbes (1990), 135.
20 Wilson (1985), 120.
21 Braddick (2018), 22–3.
22 Publishing over eighty tracts by the time of his death in 1657.
23 Rees (2016), 134.
24 Rees (2016), 153–4.
25 Lilburne (1645), 2 and Coffey (2016), 263.
26 Barber (1998), 57.
27 Not so dramatic a denouement though. Fined and stripped of office, and then retired. Gayer to Sussex, where he became president of Christ's Hospital.
28 Rees (2016), 204–7 and Braddick (2018), 133–6.
29 Manning (1992), 30, 33.
30 Woodhouse (1986), 7–8.
31 Woodhouse (1986), 1. A leading agitator, Edward Sexby began his military career as a trooper in Cromwell's famed regiment of 'Ironsides'. In October 1648 he was granted £100 by the Commons in gratitude for bringing news of Cromwell's victory at Preston. During the 1650s, however, he turned against his former mentor, even publishing a tract entitled *Killing No Murder*, justifying the attempted assassination of the 'tyrant' Oliver.
32 A very 'grave man', according to Lucy Hutchinson (2000), 76.
33 Woodhouse (1986), 19, 25–7.
34 Woodhouse (1986), 53.
35 Woodhouse (1986), 54, 59–61, 69.
36 It has been surmised that the conversation became so heated that it was decided either to cease taking notes or, later, to have them destroyed.
37 Woodhouse (1986), 107.
38 Sharp (2001), 183.
39 A last straw, it has been surmised, for prospective regicides such as Thomas Chaloner. Scott (2001), 141.
40 Matusiak (2017), 136. The assurance coming from Jack Ashburnham, based on a chance encounter, and a quick chat, 'upon the Highway at Kingston'.
41 The personal advice coming from Cromwell. Barber (1998), 100.
42 A bowling alley and a miniature golf course were built for him, in the outer bailey of the castle.
43 Collins (2016), 187.
44 Clarendon (1843), 665, holding Ireton responsible.
45 Clarendon (1843), 664.
46 Rushworth (1721), 4.1243.
47 Clarendon (1843), 664.
48 From *Ezekiel* 21:27; a much-favoured passage amongst the like-minded. See Loewenstein (2001), 79, 100–11.
49 *The Declaration and Standard of the Levellers of England Delivered in a Speech to his Excellency the Lord General Fairfax* (London, 1649), 2. In Coffey (2016), 270.
50 Gent (1663), quoted in Sachse (1973), 70.
51 See Farr (2006), 161–2, 165 and Underdown (1985), 116.
52 A referent inscribed in an elegy entitled *Veni, Vidi, Vici*, composed on Ireton's death in 1652.

53 Manning (1992), 19.
54 Holmes (2020), 302.
55 Manning (1992), 25.
56 Rees (2016), 256–7.
57 Coffey (2016), 263–4.
58 Manning (1992), 33.
59 Shakespeare (1967), 5.1.317.
60 Farr (2006), 182.
61 Farr (2006), 142–7.
62 Braddick (2009), 556–8, Holmes (2019), 593–4 and Polizzotto (2016), 34.
63 We have come across Whitelock before, ringing his hands in late summer 1642.
    A lawyer by training, he would commonly lead negotiating teams during the 1640s.
    Between 1648 and 1655 he would be a commissioner of the Great Seal, and again in
    1659, when he was also appointed Lord Keeper. Cromwell would try desperately to
    get him to assume a prominent role in the trial of the king. But to no avail.
64 Holmes (2019), 591.
65 At seventy quarto pages long, the *Remonstrance* certainly demanded some diligence.
    A full 'four hours' of reading, according to Sir Roger. The divine William Sedgwick
    was of similar opinion, full of 'dark and vain tautologies in which you are lost and
    grope'. An *Abridgement* would be drafted up, principally for circulation in the army.
    See Holmes (2019), 604 and (2020), 306.
66 Woodhouse (1986), 342–3 and Rees (2016), 265, 276.
67 Farr (2006), 159.
68 Matusiak (2017), 305.
69 Various wheezes were dreamed up to find a way to get the king through his window.
    In the end it was nitric acid which weakened the bar sufficient that it could be prised
    out. Unlike the king who balked at the prospective drop, from chamber to ground.
70 Matusiak (2017), 300.
71 Iagomarsino (1989), 33.
72 W. Allen, *A faithful Memorial of the remarkable Meeting of Many Officers of the
    Army*, 1659. In Crawford (1977), 54.
73 Holmes (2019), 597.
74 Chernaik (2017), 7–8.
75 Farr (2006), 155 and Crawford (1977), 55.
76 A courtesy title, as eldest son of the earl of Stamford. Grey was an MP.
77 Firth (1894), 1.211–12.
78 Manning (1992), 174 and Fraser (1989), 270.
79 Located in Coleman Street in the City, the Star was the home of a fiery congregation
    presided over by a former army chaplain John Goodwin.
80 Pepys records three pubs adjoining Westminster, known as *Heaven*, *Purgatory* and
    Hell. It might have been supposed that *Purgatory* would have been more appropriate.
81 Russell (1990), 142.
82 Manning (1992), 46.
83 Reynardson had made his opposition to the trial of the king well-known. On 13
    January he refused to sanction a petition in support of proceedings. The final straw
    was his refusal, in early February, to read the *Act Abolishing Kingship*. Fined £2000
    and sent to the Tower as a consequence, as well as ejected from office.
84 Woodhouse (1986), 175.
85 Woodhouse (1986), 171, 173.

86 Woodhouse (1986), 140.
87 Bray (1850), 1.248.
88 Farr (2006), 193.
89 Prynne (1649).
90 Barber (1998), 165.
91 Woodhouse (1986), 469–70. It was probably Rich who invited Lizzie.
92 Woodhouse (1986), 470.
93 Polizzotto (2014), 57–9.
94 Woodhouse (1986), 471 and Taft (2006), 193.
95 Woodhouse (1986), 138.
96 Woodhouse (1986), 175.
97 Manning (1992), 24.
98 Hill (1997), 282.
99 Spencer (2015), 27.

100 Shakespeare (1966), 3.2.156.
101 Royle (2005), 516.
102 Rees (2016), xvii.
103 Hirst (1995), 249.
104 From *Mercurious Mennippeus*. Quoted in Thomas (1984), 183. A first Ordinance authorizing the army to close the theatres was passed on 1 January 1649.
105 In the third part of his *Institutes*. Collins (2016), 173, 177.
106 The principal drafter was Henry Marten. Nalson (2016), 20.
107 Rushworth (1721), 7.1376–80.
108 Barber (1998), 125.
109 Headed by Sir Hardress Waller and Colonels Harrison and Whalley.
110 Farr (2006), 185.
111 Warwick (1813), 377.
112 Clarendon (1843), 310–11.
113 Braddick (2018), 102.
114 Orr (2002), 189. Restored to health, Steele would lead the prosecution of the Duke of Hamilton a few weeks later.
115 Robertson (2006), 9.
116 There was a third member of the prosecution team, John Aske, who appears to have made no contribution to the proceedings. Royalist commentators were understandably hostile to each. 'Babbling and brazen-faced', Sir Phillip Warwick said of Cook (1813), 377. We will catch up with Cook, who spent the bulk of the 1650s as Chief Justice of Munster, in the next chapter. Dorislaus, a close friend of Cromwell, would be assassinated by a royalist hit-squad a few months after the execution of the king. His assassins reported as exclaiming 'There lies one of the King's judges'. Near enough. See Whitelock (1853), 3.30.
117 Clarendon (1843), 310.
118 Cousins. We have encountered William 'the Conqueror' leading parliamentarian armies to significant defeats at Roundway and Cropredy Bridge. He resigned his commission in 1645. A good idea in the longer run. As was his refusal to take any part in the trial proceedings. Surviving the Restoration and dying in 1668, his final years were spent composing a *Vindication of the Character and Conduct of Sir William Waller*; making much of his refusal to take part in the trial, and skipping over all the defeats. Sir Hardress, in contrast, elected to continue his military career, accompanying Cromwell to Ireland in 1650, and becoming governor of Limerick.

The Restoration would prove to be rather more of a trial for Sir Hardress, as we will discover.

119 It was reported that Charles resorted to calling him 'my precious jewel' whenever he could catch his eye in the Hall.

120 Blencowe (1825), 54, 237.

121 And both of whom sensibly skipped abroad in 1660, ending their days in Vevey with Edmund Ludlow.

122 Hyde was convinced, albeit acting solely on hearsay (1843), 315. So too Whitelock (1853), 3.504.

123 A formal impeachment proceeding would have required the support of the Lords, as well as the king. Collins (2016), 186–9.

124 Robertson (2006), 137. Northumberland was a Presbyterian, former Lord Admiral of the Parliamentarian fleet.

125 Prominent amongst the other seven members of the committee were Henry Marten, who had drafted the 6 January Ordinance, Thomas Chaloner and Miles Corbet.

126 Orr (2002), 172.

127 Cressy (2015), 77.

128 Cressy (2015), 296.

129 Manning (1992), 19.

130 Farr (2006), 185.

131 Nalson (2016), 32–5.

132 Braddick (2009), 106.

133 Nalson (2016), 33–4.

134 The particular Pharaoh is not identified in the *Book of Exodus*. Which leaves plenty of room for surmise. The popular choice in 1649 would have been Ahmose I, who ruled between around 1550 and 1525 BC. Modern scholars commonly prefer Ramesses II or his son Meneptah. It all rather depends on trying to date the flight from Egypt.

135 Cook (1649).

136 With a due sense of caution. Several contemporary accounts of the trial exist, each a little different in its particulars. Two 'official' accounts remain, drawn up by clerks of the Court. The more renowned being that recorded by John Phelps. A later 'official' record was published at the behest of Charles II in 1683, by John Nalson. Entitled *A True Copy of the Journal of the High Court of Justice for the Tryal of King Charles I*. It drew largely on Phelps's account. In a sense this is the dominant narrative. There are, of course, various news-sheet accounts too, and later memorials. Those of Henry Walker, Gilbert Mabbott and John Rushworth being amongst the more commonly cited. Nalson used Mabbott's *Perfect Narrative of the Whole Proceedings of the High Court of Justice* quite extensively. All any historian can do is pick and choose from amongst these narratives, and then create their own. Then, as now.

137 'As of slow a pen as of speech', his personal secretary, Sir Philip Warwick, would confirm (1813), 70.

138 Royle (2005), 125–6.

139 Cressy (2015), 307.

140 Cust (2007), 348.

141 Russell (1990), 206.

142 Cressy (2015), 120, 300, 309.

143 Matusiak (2017), 33.

144 A painter named Edward Bower was in attendance during the trial and took sketches, which he later used for what would be the last portrait of Charles. Confirming the details of his dress during the trial, and the evident weariness; an impression which Charles was happy to leave. Most notable perhaps is the bushy grey beard: a consequence of refusing the services of a barber during the final weeks.

145 Nalson (2016), 35.

146 Unsurprising, perhaps, given that he was reliant on the same sources as Nalson.

147 Whitelock (1853), 3.502.

148 Nalson (2016), 36.

149 Nalson (2016), 37 and Whitelock (1853), 3.500–1.

150 Braddick (2009), 36.

151 Nalson (2016), 36–7 and Whitelock (1853), 500–1.

152 Nalson (2016), 38.

153 *Mercurius Pragmaticus*, 19–26 December 1648, in Holmes (2020), 293.

154 Nalson (2016), 39–42.

155 Nalson (2016), 40–1 and Whitelock (1853), 505.

156 Nalson (2016), 48.

157 The idea of public 'notoriety' as a species of evidence in treason trials was found in medieval common law. See Collins (2016), 190–2.

158 Nalson (2016), 50–60.

159 Wilson (1985), 151 and Wedgwood (2011), 154–5.

160 The most voluble was John Downes. Cromwell tried to get him to sit down and be quiet. But Downes refused. Wisely, as it happens. His protest was recorded, and it saved his life in 1660.

161 Aragon might seem a slightly odd diversion. Commended for having a 'Justice' who 'hath power to reform' any 'wrong' committed by the king against his subjects. As for sixth-century Fergus, recommended by Buchanan, a king who appreciated that he held his crown on trust.

162 Speech printed in Mabbott (2016), 79–86.

163 For a commentary on the development of an especially heinous crime of 'treasonable murder', in Ireland during the 1650s, see Wells (2015), 112–13. The sentiment of spring 1649 given statutory force by means of a January 1654 Council of State Ordinance.

164 Nalson (2016), 73.

165 The warrant can still be seen today, in the archives of the Houses of Parliament. Various desperate regicides would claim, at the Restoration, that they had been made to sign under duress. It would save Richard Ingoldsby, dragged, according to witnesses, to the table in tears.

166 Farr (2006), 140.

167 Quite what Denbigh had hoped to achieve remains somewhat mysterious. The French ambassador reported that the Earl had attempted to bring 'ouvertures' to the king. The extent to which, if at all, Cromwell might have been involved is similarly speculative. A last-ditch attempt, perhaps, to bring the king to his senses. See Holmes (2019), 296–7 and Adamson (2001), 57–61.

168 Maguire (1989), 13.

169 *An Elegie upon the Death of Our Dread Sovereign Lord King Charles the Martyr*, in Maguire (1989), 15.

170 Almack (1903), 296–7. The moment, we might recall, when Charles recommended they both take the time to read up on the sermons of William Laud and the *Laws* of Richard Hooker.

171 Warmstry was a moderate Anglican royalist with an apparently wide range of interests. An essay on church decoration in 1641 was followed by a defence of Christmas in 1648. Ten years later he published perhaps his most renowned work, a conversion narrative entitled *The Baptized Turk*.

172 Lacey (2001), 227.

173 In early prints, the title was given in the classical Greek; probably as an attempt to throw off the censors.

174 Thus 'literally', it has been supposed, taking the 'place of the king'. See Wheeler (1999), 122.

175 Francis Falconer Madan reached the same conclusion, rather later, in his *New Bibliography of the Eikon Basilike* in 1650. Madan would leave a substantial collection, of 133 copies of the *Eikon*, to the British Library in 1961.

176 Almack (1903), xi–xii.

177 As is the rumour that he received the king's watch and some jewellery as a reward for his services. Taylor was renowned for his devotional writings, most famously perhaps *Holy Living and Holy Dying*. Later admirers would include John Wesley and Samuel Taylor Coleridge. At the Restoration Taylor was appointed bishop of Down and Connor.

178 Russell (1990), 199.

179 Almack (1903), xi.

180 A painting with which Charles would have been undoubtedly familiar. It has been suggested that the Royal Collection included a copy, if not the original. Which would have been sold off with the rest of the Collection in the early years of the Republic. A copy was acquired by the Count of Monterrey at some point around 1653; provenance uncertain. Another Titian, on a similar theme, *Virgin and Child with Saints Catherine of Alexandria and John the Baptist*, was sold for £200 in 1650. Henrietta Maria had herself painted in the pose of St Catherine by Van Dyke in 1639.

181 For commentaries on the imagery, see Helgerson (1987), 9–11 and Zwicker (1993), 41–2.

182 Almack (1903), 267.

183 Almack (1903), 245–6, 252–3.

184 Knachel (1966), 123 and Almack (1903), 189.

185 Knachel (1966), 92, 179.

186 Knachel (1966), 147 and Almack (1903), 113, 276.

187 *The Lord Bishop of Down and Connor, The Martyrdome of King Charles or His Conformity with Christ in his Sufferings*, 1649, 11–12, in Klein (1997), 15.

188 Cable (1990), 135.

189 Knachel (1966), xi, xxvi–xxx.

190 Including the famous 'Pamela Prayer', which Milton would later denounce for reason of plagiarism, and which has since fascinated conspiracy theorists. Milton accused Charles, or whoever had edited the *Eikon*, of plagiarizing the Prayer from Sir Philip Sidney's *Arcadia*. Or, the counter-argument goes, he and Bradshaw conspired to forge spurious editions of the *Eikon*, to include the Prayer, so they could then denounce the plagiarism.

191 The musical version, the *Psalterium Carolinum*, was composed by John Wilson, and based on the versified meditations put together by Thomas Stanley.

192 Smith (2012), 80.

193 See Wilson (1985), 147, 150.

194 The Commons finally approved a list of forty-one Council members, a mix of soldiers and civilian MPs. Amongst those included were Fairfax, Skippon and Cromwell. The chair of the Council was taken, in the immediate term, by Bradshaw.

195 Barber (1998), 176–7.

196 Worden (1984), 527.

197 See Blair Worden (1984), 525 and 545, appraising a man who 'can inhabit a range of voices, each of them authentic at the moment of delivery'. His most recent biographer has reached much the same conclusion. See Smith (2012), 6–7.

198 The most renowned contribution was probably Dryden's *Upon the Death of Lord Hastings*.

199 It is not known precisely how many were slaughtered; though Hugh Peter was able to provide Parliament with the oddly precise figure of 3352 at Drogheda. Something around 2500 is commonly estimated for Wexford. Plus thousands more captured and transported into slavery.

200 Crawford (1977), 60–1.

201 All internal references from Kermode and Walker (1990).

202 The particular influence of Lucan's *Pharsalia*, which moves around the defining encounter between Caesar and Pompey at the battle of Pharsalus in 48 BC, is a critical commonplace.

203 Clarendon, as we shall see, liked to make the Machiavellian aspersion.

204 Warwick (1813), 386.

205 Worden (1984), 543.

206 Worden (1984), 533.

207 Hobbes (1985), 223.

208 Designed apparently in 'the just Figure of a Fort' (286). Gardens which looked like little fortified islands had become fashionable in the Elizabethan period, and stayed so. And the same was true of poetry which worked the garden-as-fort, or conversely garden-as-sanctuary theme. See Hamilton (1996), 173–7.

209 Chernaik (2017), 48.

210 The 'court poet of a pseudo-king' according to Norbrook (1999), 243.

211 Kermode and Walker (1990), 98, 102.

212 She was fortunate, at least, in dodging Philip, Lord Stanhope, to whom she was, for a while, engaged. The 'greatest knave in England', Swift would latter affirm.

213 Cousin of Aubrey de Vere, 20th earl of Oxford, and serial royalist plotter.

214 Wilson (1985), 170–1.

4 Milton's war

1 Lasting the week, and so 'tempestuous', Ludlow reported, 'that the horses were not able to draw against it'. Firth (1894), 2.43.

2 Article I.

3 Hobbes (1990), 191.

4 Article XXXII of the *Instrument*.

5   Norbrook (1999), 423.
6   Albeit 'gentle and virtuous'. Hutchinson (2000), 256–7.
7   Hutton (1987), 41.
8   Milton (1953–62), 3.487.
9   Shaped by Thomas Simon, formerly chief engraver to the Court of King Charles, more recently chief engraver to the Court of 'King' Oliver.
10 Firth (1894), 2.47–8.
11 Bray (1850), 1.350.
12 Kermode and Walker (1990), 116–17.
13 Milton (1991a), 84.
14 See Royle (2005), 778 and Norbrook (1999), 23–4.
15 Harvey (2017), 28.
16 Whitelock (1853), 1.131.
17 Loewenstein (2001), 51.
18 Edwards (1646) and Rees (2016), 58–9, 140–2, 338.
19 *The Fountain of Slaunder Discovered*, in Loewenstein (2001), 207.
20 Rees (2016), 69.
21 Loewenstein (2001), 21.
22 Norbrook (1999), 16.
23 Milton (2014), 132.
24 Milton (2014), 102.
25 Milton (2014), 113.
26 Milton (2014), 138.
27 Fish (2001), 56–7, 194–5 and Walker (2014), 112–13, 127, 143.
28 In which Overton managed to re-interpret *Ecclesiastes* 3:19, to prove that there was no distinction between the body of 'man' and the soul. Inspiring a little sect, calling themselves the Soul Sleepers, to wander the City distributing his dreadful blasphemies.
29 Rees (2016), 131–2.
30 Abbott (1937–47), 4.705 and Worden (2011), 237–40, 245.
31 Worden refers to Nedham's 'naked opportunism and naked pragmatism' (1998), 157. Forever 'balanced on a tightrope', according to Norbook (1999), 328.
32 Frank (1980), 90.
33 Milton (1953–62), 1.526.
34 Milton (1953–62), 1.537. Milton took particular aim at Hall in *Animadversions*, and at Ussher in *Of Prelatical Episcopacy*.
35 Milton (1953–62), 1.796, 3.493.
36 Chernaik (2017), 47.
37 Milton (1953–62), 1.615.
38 Braddick (2018), 32. Another member of Duppa's congregation was Thomas Pride.
39 The latter two, published together in March 1645, being much shorter, and essentially repeating the arguments given in *Doctrine and Discipline*.
40 The idea of 'companionate' marriage would gain traction during the later eighteenth century. Divorce law reform would only commence with the 1858 Divorce Act. No-fault divorces would come later.
41 Mary returned to the family home near Oxford. In theory for just a month or so, but in the end for three years. Of course, war had broken out and Oxfordshire was on the front line. But even so, there is no evidence that she tried very hard to return to her husband. Nor him to get her back.

42   Chernaik (2017), 81–2.
43   Campbell and Corns (2010), 180–1.
44   Making an especial friend of the Vatican librarian, Lucas Holste. And Cardinal Francesco Barberini, Pope Urban's nephew, and a hugely influential patron of the arts. It has been speculated that Milton might also have dined with Galileo.
45   In a poem entitled *On the New Forces of Conscience*. See Campbell and Corns (2010), 168.
46   Milton (1991a), 85.
47   Albeit without a Foreign Secretary.
48   In the second *Defence*, in which the recently deceased Bradshaw is also remembered as the 'most faithful' of friends.
49   Not easy, for the reasons that Sir Oliver Fleming advised. Neighbouring countries likely to 'apprehend the prosperity of the commonwealth may prove an allurement to their people to shake off their yoke'. Fleming was Master of Ceremonies. See Barber (1998), 149.
50   As Hyde described it (1843), 320.
51   Manning (1992), 188.
52   Scott (2001), 150.
53   Whitelock (1853), 2.540.
54   White (1649), in Kesselring (2016), 103–4.
55   Lilburne, in (1649), in Kesselring (2016), 107–8.
56   Manning (1992), 46.
57   Salmon (1649), in Smith (1983), 190, 193.
58   Clarendon (1843), 702–4. Owen was convicted of having shot a sheriff during fighting in south Wales.
59   For a commentary on the same legitimating strategy deployed in the 'settlement' of Ireland, see Wells (2015).
60   Bray (1850), 1.251.
61   Worden (1984), 527.
62   Manning (1992), 189–90.
63   As would be another jury, in 1653, when Lilburne was again charged with treason. And again acquitted. No divine intervention this time it seems. But the presence, once again, of Coke and his *Institutes*.
64   Rees (2016), 290–1.
65   There would be a series of mutinies during the spring. First at Bishopsgate in London, and then across the south and south-west. Amongst those rumoured to have taken a leading role was Captain George Joyce.
66   Woodhouse (1986), 477.
67   Orr (2002), 181.
68   Monitary meaning admonition.
69   Milton (1953–62), 5.255.
70   Milton (1991b), 17.
71   Milton was especially impressed by Buchanan's *Detectio*, a strident defence of the deposition of Mary Queen of Scots.
72   Milton (1991b), 4. An allusion to *Macbeth*, 5.9.19–22. Milton tries to extricate himself from the problem by claiming that the voice of 'liberty' in Scotland has been more recently corrupted by that of 'Faction'.
73   Milton (1991b), 3.
74   Milton (1991b), 3, 8–9.

75 Milton (1953–62), 3.586.

76 Milton (1991b), 10.

77 Milton (1991b), 9–11.

78 Milton (1991b), 33.

79 Milton (1991b), 13.

80 A slightly amended second edition would appear sometime in the autumn.

81 Loewenstein (2001), 11, surmises that Milton might have sympathized with Lilburne's sentiment and so quietly neglected the brief.

82 £10 for the author, £5 for the printer, 40 shillings for a bookseller.

83 Kelsey (1997), 74.

84 Loewenstein (2001), 36–7.

85 See Loewenstein (2001), 36–7 and (1990), 27–8.

86 Whitelock (1853), 2.523, recorded the scene where the old seal was broken up on the floor of the Commons. He also recorded declining an invitation to become a commissioner of the new seal, for reason of the 'trouble of the place'. Too much hassle.

87 Kelsey (1997), 73.

88 Wither (1649).

89 Milton (1953–62), 3.493.

90 Milton (1953–62), 3.341.

91 Zagorin (1982), 1.18, refers to act of 'symbolic violence'.

92 Milton (1953–62), 3.422.

93 Milton (1953–62), 3.473.

94 Milton had written up the 'Popish Plot' before, most notably perhaps in his essay *On Reformation*.

95 Milton (1953–62), 3.595.

96 Achinstein (1999), 154–5.

97 Milton (1953–62), 3.348–9, 376, 469.

98 Milton (1953–62), 3.343, 601.

99 It is difficult to be sure if the inference is directed more precisely towards Shakespeare's *Twelfth Night*. Elsewhere Milton insinuates disparagingly towards Shakespeare as the author of the king's language; the 'Closet Companion of these his solitudes'. See Zwicker (1993), 54.

100 Milton (1953–62), 3.358, 498.

101 Trevor-Roper (1988), 255, 268–9.

102 Milton (1953–62), 3.343, 406, 498–9. For a discussion of this dilemma, see Zwicker (1993), 39–40, 45–6, Hirst (1995), 245–7 and Wheeler (1999), 128–9.

103 Milton (1953–62), 3.505, 558.

104 Milton (1953–62), 3.348.

105 A pithy metaphor added to the second edition of *Eikonclastes* which came out in early 1650.

106 Milton (1953–62), 3.401–2.

107 According to Boehrer (1987), 99, 105, a 'dismal defeat'. Milton 'simply never had a chance'.

108 Sharpe (2000), 195.

109 Milton excused his tardiness on grounds of 'precarious health'. See Campbell and Corns (2010), 231.

110 Milton (1991b), 55–6, 61, 125, 181.

111 Milton (1991b), 121.

112 Milton (1991b), 94, 99–100.
113 Milton (1991b), 149–50, 180.
114 Milton (1991b), 203.
115 Milton thought it was an exiled Franco-Scottish writer named Alexander Muir, at the time professor of Ecclesiastical History at Amsterdam University. Later in 1654, Muir published a fierce rebuttal of Milton's *Second Defence*.
116 Boehrer (1987), 101.
117 See Hill (1997), 175 and Norbrook (1999), 331–2.
118 Kermode and Walker (1990), 94.
119 Who rather relished his reputation as a notorious womanizer.
120 There are various contemporary accounts of the episode. See Abbott (1939), 2.640–7 and Firth (1894), 1.351–5.
121 Firth (1894), 1.355.
122 In his second *Defence*. Milton (1962), 836–7.
123 In a predictably long address at the opening of the Parliament, on 4 July. Abbott (1939), 3.52–66.
124 In the words of John Rogers (1653). The analogy, founded in *Exodus* 18:21, was commonly deployed: 'Thou shalt provide out of all the people able men.'
125 Shapiro (2019), 131–8.
126 Abbott (1939), 4.489–90.
127 A view shared by many of a more millennial disposition. John Warr was another who warned of the distractions which attend 'judgement about the Externall Forme of Civil government'. See Morrill (1993), 27 and Barber (1998), 164.
128 Abbott (1939), 3.438, 458–60.
129 Royle (2005), 623–4.
130 Royle (2005), 635.
131 Whitelock (1853), 3.471.
132 Firth (1894), 2.9.
133 Abbott (1939), 3.434–43.
134 Knoppers (2000), 1, 70–1, 76–7.
135 Abbott (1939), 3.460.
136 Loewenstein (2001), 144.
137 Provision was made for ten thousand horses and twenty thousand foot and a 'convenient number of ships'. Parliament would be elected triennially. But not by Royalists, at least for now, and never by Catholics. And any elector had to be in possession of property worth £200. So not many.
138 Abbott (1939), 3.460.
139 Knoppers (2000), 93 and Loewenstein (2001), 78–9.
140 Chernaik (2017), 117.
141 Kermode and Walker (1990), 94, 98.
142 Kermode and Walker (1990), 98.
143 Norbrook (1999), 302–8.
144 Knoppers (2000), 80.
145 Firth (1894), 1.371. The *Instrument* made its first public appearance at the investiture ceremony. A few 'skins of parchment' as one unknowing guest observed, of the first written constitution in English history. Nedham was amongst those who had no prior knowledge of its existence. Norbrook (1999), 300–1.
146 Whitelock (1853), 4.73–5, 82–3.
147 Hutchinson (2000), 256–7 and also Norbrook (1990), 315–16.

148 Knoppers (2000), 72 and Loewenstein (2001), 122–3.

149 Overton (1649) and Norbrook (1999), 321–2, wondering the extent of Overton's authorship. He denied authorship when accused by the Council. But had distributed the piece.

150 Busy revising his *Second Defence*, wherein could be found reference to their 'sweet' friendship.

151 So over he came, to give it a go. Sexby was, at the time, fighting in the Netherlands for the Spanish. An intriguing career path. The former Ironside had remained loyal until around 1654. It was he who carried news of the success at Preston late summer 1648 to Parliament; and received a reward of £100 for his efforts. With Cromwell in Ireland and then Scotland in 1650 and 1651. And then sent abroad in the service of the Republic's secretary for Foreign Tongues. At some point though, apparently frustrated by Cromwell's reluctance to mount a serious operation against the French, Sexby had gone rogue, returning to England in late 1657, with the intention of blowing up Whitehall. Another 'powder' plot. Captured, Sexby died in the Tower the following year, having 'been a while distracted in his mind'.

152 Abbott (1939), 3.579–80.

153 Hutchinson (2000), 257.

154 Royle (2005), 728–9.

155 Spencer (2014), 93.

156 Whitelock (1853), 4.287–91.

157 Waller (1840), 164.

158 Firth (1894), 2.21.

159 In the words of a doubtful earl of Warwick. Royle (2005), 694–5.

160 It would assemble in December 1657. Sixty-three nominated members.

161 A consequence intimated during dinner the evening before, or so Firth reported (1894), 2.24–5.

162 Abbott (1939), 4.473.

163 Royle (2005), 735.

164 Norbrook (1999), 383.

165 Loewenstein (2001), 138.

166 According to his later editor, John Toland, confirming that Harrington and his captive king had passed many an evening together discussing matters 'concerning Government', though not those of republicanism which Charles could not 'indure'. Rather 'stiffe in disputation', Harrington later recalled of Charles. See Hammersley (2019), 25, 54–7, 102.

167 Hammersley (2019), 257.

168 Hammersley (2019), 249–56.

169 Norbrook (1999), 399–400.

170 Pepys recorded a walk home on 11 February, passing through King Street 'and all along burning and roasting drinking for rumps – there being rumps tied upon sticks and carried up and down'. Pepys (1993), 16.

171 Milton (1962), 333.

172 Milton (1962), 342.

173 Milton (1962), 337. As again recommended in his *Letter unto Mr Stubs*, which appeared at the beginning of February.

174 Milton liked to present himself as a Jeremiah, alternatively a Samuel. The extent to which the *Readie and Easie Way* should be read as a litany of despair remains a matter of academic debate. See Woolrych (1993), 929–43, Chernaik (2017),

90–8, Norbrook (1999), 414–16 and 420–2, Knoppers (2000), 213–25 and Hill (1997), 206–7.

175 Milton (1962), 334, 347–50, 352.
176 Milton (1962), 334–5.
177 Norbrook (1999), 335.
178 Milton (1962), 337.
179 Knoppers (2000), 157.
180 Nedham (1659), 40.
181 Ludlow (1978), 5.114.
182 Abbott (1939), 4.712–21.
183 Pepys (1993), 39.
184 Aboard what had been the *Naseby*, but which was now named the *Royal Charles*. On arrival, the Mayor presented him with a Bible. The 'thing he loved above all things in the world', Charles replied. Fraser (1979), 180.
185 Bray (1850), 1.337.
186 Clarendon (1843), 995.
187 Something which made the 'whole court nasty and stinking'. Bray (1850), 2.207.
188 Knoppers (2000), 168–9.
189 Walker (1987), 10.
190 Norbrook (1999), 426.
191 Rumours would persist that Milton was invited back into government service during the 1660s, possibly as Latin Secretary in succession to Richard Fanshawe, who died in 1666.
192 Potter (1999), 243.
193 Gardiner (1980), 465–6.
194 A committee of five members in fact.
195 Potter (1999), 244.
196 During the audience, the king suggested that it might be a good time for Bulstrode to retire.
197 Finch (2016), 128.
198 Dixwell was a former governor of Dover Castle.
199 Spencer (2014), 120–1.
200 His case helped by the fact that he secured, and then surrendered, his old comrade Major General Lambert. He would even be made a Knight of the Bath at the coronation.
201 Spencer (2014), 125.
202 Their skulls would be put on spikes and displayed at Westminster Hall until 1680, when they finally blew down in a storm.
203 Pepys (1993), 100.
204 Spencer (2014), 112.
205 Derived, of course, from contemporary accounts, having already gone into exile.
206 Finch (2016), 118–20.
207 Pepys (1993), 85.
208 Interestingly, Harrison took particular exception to this evidence.
209 Finch (2016), 137–8.
210 Finch (2016), 143.
211 Finch (2016), 138–9.
212 Finch (2016), 148.
213 Finch (2016), 149.

214 Firth (1894), 2.317.
215 The others being the prominent Fifth Monarchist John Carew, Gregory Clement, and Colonels John Jones and Thomas Scott.
216 By common account. Though Ludlow describes a more elevated scene. Firth (1894), 2.312–14.
217 Spencer (2014), 154.
218 Pepys (1993), 86.
219 Barkstead was former governor of the Tower, and Cromwell's steward. Okey had commanded the only Regiment of Dragoons in the New Model. We will briefly visit his funeral in the next chapter. Corbet was a lawyer, appointed Chief Baron of the Exchequer in Ireland during the Protectorate.
220 Ogg (1984), 179–80. Charles held Vane personally responsible for the prosecution of Strafford.
221 A slightly peculiar execution scene too. Even though Vane was despatched in the Tower, the authorities were concerned enough by what he might try to say that they had a group of musicians stood under the scaffold. With instructions to strike up as soon as Sir Henry started speaking.
222 Lenthall would later repent his actions, ordering that his headstone should simply read 'Vermis sum'; 'I am a worm.'
223 A contrition aired in A True and Humble Representation of John Downs Esq, published in 1660.
224 Huncks had been one of those entrusted with organizing the execution, despite the fact that he had not signed the warrant. A refusal which had earned a rebuke from Cromwell.
225 Chernaik (2017), 173.
226 The estate had belonged to the family of Cromwell's son-in-law Charles Fleetwood. But was passed to the duke at some point in the early 1660s.
227 See here Loewenstein (2001), 243–4.
228 By kind permission of Richard Royston no less, now warden of the Stationers Company. A license to print purchased by Samuel Simmons for the sum of £5. Another £5 due once the first run of thirteen hundred copies had sold out. And then a further £5 for each fresh run. Samuel's dad, Matthew, had published a number of Milton's earlier prose works, stretching back into the early 1640s.
229 Aubrey suggested that Satan's first soliloquy was drafted by the early 1650s. Hill suggests that the first six books might have been completed by the end of 1660, the remaining six done by 1665. Hill (1997), 365–6.
230 The 'stamp of Milton's political experience', as Campbell and Corns put it (2010), 345.
231 All internal references to Paradise Lost, taken from Milton (1991a).
232 Norbrook (1999), 467.
233 Toland would intimate so, in the preface to his 1698 reprint of the poem.
234 Milton (1953–62), 501–2.
235 Loewenstein (2001), 247, 267.
236 All internal references to Paradise Regained taken from Milton (1991a).
237 Plenty of revolutionaries liked to see themselves as latter-day Samsons, not least John Lilburne.
238 All internal references to Samson Agonistes taken from Milton (1991a).
239 Loewenstein (2001), 5.
240 Milton (1953–62), 671.

241 A term popular amongst puritans of the more apocalyptic kind, such as Winstanley, Abiezer Coppe and William Erbury.
242 Levi (1997), 233.

5 The histories of Edward Hyde

1 And Viscount Cornbury. He had already become Lord Hyde a few months earlier.
2 The etymology of the phrase borrows from the old German; 'spic' for a nail, 'span' for piece of wood. By the mid-seventeenth century it had acquired its more familiar usage, meaning neat and tidy. It is first discovered in English writing in Pepys's *Diary*. An entry for 15 November 1665, reading that Pepys saw Lady Batten walking along the street in her 'new spick-and-span white shoes'. Pepys (1993), 554.
3 The last monarch to make the procession from the Tower. Monk's regiment would later acquire the name the Coldstream Guards; in honour of their role in securing the Restoration in early 1660. Monk crossed the Tweed at the village of Coldstream. As for the sandals, it was noted that Charles struggled a bit. Two inch heels. The need for which was doubtful, given that the king was anyway well over six feet tall.
4 Pepys (1993), 866. The earl's wife, Lady Anna, has enjoyed a rather variable press. The story was put about that she attended the duel, disguised as a groom, and held the reins of the duke's horse; whilst he killed her husband. After which she and the duke made love in his blood-stained shirt. Sir Peter Lely would paint her at some point shortly after. Replete with the customary plunging neckline and stray nipple. We will take a closer look at Sir Peter's work very shortly. By then Anne had taken up residence with duke, and Mary. There is no record as to how the two women got on. Perhaps an attraction of opposites, we can hope.
5 Cromwell had the previous crown melted down.
6 Hutton (1987), 153.
7 The Dymockes of Scrivolsby had been Champions of the Crown since the reign of Richard II. Sir Edward was in his sixties, and would die not long afterwards.
8 Walker (1987), 18.
9 Pepys (1993), 132.
10 Spencer (2104), 57.
11 Pepys (1993), 114–15.
12 Walker (1987), 18.
13 In sum roughly £7000 pa. In due course he also received an eighth interest in the province of 'Carolina'. Ludlow, unsurprisingly appalled by Monk's 'treachery', confirmed that he received 'divers pensions and lands of great value'. Firth (1894), 2.284.
14 Pepys (1993), 16.
15 Warwick (1813), 216.
16 Jonathan Scott (1991), 9, deploys a more cautionary metaphor, describing England in 1660 as a 'traumatised patient'.
17 Rochester, *On King Charles*, in Ellis (1994), 30.
18 *The True-Born Englishman*, in Furbank and Owens (1998), 34.
19 Rideal (2017), 93.
20 Clarendon (1843), 915–25, 931–41.
21 Pepys (1993), 681.

22 Great Tew is about ten miles from Oxford. Hyde described it as a kind of University retreat.

23 Other members of which included Selden, and the young poets Abraham Cowley and Edmund Waller.

24 Two extended panegyrics to Falkland can be found in the *History*, at 430–4 and 925–7.

25 Clarendon (1843), 940–1.

26 Smith (1994), 70, 90.

27 Wormald (1989), 172.

28 In correspondence, hoping that 'the judgement of Heaven' would 'fall light' on the Prince. Fraser (1979), 90–1.

29 Clarendon (1843), 992–3, 100–5.

30 *To the Lord Chancellor*, in Marriott (1995), 14. Written to celebrate New Year 1662.

31 Seaward (1989), 18–19.

32 Over the coming months, the army was reconstituted into a smaller force of approximately seven thousand 'guards'. To include Monck's Coldstream Guards, the Duke of York's Life Guards and Colonel Russell's Foot Guards, later renamed the Grenadier Guards. And, after some judicious purging, the remnants of Cromwell's 'life guards', which would become the Royal Horse Guards.

33 Prosecutions under the *Five Mile Act* were, in fact, quite rare. Only one in the first year. The *Conventicle Act*, conversely, saw 230 transported from the London area alone.

34 Ogg (1984), 218.

35 Smith (1994), 302.

36 Rose (2013), 10.

37 Dunkirk had been taken by Cromwell in order to stop French privateers threatening British ships trading through the Channel.

38 Clarendon (1843), 1198.

39 Clarendon (1843), 1000–2.

40 As Defoe put it, in his *A Journal of a Plague Year* (1986), 252.

41 Morrah (1979), 202.

42 Rideal (2016), 200, 211.

43 Ogg (1984), 312. The Dutch also towed a second ship, the *Unity*. Amongst those fired were the *Royal Oak* and the *Royal James*.

44 Bray (1850), 2.11, 17.

45 Clarendon (1843), 1001–4.

46 Pepys (1993), 721.

47 Hill (1997), 402.

48 Clarendon (1843), 1009.

49 Pepys (1993), 798.

50 Clarendon (1843), 1087, 1191–3.

51 To be passed on to Orlando Bridgeman, as Lord Keeper. Hyde had apparently resisted for a few days, leading to the audience. Pepys (1993), 822–3.

52 Fraser (1979), 255.

53 Though ultimately there would be seventeen charges.

54 Opposed by the Duke of York and his allies, and virtually all the Lords Spiritual.

55 Burnet later reported the story that Hyde had fallen out of royal favour when he encouraged Frances Stuart to elope with the Duke of Lennox. Charles was mildly obsessed with 'La belle Stuart'.

56 Smith (1994), 320–2 and Fraser (1979), 337.
57 Rumour would suppose that Margaret was, in turn, mistress to Charles, his brother James and Prince Rupert.
58 Pepys (1993), 798.
59 Who was though a considerable admirer. Pepys (1993), 229.
60 Kermode (1990), 265.
61 Preface to *Annus Mirabilis*, in Walker (1987), 7.
62 Ellis (1994), 40–2.
63 All internal references to *Clarendon's Housewarming* taken from Kermode and Walker (1990), 121–4. Pepys declared Hyde's new house to be the 'noblest prospect that I ever saw in my life'. Pepys (1993), 584.
64 Firth (1894), 2.407.
65 Popularly known as 'Dunkirk House'; the inference being that it had been funded by some of the money received by the Treasury in 1662.
66 Internal references taken from Kermode (1990), 124–48.
67 Wittols being cuckolds.
68 Harry is Henry IV of France, assassinated in 1610.
69 Kermode (1990), xii.
70 The title playing on the Duke of Buckingham's *The Rehearsal*, a farce first performed in 1671. The second part of Marvell's essay appeared in 1673.
71 Kermode (1990), 264.
72 Originally commissioned by the Polish ambassador, but in the end running way past budget.
73 The statue was removed from its site in the eighteenth century, to make way for the construction of the Mansion House, and eventually found its way to Newby Park in Yorkshire.
74 Margoliouth (1971), 395.
75 *Poem of the Statue in Stocks Market*, in Margoliouth (1971), 188.
76 Margoliouth (1971), 408.
77 Margoliouth (1971), 200–1.
78 Margoliouth, *Poems*, 212.
79 Defoe would be pilloried there in 1703.
80 Potter (1999), 252. In truth, Wren probably anticipated the disappointment. He had likewise intended to top his Monument to the Fire, near Pudding Lane, with a magnificent statue of Charles II, to represent the man who rebuilt London. But money was predictably short, so in the end it was topped with a bronze flame instead.
81 Anne was pregnant seventeen times in twenty-five years of marriage, to Prince George of Denmark. But no child survived past the age of eleven. Five ended with stillborn births. Seven miscarriages.
82 As she assured Parliament in May 1702. Downie (1994), 66.
83 Lord of the Treasury and then Lord President of the Council in the final years of Charles's reign. Lord High Treasurer in the first year of James's reign.
84 Preface to Clarendon (1826), 1.1, 4–5.
85 Clarendon (1826), 8, 16.
86 Taking more coherent shape, so the prefatory comments supposed, whilst Hyde was in exile on Jersey.
87 Clarendon (1843), 1. A 'personal vindication', as Wormald puts it (1989), xxxvi.
88 Clarendon (1843), 933–7, 992–3.

89 Clarendon (1843), 1.

90 Clarendon (1843), 940–1.

91 Clarendon (1843), 79–80, 444–6, 1189–90.

92 Clarendon (1843), 79.

93 Hyde retained an especial dislike for Pym, his parliamentary sparring-partner throughout 1641. 'No man had more to answer for the miseries of the Kingdom.' Clarendon (1843), 474.

94 Clarendon (1843), 638.

95 Clarendon (1843), 104.

96 The 'brawls which were grown from religion', as he elsewhere put it. Clarendon (1843), 36–40, 122–3, 920, 929–2.

97 Clarendon (1843), 28–9.

98 A claim made more particularly in regard to the King's attempt to arrest the Five Members in January 1642. Clarendon (1843), 233.

99 Clarendon (1843), 940.

100 Clarendon (1843), 696.

101 Clarendon (1843), 698.

102 Clarendon (1843), 862.

103 Wormald (1989), 324–5.

104 A comment recorded by Pepys, in Tomalin (2003), 265.

105 Clarendon (1843), 1016.

106 Clarendon (1843), 1229–36.

107 Pepys died the following year, in 1703.

108 Hume (1983), 154.

109 Worden (2002), 194.

110 Though the conclusions did evince a certain 'partiality'. Hill (1992), 27.

111 Hutchinson (2000), 284, 308.

112 Hutchinson (1995), 66–8.

113 Hutchinson (1995), 234–5.

114 Only finally published in 1806.

115 He had previously worked as a personal secretary for Sir Orlando Bridgman. But they had long since fallen out.

116 Revealing the author to be, in the words of a later editor, Thomas Hollis, the 'perfect Englishman'. Worden (2002), 122.

117 Algernon's father, the 2nd Earl of Leicester, died in 1677, leaving his son £5100. Algernon was forced to return in order to take an action in Chancery to force his brothers, as executors, to release the money.

118 Sidney (1772), 503.

119 Sidney (1772), 291–2, 314.

120 Sidney (1772), 193–4, 227.

121 A 'gross scandal', according to Gilbert Burnet. Scott (1991), 295, 303–15, 318–29, 342–7.

122 Worden (2002), 145.

123 A few months before Ludlow died.

124 The definitive account of Ludlow's make-over is found in the opening four chapters of Worden's *Reputations*. Firming up in the idea that Toland must have been the editor of Ludlow's published *Memoirs*. The *Voice* was discovered in 1970, or at least one part, covering the years 1660 to 1677. The existence of the rest is surmised from the table of contents.

125 Firth (1984), 1.37–8, 185, 1.17.

126 Worden (2002), 51–2.

127 Gray (2009), 25.

128 Most immediately the tyrannies of enclosure. Williams (2018), 653–72.

129 Defoe (1991), 1–4.

130 Defoe (1991), 4.

131 Defoe (1991), 271, 278.

132 The two monsters are to be found in the *Book of Job*. The Behemoth a creature of the land, the Leviathan a creature of the sea.

133 Hobbes had served as a tutor to the young prince, and they remained on broadly cordial terms.

134 Rogow (1986), 124.

135 In the classical dialogic style indeed.

136 Hobbes (1990), 2–3, 38, 55.

137 Loewenstein (2001), 4.

138 Loewenstein (2001), 28

139 Hobbes (1990), 118–19.

140 Hobbes (1990), 116–17, 125.

141 Hobbes (1990), 45.

142 Hobbes (1990), 154.

143 Much like Strafford, who only came over to the king 'for his own ends'. Hobbes (1990), 72, 117.

144 Hobbes (1990), 195.

145 Sidney (1772), 144.

146 Hobbes (1985), 161.

147 Hobbes (1985), 107, 728.

148 Hobbes (1985), 189

149 Hobbes (1985), 186. The thrust of Hobbes's thesis, that the primary concern of humanity is self-preservation, had been ventured back in 1642, in an earlier treatise entitled *De Cive*.

150 Hobbes (1985), 720–1.

151 Hobbes (1985), 192–3.

152 Hobbes (1985), 202.

153 Hobbes (1985) 191–2.

154 These prerogative rights are listed in Part 2, chapter 18.

155 Hobbes (1985), 187, 223.

156 Hobbes (1985), 448.

157 As Leo Strauss famously supposed, (1963), ix–xvi, 1–2, 129–30.

158 Hobbes (1985), 105.

159 Hobbes (1985), 466–9.

160 A rhetorical strategy intended to resonate with 'witchcraft' as much as Catholicism.

161 Hobbes, *Leviathan*, 633–6, 657–9, 706.

162 Hobbes, *Leviathan*, 640–1, 668–79.

163 For alternative interpretations of the image, see Skinner (1996), 388–9, and Agamben (2015), 19–54. Both supposing the image to represent the power of the state. Skinner intimates a more secular authority, Agamben prefers a darker, theological representation.

164 Hobbes (1985), 720–1.

165 Hobbes (1985), 727–8.

166 Hobbes (1985), 371–2.
167 Rogow (1986), 190–4.
168 Wormald (1989), 304.
169 Smith (1994), 250.
170 Sir Leoline Jenkins, in Speck (1988), 36–7.
171 Burnet (1833), 3.59–66.
172 Speck (1988), 67.
173 Rose (2011), 273.
174 Comprising Danby, Devonshire, Lumley, Russell, Shrewsbury, Henry Sidney and the Bishop of London. Their interest further stimulated by news, in November 1687, that James's wife, Mary of Modena, was pregnant.
175 Lely had painted a younger Mary, at some point around 1672. As Diana the huntress.
176 Hair mounted high. Unlike the Windsor 'beauties' who all went for the flatter forehead look, decorated with a fringe of ringlets.
177 'Hey nephew, to your work', the Charles was reported to have cried, as William ventured towards the marital bed, 'St George for England'. Fraser (1979), 349.
178 The Archbishop of Canterbury, William Sancroft, refused to officiate.
179 Macaulay (1986), 286–7.
180 Locke (1989), 170–1, 179.
181 Mossner (1980), 311.
182 Blackstone (2016), 4.429–32.
183 Cromartie (1995), 62–3.
184 The interior was only open to selected visitors, of course. But, for any who were admitted to Horace's bedroom, the warrant was in plain sight.
185 Worden (2002), 216.
186 The Prelude, in Hutchinson (1936), 570.
187 Porter (2001), 447.
188 Unnamed sonnet, in Hutchinson (1936), 244.
189 Burke (1986), 137.
190 In his ballad, the History of the English Rebellion. In Loewenstein (2001), 179.
191 Trela (1998). The novel is actually set in the 1650s, starting with the aftermath of Worcester and ending with the Restoration. Charles assumes a haunting presence, mainly in Cromwell's tortured imagination.
192 Boscobel told the very romantic story of Prince Charles's escape after Worcester. The Leaguer of Lathom revisited the travails of Charlotte de Tremouille, Countess of Derby, who famously held Lathom Hall against parliamentarian troops in 1644.
193 The leading military artist of late Victorian England, Crofts's other fascination was the Napoleonic wars.
194 Captured in a rather curious painterly contest in Paris, in 1831. First in Paul Delaroche's Cromwell before the Coffin of Charles I, based on the rumour that Cromwell had snuck into the room where Charles was lying at rest. Delaroche was trying to create a parallel between Cromwell and Napoleon Bonaparte. On witnessing his efforts, an appalled Eugene Delacroix painted Cromwell with the Coffin of Charles I. In the hope of better capturing the tortured depth of Napoleon's soul. Difficult to pick a winner. Delaroche's Cromwell, lifting the lid and taking a sly peek, looks a bit shifty, and oddly short of stature. Delacroix's is neither of these, a longer glance and a much longer frame. But still strangely spare.
195 Carlyle (1871), 1.11.
196 Carlyle (1871), 1.49.

197 Carlyle (1871), 1.67.

198 Carlyle, *Letters*, 1.68. The referents being to Rushworth's vast, and slightly chaotic, eight-volume collection of tracts and treatises, and Nalson's account of the trial of the king. Both of which we have, of course, encountered.

199 Bagehot (2001), 34–7, 185–6.

200 Bagehot (2001), 66–7, 178.

201 Worden (2002), 21.

202 Hannah de Rothschild. Who had died in 1890, leaving Archibald more than enough to buy a statue.

203 Leighton Buzzard was chosen to be 'Q Central', the operational centre for a number of important radar and surveillance operations. Including the renowned code-breakers at nearby Bletchley Park, RAF Group 60 radar, RAF Central Exchange and Wireless Telegraph, and the Met Office.

204 Trevor-Roper (1978), v, xi–11.

205 Worden (2002), 21–3, 342.

206 Wormald (1989), 154.

207 Clarendon (1843), 540.

208 Clarendon (1843), 933.

209 Clarendon (1843), 1–2.

210 Clarendon (1843), 2.

211 Pepys reported Hyde being bedridden with gout as early as the later 1650s. The *Life* records a man who 'indulged his palate very much, and took even some delight in eating and drinking well'. Though never to excess. More the 'epicure', the reader is assured. See *History*, 933. The gout, and the portraiture, suggest otherwise.

SELECT BIBLIOGRAPHY

Abbott, W. (ed.) (1937–47) *Writings and Speeches of Oliver Cromwell*, Cambridge, MA: Harvard UP.

Achinstein, S. (1999) 'Milton and King Charles', in T. Corns (ed.), *The Royal Image: Representations of Charles I*, Cambridge: Cambridge UP.

Adams, J. (1854) *The Works of John Adams*, New York: Little, Brown.

Adamson, J. (2001) 'The Frighted Junto: Perceptions of Ireland and the Last Attempts at Settlement with Charles I', in J. Peacey (ed.), *The Regicides and the Execution of Charles I*, London: Palgrave, 36–70.

Agamben, G. (2015) *Stasis: Civil War as a Political Paradigm*, Edinburgh: Edinburgh UP.

Almack, A. (ed.) (1903) *Eikon Basilike, or the King's Book*, London: De la More.

Anon. (1649) *Eikon Aethine: the ourtraiture of truths most sacred majesty truly suffering, though not solely, wherein the false colours are washed off*, London.

Bagehot, W. (2001) *The English Constitution*, Cambridge: Cambridge UP.

Baker, J. (2004) 'The Common Lawyers and the Chancery: 1616', in A. Boyer (ed.), *Law, Liberty and Parliament: Selected Essays on the Writings of Sir Edward Coke*, Indianapolis, IN: Liberty Press, 254–81.

Baker, J. (2018) *The Reinvention of Magna Carta 1216–1616*, Cambridge: Cambridge UP.

Barber, S. (1998) *Regicide and Republicanism: Politics and Ethics in the English Revolution 1646–1659*, Edinburgh: Edinburgh UP.

Baxter, R. (1696) *Reliquae Baxter.iniae*, London.

Berman, H. (1994) 'The Origins of Historical Jurisprudence: Coke, Selden, Hale', *Yale Law Journal* 103: 1652–738.

Blackstone, Sir W. (2016) *Commentaries on the Laws of England*, Oxford: Oxford UP.

Blencowe, R. (ed.) (1825) *The Sydney Papers*, London: John Murray.

Boehrer, B. (1987) 'Elementary Structures of Kingship: Milton, Regicide and the Family', *Milton Studies* 23: 97–117.

Braddick, M. (2009) *God's Fury, England's Fire: A New History of the English Civil Wars*, London: Penguin.

Braddick, M. (2018) *The Common Freedom of the People*, Oxford: Oxford UP.

Bray, W. (ed.) (1850) *The Diary and Correspondence of John Evelyn*, London: Henry Colburn.

Breward, C. (2009) 'Fashioning the Modern Self: Clothing, Cavaliers and Identity in van Dyck's London', in K. Hearn (ed.), *Van Dyck and Britain*, London: Tate, 24–37.

Brooks, C. (2010) *Law, Politics and Society in Early Modern England*, Cambridge: Cambridge UP.

Burgess, G. (1992) *The Politics of the Ancient Constitution: An Introduction to English Political Thought 1603–1642*, London: Macmillan.

Burgess, G. (1996) *Absolute Monarchy and the Stuart Constitution*, New Haven, CT: Yale UP.

Burke, E. (1986) *Reflections on the Revolution in France*, London: Penguin.

Burnet, G. (1833) *History of His Own Time*, Oxford: Oxford UP.

Butterfield, H. (1931) *The Whig Interpretation of History*, London: Bell.

Cable, L. (1990) 'Milton's Iconoclastic Truth', in D. Loewenstein and J. Turner (eds), *Politics, Poetics and Hermeneutics in Milton's Prose*, Cambridge: Cambridge UP, 135–52.

Campbell, G., and Corns, T. (2010) *John Milton: Life, Work, and Thought*, Oxford: Oxford UP.

Carlton, C. (1995) *Charles I: The Personal Monarch*, London: Routledge.

Carlyle, T. (1871) *Oliver Cromwell's Letters and Speeches, with Elucidations*, London: Scribner, Welford.

Chernaik, W. (1983) *The Poet's Time: Politics and Religion in the Work of Andrew Marvell*, Cambridge: Cambridge UP.

Chernaik, W. (2017) *Milton and the Burden of Freedom*, Cambridge: Cambridge UP.

Christianson, P. (1991) 'Royal and Parliamentary Voices on the Ancient Constitution', in L. Peck (ed.), *The Mental World of the Jacobean Court*, Cambridge: Cambridge UP, 71–97.

Clarendon, Lord (1826) *The History of the Rebellion and Civil Wars in England*, Oxford: Oxford UP.

Clarendon, Lord (1843) *The History of the Rebellion and Civil Wars, Also His Life by Himself*, Oxford: Oxford UP.

Coast, D. (2016) 'Rumor and "Common Fame": The Impeachment of the Duke of Buckingham and Public Opinion in Early Stuart England', *Journal of British Studies* 55: 241–67.

Coffey, J. (2016) 'England's Exodus: The Civil War as a War of Deliverance', in C. Prior and G. Burgess (eds), *England's Wars of Religion Revisited*, London: Routledge, 253–80.

Coke, Sir E. (1823) *The Institutes of the Laws of England*, London: W. Clarke.

Coke, Sir E. (2003) *Selected Writings of Sir Edward Coke*, Indianapolis, IN: Liberty Press.

Collins, J. (2016) *Martial Law and English Laws*, Cambridge: Cambridge UP.

Cook, J. (1649) *King Charles His Case*, London.

Coquillette, D. (1992) *Francis Bacon*, Edinburgh: Edinburgh UP.

Crawford, P. (1977) 'Charles Stuart, That Man of Blood', *Journal of British Studies* 16: 41–61.

Cressy, D. (2015) *Charles I and the People of England*, Oxford: Oxford UP.

Cromartie, A. (1995) *Sir Matthew Hale, 1609–1676: Law, Religion and Natural Philosophy*, Cambridge: Cambridge UP.

Cust, R. (1985) 'Charles I, the Privy Council, and the Forced Loan', *Journal of British Studies* 24: 208–35.

Cust, R. (1986) 'News and Politics in Early Seventeenth Century England', *Past and Present* 112: 60–90.

Cust, R. (2007) *Charles I*, London: Routledge.

Defoe, D. (1986) *A Journal of a Plague Year*, London: Penguin.

Defoe, D. (1991) *Memoirs of a Cavalier*, Oxford: Oxford UP.

Defoe, D. (1997) *The True-Born Englishman and Other Writings*, P. Furbank and R. Owens (eds), London: Penguin, 1997.

Doe, N. (2017) 'Richard Hooker: Priest and Jurist', in M. Hill and R. Helmholz (eds) *Great Christian Jurists in English History*, Cambridge: Cambridge UP, 115–38.

Downie, J. (1994) *To Settle the Succession of the State: Literature and Politics 1678–1750*, London: Macmillan.

Downs, J. (1660) *A True and Humble Representation of John Downs Esq*. London.

Edwards, T. (1646) *Gangraena*, London.

Ellis, F. (ed.) (1994) *John Wilmot, Earl of Rochester: The Complete Works*, London: Penguin.

Farr, D. (2006) *Henry Ireton and the English Revolution*, Rochester, NY: Boydell and Brewer.

Farrand, M. (ed.) (1911) *The Records of the Federal Convention of 1787*, New Haven, CT: Yale UP.

Finch, Sir H. (2016) 'Exact and Most Impartial Accompt of the Indictment, Arraignment, Trial, and Judgment (according to law) of Twenty-Nine Regicides etc.' in K. Kesselring (ed.), *The Trial of Charles I*, Peterborough, ON: Broadview, 114–50.

Firth, C. (ed.) (1894) *The Memoirs of Edmund Ludlow*, Oxford: Oxford UP.

Fish, S. (2001) *How Milton Works*, Cambridge, MA: Harvard UP.

Frank, J. (1980) *Cromwell's Press Agent: A Critical Biography of Marchamont Nedham*, Lanham, MD: UP of America.

Fraser, A. (1979) *King Charles II*, London: Weidenfeld and Nicolson.

Fraser, A. (1989) *Cromwell: Our Chief of Men*, London: Mandarin.

Furbank, P., and Owens, W. (1998) *A Critical Bibliography of Daniel Defoe*, London: Routledge.

Gardiner, S. (1887–91) *History of England*, London: Longman, Green and Co.

Gardiner, S. (1901) *History of the Great Civil War, 1642-1649*, London: Longman.

Gardiner, S. (1906) *Constitutional Documents of the Puritan Revolution 1625–1660*, Oxford: Oxford UP.

Gent, J. (1663) *The History of the Life and Death of Oliver Cromwell*, London.

Gentles, I. (1992) *The New Model Army in England, Ireland and Scotland 1645–1653*, Oxford: Blackwell.

Gest, J. (1909) 'The Writings of Sir Edward Coke', *Yale Law Journal* 18: 504–32.

Gray, T. (2009) *Elegy in a Country Churchyard, and Other Poems*, London: Penguin.

Guy, J. (1982) 'Henry VIII and the Praemunire Manoeuvres of 1530–1531', *English Historical Review* 97: 481–503.

Haivry, O. (2017) *John Selden and the Western Political Tradition*, Cambridge: Cambridge UP.

Hamilton, G. (1996) 'Marvell, Sacrilege, and Protestant Historiography: Contextualizing "Upon Appleton House"', in D. Hamilton and R. Strier (eds), *Religion, Literature and Politics, in Post-Reformation England 1540–1688*, Cambridge: Cambridge UP, 161–86.

Hammersley, R. (2019) *James Harrington: An Intellectual Biography*, Oxford: Oxford UP.

Harvey, D. (2017) *The Law Emprynted: The Printing Press as an Agent of Change*, London: Bloomsbury.

Helgerson, R. (1987) 'Milton Reads the King's Book: Print, Reference and the Making of a Bourgeois Idol', *Criticism* 29: 1–25.

Hill, B. (1992) *The Republican Virago: The Life and Times of Catharine Macaulay Historian*, Oxford: Oxford UP.

Hill, C. (1997) *Milton and the English Revolution*, London: Faber and Faber.

Hirst, D. (1995) 'John Milton's *Eikonoclastes*: The Drama of Justice', in D. Smith, R. Strier and D. Bevington (eds), *The Theatrical City: Culture, Theatre and Politics in London 1576–1649*, Cambridge: Cambridge UP, 245–59.

Hobbes, T. (1985) *Leviathan*, London: Penguin.

Hobbes, T. (1990) *Behemoth, or the Long Parliament*, Chicago: Chicago UP.

Holmes, C. (2019) 'The Remonstrance of the Army and the Execution of Charles I',
    History 362: 585–605.

Holmes, C. (2020) 'The Trial and Execution of Charles I', *Historical Journal* 53: 289–316.

Hume, D. (1983) *History of England*, Indianapolis, IN: Liberty Fund.

Hutchinson, L. (2000) *Memoirs of the Life of Colonel Hutchinson*, London: Phoenix.

Hutchinson. T. (ed.) (1936) *Wordsworth: Complete Poetical Works*, Oxford: Oxford UP.

Hutton, R. (1987) *The Restoration: A Political and Religious History of England and Wales
    1658–1667*, Oxford: Oxford UP.

Iagomarsino, D., and Wood, C. (eds) (1989) *The Trial of Charles I: A Documentary History*,
    Hanover, NH: Dartmouth College Press.

Itzin, C., and Trussler, S. (1975) 'Petrol Bombs through the Proscenium Arch', *Theatre
    Quarterly* 17: 4–20.

Jardine, L., and Stewart, A. (1998) *Hostage to Fortune: The Troubled Life of Francis Bacon*,
    London: Victor Gollanz.

Jones, E. (1971) *Politics and the Bench: The Judge and the Origins of the English Civil War*,
    London: Allen and Unwin.

Kantorowicz, H. (2016) *The King's Two Bodies: A Study in Medieval Political Theology*,
    Princeton: Princeton UP.

Keenan, S. (2020) *The Progress, Processions and Royal Entries of King Charles I*,
    Oxford: Oxford UP.

Kelsey, S. (1997) *Inventing a Republic: The Political Culture of the English Commonwealth
    1649–1653*, Manchester: Manchester UP.

Kelsey, S. (2002) 'The Death of Charles I', *Historical Journal* 45: 727–54.

Kelsey, S. (2003) 'The Trial of Charles I', *English Historical Review* 118: 583–616.

Kelsey, S. (2004) 'Politics and Procedure in the Trial of Charles I', *Law and History Review*
    22: 1–26.

Kermode, F., and Walker, K. (eds) (1990) *Andrew Marvell*, Oxford: Oxford UP.

Kesselring, K. (ed.) (2016) *The Trial of Charles I*, Peterborough, ON: Broadview.

Kishlansky, M. (1999) 'Tyranny Denied: Charles I, Attorney General Heath and the Five
    Knights Case', *Historical Journal* 42: 53–83.

Kishlansky, M. (2013) 'A Whipper Whipped: The Sedition of William Prynne', *Historical
    Journal* 56: 603–27.

Klein, D. (1997) 'The Trial of Charles I', *Journal of Legal History* 18: 1–25.

Knachel, P. (ed.) (1966) *Eikon Basilike: The Portraiture of His Sacred Majesty in His
    Solitudes and Sufferings*, Ithaca, NY: Cornell UP.

Knapfla, L. (1977) *Law and Politics in Jacobean England*, Cambridge: Cambridge UP.

Knoppers, L. (2000) *Constructing Cromwell: Ceremony, Portrait, and Print 1645–1661*,
    Cambridge: Cambridge UP.

Lacey, A. (2001) 'Elegies and Commemorative Verse in Honour of Charles the
    Martyr, 1649–1660', in J. Peacey (ed.), *The Regicides and the Trial of Charles I*,
    London: Palgrave, 225–46.

Lake, P. (1988) *Anglicans and Puritans: Presbyterian and English Conformist Thought from
    Whitgift to Hooker*, London: Routledge.

Lee, M. (ed.) (1882) *Dairies and Letters of Phillip Henry*, London: Kegan Paul.

Levi, P. (1997) *Eden Renewed: The Public and Private Life of John Milton*,
    London: Macmillan.

Lilburne, J. (1645) *A Copie of a Letter*, London.

Lilburne, J. (1649) *The Legal Fundamental Liberties of the People of England Revived,
    Asserted, and Vindicated*, London.

Locke, J. (1989) *Two Treatises of Government*, London: Dent.

Lockwood, S. (ed.) (1997) *Sir John Fortescue: On the Laws and Governance of England*, Cambridge: Cambridge UP.

Loewenstein, D. (2001) *Representing Revolution in Milton and His Contemporaries: Religion, Politics and Polemics in Radical Puritanism*, Cambridge: Cambridge UP.

Loncar, K. (1990) 'John Selden's *History of Tithes*', *Journal of Legal History* 11: 218–38.

Ludlow, E. (1978) *A Voyce from the Watch Tower*, B. Worden (ed.), London: Camden Society.

Mabbott, G. (2016) 'A Perfect Narrative of the Whole Proceedings of the High Court of Justice', in K. Kesselring (ed.), *The Trial of Charles I*, Peterborough, ON: Broadview, 79–86.

Macadam, J. (2011) '*Mercurius Britannicus* on Charles I: An Exercise in Civil War Journalism and High Politics, August 1643 to May 1646', *Historical Research* 84: 470–92.

Macaulay, Lord (1986) *The History of England*, London: Penguin.

Madison, J. (1911) 'Notes of Debates in the Federal Convention of 1787', in M. Farrand (ed.), *The Records of the Federal Convention of 1787*, New Haven, CT: Yale UP.

Maguire, N. (1989) 'The Theatrical Mask/Masque of Politics: The Case of Charles I', *Journal of British Studies* 28: 1–22.

Manning, B. (1992) *1649: The Crisis of the English Revolution*, London: Bookmarks.

Margoliouth, H. (ed.) (1971) *The Poems and Letters of Andrew Marvell*, Oxford: Oxford UP.

Marriott, D. (ed.) (1995) *The Works of John Dryden*, London: Wordsworth.

Matusiak, J. (2017) *Prisoner King: Charles I in Captivity*, Stroud: History Press.

McGrade, A. (ed.) (1989) *Richard Hooker: Of the Laws of Ecclesiastical Polity*, Cambridge: Cambridge UP.

McKnight, L. (1996) 'Crucifixion or Apocalypse? Refiguring *Eikon Basilike*', in D. Hamilton and R. Strier (eds), *Religion, Literature and Politics, in Post-Reformation England 1540–1688*, Cambridge: Cambridge UP, 138–60.

Meron, T. (1993) *Henry's Wars and Shakespeare's Laws*, Cambridge: Cambridge UP.

Milton, J. (1953–62) *Complete Prose Works*, New Haven, CT: Yale UP.

Milton, J. (1962) *Collected Political Writings of John Milton*, M. Hughes (ed.), New Haven, CT: Yale UP.

Milton, J. (1991a) *A Critical Edition of the Major Works*, S. Orgel and J. Goldberg (eds), Oxford: Oxford UP.

Milton, J. (1991b) *Political Writings*, M. Dzelzainis (ed.), Cambridge: Cambridge UP.

Milton, J. (2014) *Areopagitica and Other Writings*, London: Penguin.

Monateri, P. (2018) *Dominus Mundi: Political Sublime and the World Order*, Oxford: Hart.

Morrah, P. (1979) *Restoration England*, London: Constable.

Morrill, J. (1993) *The Nature of the English Revolution*, London: Longman.

Morrill, J. (2011) 'Renaming England's Wars of Religion', in G. Burgess and C. Prior (eds), *England's Wars of Religion Revisited*, London: Routledge, 307–25.

Mossner, E. (1980) *The Life of David Hume*, Oxford: Oxford UP.

Nalson, J. (2016) 'A True Copy of the Journal of the High Court of Justice for the Trial of K. Charles I, as it was read in the House of Commons, and Attested under the hand of Phelps, Clerk to that Infamous Court', in K. Kesselring (ed.), *The Trial of Charles I*, Peterborough, ON: Broadview, 19–78.

Nedham, M. (1659) *Interest Will Not Lie*, London.

Norbrook, D. (1999) *Writing the English Republic: Poetry, Rhetoric and Politics 1627–1660*, Cambridge: Cambridge UP.

Ogg, D. (1984) *England in the Reign of Charles II*, Oxford: Oxford UP.

Orr, A. (2002) *Treason and the State: Law, Politics and Ideology in the English Civil War*, Cambridge: Cambridge UP.

Overton, R. (1649) *The Hunting of Foxes*, London.

Peck, L. (1993) 'Kingship, Counsel and Law in Early Stuart Britain', in J. Pocock (ed.), *Varieties of British Political Thought 1500–1800*, Cambridge: Cambridge UP, 80–116.

Pepys, S. (1993) *The Shorter Pepys*, London: Penguin.

Pocock, J. (1967) *The Ancient Constitution and the Common Law*, New York: Norton.

Polizzotto, C. (2014) 'What Really Happened at the Whitehall Debates? A New Source', *Historical Journal* 57: 33–51.

Polizzotto, C. (2016) 'Speaking Truth to Power: The Problem of Authority in the Whitehall Debates of 1648–9', *English Historical Review* 131: 31–63.

Pollock, P. (ed.) (1927) *John Selden: Table Talk*, London: Quaritch.

Porter, R. (2001) *Enlightenment: Britain and the Creation of the Modern World*, London: Penguin.

Potter, L. (1999) 'The Royal Martyr in the Restoration', in T. Corns (ed.), *The Royal Image: Representations of Charles I*, Cambridge: Cambridge UP, 240–62.

Price, P. (1997) 'Natural Law and Birthright Citizenship in *Calvin's Case*', *Yale Journal of Law and Humanities* 9: 73–145.

Prynne, W. (1649) *A Brief Memento to the Present Unparliamentary Junto*, London.

Raffield, P. (2004) *Images and Cultures of Law in Early Modern England: Justice and Political Power 1558–1660*, Cambridge: Cambridge UP.

Raffield, P. (2010) *Shakespeare's Imaginary Constitution: Late Elizabethan Politics and the Theatre of Law*, Oxford: Hart.

Rees, J. (2016) *The Leveller Revolution*, London: Verso.

Reeve, J. (1986) 'The Arguments in King's Bench in 1629 Concerning the Imprisonment of John Selden and Other Members of the House Commons', *Journal of British Studies* 25: 264–87.

Rideal, R. (2017) *1666: Plague, War and Hellfire*, London: John Murray.

Robertson, G. (2006) *The Tyrannicide Brief: The Story of the Man Who Sent Charles I to the Scaffold*, London: Vintage.

Rogers, J. (1653) *To His Excellency the Lord General*, and *Sagrir, or Dooms-Day Drawing Nigh*, London.

Rogow, A. (1986) *Thomas Hobbes: Radical in the Service of Reaction*, New York: Norton.

Rose, J. (2013) *Godly Kingship in Restoration England: The Politics of the Royal Supremacy 1660–1688*, Cambridge: Cambridge UP.

Royle, T. (2005) *Civil War: The Wars of the Three Kingdoms 1638–1660*, London: Abacus.

Rushworth, J. (1721) *Historical Collections of Private Passages of State*, D. Browne (ed.), London.

Russell, C. (1979) *Parliaments and English Politics 1621–1629*, Oxford: Oxford UP.

Russell, C. (1988) 'The First Army Plot of 1641', *Transactions of the Royal Historical Society* 38: 85–106.

Russell, C. (1990) *The Causes of the English Civil War*, Oxford: Oxford UP.

Sachse, W. (1973) 'England's "Black Tribunal": An Analysis of the Regicide Court', *Journal of British Studies* 12: 69–85.

Salmon, J. (1649) *A Rout, a Rout*, London.

Scott, D. (2001) 'Motives for King-Killing', in J. Peachey (ed.), *The Regicides and the Execution of King Charles I*, London: Palgrave, 138–60.

Scott, J. (1991) *Algernon Sidney and the Restoration Crisis, 1677–1683*, Cambridge: Cambridge UP.

Seaward, P. (1989) *The Cavalier Parliament and the Reconstruction of the Old Regime*, Cambridge: Cambridge UP.

Shakespeare, W. (1966) *Richard II*, London: Routledge.

Shakespeare, W. (1967) *Measure for Measure*, London: Routledge.

Shakespeare, W. (1991) *Henry V*, London: Routledge.

Shapiro, J. (2019) *Law Reform in Early Modern England: Crown, Parliament and the Press*, Oxford: Hart.

Sharp, A. (2001) 'The Levellers and the End of Charles I', in J. Peacey (ed.), *The Regicides and the Execution of Charles I*, London: Palgrave, 181–201.

Sharpe, K. (1992) *The Personal Rule of Charles I*, New Haven, CT: Yale UP.

Sharpe, K. (2000) *Remapping Early Modern England: The Culture of Seventeenth-Century Politics*, Cambridge: Cambridge UP.

Sharpe, K. (2009) 'Van Dyck, the Royal Image and the Caroline Court', in K. Hearn (ed.), *Van Dyck and Britain*, London: Tate, 14–23.

Sidney, A. (1772) 'Discourses Concerning Government', in J. Robertson (ed.), *Sydney on Government: The Works of Algernon Sydney*, London: Strahan.

Sirico, L. (1999) 'The Trial of Charles I: A Sesquitricentennial Reflection', *Constitutional Commentary* 16: 51–62.

Skinner, Q. (1996) *Reason and Rhetoric in the Philosophy of Hobbes*, Cambridge: Cambridge UP.

Smith, D. (1994) *Constitutional Royalism and the Search for Settlement, c.1640–1649*, Cambridge: Cambridge UP.

Smith, D. (1995) 'The Root and Branch Petition and the Grand Remonstrance', in D. Smith, R. Strier and D. Bevington (eds), *The Theatrical City: Culture, Theatre and Politics in London 1576–1649*, Cambridge: Cambridge UP, 209–23.

Smith, D. (2014) *Sir Edward Coke and the Reformation of the Laws: Religion, Politics and Jurisprudence 1578–1616*, Cambridge: Cambridge UP.

Smith, D. (2017) 'Sir Edward Coke: Faith, Law and the Search for Stability', in M. Hill and R. Helmholz (eds), *Great Christian Jurists in English History*, Cambridge: Cambridge UP, 93–113.

Smith, N. (ed.) (1983) *A Collection of Ranter Writings from the Seventeenth Century*, London: Pluto.

Smith, N. (2012) *Andrew Marvell: The Chameleon*, New Haven, CT: Yale UP.

Smith, P. (ed.) (2001) *Bagehot: The English Constitution*, Cambridge: Cambridge UP.

Sommerville, J. (1986) *Politics and Ideology in England 1603–1640*, London: Longman.

Sommerville, J. (1991a) 'James I and the Divine Right of Kings: English Politics and Continental Theory', in L. Peck (ed.), *The Mental World of the Jacobean Court*, Cambridge: Cambridge UP, 55–70.

Sommerville, J. (ed.) (1991b) *Sir Robert Filmer: Patriarcha and Other Writings*, Cambridge: Cambridge UP.

Sommerville, J. (ed.) (1994) *King James VI and I: Political Writings*, Cambridge: Cambridge UP.

Speck, W. (1988) *Reluctant Revolutionaries: Englishmen and the Revolution of 1688*, Oxford: Oxford UP.

Spencer, C. (2014) *Killers of the King*, London: Bloomsbury.

Stacy, W. (1985) 'Matter of Fact, Matter of Law, and the Attainder of the Earl of Strafford', *American Journal of Legal History* 29: 323–47.

Stone, L. (1967) *The Crisis of the Aristocracy 1558–1641*, New Haven, CT: Yale UP.

Strauss, L. (1963) *The Political Philosophy of Hobbes*, Chicago: Chicago UP.

Summers, C. (1985) 'Herrick's Political Counterplots', *Studies in English Literature 1500–1900* 25: 165–82,

Taft, B. (2006) 'From Reading to Whitehall: Henry Ireton's Journey', in M. Mendle (ed.), *The Putney Debates of 1647: The Army, the Levellers and the English State*, Cambridge: Cambridge UP, 175–95.

Thomas, P. (1984) 'Two Cultures? Court and Country under Charles I', in C. Russell (ed.), *The Origins of the English Civil War*, London: Macmillan, 158–93.

Thomas, V. (1991) *The Moral Universe of Shakespeare's Problem Plays*, London: Routledge.

Tomalin, C. (2003) *Samuel Pepys: The Unequalled Self*, London: Penguin.

Trela, D. (1998) 'Sir Walter Scott on Oliver Cromwell: An Evenhanded Royalist Evaluates a Usurper', *Clio* 27: 195–220.

Trevor-Roper, H. (1978) *Selections from Clarendon*, Oxford: Oxford UP.

Trevor-Roper, H. (1988) *Catholics, Anglicans and Puritans*, Chicago: Chicago UP.

Tyacke, N. (1973) 'Puritanism, Arminianism and Counter-Revolution', in C. Russell (ed.), *The Origins of the English Civil War*, London: Macmillan, 119–43.

Underdown, D. (1985) *Pride's Purge: Politics in the Puritan Revolution*, London: Allen and Unwin.

Usher, R. (1903) 'James I and Sir Edward Coke', *English Historical Review* 18: 664–75.

Walker, K. (ed.) (1987) *John Dryden: A Critical Edition of the Major Works*, Oxford: Oxford UP.

Walker, W. (2014) *Antiformalist, Unrevolutionary, Illiberal Milton*, Aldershot: Ashgate.

Waller, E. (1840) 'On a War with Spain, and Fight at Sea', London.

Walzer, M. (1973) 'Regicide and Revolution', *Social Research* 40: 617–42.

Warwick, Sir P. (1813) *The Memoirs of the Reign of King Charles I*, London: Ballantyne.

Watt, G. (2009) *Equity Stirring: The Story of Justice Beyond the Law*, Oxford: Hart.

Wedgwood, C. (2011) *A King Condemned*, London: Tauris Parke.

Wells, J. (2015) 'English Law, Irish Trials and Cromwellian State Building in the 1650s', *Past and Present* 227: 77–117.

Weston, C. (1991) 'England: Ancient Constitution and Common Law', in J. Burns and M. Goldie (eds), *The Cambridge History of Political Thought 1450–1700*, Cambridge: Cambridge UP, 374–411.

Wheeler, E. (1999) '*Eikon Basilike* and the Rhetoric of Self-Representation', in T. Corns (ed.), *The Royal Image: Representations of Charles I*, Cambridge: Cambridge UP, 122–40.

White, F. (1649) *The Copies of Several Letters Contrary to the Opinion of the Present Powers, Presented to the Lord General Fairfax, and Lieutenant General Cromwell*, London.

Whitelock, B. (1853) *Memorials of the English Affairs, from the Beginning of the Reign of Charles I to the Happy Restoration of King Charles II*, Oxford: Oxford UP.

Williams, J. (2018) 'Thomas Gray's *Elegy* and the Politics of Memorialization', *Studies in English Literature* 58: 653–72.

Willms, S. (2006) 'The Five Knights Case and Debates in the Parliament of 1628; Division and Suspicion under Charles I', *Constructing the Past* 7: 92–100.

Wilson, J. (1985) *Fairfax*, London: John Murray.

Wither, G. (1649) *The British Appeals*, London.

Woodhouse, A. (ed.) (1986) *Puritanism and Liberty: Being the Army Debates from the Clarke Manuscripts*, London: Dent.

Woolrych, A. (1991) *Battles of the English Civil War*, London: Pimlico.

Woolrych, A. (1993) 'Dating Milton's *History of Britain*', *Historical Journal* 36: 929–43.

Worden, B. (1984) 'The Politics of Marvell's *Horatian Ode*', *Historical Journal* 27: 525–47.

Worden, B. (1998) 'Milton and Marchamont Nedham', in D. Armitage, A. Himy and Q. Skinner (eds), *Milton and Republicanism*, Cambridge: Cambridge UP, 156–80.

Worden, B. (2002) *Roundhead Reputations: The English Civil Wars and the Passions of Posterity*, London: Penguin.

Worden, B. (2011) 'Oliver Cromwell and the Cause of Civil and Religious Liberty', in C. Prior and G. Burgess (eds), *England's Wars of Religion Revisited*, London: Routledge, 231–52.

Wormald, B. (1989) *Clarendon: Politics, History and Religion 1640–1660*, Oxford: Oxford UP.

Wormald, J. (1991) 'James VI and I, *Basilikon Doron* and *The Trew Law of Free Monarchies*: The Scottish Context and the English Translation', in L. Peck (ed.), *The Mental World of the Jacobean Court*, Cambridge: Cambridge UP, 36–54.

Wright, S. (2006) 'Nicholas Fuller and the Liberties of the Subject', *Parliamentary History* 25: 176–213.

Young, P. (1985) *Naseby 1645: The Campaign and the Battle*, London: Century.

Zagorin, P. (1982) *Rebels and Rulers*, Cambridge: Cambridge UP.

Zwicker, S. (1993) *Lines of Authority: Politics and English Literary Culture 1649–1689*, Ithaca, NY: Cornell UP.

INDEX

A Handkerchief for Loyal Mourners 108
*A True Relation of the King's Speech to
    the Lady Elizabeth and the Duke of
    Gloucester, the day before his death* 108
Abbott, George, Archbishop of
    Canterbury 31, 54
*Act Concerning Ecclesiastical
    Appointments* 11
*Act for an Annual Perpetuall Thanksgiving
    on the Ninth and Twentieth Day of
    May* 147–8
*Act for Erecting of a High Court of Justice
    for the Trying and Judging of Charles
    Stuart* 96
Act for the Abolishing of Kingly Office 129
*Act for the Speedy Disbandment of the
    Army* 164
Act in Restraint of Annates 11
Act in Restraint of Appeals 147
*Act of Attainder of severall persons guilty of
    the horrid murther of his Late Sacred
    Majesty King Charles I* 148
Act of Indemnity and Oblivion 147, 164
Act of Settlement 190
Act of Supremacy 11
Act of Succession 11
Act of Uniformity 165
*Act Prohibiting the Proclaiming of any
    Person to be King of England* 79
Adams, John 6
Adwalton Moor, battle of 65
Ainsworth, William Harrison 193
    Boscobel 193
    The Leaguer of Lathom 193
Alfred, King of England 137
Alleyn, Edward 21

Almack, Edward 109
Anderson, Sir Edmund, Chief Justice 8
Andrews, Lancelot 14
Andrews, Sir Thomas 92
Anne, Queen of England 175, 190
Answer to the Nineteen Propositions 65,
    164, 176
Apsley, Sir Allen 148
Aristotle 11, 132, 137
    Ethics 11
Ashburnham, John 72
Ashe, John 142
Astley, Sir Jacob, 1st Lord 67, 71–2
Athelstan, King of England 137
Aubrey, John 144, 169, 183
Axtell, Colonel Daniel 105, 107, 151–2

Bacon, Sir Francis, Attorney-General and
    Lord Chancellor 6–7, 10–11, 23, 25–6
    Letter of Advice 6
Bagehot, Walter 41, 194
    The English Constitution 194
Baillie, Robert 70
Balfour, Sir William 38
Bancroft, Thomas, Archbishop of
    Canterbury 13, 16–18, 51
Bankes, Sir John, Attorney-General 57
Barebones Assembly 116, 138
Barkstead, Colonel John 151
Basing House, siege of 71, 184
Bastwick, John 49
Bates's Case 10, 12
Baxter, Richard 81, 123, 143, 165
    A Holy Commonwealth 143
Beale, John 153
Bell, John 163

Berkeley, Sir Robert, Justice 57, 60
Bethel, Slingsby 180
Bill of Rights 3, 189–90
Biographia Britannica 178, 190
Birch, John, Colonel 71–2
Bishop, Captain George 85
Blackstone, Sir William 191
   Commentaries on the Laws of
     England 191
Blake, William 153
Book of Lawful Sports 48–9, 136
Booth, Sir George 143
Bosse, Abraham 185
Boswell, James 191
Boughton, Andrew 99, 148
Bracton 18, 132, 137
Bradshaw, John, Lord President 97, 100,
   104–7, 128, 148
Bramston, Sir John, Lord Chief Justice 58
Brandon, Richard 80
Brenton, Howard 1–2
   55 Days 1
Brereton, Major-General William 71–2,
   98
Bridgman, Sir Orlando, Chief Justice
   103, 149–50
Broome, Richard 113
Browne, Robert 79
Buchanan, George 8, 131
   De Jure Regni apud Scotus 8, 131
Bunyan, John 153
Burgh, John 49
Burgoyne, Sir Robert 90
Burke, Edmund 192
   Reflections on the Revolution in
     France 192–3
Burnet, Gilbert, Bishop of Salisbury 112,
   187–8, 195
   History of Our Own Time 187, 195
Burrough, Edward 121, 153
Burroughs, Jeremiah 46
Burton, Henry 14, 48–9, 52, 100
Butler, James, 1st Duke of Ormonde 68–71,
   90, 113, 160–1
Butler, Samuel 95
Butterfield, Herbert 2
   The Whig Interpretation of History 2
Byron, George, 6th Lord 192
Byron, William, 3rd Lord 148

Calendar of Saints 162
Calvin's Case 12, 18
Capel, Arthur, 1st Lord 87, 129
Carew, John 139, 181
Carew, Thomas 43
Carey, Henry, 1st Earl of Dover 152
Carisbrooke Castle 86, 110
Carleton, Sir Dudley 33, 50
Carlyle, Thomas 2–3, 194–6
   The Letters and Speeches of Oliver
     Cromwell 194
Carte, Thomas 190
   General History of England 190
Cartwright, Thomas 15
Cary, Lucius, 2nd Viscount Falkland 43, 45,
   53, 163, 195
Case of Commendams 24
Case of the Five Knights 31–3, 188
Case of Proclamations 19–23
Case of the Seven Bishops 188
Catherine of Braganza, Queen of
   England 168
Catherine Parr, Queen of England 99
Caudry's Case 10
Cavendish, William, 1st Earl of
   Newcastle 41
Cavendish, William, 3rd Earl of
   Devonshire 182
Cecil, Sir Robert 18, 22
Chalgrove, battle of 65
Chamberlain, John 26
Chamberlayne, Edward 166
Charles I, King of England 1–4, 12, 14,
   23, 28–47, 50–2, 54–7, 59–70, 72–4,
   78–83, 85, 88, 90–1, 93, 95–7, 100–10,
   114, 116, 122, 132–3, 135–7, 139,
   149–50, 155, 162, 168–9, 174, 177–81,
   183, 185, 191, 193–4, 196–8
Charles II, King of England 41, 108, 110,
   146, 155, 160, 164–5, 168–9, 172–3,
   175, 185, 187, 197
Chepstow Castle 152
Cheriton, battle of 45
Childerley House, 74
Christian IV, King of Denmark 30
Cicero 137
Clarendon 'Code' 152–3, 165
Clarges, Sir Thomas 147
Clifford, Lady Anne 22

Clinton, Theophilus, 4th Earl of Lincoln 31
Cockayne, George 93
Coke, Lady Frances 27–8
Coke, Lady Elizabeth 7, 27
Coke, Sir Edward, Lord Chief Justice 4,
    6–7, 11–14, 17–18, 20, 22–5, 30, 32–6,
    61–2, 64, 83, 85, 96, 100, 103, 130,
    132, 137, 163, 189–91
    Institutes 6–7, 18, 34, 85, 103, 130, 132
    Reports 4, 6, 14, 22–3, 36, 132, 191
Colchester, siege of 2, 87, 91, 127
Coleridge, Samuel Taylor 21, 192
College of Physicians 165
Company of King's Men 21
Company of Starchmakers 20
Compton, Henry, Bishop of London
    189
Conventicle Act 152, 165
Cook, John 94–5, 98, 100–1, 103, 106, 131,
    134, 151
    King Charls His Case 101, 131, 134
Corbet, Sir John 31, 59
Corbet, Miles 151
Corporation Act 165
Correr, Anthony 50, 53, 58
Corytone, Sir Robert 31
Cosin, John 46, 52–3
    Collection of Private Devotions 46, 52
Cotton House 97
Coventry, Thomas, Lord Keeper 31
Cowley, Abraham 112
Craik, Sir Henry 196
    The Life of Edward, Earl of Clarendon
        and Lord High Chancellor of
        England 196
Crofts, Ernest 193–4
    Charles I on the Way to his Execution
        193
    Cromwell at the Storming of Basing
        House 193
    Cromwellian Soldiers Leaving Warwick
        Castle 193
    Hampden Riding Away from Chalgrove
        Field 193
    The Funeral of Charles I at St George's
        Chapel 193
    The Surrender of the City of York 193
    Whitehall, January 30th 1649 193–4
Croke, Sir George, Justice 57

Cromwell, Mary 116
Cromwell, Oliver, Lord Protector 1, 3, 41,
    50, 53, 65–8, 74, 79–80, 83–5, 88, 91,
    94–5, 97–8, 102, 107–8, 113–14, 116,
    120–3, 125, 128–30, 133, 138–42,
    145–6, 148, 153, 160, 166, 168, 170,
    176, 178, 185–6, 189, 192–6
Cromwell, Richard 120, 143
Cromwell, Thomas 55
Cropredy Bridge, battle of 65
Crosfield, Thomas 31
Culpeper, Sir Nicholas 59

Dalzell, Robert, 1st Earl of Carnwath 67
Danvers, Sir John 98
Darnell, Sir Thomas 31–2
Davenant, John, Bishop of Salisbury 51
Davenant, Sir William 45
    The Temple of Love 45
Davenport, Sir Humphrey, Justice 58
Davies, Lady Eleanor 52, 126
Davies, Sir John 11
    Irish Reports 11
De Ruyter, Admiral Michiel 166, 171
Declaration of Breda 146–8, 162, 164–5
Declaration of Indulgence 188
Declaration of Right 189
Declaration of the Parliament of
    England 131
Defoe, Daniel 163, 175, 181
    Memoirs of a Cavalier 181
    The Shortest Way with Dissenters 175
Dendy, Sir Edward, Serjeant of Arms 96
Desborough, Major General John 142
Devereux, Robert, 2nd Earl of Essex 7
D'Ewes, Sir Simonds 35, 39, 50, 56
Dickens, Charles 3, 193
    A Tale of Two Cities 193
    Barnaby Rudge 193
Digby, Sir Kenelm 43, 62, 64–6, 70, 177
Digges, Sir Dudley 32, 34
Disraeli, Benjamin 194
Dixwell, Colonel John 148
Dodderidge, Sir John 12
Donne, John 27, 78
Dorislaus, Isaac 98, 100
Downes, Colonel John 107, 152
Dr Bonham's Case 23
Drogheda, massacre 113, 138

Dryden, John 116, 121, 147, 161–2,
    164, 166
    Annus Mirabilis 166
    Astraea Redux 147
    Heroic Stanzas 121
    Panegyrick on his Coronation 161
    To My Lord Chancellor 164
Dugard, William 111
Dunbar, battle of 66, 120, 131, 138
Duppa, Brian 126
Dutton, William 115
Dymocke, Sir Edward 161

Earl of Oxford's Case 23
Earle, Sir Walter 31
Edgehill, battle of 45, 65, 72, 82
Edward II, King of England 95, 107, 150
Edward the Confessor, King of
    England 137
Edwards, Thomas 123
    Gangraena 123
Egerton, John, 1ˢᵗ Earl of Bridgwater 59
Egerton, Sir Thomas, Lord Chancellor
    Ellesmere 10, 22, 24
Eikon Alethine 135
*Eikon Basilike: the Portraiture of his Sacred
    Majesty in His Solitudes and Sufferings*
    35, 109–11, 131, 133, 136, 145, 147,
    169, 178
Eliot, George 193
Eliot, Sir John 10, 35–6
    Monarchie of Men 10
Elizabeth I, Queen of England 12, 19, 21,
    36, 41, 191
Ellwood, Thomas 153
Erasmus, Desiderius 41
    The Education of a Christian Prince 41
Evelyn, Sir John 93, 135, 146, 155, 166
Exultationis Carmen 146

Fairfax, Lady Anne 99, 107, 116
Fairfax, Lady Mary 111–13, 116, 160
Fairfax, Sir Thomas, 3ʳᵈ Lord Fairfax 66–8,
    74, 81, 83, 88, 91, 98–9, 105, 111–12,
    115, 117, 127, 160, 184
Farre, Colonel Henry 87
Fawkes, Guy 7
Feilding, William, 3ʳᵈ Earl of Denbigh
    108, 112

Feltham, Owen 111
    *Epitaph to the Eternal Memory of
    Charles I* 111
Felton, John 29–30
Fiennes, William, 1ˢᵗ Viscount Saye and
    Sele 56–7, 70
Filmer, Sir Robert 9
    Patriarcha 9
Finch, Sir Heneage 148
Finch, Sir John 35, 58, 60, 138
Firth, Charles Harding 3
Five Mile Act 165
Fleetwood, Colonel Charles 71, 98, 142
Fleming, Sir Thomas, Lord Chief Justice
    and Chief Baron 10, 12, 22
Fortescue, Sir John, Chief Justice 19,
    22, 132
    In Praise of the Laws of England 19
Fox, Charles James 192
Fox, George 143
Franklin, Benjamin 3
Fraser, Antonia 3
Fraser, James 139
Fuller, Nicholas 14–16, 18
    The Argument of Nicholas Fuller 18, 54
Fuller's Case 14–19

Gardiner, Samuel Rawson 3, 14
Gascoigne, Sir Bernard 87
Gauden, John, Bishop of Exeter and
    Worcester 41, 109, 111, 131, 145
    Cromwell's Bloody Slaughter-House 145
    Religious and Loyal Protestation 131
Gayer, Sir John 83
Geddes, Jennie 59
Gentileschi, Orazio 42
Geoffrey of Monmouth 13
George I, King of England 190
George III, King of England 192
Gibbons, Grinling 173
Glanvil's Case 23–4, 26
Glynne, Sir John, Lord Chief Justice 62, 142
Goffe, William, Colonel 52, 83–5, 98, 148
Gonzaga, Duke Vincenzio 40
Goodwin, John 46, 91
    Anti-Cavalierisme 46
Gordon riots 191
Goring, George, 1ˢᵗ Earl of Norwich 43, 66,
    71, 87, 129

Gow, Andrew Carrick 193
  *Cromwell Dissolving the Long
    Parliament* 193
  The Battle of Dunbar 193
  *The Visit of Charles I to Kingston-upon-
    Hull* 193
Graham, James, 1st Marquess of Montrose
  66, 114
Grand Remonstrance 51, 63
Granger, John 178
Gray, Thomas 181, 191
  Elegy in a Country Churchyard 181, 191
Greville, Robert, 2nd Lord Brooke 92
Grey, Thomas, Lord Grey of Groby 91, 98
Greygoose, Samuel 52
Grimstone, Harbottle 54
Gwynne, Nell 168

Habeas Corpus Act 190
Hacker, Colonel Frances 78, 151–2
Hale, Sir Matthew, Lord Chief Justice
  146, 191
  History of the Common Law 191
Hall, Joseph, Bishop of Norwich 53, 126
  Episcopacy by Divine Right Asserted 53
Hamilton, James, 1st Duke of Hamilton 53,
  71, 86, 104, 129
Hammond, Colonel Robert 86, 100
Hampden, Sir Edmund 31
Hampden, John 37, 56–8, 176, 195
Hampden's Case 57–8, 60, 177
Hampton Court 39, 41, 81
Harrington, Sir James 120, 133, 143–4, 166,
  180, 192
  Oceana 120, 133, 143–4, 180
Harrington, Sir John 24, 44
Harrison, Colonel Thomas 90, 92, 95, 98–9,
  138, 149–50, 152, 174, 181, 189
Harrison, Reverend Thomas 58
Hartlib, Samuel 127
Haselrig, Sir Arthur 38, 59, 62
Hastings, Henry, 1st Lord Loughborough
  87
Hatfield House 74
Hawkins, William 51
Heads of Proposals 74
Heads of the Charge Against the King 100
Heath, Robert, Attorney-General and Chief
  Justice 32–3, 38–9, 48

Henrietta Maria, Queen 38–9, 43, 45–7, 85,
  102, 177
Henry V, King of England 28
Henry VI, King of England 95
Henry VIII, King of England 20, 51, 55,
  174, 191
Henslowe, Phillip 21
Herbert, George 78
  Devotions 78
Herbert, Philip, 4th Earl of Pembroke 30
Herbert, Sir Thomas 75, 91, 175
Herrick, Robert 66, 79
  Good Friday: Rex Tragicus 79
Hervey, John, 2nd Lord 179
Heveningham, Sir John 31
Heveningham, William 150, 152
Hewson, Colonel John 83, 91, 98, 148
Heylyn, Peter 12, 40, 49, 51
High Commission 15–17, 26–8, 129,
  164, 187–8
Hill, Christopher 3
Hoard, Samuel 53
Hobbes, Thomas 81, 100, 115, 120,
  123, 182–6
  Behemoth 182–3
  *Dialogue Between a Philosopher and
    a Student of the Common Laws of
    England* 183
  Leviathan 100–1, 115, 182, 184–5
  The Elements of Law 182, 184
Hodges, Margaret 168
Hogarth, William 54
Holdenby House 36, 73–4, 83, 110
Holinshed, Ralph 22
Holles, Denzil 35–7, 66, 149–50, 176, 180
  Memoirs of Denzil Holles 180
Holles, John, 1st Earl of Clare 31
Holmes, Clive 3
Honyman, Andrew 62
Hooker, Richard 11–14, 176
  Of the Laws of Ecclesiastical Polity 11–14
Horace 113–14
  Actium Ode 114
Horton, Sir Thomas 91
Hotham, Sir John 64
Howard, Queen Catherine 55
Howard, Sir Robert 27
Howard, Thomas, 1st Earl of Berkshire 64
Hudson, George 72

Humble Petition and Advice 120, 142
Hume, David 178, 190–1
  History of England 178, 190
Humfrey, Andrew 53
Hunks, Colonel Hercules 152
Hunne's Case 10
Hurst Castle 91
Hutchinson, Colonel John 148, 152, 179
Hutchinson, Lucy 22, 69, 120–1, 141, 179–80
  Memoirs of the Life of Colonel Hutchinson 69, 179
Hutton, Sir Richard, Justice 57–8
Hyde, Anne, Duchess of York 167, 171
Hyde, Sir Edward, Earl of Clarendon and Lord Chancellor 4, 30, 35, 38, 51, 57–8, 64–5, 67, 73, 87, 97–8, 109, 116, 129, 146–8, 160–8, 170–1, 175–81, 183, 186–90, 195–8
  A Life, by Himself 176
  History of the Rebellion 4, 57–8, 65, 162–3, 175–9, 181, 195, 197–8
Hyde, Henry, 2ⁿᵈ Earl of Clarendon 188
Hyde, Laurence, 1ˢᵗ Earl of Rochester 175–6, 197–8
Hyde, Sir Nicholas, Lord Chief Justice 32, 163

Impeachment for High Treason against Oliver Cromwell and Henry Ireton 85
Ingoldsby, Colonel Richard 148
Innocent X, Pope 69
Instrument of Government 120, 140–1
Ireton, Major-General Henry 67, 74, 83–5, 87–8, 90–1, 93–4, 97–100, 102, 105, 107, 128, 148

James I and VI, King of England and Scotland 6–10, 13–14, 17–23, 25–7, 42, 45, 100, 120–1, 131, 142, 191
  Basilicon Doron 9, 42
  Daemonology 8
  Divine Art of Poesie 8
  The Trew Law of Free Monarchies 8–9, 42, 104
James II, King of England 108, 160, 167, 175, 186–8, 194–5
Jefferson, Thomas 6

Jeffreys, George, Lord Chief Justice and Lord Chancellor 180, 187
Jenkins, Sir David 36
Jephson, Colonel William 142
Jermyn, Henry, 1ˢᵗ Earl of St Albans 171
Jones, Inigo 71, 174
Jonson, Ben 23, 45
  Bartholomew Fair 23
Joyce, Cornet George 74, 83, 92, 94
Juxon, William, Archbishop of Canterbury 78–9, 155, 161

Kelsey, Sean 3
Kilmainham Royal Hospital 169
King, Henry, Bishop of Chichester 108
  A Deep Groan Fetch'd at the Funeral of that Incomparable and Glorious Monarch K.Charles I 108
Kinnersley, Clement 120–1
Knox, John 101, 131–2
  The first blast of the trumpet against the monstrous regiment of women 131
Knyvett, Sir Thomas 58

Lachrymae Musarum 113
Ladd, Thomas 16
Lambarde, William 10–11, 41
Lambert, Major-General John 86, 91, 98, 142–3
Landsdowne, battle of 65, 71
Landseer, Sir Edwin 193
  The Battle of Naseby 193
  The Eve Before Edgehill 193
Langdale, Sir Marmaduke 67, 71, 86
Langport, battle of 71
Laud, William, Archbishop of Canterbury 10–11, 13, 29, 49, 51, 53–5, 58, 60–1, 63, 82, 98, 101–2, 109, 177–8
Lely, Peter 116, 140–1, 168, 188
  'Windsor Beauties' 168
  'Lowestoft Flagmen' 168, 171
Lenthall, William, Speaker 39, 68, 112, 138, 151
Leslie, Henry, Bishop of Down and Connor 110
  The Martyrdom of King Charles, or His Conformity with Christ in His Sufferings 110
Leslie, General John 73

Levet, William 110
Licensing of the Press Act 152
Lichfield Cathedral 92, 129
Lilburne, John 6, 13, 38, 63, 82–3, 85, 88, 90, 97, 125–6, 129–30, 133–4, 176
   An Impeachment of High Treason Against Oliver Cromwell 133
   Copie of a Letter 83
   Cry for Justice 82
   England's New Chains Discovered 130, 133
   Regal Tyranny discovered 83
   The Second Part of England's New Chains Discovered 130
Lilly, William 66, 85
Lisle, Lady Alice 187–8
Lisle, Sir George 72, 87–8
   Locke, John 190
   Treatise on Government 190
Lostwithiel, battle of 65, 87
Louis XIII, King of France 56
Louis XIV, King of France 165
Lovelace, Richard 112
Lowestoft, battle of 169
Lucan 113, 155
Lucas, Sir Charles 72, 87–8
Ludlow, Edmund 37, 70, 98, 121, 138–9, 141, 145, 148, 151, 170, 180–1, 187
   A Voyce from the Watchtower 145, 180
Lunsford, Sir Thomas 38–9, 47, 82
Luther, Martin 122, 124

Macaulay, Catharine 179
Macaulay, Thomas Babington, Lord 189, 195–6
   History of England 189
Machiavelli, Niccolo 41, 113–14
   The Prince 41, 113
Madison, James 3
Magna Carta 16, 18, 32, 34, 81–2, 183
Mainwaring, Roger 31
Mansell, Richard 16
Mantegna, Andrea 41, 69, 75, 85
   The Triumphs of Caesar 41, 69
Marshall, William 110
Marston Moor, battle of 55, 65, 82, 84, 111, 149
Marten, Henry 13, 41, 92, 98, 104, 138, 148, 152

Martin Marpriest pamphlets 82, 125
Marvell, Andrew 112–16, 121, 133, 138, 140, 144, 147, 153, 155, 157, 163, 169–75, 192
   A Dialogue Between Two Horses 173
   A Poem Upon the Death of His Late Highness the Lord Protector 121
   An Account of the Growth of Popery and Arbitrary Government 172
   An Elegy Upon the Death of My Lord Villier 112
   An Horation Ode Upon Cromwell's Return from Ireland 112–13, 115, 134, 155
   Clarendon's Housewarming 170
   Last Instructions to a Painter 155, 171, 172
   Statue at Charing Cross 173
   The Character of Holland 116
   The First Anniversary 116. 138, 140–1
   The Rehearsal Transpros'd 157, 172
   To His Coy Mistress 116
   Upon Appleton House 115
   Upon the Hill and Grove at Bilborough 115
Mary, Queen of Scots 80
Mary II, Queen of England 188–9
May, Thomas 69
Mazarin, Cardinal Jules 102, 108
Mentmore estate 196
Mercurius Britanicus 69–70
Mercurius Elencticus 90, 125
Mercurius Politicus 125, 134, 139, 142
Mercurius Pragmaticus 95
Mews, Peter, Bishop of Winchester 109
Mildmay, Sir Henry 98
Milton, John 4, 9, 14, 37, 63, 69–70, 100–1, 113, 116, 120–2, 124–8, 131–2, 134–8, 140, 144–8, 152–7, 181, 183–4, 189–90, 192–3
   A Defence of the People of England 137, 147
   A Second Defence of the People of England 137, 140
   A Treatise on Civil Power 144
   Animadversions 126
   Apology for Smectymnus 126
   Areopagitica 124
   Colasterion 126

Doctrine and Discipline of Divorce 127
Eikonoclates 135–6, 147, 154
History of Britain 131
Judgment of Martin Bucer 127
Lycidas 126
Observations upon the Articles of
    Peace Made and Concluded with the
    Rebels 133
Of Education 127
Of Prelatical Episcopacy 126
Of Reformation 126
Paradise Lost 122, 153–4
Paradise Regained 122, 153–5
Reason of Church Government 126
Samson Agonistes 122, 153–7
Tetrachordon 127
The Cabinet Council 145
The Likeliest Means to Remove Hirelings
    from the Church 144
The Present Means and Brief Delineation
    of a Free Commonwealth 144
The Readie and Easie Way to Establish a
    Free Commonwealth 144, 155
The Tenure of Kings and Magistrates
    131–2, 134
To the Lord General Cromwell 121
Mingay, Anthony 58
Mirror for Magistrates 41
Monk, George, 1ˢᵗ Duke of Albemarle 144,
    147, 149, 160, 162, 169, 174
Mont Orgueil Castle 152
Montagu, Edward, 1ˢᵗ Earl of Sandwich 29,
    149, 169
Montagu, Edward, 2ⁿᵈ Earl of
    Manchester 82
Montagu, Robert, 3ʳᵈ Earl of
    Manchester 149
Montague, Richard, Bishop of
    Chichester 51
Monumentum Regale 108
More, Sir Thomas, Lord Chancellor 41
    History of Richard III 41
Morgan, Colonel Thomas 71–2
Morice, Roger 15
Morrice, Sir Thomas 147
Morton, Thomas, Bishop of Durham
    51, 102
Muggleton, Ludowick 123
Mytens, Daniel 42

Nalson, John 103
Naseby, battle of 2, 39, 66–9, 71, 73, 81, 84,
    87, 101–2, 106, 109, 123, 149, 160,
    177, 184
Nashe, Sir Thomas 20
Nayler, James 153
Nedham, Marchamont 69–70, 85, 90, 115,
    125, 133, 193
    The Case of the Commonwealth of
        England 115
    The Leveller Levell'd 85
Neile, Richard, Bishop of Durham and
    Archbishop of York 46, 51, 63
Newburn, battle of 60, 62, 73
Newbury, first battle of 45, 163
Newbury, second battle of 65
Newcastle Propositions 73
Newton, Sir Isaac 175
Nicholas, Robert, Serjeant 98
Nicholas, Sir Edward 109
Nineteen Propositions 65
Northen, Reverend Richard 58
Noy, William 32, 48
Nun Appleton 111, 115, 169

Oath of Engagement 112, 115, 184
Okey, Colonel John 68, 98, 151
Ordinance for the Regulation of Printing
    124, 127
Osborne, Thomas, 2ⁿᵈ Earl of Danby and
    Lord Treasurer 173
Overall, John, Bishop of Lichfield 25
Overton, Colonel Robert 100, 121,
    152
Overton, Richard 83, 125, 141
    Man's Mortality 124
Owen, John 129
Owen, Sir John 129

Paine, Tom 192
Palmer, Geoffrey, Attorney-General
    103
Parker, Henry 34, 69
    Observations 34
Paulet, 5ᵗʰ Marquess of Winchester 71
Paulucci, Lorenzo 139
Paxton, Sir Joseph 196
Pecke, Thomas 143
Pennington, Sir Isaac 98, 153

Pepys, Samuel 29, 80, 144, 146, 149, 151, 160–3, 166–7, 169, 175, 178, 188
   Diary 162
Percy, Algernon, 10th Earl of Northumberland 74, 99
Peter, Hugh 12, 70, 80, 89–90, 93–4, 105, 139, 151–2, 181
Petition of Many Thousands of Freeborn People of England 85
Petition of Right 34–6, 56, 59, 61, 83, 130, 190
Phelps, John 99, 148
Philliphaugh, battle of 71
Plowden, Edmund 12
   Commentaries 12
Poole, Lizzie 93–4
Pope, Alexander 81
Powell, Vavasor 141
Preston, battle of 86–7, 91
Preston, John 46
Price, John 89
Price, Lawrence 40
   Great Britain's Time of Triumph 40
Pride, Colonel Thomas 1, 91–2, 142, 148, 197
Primrose, Archibald, 5th Earl of Rosebery 195–6
Primrose, Harry, 6th Earl of Rosebery 196
Prynne, William 6, 14, 45–50, 52, 54–5, 82, 125–7, 131, 176, 188
   A Breviate of the Prelates Intolerable Usurpations 49
   A brief memento to the present unparliamentary junto 131
   A Brief Survey of Mr Cozen's, His Cozening Devotions 46
   Animadversions on the Fourth Part of Coke's Institutes 46
   Histriomastix 47
   News from Ipswich 49
   The Unloveliness of Lovelocks, etc 47
Putney, Army Council and debates 2, 83–5, 93, 125
Pye, Sir Robert 33
Pym, John 37, 51, 54, 61, 176

Raglan Castle 68
Rainsborough, Colonel Thomas 84–5, 89–90
Raleigh, Sir Walter 7

Ralph, James 172
   Critical Review of the Public Buildings of London 172
Regni Sanguinis Clamor 137
Remonstrance of Many Thousand Citizens 82, 125
Remonstrance of the Army 90–1, 100, 107
Reresby, Sir John 188
Reynolds, Edward 50, 52
Rich, Henry, 1st Earl of Holland 129
Rich, Colonel Nathaniel 93
Richard II, King of England 95, 107, 150
Richelieu, Cardinal Armand Jean du Plessis 41
Robertson, Geoffrey 3
Robinson, Henry 13
Root and Branch Petition 53, 61
Rota club 143–4
Roundway Down, battle of 65, 71
Rous, Sir Francis 52
Rowlands, Samuel 47
   Earth's Vanity 47
Rowton Heath, battle of 45
Royal Society 175
Royston, Richard 109, 111, 133
Rubens, Peter Paul 42, 44, 78, 174
   King Phillip IV of Spain wearing the Order of the Golden Fleece 44
   The Apotheosis of James I 78
   The Peaceful Reign of James I 78
   The Union of Crowns 78
Rudyerd, Sir Benjamin 33, 47, 53
Rupert, Prince of the Rhine 66–8, 73, 87, 122
Rushworth, John 67, 96, 108, 179
   Historical Collections 179
Rutherford, Samuel 12
Rye House plot 180

Sackville, Edward, 4th Earl of Dorset 28, 38
Salmasius, Claudius 9, 133, 137
   Defensio Regia Pro Carolo I 133, 137
Salmon, Joseph 129
Sancroft, William, Archbishop of Canterbury 58, 187
Sandown Castle 152
Savile, George, 1st Marquess of Halifax 167–8, 188–9
   Character of a Trimmer 167

Scot, Thomas 14
Scott, James, 1st Duke of Monmouth 187
Scott, Sir Walter 193
  Woodstock 193
Scrope, Colonel Adrian 148, 150
Seditious Sectaries Act 15
Selden, John 13, 28, 32–3, 35–6, 64, 128,
    135, 195
  History of Tithes 32
Self-Denying Ordinance 66
Seneca 131, 137
Senhouse, Richard, Bishop of Carlisle 78
Sexby, Captain Edward 84, 140
  Killing No Murder 141
Shakespeare, William 1, 6, 21, 40–2, 67,
    102, 122
  Henry V 67–8
  Measure for Measure 21, 41
  Richard II 41–2, 122–3
  Twelfth Night 6
Shelley, Percy 153
Sherfield, Henry 52, 126
Shirley, James 45
  The Triumph of Peace 45
Sibthorpe, Robert 31
Sidney, Colonel Algernon 98–9, 138, 180,
    184, 190, 192
  Discourses Concerning Government 180
Sidney, Philip, 1st Viscount Lisle 98
Sion House 74
Sir Anthony Roper's Case 17
Skinner, Richard 51
Skippon, Phillip, Major-General 39–40,
    65, 67, 98
Slingsby, Sir Henry 60
Slyngesbie, Robert 38
Smith, Sir Thomas 132
  Commonwealth of England 132
Sobieski, John, King of Poland 172
Somerset, Edward, 1st Earl of Glamorgan 68
Somerset, Henry, 1st Marquess of
    Worcester 68
Somerset House 120, 174
Southey, Robert 192, 195
Spanish succession, war of 174
Spence, Joseph 81
Sprat, Thomas 121
Sprigge, Joshua 105
St Asaph's Cathedral 129

St George's Chapel, Windsor 80, 174
St James Palace 80
St John, Oliver, Chief Justice 57, 61–2, 97
St Paul's Cathedral 129, 166
Stanley, Thomas 63
Star Chamber 15, 27, 35, 48–9, 82, 164
Stationer's Company 124
Statute of Praemunire 24
Steele, William, Attorney-General 97
Stillingfleet, Edward 165
Stow-on-the-Wold, battle of 71, 84, 87, 184
Strawberry Hill 191
Strode, Sir William 38, 56
Stuart, Henry, Duke of Gloucester
    108, 138–9
Stuart, Lady Elizabeth 108
Stuart, Henry, Prince of Wales 42
Swift, Jonathan 175
  Tale of a Tub 175
Sydenham, Cuthbert 124

Talbot, Francis, 11th Earl of Shrewsbury 160
Taylor, Jeremy, Bishop of Down and
    Connor 109
Taylor, John 81
  The World Turn'd Upside Down 81
Temple, Sir Peter 57
Temple, Sir William 90
Tennyson, Alfred Lord 193
Test Acts 188
Thackeray, William Makepeace 193
The Agreement of the People 83–4, 92, 94
The Army Scout 88, 90
The Case of the Army Truly Stated 81–3
The Eclectic 195
The King's Cabinet Opened 69
The Literary Gazette 195
The Moderate 89–90
The Royal Charles, naval flagship 166
The Shepherd's Paradise 47
The Weekly Intelligencer 134
Thellwall, John 192
Thomason, George 109, 137
Thurloe, John 116, 125
Thuycidides 177
Tilman, Edward 28
Titian 41, 44, 110
  Charles V at Muelberg 44
  Charles V with a Hound 61

*George D'Armagnac with Guillaume
Philandrier* 61
St Catherine of Alexandria 110
Supper at Emmaus 41
Toland, John 180–1
Life of Milton 180
Memoirs of Edmund Ludlow 180–1
Toleration Act 190
Torrington, battle of 71
Tourneur, Timothy 26
Trapnel, Anna 141
Treaty of Ripon 59–60
Trevelyan, George Macaulay 163
Twysden, Sir Roger 13, 58
Tyers, Thomas 191–2

Udall, John 15
Underdown, David 3
Ussher, James, Archbishop of Armagh
63, 126

Valentine, Benjamin 35
Van Dyck, Sir Anthony 42, 44–5, 54, 168
Charles I at the Hunt 50
Charles I on Horseback 44
*Charles I on Horseback with M de St
Antoine* 44
*Lord John Stuart and his Brother Lord
Bernard Stuart* 45
*Queen Henrietta Maria with Sir Jeffrey
Hudson* 43
The Great Peece 43
The Five Eldest Children of Charles I 43
Vane, Sir Henry 53, 62, 98, 130, 151, 192
Vaughan, Sir John, Chief Justice 103
Venner, Thomas 152–3
Vere, Edward de, 18th Earl of Oxford 27
Verney, Sir Edmund 60, 65
Villiers, Barbara, Duchess of Castlemaine
167, 171, 177, 195
Villiers, George, 1st Duke of Buckingham 2,
27–31, 33–4, 43, 177
Villiers, George, 2nd Duke of Buckingham
116, 160, 167
Villiers, John, 1st Viscount Purbeck 27
Vincent, John 166
Vindicae Contra Tyrannos 99
Virgil 113
Vyner, Sir Robert 161, 172–3

Walker, William 58
Waller, Sir Hardress 91, 94, 98, 150
Waller, Edmund 121, 140, 142, 147,
171, 173
*Instructions to a Painter, for the Drawing
of a Posture and Progress of his Forces
at Sea* 171
*On the Statue of King Charles at Charing
Cross* 173
Panegyrick to my Lord Protector 140,
147
*To the King upon his Majesty's Happy
Return* 147
Waller, Sir William 65, 98, 123
Walmstry, Thomas 108
Walpole, Horace 116, 191–2
Walton, Colonel Valentine 148
Walwyn, William 123
Ward, Matthew 195
The Disgrace of Lord Clarendon 195
Warwick, Sir Philip 29, 51, 61, 63, 65, 97,
103, 108, 175, 198
Memoirs of Sir Philip Warwick 63,
175, 198
Wedgwood, Dame Cicely Veronica 3
Wedgwood, Josiah 192
Wentworth, Thomas, 1st Earl of Strafford 2,
38, 49, 60–3, 66, 79, 110, 177–8, 183
Wesley, John 175
Westminster Abbey 174
Westminster Hall 79, 91, 95–7, 101, 106,
125, 142, 163
Westminster Palace 195
Weston, Sir Richard 33, 175
Wexford, massacre 113, 138
Whalley, Colonel Edward 90, 94, 98, 148
Wharton, Sir George 66, 71
White, Major Francis 128–9
Whitehall, Council of Officers 92–4, 125
Whitehall Palace 39–40, 78, 135, 139, 155,
160, 167, 187
Whitelock, Bulstrode 45, 58, 65, 79, 90, 98,
123, 128, 139, 141, 148
Whiteway, William 48–9
Widdrington, Sir Thomas 98
Wildman, John 81–5, 144
William I, King of England 137
William II, King of England 95
William III, King of England 188–9

Williams, John, Archbishop of York and
    Lord Keeper 10, 38, 63
Williams, Sir Trevor 70
Wilmot, John, 2nd Earl of Rochester 170
    Signor Dildo 170
Windebank, Francis 56
Windsor Castle 91, 93, 95
Winstanley, Gerard 88, 123
Winstanley, WIliam 145
    England's Worthies 145
Wither, George 125, 134
    British Appeals 134
Woburn Abbey 74
Wollstonecraft, Mary 192

Wolsey, Cardinal Thomas, Archbishop of
    York and Lord Chancellor 53
Worcester, battle of 120, 131, 134, 138–9,
    146, 161, 169
Wormald, Brian 196
Wordsworth, Christopher 109
    Who Wrote the Eikon Basilike? 109
Wordsworth, William 192
Wray, Sir John 53
Wren, Sir Christopher 174
Wren, Matthew, Bishop of Norwich 49, 51
Wriothesley, Thomas, 4th Earl of
    Southampton 81